This book has been developed from Robert Carrier's series 'Great Dishes of the World' that has appeared in the *Colour Magazine* of *The Sunday Times*

Robert Carrier is one of the world's most famous food writers. One-time Food Editor of *The Sunday Times*, *Harper's Bazaar*, *Vogue* and *The Daily Telegraph Magazine*, he is the author of several important cook books – *Great Dishes of the World*, *The Robert Carrier Cookery Cards*, *Cooking for You* and *The Robert Carrier Cookery Course*.

Also by Robert Carrier and available from Sphere

THE ROBERT CARRIER COOKERY COURSE Volumes 1 – 5

Great Dishes of the World

ROBERT CARRIER

SPHERE BOOKS LIMITED
30/32 Gray's Inn Road, London WC1X 8JL

First published in Great Britain by
Thomas Nelson & Sons Ltd 1963

First Sphere Books edition 1967
Reprinted 1967 (twice), 1970, 1973 and 1976

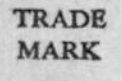

Composed in Univers and Times Roman by C. Nicholls & Company Ltd, at Manchester, England.

Printed in Great Britain by
Hazell Watson & Viney Ltd
Aylesbury, Bucks

Colour illustrations printed by Acorn Litho, Feltham, Middlesex, England.

GREAT DISHES OF THE WORLD

Foreword

The history of every nation lies visible on its table. Its wars and victories, its occupation in defeat, the marriages of its kings, its religion, its overseas empires – all have left behind them a dish or two destined to be adopted into the national life.

The Medicis, by marrying the Louis, transformed the French table, which then claimed the credit and conquered the world with its cuisine. The Auld Alliance, forged by endless interlocking marriages between the two kingdoms, still leaves many mementos in the Frenchified names of Scotland's food. A revolution gave us restaurants, when the chefs of the aristocracy were reduced to serving the very people who had so rudely cut off the heads they used to feed.

Civilisation itself, in fact, is founded upon food, for it began with the domestication of animals and the cultivation of crops. As soon as people could stay still – were released at last from the travail of following the game on which they fed – they ceased to live from hand to mouth, began to build up stocks and to store their wealth. With this wealth they bought leisure, and leisure brought them culture.

Then the wanderlust returned, forced on mankind again by the demands of food. The drives out from the Near East in search of pasture spread civilisation to Europe.

Greece and Rome flourished and fell, but Europe in the Dark Ages still needed spices. The quest for these, hidden behind the oratory of Saint Bernard and Peter the Hermit, led to the wonder of the East being rediscovered in the Crusades. For it was food, and not religion, that drove our forefathers to set out for years on the Crusades, to open up again the spice routes to the East closed down by the explosion of Mohammedanism in the Arabian desert.

It was food, once more, that made men brave uncharted seas – filled, as they thought, with monsters and evil spirits – to find the spice islands in the West. For spices were the measure by which wealth was counted in the Middle Ages, so coveted were they. So coveted, indeed, that Columbus died disgraced for having found only gold in America, and not the spices that he had promised.

This book assembles some of the most famous dishes of the world, dishes evolved from civilisations long past, dishes that have been favoured by every people that has tried them. Some still have to achieve international popularity. But each one of them is a part of the story of mankind. So let us approach them reverently. They have all history behind them. The first taste of some may surprise you, but adventure your palate as your ancestors did. And remember, the history of the world is written in this food. Culture stems from the stomach as well as the brain.

Contents

List of Plates

SUCCESS WITH RECIPES

'I dislike feeling at home when I'm abroad', said Bernard Shaw, his eyes fixed disapprovingly on those English tourists who spend their holidays searching for a good cup of tea and some plain, decent cooking. But what the master of paradox failed to mention was the delight of feeling abroad when we are at home.

The easiest way to carry yourself back to some favourite haunt is to recreate at home the dishes you enjoyed there. Or you can transport yourself to countries you have never even visited by sampling their cuisine. There is a tremendous variation in the food styles of the different nations of the world. Add to this the diverse regional cuisines of France, Italy, the United States and China, to name just a few, and you will have some idea of the delights that await you in this book.

Over the past fifteen years I have been collecting recipes on my travels abroad, experimenting with them in my own kitchens in America, Italy, Germany, France and England.

This book is the outcome of those years of pleasure, for an undoubted pleasure it has been, resulting in a collection of some of the world's most exciting recipes – GREAT DISHES OF THE WORLD – each guaranteed to bring you the delights of travel without any of its inconveniences. No visas, no endless waits at airports, no inoculations and no luggage are necessary for the enjoyment of these dishes. Only the excitement of preparing something new, of tasting a quite original flavour, of sampling the exotic.

Do not be alarmed by the foreign names of some of these dishes, or by the seeming multiplicity of the ingredients used. You will find that you already have most of them in your kitchen, and in the next few chapters I hope to show that most cooking – even of elaborate dishes – is merely the result of combining a number of very simple operations; but like everything else – walking, talking, driving a car, painting a picture – you learn best by actually *doing*.

In our grandparents' time, there were elaborate bicycling schools where people spent months learning how to stay balanced on two wheels. It seems that in the beginning we have to learn everything the hard way; later, it becomes almost second nature.

The great thing in cooking, according to the experts, is to master the principles and then to allow the application of the rules to special cases to follow as a matter of course. Thus, when you have learnt how to cook a steak to pink-centred, charcoaled perfection, you will not need special lessons for grilling a lamb chop; when you have learnt to make half a dozen sauces, you will be able to make half a hundred without extra effort.

Whenever you try a new method of cooking, do not be disappointed if you are unsuccessful at the first or even the second attempt, but try to find out the cause of failure and remedy it the next time. For recipes are not like doctors' prescriptions: they cannot be repeated too often. In every case you must use your own judgment with regard to the time required for each cooking process.

HOW TO USE THIS BOOK

Read the recipe all the way through before you start to cook. Check that you have all the necessary ingredients and equipment. If any of the general directions are not completely clear to you, read the introductory material found in the next few chapters.

Section 1, 'THE GOOD INGREDIENTS', tells you what basic ingredients are necessary; gives you French chefs' tricks with butter, olive oil and diced green bacon to add flavour and substance to stews, *ragoûts* and casseroles; and shows how finely-chopped onion, shallot and garlic can lend excitement to the simplest sauces.

Section 2, 'A SHORT GUIDE TO COOKING TERMS', defines the meaning of any cooking term used in this book that might be unfamiliar to you.

Section 3, 'BASIC EQUIPMENT', describes the equipment I find most useful in my kitchen.

And you will find Section 4, 'BASIC COOKERY METHODS', of interest whenever you are in doubt about the golden rules of cooking. To boil, to blanch, to poach, to steam, to glaze, to braise, to grill, to roast, to fry, to bake, to cook *au gratin* and *en papillote* – these twelve phrases embrace all cooking, from the first essays of the cave-man to the subtlest intricacies of Brillat-Savarin. These twelve basic methods of cooking are the foundation on which everything stands, from stewed cabbage served in its own water to the wildest experiments and triumphs that you can achieve in your own kitchen.

SECTION 1

The Good Ingredients

Many cooks today make the mistake of trying to economise on the basic necessities of good cooking: the best butter; olive oil from Provence; fat bacon; quality wines and rich stocks for cooking; coarse salt (the famous *gros sel* of French cuisine) and freshly-ground black pepper; onion, garlic and shallots; the best wine vinegar and a selection of fresh herbs and spices. But this is a false economy, for with these materials at hand, you can make any number of excellent casserole dishes using the same basic cooking techniques.

Of course, you will have to acquire a *tour de main*; you will have to know how to make stocks and soups, sauces and soufflés, and learn the techniques of roasting and baking. You must become accustomed to your oven, to your mixer, to your omelette pan . . . and to the foods you are likely to cook.

Nothing replaces quality and freshness. All food should be eaten fresh. I find that a salad picked from the garden ten minutes before Sunday luncheon is worth five of the same from the corner grocer's; and a fish caught fresh from the coastal waters of St. Tropez makes a better *bouillabaisse* than those kept on ice in the best Paris restaurants.

So avoid buying foods too far in advance. I find that meats, fish, butter, milk, fruits and vegetables all tend to lose freshness and flavour when stored too long. If you are going to refrigerate foods, fresh or cooked, keep them in covered containers to preserve moisture.

And remember, it is not necessary for you to serve highly complicated dishes when you entertain. Greatness in cooking is apparent primarily in the plain dishes – those sound traditional country casseroles of the French regional cuisine, for instance – properly prepared with butter of farmhouse freshness and simmered for hours in the lowest of ovens.

There are countless recipes for the pot roasts and *ragoûts* of lamb, veal and beef, and the great country stews of poultry, meat and game, which have many points in common in their preparation. (1) Whether or not the meat has been larded, it is usually dredged with flour and sautéed until golden in hot fat – butter, oil, salt pork, or a combination of the three. (2) It is then usually flamed in cognac, Calvados or some other alcohol, before being moistened with rich stock, wine or cream, and slowly simmered to perfection. (3) Finally, the extracts given out by the meat in the cooking process, however delicious they may be, are almost always enriched by the addition of onions, shallots, garlic and a selection of fresh herbs or spices.

These country recipes, whether *bœuf à la gardiane*, tender chunks of beef braised in red wine as cooked in the Camargue region of France, or *matelote à la bourguignonne*, a *ragoût* of freshwater fish, eel, pike and carp, flamed in brandy and served in a rich wine sauce, or any of the other delicious casserole dishes of meat, fish, poultry or vegetables which you will find described in the pages of this book, all follow the same basic cooking techniques.

COOKING FATS

There is nothing, to my mind, that quite replaces butter in cooking. If you want the best results, all butter and all cooking oils should be of the best quality. And although margarine has become very popular in recent years, I see no great advantage in using it; if a vegetable fat is called for, by far the most practical and most pleasant to use are the vegetable oils – olive, corn and peanut.

For slow frying, I like to mix olive oil and butter in equal quantities, putting the oil in the pan first to keep the butter from browning; or I use a combination of olive oil and corn oil for the lighter *ragoûts* of chicken, rabbit or vegetables.

For the earthier casseroles, I combine olive oil and butter and add diced cubes of fat salt pork or green bacon to create a rich emulsion with plenty of flavour. Lard, dripping and what the French often call the *graisses nobles* – goose, duck and chicken fats – are also indicated for certain regional specialities. And whatever cooking one intends to do, a supply of good olive oil is essential for salads and as a sauce for spaghetti and bean dishes in the Italian manner.

THE AROMATICS

ONIONS

The onion is perhaps the oldest known vegetable in the world.

Onions are said to have been one of the foodstuffs eaten by the Egyptian workmen who built the Pyramids. For centuries, the French have been particularly fond of onion soup. In Les Halles (the Paris equivalent of Covent Garden) it is served steaming hot in the early hours of the morning – a very old custom which has become a considerable tourist attraction.

The onion is a sublime flavourer for casserole dishes and stews. Try the French trick of browning finely-chopped onions, shallots and garlic in olive oil and butter before adding meat and vegetables for a meat casserole. This aromatic trio will add greatly to the end result of your dish. But a word of warning – do not let them turn colour before adding meat. They should be just transparent.

A little onion chopped finely – a tablespoon or two, no more – browned in butter with a little finely-chopped parsley and a hint of garlic, adds greatly to the savour of grilled steak or lamb chops. Add a whole onion, stuck with a pungent clove or two, to chicken or beef stock; serve a dish of creamed onions as an accompaniment to roast lamb. If onions are small enough, present them in a baked pastry case for added effect.

I like onions with a Provençal stuffing of ground veal, diced fat salt pork, finely-chopped onion and garlic, minced fresh tarragon and parsley, beaten egg, boiled rice, freshly-grated Parmesan cheese and salt and pepper, to taste.

Try small white onions, glazed, as a flavour and texture garnish for party dishes. To make glazed onions: peel small white onions and cook them very slowly, uncovered, in enough butter and water to half-cover them. Sprinkle the onions with sugar and salt, and baste them frequently. The onions should be translucent and melting.

SHALLOTS

The delicate, violet-tinted shallot, another member of the onion family, is usually finely chopped and sautéed in a little butter as a flavourful addition to casseroles, stews, sauces and grilled or sautéed meat, fish and poultry. Shallots are easy to grow if you have a patch of good soil in the sun; and once you start them, they are virtually perpetual, as they reproduce by dividing. A grilled fillet steak, served with hot melted butter and sprinkled with finely-chopped parsley and shallots, is delicious. Chopped shallots in small game birds –

quail, partridge, grouse – add greatly to the flavour; chopped shallots can also be used effectively in wine sauces and in stuffings for meat roasts. Fish dishes improve greatly with the addition of a little finely-chopped shallot to the sauce.

LEEKS

The leek, probably brought to Britain by the early Romans, was commonly cultivated in Egypt in the time of the Pharaohs. Closely allied to the onion – but with the bulbous part cylindrical and the leaves broad and flat – the leek was celebrated in Italy in the time of Pliny. It was held in great esteem by the Emperor Nero, who used to eat leeks for several days each month to clear his voice.

The leek is grown in this country as a vegetable, with properties very similar to the onion, but of a milder character. I like to combine leeks with onions and garlic as an aromatic threesome for the great French soups, *pot-au-feu* and *poule-au-pot*. They are, of course, an integral part of cock-a-leekie and Scotch broth, and puréed with chicken stock, cream and potatoes, make one of the most famous soups in the world – *vichyssoise*. Try leeks on their own, puréed with chicken stock and cream, for a delicious cream of leek soup. Serve this versatile vegetable in a variety of ways: leeks *à la grecque* (leeks boiled in dry white wine and olive oil with finely-chopped onions and carrots), leeks *à la vinaigrette* (leeks poached in water and served with a vinaigrette sauce), leeks *au gratin* (leeks baked in a cream sauce) and leeks *mornay* (poached leeks served with a well-flavoured cheese sauce).

CHIVES

The most 'polite' of the onion family, the chive is one of the most popular culinary seasonings thanks to its delicate flavour. Combine finely-chopped chives with finely-chopped chervil, parsley and tarragon to make the delicate combination for an *omelette aux fines herbes*. Carry this subtlety one step further for a *soufflé aux fines herbes*. *Vichyssoise* would not be *vichyssoise* without its sprinkling of chives. Use this plant finely chopped to add a delicious hint of onion to salad dressings and as a garnish for vegetables. Try it also with cream of asparagus and bean soup.

GARLIC

When garlic first appeared in history, it was considered to have magic properties like the mandrake root. It was a wonder drug, perhaps the oldest drug in the world – a primeval 'cure-all' for the ancients.

In describing its most potent powers, the Roman historian

Pliny claimed that garlic was so good 'the very smell of it drove away serpents and scorpions'.

Today, French and Italian cooks cannot possibly get along without this most beloved and most hated of seasoners. And in this country, garlic is slowly creeping back into favour, working its way up the social ladder in thousands of kitchens throughout the country during the post-war years.

Without this pungent bulb, many dishes would almost lack their reason for being. Who would give a second thought to *bouillabaisse* – that golden-coloured, highly-flavoured *bouillon* of fish from the Mediterranean – without the aromatic flavours of garlic and saffron? And could we call a salad – tender green lettuce leaves, bathed in olive oil, home-made wine vinegar, salt and freshly-ground black pepper – a real salad if it did not contain at least a hint of garlic? I like to add a clove or two of garlic to hearty French or Italian casseroles of meat or vegetables and to *pasta* sauces. And I always insert a sliver or two into a roast of lamb, pork or beef before cooking it.

In some cases, it is the strong, garlicky flavour that gives the dish its character; in others, the appeal comes from the special bouquet that garlic imparts to the food rather than from its own flavour.

In using garlic, I think it best to consider three basic facts. First, the heavy flavour that offends many people evaporates if you crush the garlic before using it. This seems to eliminate the strong odour and flavour and leaves a pleasing pungency. Second, this same heavy flavour of the garlic – like that of the onion – disappears if you simmer it in a liquid. And third, garlic acquires a bitter taste if allowed to cook in butter or oil long enough to take on colour. In making garlic-flavoured butter sauces for sautéed foods, add the crushed garlic to butter already heated, or lightly browned and just heated through, before you pour the sauce over the food.

One of my favourite garlic recipes in this vein is the famous Italian spaghetti dish, *spaghetti al' alio e olio*, which simply means spaghetti served with an oil and garlic sauce.

Professional chefs' recipes usually specify 'crushed' garlic. You can crush a small amount of garlic by bringing the flat side of a big heavy knife down sharply on the chopped pieces. I like to crush each clove of garlic flat with the palm of my hand – delicate fibrous casing and all – and put four or five of these crushed cloves with an equal number of sage leaves in the centre of a boned roast of pork. Roll up the meat, tie it securely and roast it in the usual way, and you will have *rôti de porc à la provençale.*

French cooks always call a small amount of crushed garlic '*une pointe d'ail*' – as much as you can pick up on the point of a small sharp knife. When they want to crush larger amounts of garlic, they use a small mortar and pestle. Cooks in this country can purchase garlic presses which are quite efficient. But whichever method you use, do not forget to clean thoroughly any boards, knives or other utensils used with garlic, because a lingering garlic flavour on kitchen equipment is far from desirable.

HERBS

The British are not adventurous with herbs: mint, parsley, sage, and possibly thyme and chives, are virtually the only ones they use. All the herbs mentioned here can be used fresh, dried or frozen. Drying them is a simple task. Harvest herbs when plant first begins to show flowers; dry in a well-ventilated room and store in air-tight containers in a cool, dry place. To quick-freeze herbs: blanch in boiling water; plunge immediately in iced water; drain off excess moisture; seal in aluminium foil and place in the freezer. Frozen herbs should be thawed at room temperature before using.

All seasoning should, of course, be to taste, and herbs – like perfume – should be used subtly. Experiment, with a light hand at first, to discover the distinction herbs can contribute to your cooking. Then, as you become more expert, use fresh herbs liberally to make your favourite dishes more personally yours.

In general, I like to add most herbs towards the end of cooking. In this way they cannot cook too long, losing savour or imparting a bitter taste to food.

THYME

Pungent, aromatic and popular, thyme is used to flavour stews, soups and sauces; it goes particularly well with dishes in which wine is used. There are many varieties of this herb, wild and cultivated. Lemon thyme adds zest and flavour to scrambled eggs, egg sandwich spreads and creamed eggs. Mix thyme to taste with salt and freshly-ground black pepper and rub over beef, lamb or veal before roasting. Casseroles of meat or poultry are greatly enhanced in flavour if a little thyme is added shortly before cooking time is up. Try this herb warmed in butter with grilled lobster, shrimps and prawns. Add it to butter to dress carrots, mushrooms, onions and potatoes.

PARSLEY

This is the best known and the most generally used of all herbs – invariably thought of in this country as a garnish for meat, fish and vegetables. Modern dieticians have discovered a wealth of vitamins in parsley. Use it chopped finely to enhance the flavour of sauces, soups and stews, fish and meat salads, stuffings, and as an intrinsic part of the traditional faggot of mixed herbs (the French call it a '*bouquet*'), which adds such a wonderful something to French country cooking. Parsley sauce is an excellent accompaniment to boiled or steamed fish, or boiled chicken.

MARJORAM

One of the most popular of herbs – and one of the most versatile. It is very pungent – a little goes a long way. Stews, soups, braised meats, sausages, pork roasts and chops, all call for interesting uses of marjoram. This herb is also very good with fish. Try a little finely chopped with buttered carrots, spinach or turnips for a subtle, new flavour. Its aromatic, slightly bitter taste is excellent in poultry stuffings.

SAFFRON

Saffron – now one of the world's most costly flavouring agents – comes from the stigma of a certain type of crocus. Once so greatly esteemed in this country as a flavourer of breads, cakes, soups and stews, saffron is now more or less forgotten. Not so in Italy, where it lends its special flavour and colour to *risotto alla milanese* (saffron rice), in France, where it is an integral part of *bouillabaisse* and Provençal fish soups, and in Spain, where it is one of the main ingredients of *paella*, Spain's national dish of chicken, sausage, seafood and saffron-flavoured rice. Use saffron to add colour and zest to rice dishes and fish soups of all kinds. Try it in baking, for example in saffron buns and saffron bread.

TARRAGON

Known to most as a flavouring for wine vinegar, this fresh, green herb is delicious when chopped finely and combined with melted butter and a little lemon juice as a sauce for fish. The delicate, pungent taste of this difficult-to-grow herb – and its delightful perfume – make it a must in any herbal list. Add chopped fresh tarragon to any salad; use it to add special interest to fricasséed or roast chicken. Use it in aspics with chicken, eggs or shellfish. Tarragon is the indispensable ingredient of a *sauce béarnaise*; adds its inimitable savour to green mayonnaise. Its faintly anise flavour is good in marinades for meat and fish.

MINT

The very smell of this popular herb is supposed to stimulate appetite. In England it is king; for there are about fourteen varieties of mint grown in this country alone. Spearmint, the most popular, is used for flavouring peas and potatoes, and in the preparation of mint sauce to accompany roast lamb. Try it, too, in salads and salad dressings. Fresh pea soup, whether served hot or cold, is the better for the clean, clear flavour of fresh mint, as are pot cheeses, ices, wine cups and, of course, mint julep.

Try the other mint varieties – grow them in your garden or on the window sill – for further flavour flourishes: pineapple and eau-de-Cologne mint snipped into salads, or crystallised for cakes, or tied in bunches to flavour wine cups and *tisanes*; apple mint for poultry stuffings, fruit cups and for jellies made from crab-apples and gooseberries.

FENNEL

Fennel is used extensively by the Italians and the Mediterranean French. This feathery herb, which looks something like dill, is excellent in fish sauces and salad dressings. Fennel seeds – famous for their use in liqueurs of the *anisette* variety – add a subtle flavour and texture to pastries.

Dried fennel stalks are used by the French for flaming *loup de mer* and as an aromatic in *bouillabaisse* and *soupe de poissons*.

The bulbs of fresh fennel (*finocchio* in Italian, *fenouil* in French) are also eaten as a salad. In this case the thickened stalk or bulb is sliced thinly and dressed with olive oil, lemon, salt and pepper. Eaten this way, it has a delightful anise or liquorice flavour.

ROSEMARY

A sprinkling of fresh rosemary leaves complements the flavour of lamb and kid. Add chopped fresh rosemary, blended with chopped parsley and butter, to any baked chicken dish for a delightful change. The fresh, sweet, pinewoods flavour of this herb, which has been used since antiquity, adds an indescribable taste to sauces, stews and cream soups. Try it with steak or veal chops, using finely-chopped rosemary leaves as you would pepper for a steak *au poivre*. No other seasoning is necessary. Rosemary is better used fresh than when dried.

CORIANDER

Fresh coriander is used in practically all cooking in Mexico and South America, where it is called *ciantro*. It is also used extensively by the Chinese and Japanese, who call it Chinese parsley. Its exotic flavour is the highlight of *ceviche* (raw fish salad), *guacamole* (mashed avocado salad) and other Mexican dishes. In this country we use coriander leaves or seeds in chutneys, with lemon sauce for venison, and with braised celery or cream of celery soup. Its flavour seems to bring out the celery taste.

CHERVIL

This delicate, feathery herb is a member of the parsley family. A little chervil is excellent in a delicate butter sauce such as *sauce hollandaise*. Finely-chopped chervil, parsley, chives and tarragon go to make the subtle combination of fresh herbs necessary for an *omelette aux fines herbes*. Chervil alone makes a cheese omelette very special. It is very good with most stews and soups and an excellent garnish for salads. Try sprinkling finely-chopped fresh chervil on grilled fish just before you remove it from under the grill.

BASIL

One of the choicest and most aromatic of herbs, basil is difficult to grow in this climate. It is very popular with the Spaniards, the Italians, the French and the Portuguese, who use the spicy and aromatic scent of basil in the preparation of many of their dishes. It has a delightful odour and some claim it is clove-like in flavour. Basil is especially fine with lamb chops to which its leaves and tender stems give a sweet, mildly pungent flavour. Combine chopped snippets of basil with *oregano*, chives and melted butter and serve with spaghetti; sprinkle a teaspoon of finely-chopped basil leaves and parsley on sliced, chilled tomatoes to make a salad that literally breathes 'South of France'. Use it to flavour salads, soups, stews and sauces.

BOUQUET GARNI

Is a bunch of herbs, either tied together or bound into a tiny cheesecloth sack, and cooked with the food. The herbs are usually bound so that they may be lifted out at the end of cooking and discarded, but my French cook, Naomi, used to chop up her *bouquet* herbs as finely as possible and incorporate them into the sauce. A simple *bouquet* consists of merely a few sprigs of parsley, chives and a bay leaf. A *bouquet garni* is made up of two sprigs parsley, two sprigs thyme, one branch celery, one sprig marjoram, one bay leaf and one sprig rosemary.

OREGANO

Closely related to marjoram and sometimes called wild marjoram, *oregano* seems to go specially well with tomatoes and tomato sauces – hence a natural for *pasta* sauces. A touch of this herb makes grilled tomatoes delicious. Try *oregano* when baking onions or roasting pork or lamb. This herb is much used in Italy to flavour the many recipes for *pizza*. Use *oregano* in stuffing for meat or fowl, in basting sauces and marinades.

SAGE

Sage is used a good deal in Italian and Provençal dishes. *Saltimbocca* rolls thin slices of veal with *prosciutto* (Parma ham) and a sage leaf, and fries them gently in butter. In Provence, *daurade au sauge* (sea-bream cooked with sage) and *carré de porc au sauge* (roast pork with sage) are well-known specialities. Because of its strong, bold flavour, it must be used with great care – especially in stuffings for chicken, duck and goose, where it is apt to swamp other, more delicate flavours. It is fragrant, though a little bitter; good with pork, goose and sausage.

DILL

A lacy, delicately-flavoured herb, dill is used in many German, Russian and Swedish recipes. Far too little is used in England today where it is best known as a flavouring for vinegar and pickles. Fresh sprigs of this herb mix well with many vegetables and with salads and fish. Try cucumbers with sour cream and fresh dill; new potatoes with lemon butter and fresh dill; potato salad with crumbled bacon and fresh dill in the dressing; fish salads with dill.

SPICES

The fortunes of Europe's greatest families were founded on the peppercorn. Medieval spice merchants became very rich men, for a pound of ginger would buy a sheep; a pound of cloves would buy a cow; a sack of pepper would buy a man. In fact, at one time pepper was so expensive that it was sold by the individual peppercorn.

We owe a lot to spices today. Not only the more exotic flavour of our foods – special dishes such as steak *au poivre*, Madras chicken curry and saffron rice – but the discovery of a whole new world. Until the thirteenth century, the Arabs, leading spice merchants to the world, had kept the secret of their source of supply so closely guarded that the West did not discover where these riches could be obtained until Marco Polo visited the Orient. His written account of his three voyages astonished the world. As a result of his tales, Columbus set out on the voyage of exploration that was to end in the discovery of the islands of the Caribbean and of America; Vasco da Gama rounded the continent of Africa

CHERVIL

DILL

BASIL

OREGANO

CORIANDER

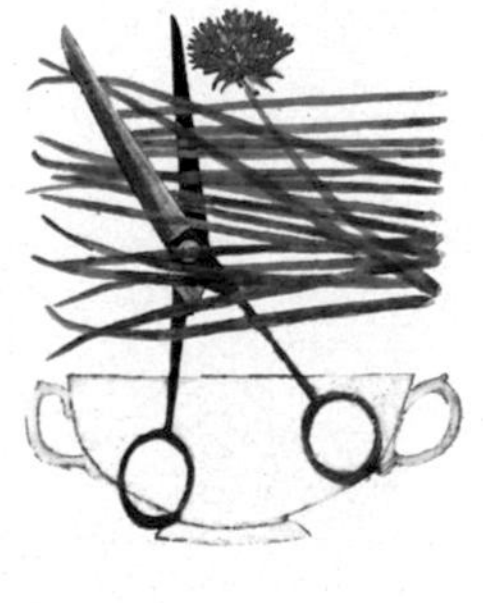

CHIVES

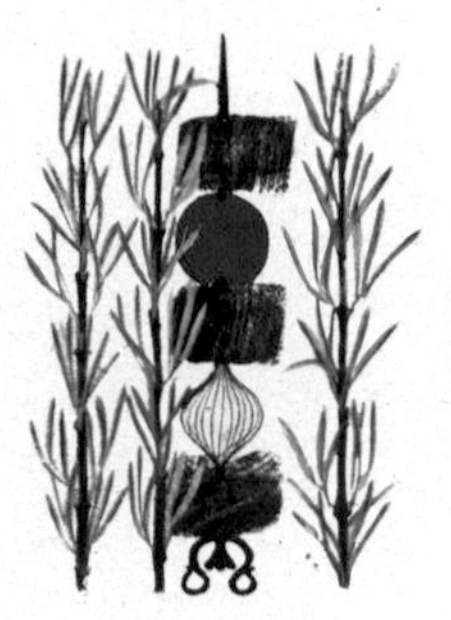

ROSEMARY

PARSLEY

FENNEL

THYME

MARJORAM

BOUQUET GARNI

to reach India for the first time by sea; and Magellan, after two years of hardship and adventure, discovered the Spice Islands of New Guinea where cloves, nutmeg, cinnamon, pepper and other spices grew in abundance.

How to use spices: Be selective. Unless you are following a tested recipe do not combine too many at one time. And remember, the correct spice combination for any food is the one that tastes right to you. There are no rules. The use of spices is an art, not a science.

Test your spices occasionally: If spices are kept too long they lose their wonderful distinctive aroma. They should then be replaced with a fresh supply.

ALLSPICE

Allspice is the dried, hard, unripe berry of the pimento or allspice tree, a member of the bay family. It was thought by Columbus to be the much sought after 'pepper', and was brought back in great triumph to Europe. Often called the Jamaican pepper, it closely resembles the true pepper in shape, but has a delicately fragrant flavour – pungent and aromatic – that tastes like a blend of cinnamon, nutmeg and mace, strongly spiced with cloves. The French call this spice '*quatre épices*'.

Allspice is excellent for game, poultry stuffings and sausage mixtures. Use it ground or whole in stews, *ragoûts*, sauces and gravies, whole for pickles and marinades; add two or three berries to a fresh pea soup; to flavour chutneys, ketchup and spiced fruits. Use it with a light hand to flavour delicate sauces for fish and eggs; let its fragrance accent hot puddings, fruit pies and some cakes.

ANISEED

Strongly flavoured and highly scented if used too lavishly, aniseed has a light, wonderfully pleasant liquorice flavour when used with a gentle touch in cooking. Sometimes called 'sweet cumin', to which it has a slight similarity in flavour, it is used widely in confectionery and cake and pastry making. French cooks pound aniseed with lump sugar to flavour sponge cakes, custards or creams.

Aniseed is distilled to make Pernod and *anisette*, two French liqueurs of distinction. Use Pernod to flavour fish chowders; you will find that a few drops lend a certain excitement to oysters Rockefeller. A 'stew' of lobsters is enhanced with the volatile essence of this Mediterranean liqueur.

Sprinkle aniseed on cakes and cookies. Use it in the Oriental manner to add flavour and excitement to fish and gammon.

CARDAMOM

Cardamom – which belongs to the ginger family – once had a reputation as an aphrodisiac and was consequently used by certain chefs of the French Court for its reputedly 'warming' qualities.

Cardamom has much of the same fire as ginger, allspice and black pepper, and is used in India as one of the prime ingredients of hot curry powders and sauces.

I like to use cardamom seeds whole for pickling and for curries; finely ground in pastries, sweet sauces and cakes.

Cardamom goes particularly well with orange. Try a little, too, sprinkled on melon, or just a hint of this fragrant spice to give a touch of the East to after-dinner coffee.

CHILE POWDER

A blend – like curry – of several ingredients, chile powder (also called chili powder; never to be confused with powdered chilli) is a delicious combination of the finely-ground pods of several kinds of hot peppers, paprika, cumin seed, dried garlic and *oregano*.

Rich in colour and in flavour, chile powder is much used in Mexican and South-Western American cooking, as well as in tropical countries to flavour native dishes, stews, meats, sauces and soups.

CINNAMON

A spice highly prized by the ancients – cinnamon is made from the dried spicy inner bark of the cinnamon tree, first cousin to the cassia and the bay. Its fragrant odour and sweet spicy flavour are the perfect foil, when used in moderation, to fish and fish sauces.

Combine cinnamon with pepper, ginger, cloves and mace. Use this mixture as a 'dry marinade' to rub on pork chops and game before cooking. Add a hint of cinnamon and cloves to Dijon mustard to flavour baked ham.

Spice 'mulled' wines with cinnamon. Let this spice add interest to sweets, cakes and puddings. Sprinkle it over coffee, sliced fresh fruits and puddings.

Its highly fragrant odour and sweet, aromatic flavour are a 'must' for apple pies, dumplings, sauces and puddings.

CLOVES

Cloves – like pepper – were one of the first Oriental spices to excite the cupidity of Western spice traders. First used by the Chinese, the clove has a hot spicy flavour and a highly aromatic scent.

Use whole cloves for pickling, for pork, ham and gammon, and fruit dishes. Take advantage of the clove's natural affinity for onion, pork and ham. Use ground cloves in spice cakes, gingerbreads, puddings and sweets.

No apple pie is considered complete without a faint hint of clove, but be careful not to overdo it.

CORIANDER

Sweet yet tart in flavour, coriander is a favourite ingredient of hot curries and sauces.

Coriander is delicious when rubbed on pork before roasting; or on pork chops before cooking. Use dried coriander to flavour Moroccan dishes; with dried bean soups, or in poultry stuffings.

Try this spice with meats, cheeses, pickles; use it sparingly in puddings and pastries.

CUMIN SEED

An important ingredient of all 'chili' and 'curry' powders, cumin is much used in Far Eastern and Oriental foods. Its strong, aromatic scent and pungent flavour (similar to caraway seed, but much stronger in flavour) are used extensively in Mexican cookery, Indian curries, and as a delicious flavourer for meat loaf, lamb and chicken dishes and anything made with dried beans.

I like to use the seeds whole as an attractive 'wrapping' for cubes of cream cheese.

CURRY POWDER

Commonly known as a spice, curry powder is in reality a blend of many herbs and spices. Commercial varieties may contain eight to thirty-eight different sorts. Connoisseurs of curry have special formulae of freshly-ground herbs and spices for various dishes. The following list – which reads like a complete herb and spice index – will give you some idea of the principal ingredients it is possible to include in a well-blended curry powder: allspice, aniseed, bay leaves, cardamom, cinnamon, cloves, coriander, cumin, dill, fennel, garlic, ginger, mace, mustard, nutmeg, black pepper, white pepper, red pepper, paprika, poppy seeds, saffron, turmeric, etc. The relative strength of the blend depends, of course, on how much hot pepper is used.

MUSTARD

Mustard was well known to the ancient Romans, who imported it into Gaul where it quickly found favour. The French moisten powdered white and black mustards with verjuice (to make Dijon mustard), with wine (to make Bordeaux mustard), and add herbs for various special mustard blends.

English mustard – produced in this country since 1720, when it was first ground and sifted commercially – is a blend of powdered white and black mustards, with a little turmeric added to give the mustard powder a rich golden yellow. It is very hot in flavour.

I like to use mustard to flavour sauces and gravies for meats and game; in pickles, chutneys and relishes, and, of course, in salad dressings.

GINGER

One of the earliest Oriental spices to be known to Europe, ginger originally came from Southern China where the ripe roots were carefully selected, boiled in several waters to remove some of their fire, and then preserved in thick syrup. Ginger was known to the ancient Greeks and Romans. It was used in India in early times. In England, ginger was well known before the Conquest.

This extremely pungent spice should be creamy-white in colour when ground. It is smooth-skinned and light buff in colour when whole.

Ground ginger adds much to apple sauces, chutneys and stewed fruits. Try blending ground ginger with black pepper and crushed salt, and rubbing it over steaks and chops before grilling. Also good with lamb.

Sprinkle ground ginger lightly on fish before grilling. Add lightly to fruit and wine sauces.

MACE

Mace is the dried outer sheath of the kernel of the fruit of the nutmeg tree, and similar, if stronger, in flavour. It is an expensive spice – only a quarter of an ounce is obtained per pound of nutmeg harvested.

Use ground mace for pickling, marinades, brines and game sauces. Use it with a lighter hand for cakes, sweets and puddings. Add mace with impunity to any sweet in which chocolate plays a leading part.

Oyster stew – a great favourite in New England – would not be the same without a dash of mace. Try mace with fish, shellfish, eggs and vegetables in a rich cream sauce. Cauliflower and carrots, particularly, take kindly to a hint of mace, and puréed potatoes, enriched with cream and butter, are all the better for a dash of this versatile spice.

NUTMEG

Delicate and at the same time very aromatic, nutmeg is the dried seed of the fruit of the nutmeg tree. Usually used as a substitute for, or as an adjunct to, mace, this spice is very stimulating to the palate.

The whole nut keeps its flavour almost indefinitely. Ground nutmeg, however, soon loses its flavour, so it is much better to keep it in nut form and grate it as you need it.

Use nutmeg as you would mace.

PAPRIKA

One of the spices the Turks brought with them to Western Europe was paprika, or Turkish pepper, as it was called in the sixteenth century – the same 'sweet' pepper or *aji* discovered by Columbus in the New World. Warmly aromatic and a rich red in colour, paprika is used a great deal in French, Spanish, Moroccan and Hungarian cookery.

Use this mild sweet cousin of the red pepper to add colour and flavour to eggs, seafood and vegetables. Fish dishes, cream soups and cooked cheese dishes all benefit from a sprinkling of paprika. And, of course, it is a prime ingredient of chicken or veal paprika, and of the Hungarian national dish *gulyas*.

PEPPER

One of the prime motivating factors for Columbus's voyage to find the Spice Islands, pepper is our most widely used spice. Columbus found two kinds of pepper: the black seeds whose aroma was much like that of cloves, cinnamon and nutmeg (our famous allspice), for centuries called Jamaican pepper – and the spicy vegetable which the Mayan natives called *aji* (the red pepper family).

BLACK PEPPER – one of the first spices to be introduced to Europe – is the dried, unripe fruit of the *piper nigrum* found in the East Indies. This spice lends flavour and excitement to most foods. It quickly loses flavour and aroma when ground. I prefer to grind it with a pepper mill as I need it.

WHITE PEPPER – less pungent and less aromatic than black pepper – is the same seed freed from its outer skin. It is perfect for lighter sauces and in any dish where specks of black pepper would be unsightly.

RED PEPPER – the most pungent of all spices – is very hot, pungent and biting. Use it sparingly to lend excitement to fish, shellfish, *canapé* spreads and salad dressings. Perfect for curry and barbecue sauces, and the hot stews and *ragoûts* of Africa and the Caribbean.

TURMERIC

Made from the dried and ground stem or root of a plant of the ginger family, turmeric is similar in flavour to ginger, but more discreet.

Famous mainly for the rich yellow tinge it gives to foods, turmeric is often used to colour and flavour mixed pickles and curry and mustard powders.

THE THICKENERS

Most of the country-styled dishes – the peasant casseroles of France, Italy and Spain which are becoming so popular in this country – need no elaborate sauces to enhance their flavour. It is the slow, careful reduction of oil, butter and wine with shallots, garlic and the juices of meat, chicken or fish, cooked slowly *en cocotte* or *en casserole*, which gives to each of these dishes its own delicious flavour and texture. They contain their own sauce, in fact, and the addition of flour, thickening or a made-up sauce to such a dish is not usually necessary.

There are times, however, when you will want to make sauces and gravies a little more full-bodied or substantial; then it is best to resort to the French chef's *beurre manié* (kneaded bits of butter and flour added to the casserole at the last minute) or, for dishes with a white stock or cream base like *blanquette de veau* or *matelote à la normande*, combine egg yolks, cream and a dash of lemon juice.

BEURRE MANIÉ

When the sauce should be very slightly thickened at the last moment a *beurre manié* is indicated. Take a piece of butter (about one good tablespoon) and knead it to a smooth paste with the same amount of flour; this is stirred into the sauce bit by bit a few minutes before serving and given just sufficient time to simmer for the flour to be cooked.

EGG YOLKS

Egg yolks are useful to bind, enrich and give substance to a sauce. If your sauce should turn out to be too thin, you can thicken it by adding the yolk of an egg or two, thoroughly beaten up. Add the beaten yolks to a little of the hot liquid; beat again and pour the combined mixture into the main body of your sauce, whisking all the time. Heat through without boiling, or the yolks will cook and disintegrate.

THE MOISTENERS

WINE

The use of wine in Continental cooking dates back to Roman days. In a certain number of French and Italian dishes – *ragoûts*, soups, *daubes* – it is indispensable. When wine is cooked, the alcohol evaporates, leaving a wonderful flavour which permeates the dish. Never throw away the dregs of wine left in bottles . . . this is the best cook's trump card.

Use wine to flavour gravies; drop a spoonful into your salad dressing; add a touch at the last minute to veal chops sizzled in butter. To attempt wine cookery with poor wine is more than just a mistake, it is pure heresy.

STOCK
Most country casseroles, sauces and a great many delicious soups are based on good chicken or beef stock of the rich home-made variety. A pint or two of stock can be kept on hand for one week in a covered jar in the refrigerator, or stored indefinitely in the freezer. I make stock in regular weekly bouts; the butcher send the appropriate boiling fowl, veal and beef bones, and meat, as a regular weekly order. In this way, I am free, throughout the week, to make any number of *consommés*, *risottos*, soups and sauces. Liquids from the stock-pots enrich casseroles of meat and poultry; vegetables are cooked in stock for extra tastiness. Stock on hand is a must for good cooking.

CREAM
Cream is a luxurious complement to the domain of sumptuous cookery. It is used by the Norman French mainly in the form of *sauce normande*, which begins with a *roux* made of butter and flour. To this is added a condensed liquid obtained by boiling vegetables and herbs until the *bouillon* has become an essence of their flavours, enriched either by white wine or egg yolks, depending on the dish for which the sauce is destined. The cream is added last, along with more butter and a dash of lemon. *Sauce normande* is particularly good with various egg dishes, and a wonderful accompaniment to fish and chicken dishes.

COOKING WITH WINE

Wine is much more than just a flavouring agent; used with discretion, it gives an unmistakable fillip to the simplest dishes; and in *ragoûts* and marinades it is a wonderfully effective 'tenderiser' for the drier or tougher cuts of meat.

Wine in this country is sufficiently low in cost to allow it to be used generously in cooking. Try wine for stewing and basting; use it adventurously as a delicious substitute for other liquids or as an agent to blend flavours in a *ragoût* or a casserole. Add red wine to a marinade for beef, lamb, pork or game. Use wine – both red and white – to lend excitement to soups and sauces.

Think of wine in cooking as just another of the necessary good ingredients like butter, olive oil, parsley, onions and herbs. Allow it to round out and add savour to the general flavour of your cooking. And a note for teetotallers: wine loses its alcohol content in cooking and its taste actually changes.

There are no set rules for cooking with wine. White wines go well with the white meats of veal, poultry and fish, but they also add body and flavour to a Provençal *daube* of beef. And one of the most delicious fish recipes I know is turbot cooked in red wine.

Wine can be used to add savour to many, many good things. *Bœuf à la bourguignonne* was my first introduction to the delights of wine cookery, tender chunks of beef sautéed until golden in butter and olive oil with a few *lardons* of fat salt bacon, and then simmered to tender perfection in red wine with tiny white onions and button mushrooms. Steak *à la bordelaise* features rump steak or fillet sautéed for a minute or two on each side, sliced thinly and served with a delicious red wine sauce which is simplicity itself to make.

Try *salmis* of grouse this season. This age-old recipe roasts birds until partially cooked, cuts them into serving pieces and serves them with golden *croûtons* in a rich wine sauce. Chicken, too, is delicious when prepared in this way, as are pheasant and partridge.

Coq-au-vin, a tender chicken browned in butter, flamed in brandy and then simmered in a stock made rich with wine and herbs, is also a favourite of mine. Ham goes especially well when cooked with dry white wine. We all know gammon served with a Madeira sauce; but have you tried simple pork sausages simmered in red wine which has been thickened with a tablespoon or two of fresh breadcrumbs?

Dry sherry, Marsala or Madeira add immediate savour to a clear soup, but be careful to only use a very small amount. Baste fish and seafood with a mixture of equal parts of melted butter and dry sherry, vermouth or dry white wine.

Transform a potato salad by dressing it with olive oil, salt, freshly-ground black pepper, wine vinegar and dry white wine. Just two or more tablespoons make all the difference.

Marinate duck or game overnight in red wine with sliced carrots and onions, fresh herbs and a dash of cognac for added tenderness and flavour. Brown meat first in butter and then simmer in marinade juices until done.

Fruit, too, gains in flavour when cooked in wine. Poach hard-fleshed fruits such as pears, peaches, cherries, nectarines and apricots – with or without skins – in red or white wine, water and sugar until tender. After poaching, remove fruit from its liquid and chill. Serve in its own liquid which has been separately chilled.

And remember, the better the wine you use, the better the final dish.

THE EMERGENCY SHELF

No household should be without its emergency shelf, well stocked with tinned and packaged 'convenience' foods, ready for unexpected guests or an impromptu dinner party.

I like to entertain and I always make sure that I have the ingredients for one or two surprise menus ready for use in case I invite guests back after a cocktail party or after the theatre. For impromptu meals – whipped up in a minute without the fuss and bother that often go into a full-scale dinner party – can be enormous fun. And success is practically assured with a little forethought and planning.

In the country, particularly, where friends are more apt to drop in for just drinks and stay for supper, I rely on my emergency shelf for simple casseroles or knife-and-fork soups that come almost entirely from package or tin. Spaghetti, for instance, with an Italian tomato sauce simmered for an hour before the meal, allows just enough time for a drink or two in front of the fire with guests before lunch or dinner is served. Precede with an Italian *antipasto* platter – tinned or bottled artichoke hearts, green and black olives, a slice or two of foil-wrapped *salame*, tinned anchovies and sardines and fresh tomatoes – follow with a green salad and brandied fruits – pears, peaches, apricots and cherries – and your reputation is made.

Or, instead of spaghetti, serve a quick *paella* made with saffron rice liberally spiked with prawns, minced clams, quartered mushrooms, peas and strips of pimento. Easy to prepare, if you make sure that you have the following ingredients in store: rice for *risotto*, saffron, chicken stock cubes for *bouillon*, a Spanish onion and one tin each of prawns, minced clams, mushrooms, peas and pimento. Tiny cocktail sausages and a small roast chicken or cooked lobster, cut into serving pieces, make this dish almost regal. Follow with a green salad, a chocolate mousse or fruit fool and coffee. More than enough to keep any party going.

The egg, of course, reigns supreme as a stand-by for emergency meals. An omelette, filled with creamed tuna or curried ham and shrimp, makes an excellent light luncheon dish or a hot first course before a cold meat. Try a cheese soufflé with garlic *croûtons*, or one made with tinned salmon flavoured with freshly-grated Parmesan, lemon juice and cayenne pepper. Make a chocolate or lemon-flavoured soufflé for a festive finish to a family meal.

Paper-thin pancakes filled with emergency-shelf ingredients – curried seafood, diced tinned ham and mushrooms in a cheese sauce, mashed sardines, minced clams – can turn a simple country lunch into party fare. Try a ham and chicken salad in a fruit dressing made of sliced oranges, bananas, whipped cream and mayonnaise flavoured with a dash of brandy. Perfect after a hot seafood chowder.

Keep these stand-by supplies on your emergency shelf

When shopping for emergency-shelf items, remember that most can be kept for an almost unlimited time. So buy in quantity when you find them reduced in a sale; you will save both time and money. Best for quick meals are tinned ham, chicken, fish, seafood and luncheon meats.

I always have eggs, milk, cream, Parmesan cheese and a small supply of Spanish onions, garlic, carrots, tomatoes and lettuce on hand. In addition to these 'perishables', I like to keep the following staples for emergency entertaining:

Soups and stock cubes

CREAM OF MUSHROOM
TOMATO
TURTLE
GREEN PEA
CLAM BROTH
CHICKEN STOCK CUBES
BEEF STOCK CUBES

Tinned or bottled meats

HAM
CHICKEN
LIVER PÂTÉ

Pasta and rice

SPAGHETTI
NOODLES
GREEN NOODLES
RISOTTO RICE

Tinned vegetables

MUSHROOMS
SMALL WHITE ONIONS
ITALIAN PEELED TOMATOES
TOMATO CONCENTRATE
TOMATO JUICE
ARTICHOKE HEARTS
PEAS

Tinned fruits

PEARS
PINEAPPLE
PEACHES
APRICOTS
CHERRIES

Tinned fish

SALMON
TUNA
CRABMEAT
SARDINES
ANCHOVIES
MINCED CLAMS
COD'S ROE

Miscellaneous

OLIVE OIL
WINE VINEGAR
TINNED MILK
MAYONNAISE
OLIVES
PICKLES
RELISHES
TRUFFLES

SECTION 2

A Short Guide to Cooking Terms

Acidify: To add lemon juice or vinegar to a sauce or cooked dish.

Acidulated water: (1) Water mixed with an acidifying agent – lemon juice or vinegar – used to blanch sweetbreads, veal or chicken. (2) Lemon juice and water in equal quantities added to sliced apples, pears or bananas to stop them turning brown.

Aspic: The culinary name for calf's foot jelly, or jelly made with bones of meat, fish or poultry. Any meat, fish, poultry, game or vegetable may be served 'in aspic'.

Bain-marie: A French kitchen utensil designed to keep liquids at simmering point without coming to the boil. It consists of a saucepan standing in a larger pan which is filled with boiling water. A *bain-marie* is a great help in keeping sauces, stews and soups hot without overcooking. In domestic kitchens, a double saucepan can do double duty as a *bain-marie.*

Bake: To cook in dry heat in the oven. This term is usually used only for breads, cakes, cookies, biscuits, pies, tarts and pastries. When meats are cooked in the oven, the term used is 'to roast'.

Barbecue: To cook meat, poultry, game or fish in the open on a grill or spit over charcoal. Originally this term meant cooking a whole animal over an open fire, or in a pit. Barbecued foods are usually basted with a highly-seasoned sauce during cooking time.

Bard: To cover meat, poultry, game (and sometimes fish) with thin strips of pork fat or green bacon before roasting or braising.

Baste: To pour or spoon liquid over food as it cooks to moisten and flavour it.

Batter: Something that is beaten. Usually means the mixture from which pancakes, puddings and cakes are made. The batter used for pancakes and for coating purposes is made of eggs, flour and milk (or sometimes water) and is fairly liquid in consistency.

Beat: To mix with a spoon, spatula, whisk, rotary beater or electric blender; to make a mixture smooth and light by enclosing air.

Beurre manié: Equal quantities of butter and flour kneaded together and added bit by bit to a stew, casserole or sauce to thicken it. See page 30.

Blanch: To pre-heat in boiling water or steam. This can be done for several reasons: (1) to loosen outer skins of fruits, nuts or vegetables; (2) to whiten sweetbreads, veal or chicken; (3) to remove excess salt or bitter flavour from bacon, gammon, ham, Brussels sprouts, turnips, endive, etc.; (4) to prepare fruits and vegetables for canning, freezing or preserving. See page 50.

Blend: To mix two or more ingredients thoroughly.

Boil: To cook in any liquid – usually water, wine or stock, or a combination of the three – brought to boiling point and kept there. See page 48.

Boiling point: The temperature at which bubbles rise continually and break over the entire surface of a liquid.

Bone: To remove the bones from fish, chicken, poultry or game.

Bouillon: A clear soup, broth or stock made with beef, veal or poultry and vegetables. Strained before using.

Bouquet garni: A bunch or 'faggot' of culinary herbs. Used to flavour stews, casseroles, sauces. A *bouquet garni* can be small, medium or large, according to the flavour required for the dish and, of course, according to what the cook has at hand. See page 23.

Bread: To roll in, or coat with, breadcrumbs before cooking.

Broil: See 'grill'.

Brunoise: Finely-diced vegetables – carrots, celery, onions, leeks (and sometimes turnips) – simmered in butter and stock until soft. Used to flavour soups, stuffings, sauces and certain dishes of fish and shellfish.

Caramelise: To melt sugar in a thick-bottomed saucepan, stirring continuously until it is a golden-brown syrup.

Chaud-froid: A jellied white sauce made of butter, flour, chicken stock, egg yolks, cream and gelatine. Used to give a handsome shiny white glaze to chicken, ham, etc.

Chill: To place in refrigerator or other cold place until cold.

Chop: To cut into very small pieces with a sharp knife or a chopper.

Clarify: To clear a stock or broth by adding slightly-beaten egg whites and crushed egg shells and bringing liquid to the boil. The stock is then cooled and strained before using.

Cool: To allow to stand at room temperature until no longer warm to the touch. (*Not* to put in the refrigerator.)

Court-bouillon: The liquid in which fish, poultry or meat is cooked to give added flavour. A simple *court-bouillon* consists of water to which you have added 1 bay leaf, 2 stalks celery, 1 Spanish onion, 2 carrots and salt and freshly-ground black pepper, to taste. Other additives: wine, vinegar, stock, olive oil, garlic, shallots, cloves, etc.

Cream: To work one or more foods with a heavy spoon or a firm spatula until the mixture is soft and creamy. To cream butter and sugar: beat softened butter with electric mixer (or rub against sides of bowl with a wooden spoon) until smooth and fluffy. Gradually beat or rub in sugar until thoroughly blended.

Croûton: Bread trimmed of crusts, cut to shape (triangles, hearts, dice), rubbed with garlic (optional) and sautéed in oil or butter.

Cut in: To combine fat and dry ingredients with two knives, scissor-fashion, or with a pastry blender. When making pastry.

Deep-fry: To cook in deep hot fat until crisp and golden. Also known as French-fry. See page 54.

Devil: (1) To grill food with a mixture of butter, mustard, Worcestershire sauce and fresh breadcrumbs. (2) To cook or serve with a hot 'devil' sauce.

Dice: To cut into small even cubes.

Disjoint: To cut poultry, game or small animals into serving pieces by dividing at the joint.

Dissolve: To mix a dry ingredient with liquid until it is absorbed.

Dredge: To coat food with a fine-particled substance by dusting, sprinkling, or rolling the food in flour, cornflour, cornmeal, sugar, etc.

Dust: To sift or sprinkle lightly with a fine-particled substance such as flour, sugar or seasonings.

Duxelles: Finely-chopped mushrooms and onion (or shallots), sautéed in butter until soft. Mixture should be quite dry. Used to flavour poached fish and shellfish; dress a fillet of beef or leg of baby lamb before it is wrapped in pastry; or (see page 59) to garnish a *papillote.*

Fillet: (1) Special cut of beef, lamb, pork or veal; breast of poultry and game; fish cut off the bone lengthwise. (2) To cut any of the above to use in cooking.

Fish fumet: A highly concentrated fish stock, made by reducing well-flavoured fish stock. Used to poach fish, fish fillets or fish steaks, and flavour sauces. Corresponds to essence for meats.

Flake: To break into small pieces with a fork.

Flame: To pour or spoon alcohol over a dish and ignite it.

Fold in: When a mixture has been beaten until light and fluffy, other ingredients must be 'folded in' very gently with a spatula so that the air will not be lost. Blend in new ingredients little by little, turning mixture very gently. Continue only until the ingredients are evenly blended.

Fricassée: To cook chicken or veal in fat until golden, and then in a sauce. Fricassée is in fact a form of braising.

Fry: To cook in a little fat or oil in a frying pan. See pages 53-4.

Garniture: The garnish or trimming added to a cooked dish (or served at the same time on a separate dish): vegetables, rice, *pasta*, pastry shapes, *croûtons*, etc.

Glaze: A thin coating of syrup or aspic – sometimes coloured with caramel – which is brushed over sweets, puddings, fruits (syrup), or cooked ham, tongue, chicken, beef, pork, veal, etc. (aspic). Food must be cold and quite dry before aspic will set.

Grate: To reduce to small particles with a grater.

Gratin: To cook '*au gratin*' is to brown food in the oven – usually covered in a sauce and dotted with breadcrumbs, cheese and butter – until a crisp, golden coating forms.

Grease: To rub lightly with butter, margarine, oil or fat.

Grill: To cook by direct heat such as an open fire. In our day, by charcoal, gas or electricity. See pages 51-3.

Julienne: Cut into fine strips the length of a matchstick.

Knead: To work dough with hands until it is of the desired elasticity or consistency.

Lard: (1) Common cooking fat obtained by melting down of pork fat. (2) Culinary process by which *lardons* of pork fat or green bacon are threaded through meat, poultry, game (and sometimes fish) to lend flavour and moisture to food.

Lardons: (1) Strips of fat or green bacon used as above. (2) Diced pork fat or green bacon, blanched and sautéed to add flavour and texture contrast to certain stews, *daubes*, *ragoûts* and casseroles.

Liaison: To thicken a sauce, gravy or stew: (1) by the addition of flour, cornflour, arrowroot, rice flour, potato flour, or a *beurre manié* (flour and butter); (2) by stirring in egg yolk, double cream, or in the case of certain dishes of poultry or game, blood.

Macédoine: (1) A mixture of raw or cooked fruit for a fruit salad. (2) A mixture of cooked diced vegetables garnished with a cream sauce, mayonnaise or aspic, usually served as an *hors-d'œuvre* salad, or as a garnish.

Marinade: A highly-flavoured liquid – usually red or white wine or olive oil or a combination of the two – seasoned with carrots, onion, bay leaf, herbs and spices. Marinades can be cooked or uncooked. The purpose of a marinade is to impart flavour to the food and to soften fibres of tougher foods.

Marinate: To let food stand, or steep, in a marinade. See above.

Mask: To cover cooked food with sauce.

Mince: To reduce to very small particles with a mincer, chopper or knife.

Mirepoix: Finely-diced carrots, onion, celery (and sometimes ham), simmered in butter until soft. Used to add flavour to dishes of meat, poultry, fish and shellfish.

Oven-fry: To cook meat, fish or poultry in fat in the oven, uncovered, basting food with fat from time to time. See page 54.

Parboil: To pre-cook, or boil until partially cooked.

Pare or peel: (1) To cut off outside skin or covering of a fruit or vegetable with a knife or parer. (2) To peel fruits such as oranges or bananas without using a knife.

Papillote: To cook '*en papillote*' is the culinary term for cooking food enclosed in an oiled paper or foil case (*papillote*). See page 59.

Poach: To cook gently in simmering (not boiling) liquid so that the surface of the liquid barely trembles. See page 48.

Pit: To remove pit, stone or seed, as from cherries.

Pound: To reduce to very small particles, or a paste, with a mortar and pestle.

Purée: To press through a fine sieve or food mill to produce a smooth soft food.

Quenelle: The finely-pounded flesh of fish, shellfish, veal, poultry or game; mixed with egg whites and cream and pounded over ice to a velvety smooth paste. These feather-light dumplings are then poached in a light stock or salted water.

Ragoût: A stew made from regular-sized pieces of meat, poultry or fish, sautéed in fat until brown and then simmered with stock, meat juices or water, or a combination of these, until tender. *Navarin de mouton* is an example of a 'brown' *ragoût*; Irish stew is a typical 'white' *ragoût*, in which meat is not browned before stewing.

Reduce: To cook a sauce over a high heat, uncovered, until it is reduced by evaporation to the desired consistency. This culinary process improves both flavour and appearance.

Render: To free fat from tissue by melting at low heat.

Roast: To cook meat by direct heat on a spit or in the oven, although 'baking' would be a better term, for when meat is cooked in a closed area (oven) vapour accumulates and changes texture and flavour of true roast. See page 55.

Roux: The gentle amalgamation of butter and flour over a low heat; capable of absorbing at least six times its own weight when cooked. (1) To make a white *roux*: melt 2 tablespoons butter in the top of a double saucepan; add 2 tablespoons of sieved flour and stir with a wire whisk for 2 or 3 minutes over water until the mixture amalgamates but does not change colour. (2) A pale *roux*: cook as above, stirring continuously, just a little longer (4 to 5 minutes) or until the colour of *roux* begins to change to pale gold. (3) A brown *roux*: cook as above until mixture acquires a fine light brown colour and nutty aroma.

Salmis: To cook jointed poultry or game in a rich wine sauce after it has been roasted until almost done. Often done in a chafing dish at the table.

Salpicon: Finely-diced meat, poultry, game, fish, shellfish or vegetables, bound with a savoury sauce and used to fill *canapés* and individual *hors-d'œuvre* pastry cases. Also used to make rissoles, *croquettes* and stuffings for eggs, vegetables and small cuts of poultry or meat.

Sauté: To fry lightly in a small amount of hot fat or oil, shaking the pan or turning food frequently during cooking. See page 53.

Scald: To heat to temperature just below boiling point. I use a double saucepan to scald cream or milk. This prevents scorching.

Score: To make evenly-spaced, shallow slits or cuts with a knife.

Sear: To brown and seal the surface of meat quickly over high heat. This prevents juices from escaping.

Sift: To put through a sifter or a fine sieve.

Simmer: To cook in liquid just below boiling point, with small bubbles of steam rising occasionally to the surface.

Skewer: (1) To keep in shape with skewers. (2) The actual 'skewer' – made of metal or wood – which is used to keep meats, poultry, game, etc., in shape while cooking. (3) The 'skewer' – piece of metal or wood – sometimes called '*brochette*', used to hold pieces of chicken, fish, poultry, etc., to be grilled over charcoal, or under gas or electricity.

Sliver: To cut or shred into long, thin pieces.

Steam: To cook food in vapour over boiling water or stock. This process is often used in Oriental cooking. See page 50.

Steep: To let food stand in hot liquid to extract flavour or colour.

Stir: To mix with a spoon or fork with a circular motion until ingredients are well blended.

Whisk: To beat rapidly with a whisk, rotary beater or electric mixer in order to incorporate air and increase volume.

Zest: The finely-grated rind of lemon or orange.

SECTION 3

Basic Equipment

When Catherine de Medici brought Italian cooks to France, she also brought the key to the whole future of eating in one kitchen gadget – the fork. The knife, I grant you, is pretty important, and so is the spoon. A knife alone, however, meant that you still had to use your hands for a good part of the meal, and that restricted you to roasts and boiled meats and all the rigmarole of medieval food. But with the introduction of the fork, sauces and every subtlety became possible and the art of present-day cookery was born.

There are gadgets and gadgets. Some are indispensable, some so complicated that it is almost easier to beat by hand for twenty minutes than to assemble and dismantle the monster. You may have your own idiosyncracies – I have my automatic slicing machine, bought in a weak moment, which I have used six times during the past two years. But for the most part the equipment I use in my kitchen is as simple as Catherine de Medici's fork.

INDISPENSABLE ITEMS

CHOPPING BOWL One of the most used utensils in my kitchen is a small wooden chopping bowl with a knife which has a curved blade specially designed to fit it. In this I cut all parsley, *fines herbes*, garlic, shallots and onions. It is always in view, ready for use, in my kitchen, as is a thick chopping board. I hate to have to search for such necessary and constantly used items.

CHOPPING BOARD Make sure your chopping board is thick enough to withstand many washings without warping, and large enough to hold food that falls away from the knife.

MORTAR AND PESTLE A rather more esoteric bit of basic equipment in my kitchen is the stone mortar and pestle which are also always in readiness for pounding dried breadcrumbs, herbs to make a sauce, or meats for a pâté. I like a large-sized mortar, so that I can use it to pound anchovies for a Provençal *anchoïade* or poached salt cod for a *brandade de morue*.

ELECTRIC MIXER OR BLENDER I have both – a free-standing electric mixer, designed to take the hard labour out of soufflés, meringues, bread and cake-making; and a built-in, counter-top blender, onc of the most useful gadgets ever invented. There is hardly anything in the way of chopping and blending – from making puréed soups, to fruit drinks and such artefacts of French *haute cuisine* as *quenelles* – that this machine cannot do for you, even so far as making a perfectly delicious frozen *daïquiri*.

CUTLERY FOR THE KITCHEN

Most food preparation calls for some kind of cutting, slicing or chopping. You will find that a well-chosen selection of kitchen knives is one of the first requisites of a well-equipped kitchen. I have had special slots cut into a kitchen table top to hold each of my regularly used knives.

BASIC KNIFE WARDROBE In any department store or ironmonger's you will find an extensive array of kitchen knives with different shapes, lengths and edges. Many of the imported modern German knives have scalloped or serrated edges which offer special advantages in cutting and hold their cutting edge indefinitely. These are the knives I find most useful:

HAM SLICER The long (9 to 9½ inch) ham knife is perfect for cutting thin, parallel slices of ham or gammon and is also good for poultry.

CARVING KNIFE You will need one straight edge and one serrated edge. Use for all roasts and steaks. The blade should be 7 to 9 inches long. I find a serrated edge good for cold meats, cheeses and sausages, as well as for most bread and pastry cutting.

FRENCH COOK'S KNIFE You will need one large and one small. Use to dice, chop or slice raw vegetables and fruits.

SMALL PARING KNIFE Good for paring potatoes, cucumbers, carrots and onions. A paring knife with a pointed tip and a 3-inch blade is most satisfactory.

UTILITY KNIFE Just what its name implies; good for everything.

CLEAVER Useful for sectioning heavy pieces of meat, cutting joints, and for game and lobster. I also use mine, flat-sided, as a meat tenderiser.

KITCHEN IMPLEMENTS

Of all the everyday tools that are in constant use in every kitchen, these are among the most versatile:

COOKING FORK Select one with a long handle and stainless steel prongs.

WOODEN AND METAL SPOONS Both long and short are necessary to fit a variety of saucepan sizes.

A SLOTTED METAL COOKING SPOON is useful for making sauces and gravies smooth and for skimming stocks and sauces.

SPATULA A flexible spatula of stainless steel for icing cakes, loosening food and turning omelettes.

LADLE Available in a variety of sizes; for ladling soups, sauces and gravies.

WIRE WHISKS Either round or flat, for whisking sauces and egg whites.

MEASURING EQUIPMENT Accurate measurements are essential to any kind of cooking. If they are kept within easy reach of cooking and preparation areas, measuring becomes automatic. A set of individual MEASURING SPOONS in plastic or metal – 1 tablespoon, 1 dessertspoon, 1 teaspoon, ½ teaspoon and ¼ teaspoon – is ideal for measuring small quantities of ingredients. A PINT MEASURING CUP marked off in fluid ounces is also useful, as is a pair of KITCHEN SCALES.

METAL GRATER Round or square-shaped with different-sized cutting sides for grating cheese, lemon and orange rinds, nutmeg, etc. New stainless steel graters are on the market which make maintenance much easier.

PEPPER AND SALT MILLS While far from essential, these kitchen aids offer the extra advantage of freshly-ground seasonings.

SIEVES A conical sieve used for the straining of sauces is one of the most useful kitchen utensils. A 6-inch conical sieve is a good size for all purposes. I also find the ordinary round-bottomed sieves useful for the sieving and draining of vegetables.

MIXING BOWLS Every kitchen should have a series of mixing bowls large enough for the ingredients to be used. I like a series of three bowls in assorted sizes, as well as a mammoth bowl with a lip from Sweden which I find most useful.

COOKWARE

SAUCEPANS When buying new equipment, make sure you choose good sturdy saucepans of heavy metal. Though more expensive at first, they are well worth the initial outlay, for heavy saucepans will hold the heat better, will not dent or warp so easily and will not allow foods to scorch.

I prefer aluminium, aluminium combined with copper, or copper saucepans, in the largest sizes available. I find that if I cook for more than three persons, it is always the largest saucepan that I reach for. I prefer saucepans with straight sides.

DOUBLE SAUCEPAN Used for making most sauces and for keeping sauces hot without danger of curdling or separating. It is absolutely necessary for delicate emulsion sauces such as *béarnaise* or *hollandaise*.

FRYING PANS A large black-iron frying pan with a thick bottom is one of the best cook's aids ever invented. I have two, a 6-inch pan for omelettes and a large all-purpose pan. To keep frying pans in good condition, never put them away dirty and never clean with a metal knife or metal sponge. *A frying pan should be cleaned by heat*, with salt applied when the pan is very hot, and a paper towel.

Before using your iron frying pan for the first time, prepare it by heating it over a hot flame until all protective varnish or grease has disappeared. Then wipe it clean with a towel. Cover the bottom generously with oil or lard and heat this fat in the oven or over a flame. Pour off the excess grease and leave the residue in the pan. If it still sticks when you use it, repeat the process.

CASSEROLES

You will soon find you want a casserole 'wardrobe' – several sizes of every type of casserole made – but if your kitchen is on the small side I suggest you start with the following: two large casseroles for buffet suppers and large gatherings; two medium-sized casseroles for dinners of four to eight; and several small casseroles for vegetables and for intimate dinners for two.

The choice is large: flame-proof, classic copper and oven-proof earthenware from France; modern Swedish metal designs in all shapes, colours and sizes; and from England, beautiful new creations in coated cast iron by the Marquis of Queensberry, as well as an elegant set of graduated copper and brass casseroles from Royal Normandy.

IRON CASSEROLES I am particularly happy to see the arrival in this country of iron *cocottes* and casseroles such as I have been used to in America. There, our 'Dutch oven', a large round casserole in heavy black iron with a close-fitting iron lid, was the stand-by for every kind of cooking. Wonderful for pot roasts and for casseroles of chicken, meat and game, it worked very well as an emergency frying pan . . . and I have even baked an upside-down peach pudding in one.

These new iron casseroles, imported from Finland, come in three or four practical sizes. They are prepared and maintained in the same way as iron frying pans. Be sure to keep them well oiled as they have a tendency to rust in this climate if left dry.

ASBESTOS MAT If your casserole is not flame-proof, you will need an asbestos mat to put under it for top-of-the-stove cookery.

SECTION 4

Basic Cookery Methods

COOKING IN WATER

BOILING

You can cook anything in water – from the ubiquitous chicken to the unusual *gigot à l'irlandaise* (a tender leg of lamb, boned and stuffed with herbs, then rolled in a suet pastry and simmered gently in water until deliciously tender).

Cooking in water does not, however, mean that you should not flavour it. Salt is, of course, used even when boiling a potato. But many cooks in France never think of preparing their *bouillon* (the liquid in which anything is boiled) without adding a few peppercorns, a sprig of thyme or other herbs, a bay leaf, some onions, a little vinegar or equal quantities of wine and stock. I like to cook new potatoes, for instance, in a covered saucepan with just ½ inch of water and 2 to 3 tablespoons of butter or olive oil. Try this with peas, spinach, carrots or sliced *courgettes*.

You will find it makes all the difference, whether you are cooking a fish in a delicately prepared *court-bouillon*; a fat, herb-stuffed chicken in a rich stock spiked with dry white wine; or fresh egg noodles in a light white stock flavoured with a little olive oil and a touch of garlic.

POACHING

Other than when making tea or coffee, or when cooking the occasional new potato, green vegetable or hard-boiled egg, I prefer to think of boiling in terms of poaching (a boiling that does not quite boil), for the term 'poaching' extends to all slow processes of cooking which involve the use of a liquid, not necessarily water, no matter how small the quantity. Thus the term 'poach' applies equally as well to the cooking of a large fish – a turbot or a salmon – in an aromatic *court-bouillon*, as it does to fillets of sole simmered in a little

fish *fumet*, or to eggs or vegetables cooked in stock or water.
Poached foods are usually served with a butter or cream-based sauce or, more simply, with butter, olive oil or cream.

BLANCHING

Blanching is not, properly speaking, a method of cooking at all, but a preliminary preparation. To blanch vegetables, meat or fish, put the ingredient into a generous saucepan of cold water; bring the water to boiling point; remove the pan from the fire and drain the ingredient, which is then 'blanched'.
Almonds and chestnuts are blanched to facilitate removing their skins. Certain vegetables – onions, cabbage and even Brussels sprouts – are blanched to remove bitterness before they are tossed in butter. Diced fat bacon is usually blanched to remove excess salt before it is sautéed in butter and oil and used as a flavouring agent in many stews and *ragoûts*. Veal and lamb are blanched to preserve their whiteness for certain 'white' stews such as *fricassées* and *blanquettes*.

STEAMING

Cooking by steam is one of the principal forms of Oriental cooking and one not to be bypassed in Western kitchens. It is rapid and also one of the most effective methods of cooking I know for preserving the maximum degree of original taste.
Cooking by steam in the Chinese manner is simple in preparation: all you do is to have the food concerned (a whole fish, fish fillets or steaks, or a fillet of beef, a lean loin of pork, breast of chicken or turkey) sliced thinly across the grain. Moisten the slices in soy sauce and dry white wine, with a little cornflour added to thicken the sauce. Then add 6 to 8 thinly-sliced button mushrooms for every pound of food used. Place the meat, fish or poultry, and mushroom slices, in a heat-proof gratin dish or shallow casserole with one or two thinly-sliced shallots or green onions; and season to taste with salt and freshly-ground black pepper. When ready to cook, set dish on a stand in a large pan containing about 2 inches of rapidly boiling water.

STEAMED POULTRY

A whole chicken, a duck (or even a lean leg of baby lamb) may be steamed in this way if your steamer is large enough. Alexandre Dumaine, often called the world's greatest chef, serves a steamed chicken at his famous restaurant, La Côte d'Or, in Saulieu, Upper Burgundy. The chicken is marinated overnight in a few tablespoons of port or Madeira before being steamed in its own juices and a little butter in a heat-proof dish. The secret here is that the chicken is steamed for an hour over a superbly flavoured beef *bouillon* complete with onions, carrots, turnips and fresh herbs, which lend their flavours and juices to the finished dish.

STEAMED VEGETABLES
Most vegetables – cauliflower, peas, Brussels sprouts, green beans – steam to pefection in 15 to 20 minutes. Try steamed peas dressed with sautéed onion, diced ham, sugar and mint leaves. Dress steamed cauliflower with lemon juice and fresh breadcrumbs or slivered almonds sautéed in butter. Serve steamed Brussels sprouts with a sprinkling of fresh breadcrumbs sautéed in butter until golden. Dress steamed green beans with butter, finely-chopped parsley and crumbled bits of crisp-fried bacon.

EQUIPMENT
I use a special steamer which consists of a double saucepan with a perforated bottom which allows the steam to rise; or, failing this, I just place a metal trivet or tin pâté mould under the dish holding the food to be cooked. Whatever pan you use, cover it tightly so that the food is completely surrounded by steam and continues to cook in it until tender. Wet towels wrapped around the join between lid and pan help to prevent the steam from escaping.

1. Your cooking utensil should be large enough to hold comfortably, with a stand, the dish containing the food to be cooked.
2. Heat the dish; place the food in it and put the dish in the pan only when the water is actually boiling and steam is rising. To cook: cover the pan immediately and turn up the heat so that the steam is at its height.
3. Steamed food cooks quickly. It should be neither overdone nor underdone. All meat – except pork, which must be well done – should be a little pink when removed from the steamer.
4. Serve steamed food the moment it is considered cooked. Otherwise it will be overdone, for because of the intense heat it has absorbed, the cooking process will continue away from the heat until the food cools. Steam-cooked food should be eaten hot. Otherwise it loses flavour and texture.

GRILLING OR BROILING

Grilling or broiling – the roasting of meat on an open fire – was probably the starting point of all cooking. It is best to remember when grilling today, whether over charcoal or under gas or electricity, that the metal grid of the grill should always be very hot when the objects to be grilled are placed upon it; otherwise they tend to stick to the bars of the grid. I like to heat the grid thoroughly, wipe it clean with a damp cloth and then rub a bit of suet over the bars to prevent the meat from sticking.

Grilling is a wonderfully quick way to cook; but because it is so quick, it is difficult to grill perfectly. A minute too long under the grill, or the wrong temperature – too hot for a thin slice of ham or gammon or a joint of chicken; not hot enough for a thick slice of beef – will ruin the end result.

Practice, of course, will teach you how to deal most successfully with your grill. Two easy rules to remember: thick cuts of meat and fish should be cooked at a greater distance from the heat – thinner cuts, near the heat.

To grill steaks or chops successfully: season meat with freshly-ground black pepper and place on pre-heated grid. The thicker cuts of meat should be 'seized' on both sides with a very high heat to preserve their juices, before cooking at a more moderate heat to allow its gradual penetration into the juicy centre of the meat. The smaller cuts – *tournedos*, chops, fillets, cutlets – can be cooked without lowering the heat once the juices have been sealed in. For best results, season meats to taste with salt after cooking.

PAN-GRILLING

An excellent method of grilling steaks at home is to grill them in an iron frying pan or in one of the special grill pans made for this purpose. If the pan or grill is hot enough, it should not be necessary to add fat. If desired, rub the pan with a piece of suet. Season meat to taste with freshly-ground black pepper, sear quickly on one side, reduce the heat and cook for a minute or two longer. Turn the steak; sear on the other side and continue cooking and turning until the steak is done to your taste.

BASTING

Baste all meats with butter or oil before placing them on the hot grid, and repeat this operation several times during the cooking process to keep the meat from drying out during cooking. Little beads of blood on the outside surfaces indicate that the meat is done.

MARINATING

Meat is often marinated in olive oil and wine to tenderise and flavour it before cooking. Add freshly-ground black pepper and salt, to taste, and one or more of the following: sliced onion, shallot, garlic, soy sauce, bay leaf, thyme or parsley. Marinate meat for at least 2 hours in this mixture, turning it occasionally to ensure maximum penetration. Pat dry with a clean tea towel before grilling.

BEEF

Beef is the most popular meat for grilling. The best cuts to use for grilling are the fillet, the rump and the upper cut of sirloin. I like a good thick rib steak, cut from the sirloin, complete with bone. The most expensive cuts of beef for grilling are those cut from the fillet. Slices of fillet are usually named according to their thickness: a *tournedos* is a small piece of fillet about 1½ inches thick; the famous *filet mignon* of American restaurant parlance is a piece 1¾ to 2 inches thick; while a piece 2 to 3 inches thick is known as a *chateaubriand*.

WHITE MEATS

When grilling white meats – veal, lamb and chicken – a moderate heat will ensure that you cook and colour the meat simultaneously. Baste white-meat grills fairly often with butter, or butter and oil. They are done when the juices coming from them are colourless.

FISH

When grilling fish – with the exception of the fatty varieties such as mackerel, herrings and *rougets* – always roll the fish to be grilled in a little flour before sprinkling them with melted butter to give a golden outside crust. For best results, both the oven and grid should be very, very hot, and the grid itself should be rubbed with oil to prevent sticking.

FRYING

Frying, strictly speaking, is simply the immersing of food in very hot fat or oil. The term is sometimes extended, in this country, to pan-frying, which has come to mean the same as sautéeing, and in America many foods are oven-fried, a new combination of sautéeing and baking which has much to recommend it for simple dishes.

PAN-FRYING

This popular method of cooking uses butter to sauté meat, fish or fresh vegetables in a frying pan. Finely-chopped fresh parsley, lemon juice or slivered almonds are sometimes added to the sauce obtained. It is a good idea to add a little olive oil (but only a very little) to the butter at first; then, when the meat or fish begins to take on colour, add more butter. This will prevent butter from browning during the cooking process.

Only very tender foods are suitable for pan-frying: fish, young chicken, chops, liver, beef fillets and vegetables. Thick slices of meat cannot be pan-fried successfully. Do not crowd food in the pan and do not cover the pan when frying because the steam thus held in will moisten and destroy the surface crispness of the food.

OVEN-FRYING

Beloved by American cooks, this process is a very useful method of cooking fish or chicken. Heat the oven to 400°F. (Mark 5). Use enough oil, or oil and butter, to cover the bottom of a shallow baking dish. Heat the dish in the oven and then put in the food which you have first basted with melted butter and rolled in breadcrumbs mixed with chopped fresh herbs (parsley, chervil, chives, etc.) and a little grated lemon rind. Cook in the oven until tender.

DEEP-FRYING

The way you fry is more important than the fat or oil you use. If anyone asked me to define the quality of a fried food, I would say that its quality was in inverse proportion to the oil or fat absorbed by the food. Deep-fried food should never be greasy. *Thus, the temperature of the fat is of prime importance:* it must be hot enough to 'carbonise' the exterior of what is being fried at the very moment of immersion. This prevents grease from penetrating the food, conserves the juices and allows the food to retain all its taste.

Deep-frying is simple and quick when you know how. Vegetable fats and salad oils are good for all deep-frying. Rendered beef fat is a good choice for meats, fish *croquettes* and less delicate foods. Chicken fat and butter are not suitable for deep-frying because they scorch at low temperatures.

The quality and freshness of the oil or fat used is of great importance.

A frying medium uses itself quickly, especially when it is heated to excess. I have found that I can double the life of my frying oil if I never allow it to smoke. Use the bread test instead: drop an inch cube of day-old bread in the hot oil. If your temperature is right for deep-frying the bread should brown on one side in about 40 seconds.

1. Do not allow fat to smoke or boil.
2. The temperature of the fat should vary as little as possible during cooking.
3. If you plunge food into the fat a second time, the temperature of the second cooking must be higher than the first.

ROASTING

Now that many of us have infra-red 'rotisserie' grills, free-standing, open grill units or cookers with built-in spits, the roasting of meats in its true sense is once again possible. If the meat is cooked in an oven, baking would be a far better description, for, in spite of every precaution, it is impossible to avoid an accumulation of vapour around a cooking object in a closed oven. The spitted roast, on the contrary, cooks in a dry atmosphere and retains its own particular flavour.

But baking or roasting, as the case may be, is a simple operation and needs little attention other than frequent basting during the cooking process to keep the meat from drying out.

The cuts of beef suitable for roasting are the ribs, the sirloin, the fillet and, in best-quality beef, the rump. Suitable cuts of lamb are the leg, the saddle, the loin and the shoulder. Pork roasts include the leg, the loin and the spare rib. The loin, the saddle, the leg, the shoulder, the rump, and often the breast of veal, can all be roasted.

Roast beef can be tested with a sharp kitchen fork or skewer. Blood-red juice means that the meat is very rare, pink, that is medium done, and a clear liquid indicates that the meat is well cooked. For pork or veal: the juices that run out should be perfectly clear. For lamb: the liquid should be clear or lightly touched with pink.

1. Take meat out of the refrigerator sufficiently ahead of roasting time to allow it to acquire room temperature.
2. Roast beef in a very hot oven – 400° to 425°F. (Mark 5 to 6) – for 15 to 30 minutes to seal it. Then reduce oven heat to 325°F. (Mark 2) and continue to cook until done.
3. Baste meat frequently with fat, whether it is cooked on the spit or in the oven, beginning about 45 minutes after the meat has started to cook. Baste every 10 to 15 minutes.
4. An oven roast should always be placed on a grid so that the meat will not come in contact with the juices and fat which have drained from it into the pan underneath.
5. No liquid, gravy or water should be put in the baking pan when roasting meat as it will add to the vapour already inherent in an oven roast.

BRAISING

Braising is simply a combination of roasting, stewing and steaming. The meat to be braised is sometimes (Step 1) larded; often (Step 2) marinated; always (Step 3) browned in fat and then (Step 4) cooked gently, covered, in a little liquid to preserve juices and flavour. In the classic French method, the casserole is lined with a layer of sliced vegetables before slow simmering begins.

For the most part meat, poultry or fish to be braised is not cut up, but is braised in the piece. The braising techniques listed below can also be used with great facility for cut-up pieces of meat, poultry or fish in stews, *ragoûts*, *daubes* and casseroles of many countries.

1. LARDING

Top-quality beef – rib or fillet – does not have to be larded; but it is usually wise to lard a rump or round of beef, a roast of veal or a leg of mutton with strips of bacon fat as long as the piece of meat to be cooked and about ½ inch wide. Season these first with pepper and spices, sprinkle with chopped parsley and marinate for about 2 hours in a little brandy; then insert the strips into the meat with a special larding needle. Most butchers will lard meat for you.

2. MARINATING

The flavour of meat intended for braising is greatly improved by marinating it for a few hours in the wine which is to be the moistening agent in cooking. Roll the meat in a mixture of salt, pepper and finely-chopped herbs, and place it in an earthenware casserole just large enough to hold it, on a bed of thickly-sliced and fried carrots and onions, a generous *bouquet garni*, a clove or two of garlic, and some blanched, fried fat bacon. Cover the meat with wine and marinate for at least 2 hours in this mixture, taking care to turn it several times during this period.

3. SAUTÉEING

After having marinated the meat, drain it well and wipe it dry with a clean cloth. Sauté in a little olive oil, bacon fat, butter or lard, or a combination of these, to colour it and seal in its juices. Then place the vegetables and herbs from the marinade in the bottom of a heavy casserole or braising pan just large enough to hold the meat; place the meat on this bed of aromatics and pour in enough of the juices from the marinade to cover the vegetables amply.

4. CASSEROLING

Add well-flavoured beef stock; bring it to the boil; cover the casserole and cook gently on top of the stove or in a moderate oven until the meat can be pricked deeply with a fork without giving blood. Remove the meat to another casserole just large enough to hold it; strain the sauce through a piece of muslin and return the casserole, covered, to the oven. Cook until tender, basting from time to time to keep the top of the meat moist. Before serving, correct seasoning and thicken the sauce, if necessary, with a *beurre manié* (equal quantities of flour and butter kneaded together).

Cook very slowly so that the meat will be tender and the fat will rise gradually to the surface of the liquid.

Vegetables – as well as meats, poultry and fish – can be braised in this way with excellent results.

Any casserole can be used for braising and for stews, provided that it is thick enough to prevent scorching during the long cooking process and has a tight-fitting lid.

COOKING 'AU GRATIN'

Cooking *au gratin* (from the French verb *gratiner*: to brown) applies to oven-cooked dishes – macaroni, noodles, *gnocchi*, meats, fish and vegetables – which are baked in shallow, heat-proof gratin dishes, usually covered with a sauce, sprinkled liberally with breadcrumbs, dotted with butter and browned in the oven or under the grill until a crisp *gratin* coating forms. Cooking *au gratin* is associated in most people's minds with cheese, but although dishes *au gratin* often contain cheese, this is not an essential ingredient.

In order that there may be plenty of the characteristic crisp, golden-brown top, a shallow heat-proof dish is used, hence the familiar term, 'gratin dish'.

When browning in the oven, it is wise to set the dish in a pan half full of hot water. This prevents the sauce from spoiling or separating.

FISH AND SHELLFISH

Gratins can be made with either raw foods or left-overs. The most common raw *gratins* are made of whole fish, fish fillets or fish steaks, which are sautéed in butter or oil and covered with a *sauce duxelles* (finely-chopped mushrooms, onion and parsley, sautéed until smooth in butter) or a well-flavoured cream or cheese sauce.

Fish prepared with a white *gratin* sauce is usually poached in a concentrated fish stock, drained, covered with cream or cheese sauce, sprinkled with breadcrumbs or cheese and browned quickly in the oven.

VEGETABLES

Most vegetables can be gratinéed. Perhaps the most famous of these is *gratin dauphinois* (thinly-sliced new potatoes, cream and grated cheese, browned in the oven until smooth and flavourful, with a crisp golden crust), a wonderful accompaniment to steaks and roasts. *Gratin savoyard* exchanges beef stock for cream in an equally delicious variation of this great dish. Try adding diced celery, finely-chopped onions or shallots, or a hint of garlic to this basic recipe. You will be delighted with the result.

Larousse Gastronomique (published by Paul Hamlyn) talks of a delicious *gratin languedocien* of peeled and sliced aubergines and tomato halves sautéed in oil and then placed in alternate layers in a buttered baking dish. The vegetables are covered with a mixture of fresh breadcrumbs and finely-chopped garlic and parsley, sprinkled with olive oil (or dotted with butter), brought to the boil on the top of the stove and then baked slowly in the oven till the top is crisp and well browned.

Other vegetables – French beans, broccoli, endive, celery, leeks, onion and marrows – can be gratinéed in a similar fashion.

LEFT-OVERS – poached fish, chicken or turkey and sliced hard-boiled eggs – make excellent luncheon or supper dishes when cooked *au gratin.*

CREAMED HADDOCK AU GRATIN: Melt 2 level tablespoons butter in a saucepan; add 2 level tablespoons flour and cook until the *roux* just starts to turn golden. Add ¾ pint of milk and cook, stirring constantly, until sauce is reduced to about half the original quantity. Stir in ¼ pint double cream. Add ½ pint of this sauce to poached, flaked smoked haddock; season to taste with a little salt and pepper and pour into a heat-proof gratin dish. Combine the remaining sauce with 1 beaten egg; fold in 2 tablespoons whipped cream and spread over creamed haddock mixture. Sprinkle with fresh breadcrumbs; dot with butter and brown in a hot oven (450°F. Mark 7) or under the grill.

CREAMED CHICKEN OR TURKEY AU GRATIN: As above, using diced poached chicken or turkey instead of smoked haddock.

CREAMED EGGS AU GRATIN: As above, using sliced hard-boiled eggs instead of smoked haddock. Add freshly-grated cheese, to taste.

COOKING 'EN PAPILLOTE'

Cooking '*en papillote*' is only half-cooking really, for when you enclose an ingredient in a *papillote*, it is already half-cooked, or has at the very least been 'seized' in hot fat before being folded into the paper case which gives this process its name.

There is nothing magic about this *haute cuisine* phrase: a *papillote* is just a piece of thin, strong paper or aluminium foil, about 8½ by 11 inches, cut into an oval or heart shape, greased with oil or butter and folded to enclose the ingredient to be cooked.

Cooking *en papillote* is not only colourful but gastronomic, for the ingredient cooked in this way simmers gently in its own juices, hermetically sealed so that it loses none of its special flavour and aroma. It is almost always necessary to colour the ingredient to be cooked in butter or oil before enclosing it in its casing, but it is important not to cook it too much in the process or you will lose the advantages and virtues of this exciting cooking method.

Nothing adds more glamour to a meal than individual servings of trout, *rouget* or sole, veal cutlets, veal chops, or fat slices of salmon or turbot, first coloured in a little butter or oil, seasoned with freshly-ground black pepper, salt, fresh herbs and chopped shallots and mushrooms. The whole is then enclosed in its prepared paper case, fried for a moment in hot oil to colour and puff the case, and cooked in the oven to succulent and savoury goodness. Serve your *papillotes* in their puffed paper shells and let guests cut them open at the table with a knife. Aluminium foil cases are cooked in the oven only.

1. To cook *en papillote*: cut paper in an oval shape or in the form of a heart large enough to enclose, when folded, the food to be cooked.

2. Brush the insides of the heart shapes with melted butter or oil.

3. Sauté the food for a few moments to colour it before placing on paper or aluminium shapes.

4. Place food on bottom half of shape; add butter and aromatics – finely-chopped onion, shallot and mushrooms; and season to taste with salt and freshly-ground black pepper.

If *papillote* is paper: fold shapes and puff up shells by frying for a minute or two in hot oil in a frying pan. Then put shells on a baking sheet in the oven where they will keep their puffed-up appearance while the ingredients continue to cook.

If *papillote* is foil: fold shapes and seal edges well by crimping them together. Put shells on a baking sheet in the oven where they will continue to cook.

GREAT DISHES OF THE WORLD

CHAPTER 1

APPETISERS

Hors-d'œuvre Variés

Most of the glamorous restaurants of the world serve a galaxy of titbits, both hot and cold, which fly under the banner of *hors-d'œuvre variés*. These appetite stimulants are usually wheeled up to your table on a two- or three-tiered trolley, each tier of which can hold up to twenty small dishes or *raviers* containing a colourful assortment of vegetables, marinated in olive oil and lemon juice and served *à la vinaigrette*, or prepared *à la grecque* with wine, olive oil, finely-chopped onion, carrot and herbs. These trolleys come to us via France from Russia where the *hors-d'œuvre* idea originated in the Russian *zakouski* table, set up in a room adjoining the reception room and wheeled in to satisfy far-travelling guests before dinner. Thus it is not surprising to find Russian salad, hard-boiled eggs with a mayonnaise or sour cream dressing, and pickled and preserved fish of all kinds included in the usual *hors-d'œuvre* assortment.

The formula for *hors-d'œuvre* and *entrées chaudes* varies according to the whim of the *maître de la maison.* At the Restaurant de la Boule d'Or in Paris, for example, the *hors-d'œuvre* is limited to cucumbers in cream, sliced *saucisson*, tomato salad, asparagus *vinaigrette*, a duck pâté and a delicious dish of artichoke hearts, button onions and mushrooms *à la grecque*. The three hot *entrées* of the house are *quiche Lorraine*, a savoury tart of eggs, cheese and bacon; *pissaladière*, a Provençal tomato and onion tart; and delicately browned ham patties.

La Petite Auberge, famous three-star restaurant of Noves, in the South of France, offers an *hors-d'œuvre* dish that is in reality a meal in itself. Their famous vegetable appetiser consists of the following cooked and raw vegetables: button onions cooked in white wine and lemon juice, flavoured with nutmeg, pepper and herbs; leeks with a herb-flavoured vinaigrette sauce; coarsely-grated raw carrots dressed with mustard-flavoured mayonnaise; finely-sliced green peppers with an onion dressing; raw mushroom salad; poached celery with a Provençal dressing in which pounded anchovies, olive oil and wine vinegar play their part; highly-spiced saffron rice studded with raisins; tomato slices with a tarragon cream sauce; marinated artichoke hearts; and asparagus tips, topped with puréed tomatoes, lightly flavoured with mustard and mayonnaise. Any one of these would be delicious by itself as an *hors-d'œuvre*; or try a combination of two or more to provide colour, flavour and texture contrast.

The real purpose of the *hors-d'œuvre* course is to stimulate the appetite, not to drown it. A correctly chosen complement of dishes should not contain too much mayonnaise or other different dressings but it should contain both cooked and raw foods so that tastes and textures will vary as much as possible. Serve *hors-d'œuvre* to best advantage in individual dishes or bowls.

LENTILS AND SAUSAGES 'FORUM OF THE TWELVE CAESARS'

½ POUND LENTILS
HAM BONE OR ¼ POUND BACON
16 COCKTAIL SAUSAGES OR 8 SMALL CHIPOLATA SAUSAGES
¼ PINT OLIVE OIL
6 TABLESPOONS WINE VINEGAR
SALT AND FRESHLY-GROUND BLACK PEPPER
LETTUCE AND QUARTERED TOMATOES

Cook lentils in normal way with ham bone or bacon, and cool. Bake sausages in oven and cool. Mix lentils with oil, vinegar, salt and pepper, and arrange on bed of lettuce. Place sausages on top. Serve with quartered tomatoes. Serves 4.

BEAN SALAD VINAIGRETTE

1½ POUNDS GREEN BEANS
SALTED WATER
6–8 TABLESPOONS OLIVE OIL
2–3 TABLESPOONS WINE VINEGAR
SALT AND FRESHLY-GROUND BLACK PEPPER
FINELY-CHOPPED PARSLEY AND GARLIC

Top and tail young green beans and cook them in boiling salted water until they are barely tender. Drain and toss immediately while still warm in a well-flavoured French dressing (olive oil, wine vinegar, salt and pepper) to which you have added finely-chopped parsley and garlic, to taste. Serves 4 to 6.

MEDITERRANEAN FISH SALAD

¾ POUND TURBOT
¾ POUND HALIBUT
SALTED WATER
A LITTLE MILK
¼ POUND COOKED SHRIMPS
¼ PINT OLIVE OIL
JUICE OF 2 LEMONS
SALT AND FRESHLY-GROUND BLACK PEPPER
2–4 TABLESPOONS FINELY-CHOPPED PARSLEY
2–4 TABLESPOONS FINELY-CHOPPED SHALLOTS
1 CLOVE GARLIC, FINELY CHOPPED

Cut turbot and halibut into cubes about ½ inch thick and poach in boiling salted water to which you have added a little milk to make fish white. Reduce heat so that water barely bubbles. When fish can be flaked with a fork, drain. Remove skin and bones while fish is still warm. Combine with cooked shrimps and dress immediately with olive oil, lemon juice and salt and pepper, to taste.

When ready to serve: add finely-chopped parsley, shallots and garlic. Serves 4 to 6.

ONIONS 'MONÉGASQUE'

2 CARROTS, COARSELY CHOPPED
4 TABLESPOONS OLIVE OIL
2 POUNDS BUTTON ONIONS, PEELED
¾ PINT WATER
¼ PINT DRY WHITE WINE
4 TABLESPOONS LEMON JUICE
2 OUNCES SULTANAS
2 TABLESPOONS TOMATO PURÉE
2 BAY LEAVES
½ LEVEL TEASPOON THYME
SALT AND FRESHLY-GROUND BLACK PEPPER
CAYENNE
OLIVE OIL
FINELY-CHOPPED PARSLEY

Sauté chopped carrots in olive oil until soft and golden. Combine in a saucepan with peeled onions, water, dry white wine, lemon juice, sultanas, tomato purée, bay leaves, thyme and salt, pepper and cayenne, to taste, and simmer for about 1 hour, or until onions are cooked through and sauce has reduced a little. Chill. Just before serving: correct seasoning; add a little olive oil and sprinkle with finely-chopped parsley. Serves 8.

ORIENTAL RICE

½ LEVEL TEASPOON POWDERED SAFFRON
¼ LEVEL TEASPOON POWDERED CUMIN
6 TABLESPOONS DRY WHITE WINE
1 PINT HOT CHICKEN STOCK
¾ POUND RISOTTO RICE
½ GREEN PEPPER, SEEDED AND DICED
½ RED PEPPER, SEEDED AND DICED
½ SPANISH ONION, COARSELY CHOPPED
SALT AND FRESHLY-GROUND BLACK PEPPER

DRESSING:

6–8 TABLESPOONS OLIVE OIL
2–3 TABLESPOONS WINE VINEGAR
2 TABLESPOONS FINELY-CHOPPED PARSLEY
SALT AND FRESHLY-GROUND BLACK PEPPER

Dissolve saffron and cumin in white wine and chicken stock and combine in a large saucepan with rice, diced peppers, chopped onion, and salt and pepper, to taste. Cover pan and simmer until all the liquid is absorbed and the rice is tender. Add some more liquid if necessary.

Drain well and toss with olive oil, wine vinegar, finely-chopped parsley and salt and freshly-ground black pepper, to taste. Add more olive oil or vinegar if necessary. Serves 4 to 6.

HARICOTS BLANCS EN SALADE

¾ POUND DRY WHITE BEANS
1 SPANISH ONION, FINELY CHOPPED
2 TABLESPOONS OLIVE OIL
1 CLOVE GARLIC
1 BAY LEAF
1 TEASPOON SALT
1 SMALL GREEN PEPPER
4–6 TABLESPOONS OLIVE OIL
WINE VINEGAR
SALT AND FRESHLY-GROUND BLACK PEPPER

DRESSING:
½ SPANISH ONION, FINELY CHOPPED
4 TABLESPOONS PARSLEY, FINELY CHOPPED
1 TEASPOON PREPARED MUSTARD
1 CLOVE GARLIC, FINELY CHOPPED
SALT AND FRESHLY-GROUND BLACK PEPPER
OLIVE OIL
JUICE OF ½ LEMON
GARNISH: FINELY-CHOPPED PARSLEY, ANCHOVY FILLETS, BLACK OLIVES

Soak beans overnight in water to cover. Drain. Sauté finely-chopped onion in olive oil until golden brown. Add garlic, bay leaf, salt and 2½ pints water, and simmer beans in this stock for about 2 hours, or until beans are tender. Drain. Seed and dice green pepper and add to beans along with 4 tablespoons olive oil, and vinegar, salt and freshly-ground black pepper, to taste.

To make dressing: Combine finely-chopped onion, parsley, mustard, garlic, salt and freshly-ground black pepper in a bowl. Mix well, and then pour in olive oil, drop by drop as if you were making a mayonnaise, beating the mixture all the time until sauce thickens. Flavour with lemon juice.

Arrange salad in a salad bowl; add salad dressing and toss until well mixed; garnish with finely-chopped parsley, anchovy fillets and black olives. Serves 4 to 6.

JEWISH CHOPPED CHICKEN LIVERS

¾ POUND CHICKEN LIVERS
¼–½ SPANISH ONION, FINELY CHOPPED
CHICKEN FAT
2 HARD-BOILED EGGS
1 STALK CELERY, FINELY CHOPPED
¼–½ SMALL GREEN PEPPER, FINELY CHOPPED
SALT AND FRESHLY-GROUND BLACK PEPPER

Sauté chicken livers in a little chicken fat until they are firm, but not cooked through. Sauté finely-chopped onion in chicken fat until transparent.

Chop hard-boiled eggs coarsely and put through the finest blade of your mincer with chicken livers and onions.

Combine in a large bowl with celery, green pepper, and enough additional chicken fat to make mixture smooth. Season to taste with salt and freshly-ground black pepper.

MARINATED HERRING

12 HERRING FILLETS
1 PINT DOUBLE CREAM
6 TABLESPOONS WINE VINEGAR
1 TABLESPOON OLIVE OIL
3 MEDIUM-SIZED ONIONS, FINELY SLICED
6 BLACK PEPPERCORNS
1 LARGE SOUR APPLE, PEELED AND CUT IN THIN STRIPS
1 SMALL COOKED BEETROOT, CUT IN THIN STRIPS
½ LEMON, THINLY SLICED
3–6 SMALL BAY LEAVES

Wash herring fillets; pat dry and arrange in a bowl. Mix cream, vinegar and olive oil. Add finely-sliced onions, peppercorns, apple, beetroot, lemon and bay leaves, and pour over herrings. Cover and place in the refrigerator. Marinate 24 hours before serving ice-cold as an appetiser. Serves 6 to 12.

TURBOT SALAD 'WHITE TOWER'

2 POUNDS TURBOT
1 QUART WATER
¼ PINT MILK
10 TABLESPOONS OLIVE OIL
JUICE OF 2 LEMONS
SALT AND FRESHLY-GROUND BLACK PEPPER
2–4 TABLESPOONS FINELY-CHOPPED PARSLEY
2–4 TABLESPOONS COARSELY-CHOPPED ONION

Cut turbot into slices about ½ inch thick and place in boiling salted water to which you have added milk to make fish white. Reduce heat so that water barely bubbles. It is important that the turbot cooks very slowly so that it does not lose its juices in the stock. When fish can be flaked with a fork, drain. Remove skin and bones while still warm. Dress immediately with olive oil, lemon juice and salt and pepper, to taste. Add finely-chopped parsley and coarsely-chopped onion, and allow to cool. Just before serving, correct seasoning and add more olive oil and lemon juice if necessary.

This dish is best served soon after it has been prepared as it tends to lose flavour if kept too long. Serves 4 to 6.

CEVICHE (MEXICAN SEAFOOD COCKTAIL)

1 POUND HALIBUT, OR ANY FIRM WHITE NON-FATTY FISH
2 LEMONS OR LIMES
½ POUND TOMATOES, PEELED AND SEEDED
1 SMALL GREEN PEPPER, DICED
4 TABLESPOONS OLIVE OIL
4 TABLESPOONS FINELY-CHOPPED PARSLEY
1–2 TABLESPOONS WINE VINEGAR
DASH TABASCO SAUCE
½ TEASPOON OREGANO
SALT AND FRESHLY-GROUND BLACK PEPPER
1 AVOCADO PEAR
6 STUFFED OLIVES

Fillet, skin and dice raw fish. Place in a glass bowl; pour lemon or lime juice over it and marinate for 3 hours, turning fish pieces with a wooden spoon from time to time, so that juice turns the fish snowy-white and non-transparent. It will look and flake like cooked fish.

Dice the tomatoes and add to the fish. Add diced green pepper to fish mixture with olive oil, parsley, vinegar, Tabasco, *oregano* and salt and pepper, to taste. Serve chilled, garnished with diced avocado pear and sliced stuffed olives. Serves 4.

TARAMASALATA

1 JAR SMOKED COD'S ROE
6 SLICES WHITE BREAD
¼ SPANISH ONION, GRATED
1–2 CLOVES GARLIC, MASHED
8 TABLESPOONS OLIVE OIL
JUICE OF 1 LEMON
1 TABLESPOON FINELY-CHOPPED PARSLEY
GREEN OLIVES
HOT TOAST

Place cod's roe in a mortar. Trim crusts from bread; soak bread in water; squeeze and add to cod's roe. Pound mixture to a smooth paste. Stir in grated onion and garlic. Then add olive oil and lemon juice alternately in small amounts, stirring well, until mixture acquires a smooth, uniform consistency. Strain through a fine sieve. (The above can be done in an electric blender and in that case mixture does not need to be sieved.)

Serve in a salad bowl; sprinkle with finely-chopped parsley and garnish with green olives. Serve with hot toast. I also like to stuff 2-inch lengths of crisp celery with this mixture as a light appetiser. Serves 4 to 6.

COLD SALMON PÂTÉ

2 POUNDS RAW FRESH SALMON
6 TABLESPOONS DRY SHERRY
2 BAY LEAVES
SALT AND FRESHLY-GROUND BLACK PEPPER
6 OUNCES RAW WHITING
6 OUNCES RAW COD
2 SLICES STALE BREAD
MILK
2 EGG YOLKS, LIGHTLY BEATEN
2 OUNCES BUTTER

Skin and bone salmon; cut the best parts of it into fingers

about 1 inch thick and marinate these for about 2 hours in dry sherry with bay leaves and salt and freshly-ground pepper, to taste. Turn salmon fingers occasionally so that all sides are impregnated with sherry mixture.

Skin and bone whiting and cod and place in electric blender with the remainder of the salmon. Add bread dipped in milk, egg yolks, butter, and salt and pepper, to taste. Moisten with sherry marinade and blend well. Pass mixture through a fine sieve.

Butter a terrine or oven-proof pâté dish and cover the bottom with a layer of fish mixture; place fingers of salmon on this; cover with a layer of fish mixture, and so on until terrine is full, finishing with a layer of the fish mixture. Cook with the lid on in a slow oven (350°F. Mark 3) for 45 to 60 minutes. Serve cold. This dish will keep for 2 or 3 days in the refrigerator.

GUACAMOLE (AVOCADO APPETISER)

2 RIPE AVOCADO PEARS
JUICE OF 1 LEMON
1 CLOVE GARLIC, MASHED
4 TOMATOES, PEELED, SEEDED AND COARSELY CHOPPED
½ SPANISH ONION, FINELY CHOPPED
4 TABLESPOONS FINELY-CHOPPED CELERY OR GREEN PEPPER
1 TABLESPOON FINELY-CHOPPED CORIANDER LEAVES OR PARSLEY
2–4 TABLESPOONS OLIVE OIL
SALT AND FRESHLY-GROUND BLACK PEPPER

Peel and mash avocados lightly with a wooden spoon. Add lemon juice, mashed garlic, chopped tomatoes, onion and celery or pepper to mashed avocado mixture. Stir in chopped coriander or parsley, olive oil, and salt and pepper, to taste. Leave the avocado stones in the sauce until ready to serve to keep from browning. Mexicans serve *guacamole* with *tostaditos* (deep-fried wedges of *tortilla*).

TOMATOES GUACAMOLE

8 LARGE RIPE TOMATOES
2 RIPE AVOCADO PEARS
JUICE OF 1 LEMON
1 TABLESPOON ONION JUICE
1 CLOVE GARLIC, MASHED
SALT AND FRESHLY-GROUND BLACK PEPPER
CHILI POWDER
4 TABLESPOONS FINELY-CHOPPED CELERY OR GREEN PEPPER
1 TABLESPOON FINELY-CHOPPED CORIANDER OR PARSLEY

Tomato cases: Plunge tomatoes into boiling water, one by one, and remove their skins. Slice cap off each and carefully scoop out all pulp and seeds. Cover loosely with aluminium foil and chill in refrigerator until ready to use.

Guacamole filling: Peel and mash avocados lightly with a wooden spoon. Add lemon juice and seasonings. Fold in finely-chopped celery or pepper, and chill. Just before serving, fill each tomato case with *guacamole* mixture; sprinkle with finely-chopped coriander or parsley. Serves 4.

Terrine de Canard à l'Orange

Every French restaurant boasts its *pâté maison*; every great chef cherishes his own special *terrine* recipe incorporating chicken, duck or game. My favourite – and one of the world's great dishes – is *terrine de canard à l'orange*, a *terrine* made with the fillets of breast of duck marinated in orange juice, cognac, Noilly Prat and Madeira and encased in a savoury *farce* made up of the finely-ground meats of the duck, together with pork, pork fat and veal, flavoured with the marinade juices, herbs and spices.

Far from being difficult to prepare, a *terrine* such as this one fits particularly well into the scheme of the busy host- or hostess-cum-cook. It can be prepared in advance – several days in fact – and chilled, thus eliminating much last-minute cooking. And it is easy to serve.

Terrines are usually baked in heavy earthenware baking dishes, round or oval in shape with straight sides and with a small hole in the cover to allow the steam to escape. Always line the bottom and sides of the dish with thin slices of fat pork or fat bacon. I usually cut mine paper-thin on a rotary cutter. Failing this, a useful trick is to cut the slices at least ¼ inch thick; place them between two pieces of greaseproof paper; and then pound them with a wooden mallet to about ⅛ inch in thickness. You will find that they cover the sides of your pâté dish better this way.

Aspic plays a major part in most *terrine* recipes. When I make a *terrine*, I always place a board or flat plate on top of it to weigh it down as it cools. The *terrine* shrinks in cooling and this weight (use an iron, tinned foods or a brick) compresses it just enough to eliminate the tiny air holes that make it difficult to slice when chilled. The *terrine* should be firm and moist, and must not fall apart as you cut it. The aspic serves to hold it together, as well as add to the general flavour and appearance of the finished dish.

Any well-flavoured *consommé* will serve as a base for your aspic. For *terrines* of game and poultry, the bones of the animal or bird should be used in making the stock. It is usually wise to make sure that the aspic will set by chilling it thoroughly and re-melting it just prior to use. If the aspic fails to set during this preliminary chilling, strengthen it by adding a little unflavoured gelatine to the mixture.

TERRINE DE CANARD À L'ORANGE

1 DUCK (AND LIVER)
4 TABLESPOONS COGNAC
4 TABLESPOONS NOILLY PRAT
4 TABLESPOONS MADEIRA
4 TABLESPOONS ORANGE JUICE
½ SPANISH ONION, FINELY CHOPPED
½ LEVEL TEASPOON POWDERED THYME
½ LEVEL TEASPOON POWDERED SAVORY
1 LEVEL TEASPOON GRATED ORANGE RIND
1 LEVEL TEASPOON FINELY-CHOPPED PARSLEY
2 BAY LEAVES, CRUMBLED
SALT AND FRESHLY-GROUND BLACK PEPPER
¼ POUND DUCK OR CHICKEN LIVERS
¼ POUND VEAL
¼ POUND LEAN PORK
¼ POUND FRESH PORK FAT
1 EGG, WELL BEATEN
THIN STRIPS PORK FAT
3 THIN SLICES ORANGE
MADEIRA ASPIC

Skin and bone the duck; remove the breast fillets and meat of the breast and cut into long, thin strips about ¼ inch in diameter. Marinate strips overnight in cognac, Noilly Prat, Madeira and orange juice with finely-chopped onion, powdered thyme, savory, grated orange rind, parsley, crumbled bay leaves, and salt and freshly-ground black pepper, to taste.

Chop remaining duck meat finely with duck or chicken livers, veal, pork and fresh pork fat. Reserve carcass. Stir in liquid in which the fillets were marinated, and also beaten egg. Bake a spoonful of finely-ground meat mixture in the oven until cooked through. Taste and correct seasoning.

Garnish the bottom and sides of an oven-proof terrine dish with thin strips of pork fat. Press in a thick layer of the mixture; arrange strips of duck fillets over pâté mixture with a few strips of pork fat ¼ inch in diameter, if available. Cover with another layer of mixture. Top with thin strips of fat.

Cover *terrine*, place in a pan of hot water and bake in a moderate oven (375°F. Mark 4) for about 1 to 1¼ hours.

Remove cover and place a weighted plate on the *terrine* to compress it gently as it cools. Take *terrine* from its container, remove outside fat and replace in a clean dish. Decorate with 3 thin slices of orange and cover with Madeira aspic.

PÂTÉ MAISON

- ½ POUND BACON, THINLY SLICED
- 6 TABLESPOONS BRANDY
- 2 POUNDS CALF'S LIVER, MINCED
- ½ POUND PORK LIVER, MINCED
- 2 EGGS
- 4 TABLESPOONS DOUBLE CREAM
- 2 TABLESPOONS LEMON JUICE
- 1 CLOVE GARLIC, CRUSHED
- SALT AND FRESHLY-GROUND BLACK PEPPER
- 1 TRUFFLE, COARSELY CHOPPED (OPTIONAL)
- ¼ POUND CHICKEN LIVER, COARSELY CHOPPED

Cut rinds from bacon slices and line a pâté mould with bacon; sprinkle with a little brandy. Mix minced livers with eggs, cream, lemon juice, garlic, pepper and salt, to taste. Pour on flaming brandy. Mix well with fork and half-fill pâté mould with mixture. Place coarsely-chopped truffle and chicken liver in a row down centre. Cover with rest of pâté; then cover top with bacon. Stand mould in pan of water and bake in a slow oven (325°F. Mark 2) for about 2 hours, covered with foil. Remove and cool. Put weight on top to press down firmly, and chill overnight in the refrigerator. Turn out of mould just before serving.

TRUFFLED DUCK PÂTÉ

- 1 MEDIUM-SIZED DUCK
- 2 SHALLOTS, CHOPPED
- PINCH OF THYME
- 4 BAY LEAVES
- SALT
- FRESHLY-GROUND BLACK PEPPER
- 4 FLUID OUNCES DRY WHITE WINE
- 1 POUND CALF'S LIVER, DICED
- 6 TABLESPOONS BUTTER
- 4 COX'S ORANGE PIPPINS
- 1 TEASPOON SUGAR
- JUICE OF ½ LEMON
- 1 EGG, BEATEN
- ½ POUND FAT SALT PORK, THINLY SLICED
- TRUFFLES
- MADEIRA ASPIC

Bone and skin duck. Cut the breast in long thin strips. Combine shallots, thyme, 2 bay leaves, crumbled, ½ teaspoon salt and a little freshly-ground pepper and dry white wine. Marinate fillets in this mixture for at least 2 hours. Sauté calf's liver and duck liver in 4 tablespoons butter until medium rare. Peel apples; add sugar and cook in lemon juice and remaining butter until soft. Pass livers and apples through a sieve; add beaten egg and season to taste with salt and pepper. Blend mixture until it is very smooth.

Line a pâté dish or earthenware casserole with thin slices of fat salt pork. Add half the liver and apple mixture and place layers of marinated duck fillets on it. Stud with truffles rolled in thin slices of fat salt pork; cover with remaining liver and apple mixture and top with fat salt pork. Place 2 bay leaves on the pâté; cover casserole; place in a pan of hot water and bake for about 1½ hours in a slow oven (350°F. Mark 3).

Remove cover and place a weighted plate on the pâté to compress it gently as it cools. Take pâté from casserole; remove outside fat and replace in a clean pâté dish. Decorate with slices of truffle and cover with Madeira aspic.

MOUSSE DE FOIE GRAS EN BRIOCHE

4 TABLESPOONS DOUBLE CREAM
½ POUND TINNED PÂTÉ DE FOIE GRAS
4 TABLESPOONS COGNAC
2 TABLESPOONS FINELY-CHOPPED PARSLEY
2 OUNCES FINELY-CHOPPED MUSHROOMS
4 OUNCES BUTTER
SALT
FRESHLY-GROUND BLACK PEPPER
BRIOCHE DOUGH
1 EGG YOLK
A LITTLE MILK

Whip cream in electric blender. Combine pâté, cognac and chopped parsley, and blend thoroughly with whipped cream. Sauté mushrooms in butter over a low heat for 5 minutes or until golden. Season to taste with salt and freshly-ground black pepper. Stir mushrooms and butter into pâté mixture and let stand at room temperature for at least 1 hour.

Line a large well-buttered *brioche* mould with a sheet of *brioche* dough 1½ inches thick and about 1 inch wider in circumference than is required to line the mould. Set the pâté in a ball in the mould and cover it with the overhanging dough. Form a piece of the dough the size of a cup into a ball and set the ball on top of the *brioche*. Let the mould stand for 20 minutes in a warm place to allow the dough to rise. Brush the top with egg yolk diluted with a little milk and bake in a hot oven (450°F. Mark 7) until the *brioche* is browned and a wire tester comes out clean. Cool the *brioche* and lift it out on to a serving dish. Serve warm or cold.

Quiche Lorraine

This hot cheese pie, a native of Alsace-Lorraine, makes frequent and delicious appearances on tables throughout France. Slender wedges are served as an appetiser before dinner; larger portions make a perfect light luncheon dish when accompanied by a tossed green salad; and individual *quiches* provide a delectable first course for a more substantial meal.

Essentially custard, well flavoured with cheese and baked in a pie shell, the *quiche* varies from country to country. Germany and Switzerland have their own versions of this popular dish, but the most famous of all is the French *quiche Lorraine*. In Alsace-Lorraine, the home of the *quiche*, each village has its own special recipe and each jealously proclaims that its *quiche* is the authentic one. In some recipes, only cheese and custard are used; in others, finely-chopped onions sautéed in butter add their subtle flavour; and in still others, *lardons* of fat salt pork or green bacon are added.

I find the *quiche* an easily and quickly made, light-hearted *entrée*. But be careful, for your *quiche* should be satin-smooth on the inside with a crisp, golden crust. So do not let the *quiche* wait for guests. Serve it immediately, for it is at its best when piping hot.

Traditionally, *quiche Lorraine* is made with *lardons* of fat salt pork or green bacon, but try these variations on the basic theme, substituting for the bacon one of the following:
Quiche aux crabes: Remove tendons and bits of shell from cooked crab; flake and add to *quiche* mixture. Shrimps, prawns and diced lobster may also be added for a *quiche aux fruits de mer*.

Illustration on facing page

The World's Spices

– once so rare that they were worth their weight in gold – are familiar captives on our kitchen shelves today: golden sticks of cinnamon from the Malabar Coast of India; fat berries of allspice from Jamaica; pungent cloves from Penang; creamy white ginger from China and Hindustan, and heady, hot cayenne from Zanzibar. Make the most of these riches to give a magic touch to your cookery.

Illustration on following page

The busy kitchens of the

Restaurant Lapérouse

one of the most exciting restaurants in Paris.
A restaurant of great charm, Lapérouse is famous for its *haute cuisine* and its *cabinets privés*, private dining-rooms where lovers – and businessmen – can dine without being disturbed. A bell or *sonnette* is handy to call for service when desired. M. Topolinski, the present proprietor, states emphatically that 'Lapérouse never reveals the secrets of its *salons particuliers*'.

Quiche aux champignons: Clean and slice mushrooms thinly; sauté in butter and lemon juice; drain well and add to *quiche* mixture.
Quiche au poisson: Poach halibut or turbot fillets in a well-flavoured *court-bouillon* of water and white wine, flavoured with onion, carrot, bay leaf, salt and pepper; drain well, remove skin and bones, and flake fish into *quiche* mixture.
Quiche aux courgettes: Sauté thinly-sliced baby marrow in olive oil with a little finely-chopped onion and garlic and peeled, seeded and coarsely-chopped tomatoes; drain and stir into *quiche* mixture.

QUICHE LORRAINE

SHORTCRUST PASTRY FOR 8-INCH PIE
4 EGG YOLKS
½ PINT SINGLE CREAM
SALT AND FRESHLY-GROUND BLACK PEPPER
GRATED NUTMEG
¼ POUND GREEN BACON (CUT IN ONE PIECE)
2 TABLESPOONS BUTTER
¼ POUND GRUYÈRE CHEESE, DICED

Line pastry tin with shortcrust pastry. Prick bottom with a fork, brush with a little beaten egg and bake 'blind' for 15 minutes.

Whisk egg yolks in a bowl; add cream and whisk until thick and lemon-coloured. Flavour to taste with salt, pepper and freshly-grated nutmeg.

Cut green bacon, or fat salt pork, into thin strips; remove rind and blanch bacon in boiling water for 3 minutes; sauté strips in 2 tablespoons butter until golden.

Arrange diced cheese and green bacon strips in pastry case. Pour over the cream and egg mixture and bake in a moderate oven (375°F. Mark 4) for about 30 minutes. Serve hot. Serves 4 to 6.

Illustration on previous page

Terrine de Canard à l'Orange

Breast of duck, cut in long even strips and marinated for hours in orange juice, cognac, Noilly Prat and Madeira, is the secret here; the whole seasoned with finely-chopped onion and fresh herbs. These tender morsels are then encased in a smooth *farce* (made of pork and veal, finely chopped and pounded with the remainder of the duck) and baked in the oven. (Recipe on page 69.)

Illustration on facing page

French Onion Soup

– one of the most famous soups in the world – is almost invariably associated with late-night revelries. Its 'restorative' powers are almost legendary. Make one of the three versions your own. (Recipe on page 78.)

AMERICAN CLAM TART

1 PASTRY CASE
1 TIN CHOPPED CLAMS
3 SLICES BACON
BUTTER
3 TABLESPOONS FINELY-CHOPPED ONION
3 TABLESPOONS FINELY-CHOPPED PARSLEY
3 EGGS, LIGHTLY BEATEN
¼ PINT CREAM
SALT AND FRESHLY-GROUND BLACK PEPPER

Line a pie tin with pastry, fluting the edges; chill. Prick bottom with a fork and bake 'blind' in a hot oven (450°F. Mark 7) for about 15 minutes, just long enough to set the crust without browning it. Allow to cool.

Drain clams, reserving liquor. Sauté bacon in butter until crisp. Sauté chopped onion in resulting fat until transparent, and drain. Crumble bacon and combine with chopped clams, sautéed onion and chopped parsley. Spoon mixture into pastry shell.

Lightly beat eggs; add cream, reserved clam liquor, and salt and pepper, to taste. Pour custard mixture into pastry shell and bake the tart in a moderate oven (375°F. Mark 4) for 30 minutes, or until the crust is brown and the custard has set.

ITALIAN SPINACH PIE

1 PASTRY CASE
¾ POUND FROZEN SPINACH
2 TABLESPOONS BUTTER
SALT AND FRESHLY-GROUND BLACK PEPPER
½ POUND COTTAGE CHEESE
3 EGGS, LIGHTLY BEATEN
1–2 OUNCES FRESHLY-GRATED PARMESAN
6 TABLESPOONS DOUBLE CREAM
GRATED NUTMEG

Line a pie tin with pastry, fluting the edges; chill. Prick bottom with a fork; and bake 'blind' in a hot oven (450°F. Mark 7) for about 15 minutes, just long enough to set the crust without browning it. Allow to cool.

Cook spinach with butter, and salt and pepper, to taste. Drain thoroughly and then add cottage cheese with beaten eggs, grated Parmesan, cream and nutmeg, to taste.

Spread mixture in pastry shell and bake the tart in a moderate oven (375°F. Mark 4) for 30 minutes, or until the crust is brown and the cheese custard mixture has set.

PISSALADIÈRE

- 4 TABLESPOONS OLIVE OIL
- 6 LARGE RIPE TOMATOES
- 2 TABLESPOONS TOMATO CONCENTRATE
- 3 SPANISH ONIONS
- 2 TABLESPOONS BUTTER
- ROSEMARY OR TARRAGON
- 2 TABLESPOONS GRATED PARMESAN
- 1 TIN ANCHOVY FILLETS
- BLACK OLIVES

Dough – bread, brioche or rich pastry – for the case.
Butter or egg yolk for case. Extra oil for anchovies and olives.

Use bread dough, *brioche* dough or rich pastry for this savoury tomato and onion tart. If you use bread or *brioche* dough, roll out ¼ inch thick and line a 9-inch pie tin. Brush with butter and put in a warm place to rise slightly while you prepare the filling. If you use pastry, roll out ¼ inch thick; line the pan, fluting the edges, and chill. Then brush with a little slightly-beaten egg yolk and bake in a 450°F. (Mark 7) oven just long enough to set the crust without browning it. Allow to cool.

Heat olive oil in a pan; add ripe tomatoes, peeled, seeded and chopped, and 2 tablespoons tomato concentrate. Cook over a low heat until excess moisture is cooked away, mashing occasionally with a wooden spoon to form a purée. Slice Spanish onions and simmer in butter with a little freshly-chopped rosemary or tarragon until soft and golden but not brown.

Sprinkle bottom of pastry or dough case with Parmesan; add onions and then cover with the tomato purée. Arrange anchovies in a lattice-work on top and place a black olive in the centre of each square. Brush olives and anchovies lightly with oil and bake in a moderate oven (375°F. Mark 4) for about 30 minutes.

MINIATURE FISH CRESCENTS

4 OUNCES BUTTER
4 OUNCES CREAM CHEESE
4 OUNCES FLOUR
2 TINS SARDINES, DRAINED
LEMON JUICE AND CURRY POWDER
SALT AND FRESHLY-GROUND BLACK PEPPER
2 HARD-BOILED EGGS, FINELY CHOPPED
1 TABLESPOON FINELY-CHOPPED PARSLEY

Combine butter and cream cheese and stir until mixture is well blended. Add flour and mix with a fork. Knead dough and form it into a ball before chilling. Refrigerate for 1 hour.

To prepare filling: mash sardines. Add a little lemon juice, curry powder, and salt and pepper, to taste. Add finely-chopped eggs and parsley and mix well. Roll dough on floured surface to about ¼-inch thickness. Cut into 4-inch squares. Cut squares in half to form triangles. Place a teaspoon of sardine filling in centre of each triangle. Roll from wide edge towards point, twisting ends to seal. Turn ends to form a crescent. Place on baking sheet and store, covered, in refrigerator until ready to bake. Bake at 450°F. (Mark 7) for about 10 minutes or until golden brown.

GREAT DISHES OF THE WORLD

CHAPTER 2

SOUPS

French Onion Soup

French onion soup spells Paris in its most romantic mood, an aromatic vision of Les Halles at four in the morning, busy crowded streets filled with the clamorous cries of an awakening city, where home-returning revellers mingle with hard-working marketmen for their one communal meal of the day.

In the very heart of the market, I used to love a tiny, crowded, smoky little workman's café which stayed open all night. There, porters and fruiterers, *camioneurs* and butchers complete with blood-stained aprons used to eat and drink around the crowded *zinc* in the early hours of the morning, and consume countless portions of the house speciality: an appetising *soupe à l'oignon*, served with a piping-hot crust of bubbling cheese.

Today, the café – enlarged and bedizened – has a smart upstairs restaurant for chic Parisians and foreign visitors. But downstairs it is still the same noisy, crowded, smoky room where the marketmen gather to swap early-morning stories, and the onion soup is as good and as famous as it ever was.

French onion soup is nothing if not adaptable. Take a few onions, a little water or a little stock, a slice or two of toasted bread and a sprinkling of grated cheese, and you have a deliciously warming and inexpensive soup. Add a little dry white wine, a glass of champagne, or a dash or two of brandy, and you have a soup fit for the gods.

Pile an oven-proof earthenware dish high with slices of oven-toasted French bread; cover each layer with freshly-grated Gruyère cheese; fill the bowl with your favourite French onion soup, place it in the oven until the bowl is smoking hot, golden with melted cheese and toasted bread, and you have *soupe à l'oignon gratinée* as it is served in Les Halles.

SOUPE À L'OIGNON

24 SMALL WHITE ONIONS
4 TABLESPOONS BUTTER
SUGAR
2½ PINTS BEEF STOCK
4 FLUID OUNCES COGNAC
SALT AND FRESHLY-GROUND BLACK PEPPER
4–6 ROUNDS TOASTED FRENCH BREAD
GRATED GRUYÈRE CHEESE

Peel and slice onions thinly. Heat butter in a large saucepan with a little sugar; add the onion rings and cook them very, very gently over a low flame, stirring constantly with a wooden spoon until the rings are an even golden brown. Add beef stock gradually, stirring constantly until the soup begins to boil. Then lower the heat, cover the pan, and simmer gently for about 1 hour.

Just before serving, add cognac, and salt and pepper, and serve in a heated soup tureen or in individual serving bowls, each one containing toasted buttered rounds of French bread heaped with grated Gruyère cheese. Serves 4 to 6.

SOUPE À L'OIGNON GRATINÉE

2½ PINTS WELL-FLAVOURED ONION SOUP
OVEN-TOASTED FRENCH BREAD
FRESHLY-GRATED GRUYÈRE CHEESE

Fill oven-proof earthenware dish with oven-toasted rounds of French bread; cover each layer with freshly-grated Gruyère cheese; fill the bowl with well-flavoured onion soup and bake in a pre-heated hot oven (450°F. Mark 7) until cheese is bubbling and golden brown. Serves 4 to 6.

ONION SOUFFLÉ SOUP

2½ PINTS WELL-FLAVOURED ONION SOUP
4–6 ROUNDS OVEN-TOASTED FRENCH BREAD
¾ PINT THICK BÉCHAMEL SAUCE
6 TABLESPOONS FRESHLY-GRATED GRUYÈRE CHEESE
2 EGG WHITES, STIFFLY BEATEN
SALT, FRESHLY-GROUND BLACK PEPPER AND NUTMEG

To make soufflé: prepare a thick béchamel sauce, remove from heat and stir in freshly-grated cheese. Allow to cool and fold in stiffly beaten egg whites. Season to taste.

Pour French onion soup into individual oven-proof dishes (or one large oven-proof dish); top with toasted and buttered rounds of French bread and spoon cheese soufflé mixture over this. Bake in a pre-heated hot oven (450°F. Mark 7) for 8 to 10 minutes, or until soufflé has risen and is golden. Serve immediately. Serves 4 to 6.

COLD BORSCH

1½ POUNDS LEAN BEEF
2 QUARTS SALTED WATER
3 SPRIGS PARSLEY
2 LEEKS
2 CARROTS
1 BAY LEAF
1 CLOVE GARLIC
6 PEPPERCORNS
1 POUND COOKED BEETROOT, DICED
½ RED CABBAGE, COARSELY CHOPPED
2 POTATOES
2 ONIONS
½ POUND MUSHROOMS
½ PINT SOUR CREAM

Dice the lean beef and put it into a saucepan with 2 quarts of salted water. Bring the water slowly to the boil; skim carefully, and add parsley, coarsely-chopped leeks and carrots; add bay leaf, garlic and peppercorns. Simmer, covered, for 1½ hours, skimming from time to time. Remove the meat from the soup; strain soup into a saucepan and add diced beetroot, coarsely-chopped red cabbage, potatoes, onions and mushrooms. Bring to the boil; skim; and simmer, uncovered, for 1½ hours. Strain through a sieve; chill, and stir in sour cream before serving. Serves 6 to 8.

ITALIAN LEEK AND PUMPKIN SOUP

1 POUND PUMPKIN
½ POUND POTATOES
1 SPANISH ONION
2 OUNCES BUTTER
¼ POUND FRESH HARICOT OR BROAD BEANS
1 PINT MILK
SALT AND CAYENNE PEPPER
2 OUNCES LEEK, CUT IN STRIPS
1 PINT HOT CHICKEN STOCK
¼ PINT DOUBLE CREAM
¼ POUND BOILED RICE
2 TABLESPOONS CHOPPED CHERVIL OR PARSLEY

Peel and dice pumpkin and potatoes. Chop onion and simmer in half the butter until golden; add diced pumpkin and potatoes, beans and milk. Bring to the boil and simmer for 45 minutes, stirring from time to time to prevent scorching. Strain through a fine sieve into a clean saucepan; add salt and pepper, to taste.

Cut leeks into fine strips and 'melt' in the remaining butter. Add to the soup, along with hot chicken stock, and bring slowly to the boil. Just before serving, stir in fresh cream, boiled rice and chopped chervil or parsley. Serves 4 to 6.

'FONDA DEL SOL' ARGENTINIAN PUMPKIN SOUP

2½ POUNDS PUMPKIN MEAT
1¾ PINTS CHICKEN STOCK
1 MEDIUM ONION, CHOPPED
6 SPRING ONIONS
4 TOMATOES
½ PINT SINGLE CREAM
SALT AND FRESHLY-GROUND BLACK PEPPER
¼ PINT WHIPPED CREAM

Cut pumpkin in pieces; add stock, onion, spring onions and tomatoes, and simmer until tender. Cool. Blend – or purée;

add cream; season to taste with salt and pepper. Pour into pre-chilled cups. Just before serving, place a dollop of whipped cream on each portion. Serves 6.

CORN AND TUNA BISQUE

1 TABLESPOON BUTTER
1 TABLESPOON FLOUR
¾ PINT MILK
1 CHICKEN STOCK CUBE
1 TIN SWEET CORN
1 TIN TUNA
SALT AND FRESHLY-GROUND BLACK PEPPER
CURRY POWDER OR DRY SHERRY

Melt butter in the top of a double saucepan; add flour and cook for a few minutes, stirring constantly until well blended. Add milk and chicken stock cube and simmer, stirring from time to time, until the sauce has thickened.

Stir in sweet corn and bring to the boil; add shredded tuna and heat through. Correct seasoning and serve immediately. A little curry powder or sherry may be added if desired. Serves 4.

SCANDINAVIAN FRUIT SOUP

3 POUNDS ASSORTED FRUITS (PEACHES, PLUMS, PEARS, CHERRIES, APRICOTS, BERRIES, ETC.)
1½ PINTS WATER
3 TABLESPOONS LEMON JUICE
SUGAR
POWDERED CINNAMON
1 TABLESPOON CORNFLOUR
¼ PINT SOUR CREAM

Pit the fruit, but do not peel. Slice larger fruits. Combine fruit in saucepan with water, lemon juice, and sugar and cinnamon, to taste. Cover and simmer until fruit is soft. Purée. Dissolve cornflour in a little cold water; add to fruit, and bring to the boil, then simmer gently until soup thickens. Chill. Serve cold with sour cream. Serves 6.

Pot-au-Feu

Pot-au-feu – the great knife-and-fork soup often called the national soup of France – is one of the most rewarding dishes in the world to make. Although it looks complicated at first glance, you will find that this soup of many parts is well worth the effort involved. It is, in fact, two dishes – a beef broth or *bouillon*, and a main dish of boiled beef or, as the French term it, '*le bouilli*', ancestor via Scotland of British 'bully beef'.

Serve the soup first and follow with the *bouilli* accompanied by vegetables from the *bouillon:* carrots, leeks, onions, and sometimes – cooked separately rather than in the *bouillon* – cabbage and potatoes.

To make a pot-au-feu for eight, you will need:

- 4 POUNDS LEAN BEEF
- 2 POUNDS SHIN OF BEEF (MEAT AND BONE)
- ¼ POUND OX LIVER
- 2 CHICKEN LIVERS
- 4 QUARTS WATER
- COARSE SALT
- 4 CARROTS
- 4 LEEKS
- 2 TURNIPS
- 2 STALKS CELERY
- 1 FAT CLOVE GARLIC
- 1 SPANISH ONION
- 2 CLOVES
- 1 BOUQUET GARNI (BAY LEAF, FEW SPRIGS PARSLEY, THYME)

The secret of making a good *pot-au-feu* is to begin by covering the ingredients with cold water, bringing it slowly to the boil, a mere ripple on the surface, and then allowing it to simmer gently for hours without interruption at a low, regular heat.

Have your butcher bone the meat – chosen from the silverside, shoulder, top rib, or top round, although the last-mentioned is inclined to be a little tough in comparison to the others, or a combination of two of these, plus some shin of beef, meat and bone, so useful in making a *bouillon* for its gelatinous qualities. If I have it at hand, I sometimes add a knuckle of veal or a good-sized marrow bone to these basics for extra flavour.

Your butcher will also cut the meat into large pieces, tie it up securely and break the bones for you. All you have to do when you are ready to make your *pot-au-feu* is to lay the bones in the bottom of a large stock-pot; place the meat, ox liver and chicken livers on top and add 4 quarts of water, or water and stock, and put the stock-pot on the lowest possible heat so that the water comes to the boil very slowly. As it does so, the gradual heating of the water will enlarge the fibre of the meat and dissolve the gelatinous substances which it contains.

When the liquid barely begins to simmer in the pot, add a little salt to help the scum rise to the surface of the *bouillon.*

The scum which forms is thick and brownish-grey in colour. Let it become sufficiently compact and then skim it off with a perforated spoon, being careful to scrape away any remaining at the sides of the pot. When the water just begins to tremble, add half a glass of cold water to stop the boiling and to bring a new rise of scum to the surface. Skim and repeat this process several times for a matter of 10 to 15 minutes, until the scum is just a white froth which will of its own accord be consumed in the cooking.

Add the carrots, leeks, turnips, celery and garlic, the onion, stuck with cloves, and a *bouquet garni.* If the vegetables bring a little more scum to the surface, skim carefully and cover the stock-pot with a lid, tilting it so that the steam can escape. Keep heat as low as possible so that the stock just trembles gently at one point only. The cooking time for your *pot-au-feu* varies a little according to the size of the pieces of meat. But as none should weigh more than 2 pounds, 3 hours from the time you add the vegetables to the *bouillon* will be about right.

THE VEGETABLES

The flavour and appearance of the vegetables in your *pot-au-feu* will be better if they are not overcooked. For the best results, carrots and turnips, cut in quarters, can be added to the *bouillon* immediately after it has been skimmed. Leeks, split if they are big and with most of the green cut off, should be tied together with the celery and added an hour after the other vegetables along with an onion, stuck with cloves, garlic and a *bouquet garni*. In the North of France they add a small *bouquet* of fresh chervil to the stock when the *pot-au-feu* is three-quarters cooked, and some cooks like to improve the colour of the *bouillon* by adding a few pea pods dried in the oven. Cabbage, not usually a part of the classic *pot-au-feu*, can be cooked separately, in water at first and then in a little of the *bouillon*, and served with the meat and vegetables. Potatoes, too, are sometimes boiled or steamed and served with a *pot-au-feu*.

THE BOUILLON

Bring 3½ pints of the *bouillon* to a fast boil; dip soup ladle into the *bouillon* at the point where the boiling is most active. The fat will be forced to the side of the pot and your resultant *bouillon* will be less greasy. Pass the *bouillon*, ladle by ladle, through a fine muslin laid in a sieve, into a clean saucepan. Allow it to cool for a few minutes; skim any remaining fat from the surface; pour *bouillon* into a clean saucepan and re-heat.

THE MEAT AND VEGETABLES

Remove the beef and vegetables carefully from the stock-pot and drain. Cut the strings from the meat and remove any small bones separated in cooking. Cut the meat to facilitate serving and place it in the centre of a large hot serving dish. Surround with cooked vegetables, grouping them by colour. If you have added cabbage, place it in a sort of *bouquet* at one side of the dish. Potatoes can be served with the other vegetables or apart.

You can serve the *bœuf bouilli* alone '*au gros sel*', or you can accompany it by one or two kinds of mustard and small bowls of pickled gherkins, cocktail onions and small carrots, pimentos and green tomatoes in vinegar. I personally like to serve it with a sauce of whipped cream and grated horse-radish or, as in Italy, with *salsa verde*, a piquant green sauce.

OTHER USES FOR REMAINING BOUILLI

Put beef through the mincer; mash equal quantities of boiled potatoes. Mix all together and work them well to blend, then bind with an egg and add salt and pepper, to taste. Butter a mould; fill with meat mixture; cover with a buttered paper and cook in a moderate oven (375°F. Mark 4) for half an hour. This is delicious when served with a tomato or sour cream sauce.

Quite good meat balls or croquettes can be made in the same manner: mince the beef; combine with mashed potatoes and grated Gruyère or Parmesan cheese; season with a little nutmeg, salt and freshly-ground black pepper and sauté in butter until golden.

POULE-AU-POT

1 6-POUND BOILING FOWL
1 POUND LEAN PICKLED PORK
1 SMALL CABBAGE, QUARTERED
1 LARGE TURNIP
1 LARGE ONION
4 CLOVES
FRESHLY-GROUND BLACK PEPPER
THYME
BAY LEAF

VEGETABLE GARNISH:
12 SMALL WHITE ONIONS
12 SMALL CARROTS
12 SMALL POTATOES
1 POUND GREEN BEANS

Clean, singe and truss the boiling fowl. Wash the pickled pork thoroughly and halve it. Clean and quarter cabbage and turnip, and place the vegetables in the bottom of a large stock-pot together with an onion stuck with cloves.

Place the fowl and pickled pork on the vegetables and sprinkle with freshly-ground black pepper and a little thyme. Add enough hot water or water and stock barely to cover; place a bay leaf on top of the fowl and cover with a piece of buttered paper. Place lid tightly on the stock-pot; bring the stock slowly to the boil and simmer gently for about 2 hours. Add small onions, carrots, potatoes and green beans tied in bundles, and cook for about 45 minutes longer, or until the fowl is tender and the vegetables are cooked through.

To serve: place the fowl in the centre of a very large hot platter, place a piece of pork on each side and surround the meat with the vegetables, grouped according to colour. Reserve the broth for soup.

Basic Stocks

It has been said that a cook's reputation rises or falls by the quality of her soups. A soup must be substantial enough to satisfy and at the same time light enough not to slacken enthusiasm for what follows. What an easy way to gain a reputation, for with the best home-made stocks you can provide a whole series of delicious soups, from the world-famous *soupe à l'oignon* of the French (onions melted in butter and moistened with rich beef stock, served with grated cheese and rounds of toasted bread) to the pride of the Greek cuisine, *avgolemono* (a handful of cooked rice, eggs whisked with the juice of a lemon and some fine rich chicken stock), a gold-tinted soup that is deliciously creamy and fresh.

BASIC BEEF STOCK

2 POUNDS SHIN OF BEEF (MEAT AND BONE)
2 POUNDS SHIN OF VEAL (MEAT AND BONE)
¼ POUND LEAN RAW HAM
6 SMALL CARROTS, ROUGHLY CHOPPED AND BROWNED IN BUTTER
1 SPANISH ONION, ROUGHLY CHOPPED AND BROWNED IN BUTTER
2 STALKS CELERY, SLICED
1 BOUQUET GARNI (PARSLEY, 1 SPRIG THYME AND 1 BAY LEAF)
1 FAT CLOVE GARLIC
4–6 PEPPERCORNS
3 QUARTS COLD WATER

Bone meat, cut into large pieces and tie together. Break up the bones as finely as possible; sprinkle them with a little fat and brown them in the oven, stirring round from time to time. When they are slightly browned, put them in a large saucepan with carrots, onion, celery, *bouquet garni*, garlic and peppercorns, but no salt. Add cold water and bring to the boil. Skim carefully; wipe the edge of the saucepan, put the lid half on and allow the stock to cook gently for 4 hours. Then remove fat; pass the liquid through a sieve and allow it to cool.

Put the meat in a saucepan just large enough to hold it. Brown it a little in some fat; then clear it entirely of fat. Add ½ pint of the prepared stock; cover the saucepan and let the meat simmer over a low flame until the stock is almost reduced, turning the meat from time to time so that it is bathed on all sides in the stock. Pour the remainder of the stock into the saucepan; bring to the boil and then simmer very slowly and evenly with the lid off. As soon as the meat is well cooked, remove fat from the stock; strain through a fine sieve; cool and store in the refrigerator. The meat may be served in a great variety of ways.

BASIC BEEF STOCK (QUICK METHOD)

1 POUND VEAL KNUCKLE
1 POUND BEEF KNUCKLE
4 TABLESPOONS BEEF, VEAL OR PORK DRIPPING
2 POUNDS LEAN BEEF
2 CHICKEN FEET (OPTIONAL)
2 LEEKS (WHITE PARTS ONLY)
1 LARGE ONION STUCK WITH 2 CLOVES
2 STALKS CELERY, TOPS INCLUDED
2 CARROTS, COARSELY CHOPPED
4 SPRIGS PARSLEY
1 FAT CLOVE GARLIC
3 QUARTS WATER
SALT AND FRESHLY-GROUND BLACK PEPPER

Have veal and beef knuckles coarsely chopped by your butcher, brush with meat dripping and brown them in the oven. Place in a large stock-pot with lean beef, chicken feet, if you have any, and leeks, onion, celery, carrots, parsley and garlic. Cover with 3 quarts cold water and bring slowly to the boil, removing the scum as it accumulates on the surface. Simmer gently for 1 hour; add salt and pepper to taste, and continue to simmer for another hour, or until the meat is tender. Correct seasoning and strain the stock through a fine sieve. Cool, remove the fat and re-heat, or store in the refrigerator for later use.

BASIC CHICKEN STOCK

1 6-POUND BOILING FOWL
1 VEAL KNUCKLE
2 CHICKEN FEET
3 QUARTS WATER
SALT
6 PEPPERCORNS
2 LEEKS
6 SMALL CARROTS
1 SPANISH ONION
2 CLOVES
2 STALKS CELERY
1 BOUQUET GARNI (PARSLEY, 1 SPRIG THYME AND 1 BAY LEAF)
1 CLOVE GARLIC

Place boiling fowl in a large stock-pot (with veal knuckle and chicken feet for their extra gelatine content) and cover with water. Add salt and peppercorns and bring slowly to the boil. Simmer, with the water barely bubbling, for at least 1 hour, skimming the scum from the surface frequently. Then add leeks, carrots, onion stuck with cloves, celery, *bouquet garni* and garlic, and continue to cook for 1½ to 2 hours longer, or until the chicken is tender. Remove the fat, correct the seasoning and strain through a fine sieve. Cool and store in the refrigerator.

BASIC CHICKEN STOCK (QUICK METHOD)

1 CHICKEN (ABOUT 4 POUNDS)
1 POUND VEAL KNUCKLE
3 QUARTS WATER
2 LEEKS, WHITE PARTS ONLY
1 SPANISH ONION, STUCK WITH CLOVES
2 CARROTS, COARSELY CHOPPED
2 STALKS CELERY, TOPS INCLUDED
1 FAT CLOVE GARLIC
4 SPRIGS PARSLEY
SALT AND FRESHLY-GROUND BLACK PEPPER

Place chicken and veal knuckle in a large stock-pot with 3 quarts water and bring to the boil, skimming until the scum no longer rises to the surface. Simmer for 1 hour. Add leeks, onion, carrots, celery, garlic and parsley; add salt and pepper to taste, and continue to simmer for 1 hour. Correct seasoning and strain the stock through a fine sieve. Cool, remove the fat and re-heat, or store in the refrigerator.

BASIC ASPIC

½ POUND BEEF BONES
DUCK'S CARCASS
1 CALF'S FOOT (OR 4 CLEANED CHICKEN FEET)
1 ONION, SLICED
1 LEEK, SLICED
1 CARROT, SLICED
1 STALK CELERY, CHOPPED
1 QUART COLD WATER
SALT AND FRESHLY-GROUND BLACK PEPPER
1 BOUQUET GARNI (PARSLEY, 1 SPRIG THYME AND 1 BAY LEAF)
1 EGG WHITE
¼ POUND RAW LEAN BEEF, CHOPPED

Combine first ten ingredients in a large stock-pot; bring slowly to the boil and simmer gently for about 4 hours, skimming from time to time. Strain and cool before skimming off the fat.

To clarify the stock, beat egg white lightly, combine with chopped raw lean beef and add to the stock; bring very slowly to the boil, stirring constantly. After the stock has boiled up a few times, it will be clarified. Lower the flame and simmer the stock very gently for about 25 minutes. Strain while hot through a flannel cloth.

For Sherry Aspic: stir in 4 tablespoons dry sherry.

For Madeira Aspic: stir in 4 tablespoons Madeira.

For Tarragon Aspic: when clarifying aspic jelly, add several sprigs of tarragon.

This recipe will make 1 quart of jelly and will keep for several days in the refrigerator.

CHICKEN CONSOMMÉ

2–2½ QUARTS CHICKEN STOCK
WHITES AND SHELLS OF 2 EGGS

Strain chicken stock into a large saucepan. Add egg whites and shells and bring to the boil. Simmer for 1 hour; strain through a fine cloth and cool. Skim and keep as above.

BEEF CONSOMMÉ

2–2½ QUARTS BEEF STOCK
1 POUND MINCED LEAN BEEF
2 LEEKS, CHOPPED
2 STALKS CELERY, CHOPPED
2 CARROTS, CHOPPED
½ SPANISH ONION, CHOPPED
FRESHLY-GROUND BLACK PEPPER
WHITES AND SHELLS OF 2 EGGS

Strain beef stock and combine in a large saucepan with minced beef, chopped leeks, celery, carrots, onion, pepper and the whites and shells of 2 eggs. Simmer for 1 hour; strain through a fine cloth and cool. Skim grease from the surface and pour stock carefully into storage jars, being careful not to disturb any sediment which lies at bottom of stock. Stock will keep for weeks in the refrigerator, ready for use, if you boil it up once every 7 days.

STRACCIATELLA ALLA ROMANA

3 EGGS, WELL BEATEN
2 TABLESPOONS CHOPPED PARSLEY
2 TABLESPOONS GRATED ROMANO OR PARMESAN CHEESE
2½ PINTS WELL-SEASONED CHICKEN STOCK

Beat eggs. Stir finely-chopped parsley and finely-grated cheese into egg mixture. Bring chicken stock to a fast boil and add egg mixture slowly, stirring constantly. Continue stirring while soup simmers 5 minutes more. Serves 4 to 6.

TORTELLINI IN BRODO

8 OUNCES FLOUR
2 EGGS
2 OUNCES PROSCIUTTO, MINCED
¼ POUND COOKED CHICKEN, MINCED
2 OUNCES COOKED PORK, MINCED
1 EGG
1 TABLESPOON CHOPPED BASIL, TARRAGON OR CHERVIL
SALT, FRESHLY-GROUND BLACK PEPPER AND NUTMEG
1 TABLESPOON GRATED PARMESAN CHEESE
2½ PINTS CHICKEN STOCK

Make a well of the flour on a large pastry board; break eggs into the well and slowly mix flour and eggs together. Work dough with hands for 15 minutes, adding more flour if necessary. Sprinkle board with more flour and roll dough as thin as possible with a rolling pin. Cut rolled dough into circles about 2 inches in diameter.

To make stuffing: combine finely-chopped meats, egg, herbs, seasoning and cheese, and place 1 teaspoon of this mixture in the centre of each circle. Fold dough over, closing in the stuffing, and press edges together with fingers to give the shape of a little cap.

Bring chicken stock to the boil; add the *tortellini* and cook for about 20 minutes, or until pastry caps are tender. Serves 4 to 6.

Blender Soups

It is the destiny of some new instruments of modern times to change at one fell swoop the whole structure and habit of today's living. Such an instrument was the fork; such were the rotary whisk, the refrigerator, the deep-freeze – and such, I am sure, is the electric blender.

Here, with one relatively inexpensive attachment, all the hitherto hard-to-create dishes of French *haute cuisine* are yours for the making: delicious pâtés and terrines of meat, game and poultry; featherlight *quenelles*, those delicate morsels of forcemeat of pike, salmon and lobster; creamy purées of peas, artichoke hearts, leeks and potatoes; and the whole delightful gamut of cooling summer soups, based on a purée of vegetables, simmered in chicken stock and thickened with egg yolks and cream.

The blender is a wonderful tool and, if used correctly, will perform any number of difficult culinary operations in a wink of the proverbial eye. It can whisk soups at a speed that is spectacular, smoothing almost any miscellaneous collection of ingredients into a rich flavoursome purée. The following recipes for refreshing summer soups can all be made with the blender in shorter time than it takes me to tell you about them; and without this magic tool, they can be quickly and easily made in minutes, if not in seconds, with the aid of a *mouli légume* (food mill), available from the kitchen departments of better stores throughout the country.

Without either of these two machines, one coming to us via America and the other from France, you will have to resort to a large, fine-meshed sieve and a wooden spoon to achieve your smooth purée. This, of course, takes a little more time, yet is quite easy to do once your vegetables have been cooked.

Most vegetable soups are more rich and mellow when prepared in a well-flavoured stock rather than milk or water. If the soup is of spinach, celery, watercress, cauliflower, or other vegetables that cannot be satisfactorily simmered in butter, the vegetables should be parboiled from 8 to 10 minutes, well drained, chopped and added to the simmering chicken or beef stock. When I use leeks, onions, carrots, mushrooms or cucumber, they are first chopped, then sautéed gently in butter without being allowed to colour, and then added to the stock.

From this point on, the preparation of most vegetable cream soups is the same, whether they are to be served hot or cold. The vegetables are cooked in the gently simmering stock until quite soft; vegetables and stock are whisked in the blender or pressed through a fine sieve; seasoning is added; cream and egg yolks are stirred in and the soup is allowed to thicken in a double saucepan until it is of the right consistency.

COLD BEET SOUP

½ SPANISH ONION, SLICED
2 TABLESPOONS BUTTER
½ POUND COOKED BEETROOT, PEELED AND SLICED
1 BOILED POTATO, PEELED
SALT AND FRESHLY-GROUND BLACK PEPPER
JUICE OF 1 LARGE LEMON
½ PINT CREAM
½–¾ PINT CHILLED CHICKEN STOCK

Sauté sliced onion in butter until soft.

Put peeled sliced beetroot, sautéed onion and boiled peeled potato through electric blender (to press through a fine sieve); add salt, pepper, lemon juice and cream, and blend until smooth. Chill. Just before serving, add chilled chicken stock and blend for 1 minute. Serves 4.

CURRIED APPLE SOUP

2 TABLESPOONS BUTTER
1 SPANISH ONION, COARSELY CHOPPED
1 PINT CHICKEN STOCK
1 LEVEL TEASPOON CURRY POWDER
1 TABLESPOON CORNFLOUR
2 EGG YOLKS
¼ PINT HOT DOUBLE CREAM
2 EATING APPLES
SALT AND FRESHLY-GROUND BLACK PEPPER
JUICE OF ½ LEMON
WATERCRESS LEAVES

Melt butter; add chopped onion and cook until soft, but not brown. Stir in chicken stock and curry powder; add cornflour mixed with a little water. Bring to the boil and then simmer for 8 minutes. Add egg yolks to hot cream and stir gradually into hot soup.

Remove from fire immediately and transfer mixture to electric blender with 1 apple, peeled, cored and sliced. Blend until smooth or pass through a fine sieve. Season to taste with salt and pepper. Chill. Peel, core and dice remaining apple and marinate in lemon juice to keep colour. Just before serving, stir in diced apple and enough watercress leaves to garnish. Serves 4.

GAZPACHO (SPANISH ICED SOUP)

1 SMALL CLOVE GARLIC
6 LARGE RIPE TOMATOES
1 SPANISH ONION
1 LARGE GREEN PEPPER
1 CUCUMBER
6 TABLESPOONS OLIVE OIL
4 TABLESPOONS LEMON JUICE
SALT AND CAYENNE PEPPER
¾ PINT TOMATO JUICE
2 TABLESPOONS BUTTER
2 SLICES BREAD, DICED

Remove garlic skin. Blend 4 tomatoes and 1 clove garlic in electric blender; add ½ onion and ¼ green pepper, cut in rough pieces, and ½ cucumber, peeled and cut in cubes, and blend again. Strain mixture into a large tureen or serving bowl and chill in the refrigerator. Just before serving, blend together olive oil, lemon juice, salt, cayenne pepper and tomato juice; stir into the above mixture and add a block of ice.

Gazpacho is traditionally served accompanied by individual small bowls of raw vegetables and garlic *croûtons*. Guests help themselves to a little of each. To prepare: chop remaining vegetables – tomatoes, onion, cucumber and green pepper – and put each vegetable into a separate bowl. Heat butter with remaining clove of garlic; toss in diced bread; fry until crisp and golden and put into small serving bowl.

'FOUR SEASONS' WATERCRESS VICHYSSOISE

5 POTATOES, PEELED AND SLICED
2 LARGE LEEKS, SLICED
1½ BUNCHES WATERCRESS
1 QUART CHICKEN STOCK
1 HAM BONE (OPTIONAL)
SALT AND FRESHLY-GROUND BLACK PEPPER
1 PINT DOUBLE CREAM
SPRIGS OF WATERCRESS, TO GARNISH

Cook sliced vegetables with ham bone in stock until done. Put through a blender or purée through a fine sieve. Season with salt and pepper, and chill. Just before serving, add chilled cream. Serve with watercress. Serves 6.

VICHYSSOISE VERTE

½ POUND RAW POTATOES, DICED
2 OUNCES RAW LEEKS, CHOPPED
½ POUND RAW GREEN PEAS
1½ PINTS CHICKEN STOCK
SALT, FRESHLY-GROUND BLACK PEPPER AND CELERY SALT
¾ PINT DOUBLE CREAM
CHIVES

Simmer diced potatoes, chopped leeks and peas in chicken stock until barely tender. Put vegetables and *consommé* through an electric blender or fine sieve so that vegetables are puréed. Season to taste with salt, pepper and celery salt. Cool mixture slightly and stir in double cream. Chill thoroughly and sprinkle with finely-chopped chives. Serves 4 to 6.

LEEK AND POTATO SOUP

6 LARGE LEEKS
4 TABLESPOONS BUTTER
4 MEDIUM POTATOES
1½ PINTS CHICKEN STOCK
SALT, FRESHLY-GROUND BLACK PEPPER AND NUTMEG
½ PINT DOUBLE CREAM
FINELY-CHOPPED CHIVES

Cut the green tops from the leeks and cut the white parts into 1-inch lengths. Sauté the white parts gently in butter until soft. Do not allow to brown.

Peel and slice potatoes and add to leeks with chicken stock, and salt, pepper and finely-grated nutmeg, to taste, and simmer until vegetables are cooked. Strain vegetables and stock. Add cream and serve sprinkled with chives. Serves 4 to 6.

CREAM OF CAULIFLOWER SOUP

1 CAULIFLOWER (ABOUT 2 POUNDS)
4 TABLESPOONS BUTTER
4 TABLESPOONS FLOUR
1½ PINTS CHICKEN STOCK
1 ONION, COARSELY CHOPPED
1 STALK CELERY, COARSELY CHOPPED
2 SPRIGS CHOPPED PARSLEY
2 EGG YOLKS
¼ PINT DOUBLE CREAM
SALT AND FRESHLY-GROUND BLACK PEPPER
GRATED NUTMEG

Poach cauliflower in boiling salted water for 5 minutes and drain. Melt butter in a saucepan; add flour and cook, stirring continuously, until a smooth paste is formed. Add chicken stock, coarsely-chopped onion, celery and parsley, and simmer for 20 minutes. Strain stock; add cauliflower and cook until cauliflower is softened. Rub soup through a sieve. Bring back to the boil; stir in 2 egg yolks and cream. Simmer, stirring, for about 3 minutes, taking care that the soup does not boil, or it will curdle. Correct the seasoning with salt, pepper and a little grated nutmeg, and serve. Serves 4.

Italian Minestrone

If, as has been claimed, one of the best things ever to come out of Italy is spaghetti in all its myriad variations, one of the finest uses for *pasta* is in the many wonderful soups and *brodi* of the Italian provinces. Delicate broths of chicken or beef – *cappelletti in brodo* (chicken stock studded with subtly flavoured 'little monks' caps' of meat and herbs) and *farfellini in brodo* (beef stock with small *pasta* bows) vie with the thick fish soups of the coastal regions – *zuppa di pesce alla romana* (fish soup Roman style), *burrido* and *cacciucco* (squid, lobster, scallops and sliced fish, simmered in stock with olive oil and dry white wine) – for first place in our affections. But the most famous of them all, and certainly one of the 'great dishes of the world', is Italian *minestrone.*

Minestrone is, by its very nature, a peasant soup, basically a mixture of beans and fresh vegetables simmered in bean broth and rich beef stock or water with meats, herbs, olive oil, *pasta* and freshly-grated cheese. But like most great peasant dishes, it is fit for the most sophisticated palate.

Italian restaurants serve it as a first course, but in some Italian homes it often provides the whole meal. I like *minestrone* so thick, so full-bodied, so rich with meat and vegetables, that you can practically cut it with a knife.

The variations on the *minestrone* theme are legion. I sometimes add celery, spinach or sliced *courgettes* to the vegetables in the following recipe; diced Italian sausage, ham or ham bone do no real harm; and when in season, a handful of finely-chopped fresh basil elevates this country soup into the gourmet class.

Serve *minestrone* with additional cheese, freshly-grated Parmesan or, if available, Roman *pecorino* and a slice or two of Italian bread, even though the Italians themselves frown on eating bread with a soup that contains *pasta.*

MINESTRONE

½ POUND DRIED KIDNEY OR HARICOT BEANS
¼ POUND SALT PORK
2 CLOVES GARLIC
1 SPANISH ONION
2 QUARTS BEEF STOCK
4 CARROTS
4 STALKS CELERY
½ SMALL HEAD CABBAGE
4 SPRIGS CURLY ENDIVE
4–6 TOMATOES
½ POUND GREEN BEANS
¼ POUND FROZEN PEAS
4–6 OUNCES MACARONI, BROKEN INTO 2-INCH LENGTHS
SALT AND FRESHLY-GROUND BLACK PEPPER
2 TABLESPOONS FINELY-CHOPPED PARSLEY
2 TABLESPOONS OLIVE OIL
4 TABLESPOONS FRESHLY-GRATED PARMESAN

Soak dried kidney or haricot beans overnight. Drain. Simmer beans in 1 quart salted water for 2 hours.

Dice salt pork and sauté in a thick-bottomed frying pan until brown. Finely chop garlic; cut onion into quarters or eighths; sauté with pork until golden. Add beef stock and simmer gently with finely-sliced carrots and celery. Slice cabbage, endive, tomatoes and green beans in fairly large pieces. Add all vegetables, except peas; bring to the boil, cover, and reduce heat until soup barely simmers. Simmer for 1½ hours.

Twenty minutes before serving, add peas and macaroni lengths, or other *pasta*, bring to the boil and then simmer until macaroni is tender. If soup is too thick, add a little water. Add salt and pepper to taste, and just before serving, stir in finely-chopped parsley and olive oil. Serve hot, sprinkled with freshly-grated Parmesan. Serves 6 to 8.

PASTA E FAGIOLI

- ½ POUND DRIED KIDNEY OR HARICOT BEANS
- 1 BEEF MARROW BONE, ABOUT 4 INCHES LONG
- 4 TABLESPOONS TOMATO CONCENTRATE
- 2 QUARTS COLD WATER
- 1 SPANISH ONION
- 1 CLOVE GARLIC
- 3 TABLESPOONS OLIVE OIL
- 2 TABLESPOONS FRESHLY-CHOPPED PARSLEY
- 1 TEASPOON SALT
- PEPPER AND CAYENNE PEPPER
- 1 TABLESPOON DRIED OREGANO
- ½ POUND MACARONI, BROKEN INTO PIECES
- FRESHLY-GRATED PARMESAN

Soak dried beans overnight in cold water. Drain. Combine beans, marrow bone, tomato concentrate and 2 quarts water in a large saucepan. Bring to the boil; lower heat, cover and simmer for 2 hours.

Chop onion and garlic finely and sauté in olive oil until transparent. Add finely-chopped parsley, salt, pepper, cayenne and *oregano* and simmer, covered, for about 20 minutes. Add macaroni and continue cooking until tender. Serve sprinkled with Parmesan cheese. Serves 6 to 8.

SOUPE AU PISTOU

- 1 POUND FRENCH BEANS
- 1 POUND DRIED HARICOT BEANS
- 2 BABY MARROWS, SLICED
- 4 MEDIUM-SIZED CARROTS, SLICED
- 2 POTATOES, DICED
- 2 LEEKS, SLICED
- 4 PINTS BOILING WATER
- SALT AND FRESHLY-GROUND BLACK PEPPER
- PISTOU SAUCE (SEE DIRECTIONS)
- GRATED PARMESAN

Put French beans cut in ¼-inch slices, dried haricot beans which you have previously soaked, sliced baby marrows, carrots, potatoes and leeks, into 4 pints of boiling water. Season with salt and pepper and let them cook fairly quickly. When vegetables are cooked, add pistou sauce and cook gently for 5 minutes more. Serve this hearty soup with grated Parmesan.

To make pistou sauce: Mash well 8 large cloves of garlic in a mortar; add 8 sprigs fresh basil and mash with garlic. Add a glass of olive oil to this sauce very gradually and blend thoroughly. Then add 8 tablespoons of grated Parmesan and pound smooth. Serves 6 to 8.

ZUPPA DI FAGIOLI

½ POUND WHITE BEANS
2½ PINTS WATER
SALT AND FRESHLY-GROUND BLACK PEPPER
4 TABLESPOONS OLIVE OIL
2 CLOVES GARLIC, CHOPPED
2 TABLESPOONS CHOPPED PARSLEY

Soak beans overnight in cold water. Drain and put them into a stock-pot with 2½ pints cold water. Bring to the boil and simmer beans as slowly as possible for 2 to 3 hours, or until they are tender. Remove half the beans, blend them to a smooth purée in an electric blender – or press them through a fine sieve – add this purée to the soup and season to taste with salt and pepper.

Heat olive oil in a small saucepan and simmer chopped garlic in it until just golden. Add chopped parsley to this mixture and pour it into the soup. Serve very hot. Serves 4 to 6.

LENTIL SOUP

6 OUNCES DRIED LENTILS
2½ PINTS BEEF STOCK
HAM KNUCKLE OR ¼ POUND SALT PORK
2 POTATOES, DICED
1 TABLESPOON BUTTER
1 TABLESPOON FLOUR
FRESHLY-GROUND BLACK PEPPER

Wash lentils and drain. Cover with cold water and leave to soak for 2 hours. Drain. Cover with cold water again and bring to the boil. Boil for 10 minutes. Drain again; add beef stock and ham knuckle and bring to the boil. Lower heat; cover the pan and simmer gently for 2½ to 3 hours, or until lentils are tender.

Twenty minutes before lentils are done, add potatoes. Just before serving, make a *beurre manié* by creaming together butter and flour. Stir this into the soup, bit by bit, and continue to cook for a few minutes longer. Add pepper, to taste. Serves 4 to 6.

GREEN PEA SOUP

2 SPANISH ONIONS, THINLY SLICED
¾ POUND DRIED GREEN PEAS
3 PINTS WATER
6–8 PEPPERCORNS
1 LEVEL TABLESPOON SALT
4 CLOVES
1 LEVEL TEASPOON DRY MUSTARD
2 STALKS CELERY, THINLY SLICED
¼ POUND BACON, CUT IN THIN STRIPS
¼ LEVEL TEASPOON OREGANO
FRIED CROÛTONS

Combine first nine ingredients in a large saucepan and bring to the boil; skim and then cook very slowly, covered, for 2 to 3 hours, adding more water if soup becomes too thick. Add *oregano* after soup has cooked for 2 hours. Serve with *croûtons*. Serves 6.

GREAT DISHES OF THE WORLD

CHAPTER 3

SAUCES

Great Sauces

'A sauce-maker' according to the *Dictionary of Jovial Gastronomy* 'must be adroit and sensitive to the most delicate nuance as sauce-making includes chemistry, harmony, flavour, voluptuousness, vigilance and other virtues . . . all crossed by the lightning stroke of genius'. No wonder so many cooks hesitate to look into this awesome subject and discover for themselves that, given a few practical rules and a little experience, the whole magic realm of sauce-making is theirs for the asking. But don't get me wrong, I don't claim that your version of *quenelles de brochet* will ever equal the ethereal *pain de poisson* served with an unctuous *sauce Cardinale* created daily by Alexandre Dumaine in his restaurant at Saulieu.

Yet sauces, like soups and stocks, have their place in everyday good cooking as well as in the kitchens of international hotels. A home-made sauce can lend certain magic to the simplest ingredients and make a memorable meal out of humble beginnings.

The French have a way with sauces. Ever since the days of the famous Careme, sauce-making has been the key to French *haute cuisine*, ranking foremost among the many skills that any aspiring cook must learn, practise and finally master.

White Sauces

Béchamel – named after the *maître d'hôtel* of Louis XIV – is the mother sauce of all white sauces and is exceedingly simple to prepare. A simple *béchamel* can be made with just flour, butter, milk and a little minced onion, but I think you will find that the following classic recipe which includes chopped veal adds greatly to the savour of this delicious sauce. The secret of making a good white sauce – and most other sauces – is to cook it slowly.

BÉCHAMEL SAUCE

3 TABLESPOONS BUTTER
½ ONION, FINELY CHOPPED
3 TABLESPOONS FLOUR
1½ PINTS HOT MILK
2 OUNCES LEAN VEAL OR HAM, CHOPPED
1 STALK CELERY, FINELY CHOPPED
1 TABLESPOON BUTTER
1 SMALL SPRIG THYME
½ BAY LEAF
WHITE PEPPERCORNS
FRESHLY-GRATED NUTMEG

In a thick-bottomed saucepan, or in the top of a double saucepan, melt butter and cook onion over a low heat until it is transparent. Stir in flour and, stirring constantly, cook for a few minutes or until mixture cooks through but does not take on colour.

Add hot milk and cook, stirring constantly, until the mixture is thick and smooth.

In another saucepan, simmer finely-chopped lean veal (or ham) and celery in butter over a very low heat. Season with thyme, bay leaf, white peppercorns and grated nutmeg. Cook for 5 minutes, stirring to keep veal from browning. Add veal to the sauce and cook over hot water for 45 minutes to 1 hour, stirring occasionally. When reduced to the proper consistency (two-thirds of original quantity), strain sauce through a fine sieve into a bowl, pressing meat and onion well to extract all the liquid. Cover surface of sauce with tiny pieces of butter to keep film from forming. Makes about 1 pint.

BÉCHAMEL SAUCE (SHORT METHOD)

2 TABLESPOONS BUTTER
½ ONION, FINELY CHOPPED
1 STALK CELERY, FINELY CHOPPED
2 TABLESPOONS FLOUR
1 PINT HOT MILK
1 SMALL SPRIG THYME
½ BAY LEAF
WHITE PEPPERCORNS
FRESHLY-GRATED NUTMEG

Melt butter for the *roux* in a thick saucepan or in the top of a double saucepan. Cook finely-chopped onion and celery in it over a low heat until onion is soft but not browned. Remove pan from heat, stir in flour, return to heat and cook gently for 3 to 5 minutes, stirring constantly, until flour is cooked through. Add a quarter of the milk, heated to boiling point, and cook over water, stirring vigorously. As the sauce begins to thicken, add the remainder of the milk, stirring constantly with a wooden spoon until sauce bubbles. Add thyme, bay leaf, and pepper and nutmeg, to taste, and simmer sauce gently for 15 minutes. Strain through a fine sieve and dot surface with butter. Makes about 1 pint.

Using either version of the béchamel sauce above, you can make a variety of sauces to accompany meat, fish, eggs and vegetables.

CREAM SAUCE . . . for fish, poultry, eggs and vegetables.

Add 4 tablespoons double cream to 1 pint hot béchamel and bring to boiling point. Add a few drops lemon juice.

MORNAY SAUCE . . . for fish, vegetables, poultry, poached eggs, noodle and macaroni mixtures.

Mix 2 slightly-beaten egg yolks with a little cream and combine with 1 pint hot béchamel sauce. Cook, stirring constantly, until it just reaches boiling point. Add 2 tablespoons butter and 2 to 4 tablespoons grated cheese (Parmesan or Swiss cheese is best).

AURORE SAUCE . . . excellent with eggs, chicken or shellfish.

Add 2 to 3 tablespoons tomato purée to 1 pint hot béchamel sauce.

ONION SAUCE . . . for fish, lamb or veal.

Chop 1 Spanish onion, cover with hot water and parboil for 3 to 5 minutes. Drain and cook onion in a saucepan with a little butter until soft. Add 1 pint hot béchamel sauce and cook for approximately 15 minutes longer. Strain through a fine sieve, pressing the vegetables well to extract all juice; return to the fire and gradually add 4 tablespoons double cream. Correct seasoning with salt and white pepper, and serve.

VELOUTÉ SAUCE

2 TABLESPOONS BUTTER
2 TABLESPOONS FLOUR
1 PINT WHITE STOCK (CHICKEN OR VEAL)
SALT
WHITE PEPPERCORNS
4 BUTTON MUSHROOMS, CHOPPED

Melt butter in saucepan; add flour and cook for a few minutes to form *roux blond.* Add boiling stock, salt and pepper and cook, stirring vigorously with a whisk. Add mushrooms and cook slowly, stirring occasionally, skimming from time to time, until the sauce is reduced to two-thirds of its original quantity and is very thick but light and creamy. Strain through a fine sieve.

RICH CHEESE SAUCE

3 TABLESPOONS BUTTER
3 TABLESPOONS FLOUR
$\frac{3}{4}$ PINT HOT CHICKEN STOCK
$\frac{1}{2}$ PINT DOUBLE CREAM
2 TABLESPOONS FRESHLY-GRATED GRUYÈRE
2 TABLESPOONS FRESHLY-GRATED PARMESAN
SALT, FRESHLY-GROUND BLACK PEPPER AND NUTMEG

Melt butter in the top of a double saucepan; stir in flour and cook over water for 3 minutes, stirring continuously until smooth. Blend in hot chicken stock and then cream with a wire whisk to avoid lumps.

Stir in grated Gruyère and Parmesan and season to taste with freshly-ground black pepper, salt and a little grated nutmeg. Continue to cook over water on the lowest of heats for about 20 minutes, stirring from time to time to keep skin from forming. Makes about 1 pint. Good for poultry, fish, vegetables and eggs.

RICH PRAWN SAUCE

3 TABLESPOONS BUTTER
3 TABLESPOONS FLOUR
$\frac{3}{4}$ PINT FISH FUMET OR RICH FISH STOCK
$\frac{1}{2}$ PINT DOUBLE CREAM
$\frac{3}{4}$ POUND FROZEN PRAWNS, COARSELY CHOPPED
2 TABLESPOONS BUTTER
SALT, FRESHLY-GROUND BLACK PEPPER AND CAYENNE
2 TABLESPOONS COGNAC

Melt butter in the top of a double saucepan; stir in flour and cook over water for 3 minutes, stirring continuously until smooth. Add strained fish *fumet* slowly, stirring continuously until sauce is rich and creamy. Simmer gently for 20 minutes; then add cream and continue cooking, uncovered, stirring from time to time to keep skin from forming, until the sauce is reduced to the desired consistency.

Sauté chopped prawns in butter until heated through; season to taste with salt, pepper and cayenne pepper. Flame with cognac and add to sauce. Makes about 1 pint. Good for poached fish, and fish and shellfish soufflés.

Brown Sauces

There is only one basic brown sauce – *sauce espagnole* – used as the base for many famous French sauces. As this sauce keeps very well, make it by the quart and store it in the refrigerator in a covered jar for future use. *Sauce espagnole*, or basic brown sauce, will keep indefinitely in the refrigerator if it is boiled up again once a week, and returned to the refrigerator in a clean jar.

Use *sauce espagnole* as a base for many exciting sauces, and as it is to lend interest to braised onions, carrots and celery, or to add to the butter in which steaks and chops have been cooked.

SAUCE ESPAGNOLE

3 TABLESPOONS BEEF DRIPPING
3 OUNCES FAT SALT PORK OR GREEN BACON, DICED
3 CARROTS, COARSELY CHOPPED
1 SPANISH ONION, COARSELY CHOPPED
2 STALKS CELERY, COARSELY CHOPPED
3 TABLESPOONS FLOUR
1½ QUARTS HOME-MADE BEEF STOCK
1 BOUQUET GARNI (3 SPRIGS PARSLEY, 1 SPRIG THYME, 1 BAY LEAF)
1 CLOVE GARLIC
¼ PINT RICH TOMATO SAUCE OR 3 TABLESPOONS TOMATO CONCENTRATE

Melt fat in a large, heavy saucepan; add diced salt pork (or green bacon), carrots, onion and celery, and cook until golden. Sprinkle with flour and cook gently on a very low flame, stirring frequently, until well browned. Add a third of the boiling stock together with *bouquet garni* and garlic, and cook, stirring frequently, until sauce thickens.

Add half of remaining stock and cook very slowly over a very low heat, uncovered, stirring occasionally, for about 1½ to 2 hours. Skim off scum and fat rising to surface as it cooks. Add tomato sauce (or concentrate) and cook for a few minutes longer. Then strain through a fine sieve into a bowl, pressing the vegetables against the sieve to extract all their juice.

Clean the saucepan; return the mixture to it; add remaining stock and continue cooking slowly until the sauce is reduced to about 1 quart, skimming the surface from time to time.

Strain again. Cool, stirring occasionally. Store *sauce espagnole* in a covered jar in the refrigerator until ready to use. Makes 1 quart.

MADEIRA SAUCE

Reduce 1 pint *sauce espagnole* until it is half the original quantity. Add 6 tablespoons Madeira. Heat the sauce well, but do not let it boil, or the flavour of the wine will be lost.

SAUCE BORDELAISE

Cook 2 finely-chopped shallots in ¼ pint red wine until liquid is reduced to a third of its original quantity. Add ½ pint *sauce espagnole* and simmer gently for 10 minutes.

Remove the marrow from a split beef bone; cut it into small dice and poach it in boiling salted water for 1 or 2 minutes. Drain, and just before serving sauce add 2 tablespoons diced beef marrow and a little finely-chopped parsley.

SAUCE LYONNAISE

Sauté ½ Spanish onion, finely chopped, in 2 tablespoons butter until golden. Add 6 tablespoons dry white wine and simmer until reduced to half the original quantity. Add ½ pint *sauce espagnole*; cook gently for 15 minutes; add 1 tablespoon chopped parsley and 'finish' sauce by swirling in 1 tablespoon butter.

SAUCE PERIGUEUX

1 PINT SAUCE ESPAGNOLE
3 TABLESPOONS MADEIRA
1 TABLESPOON TRUFFLES, FINELY DICED
1 TABLESPOON TRUFFLE LIQUOR
1 TABLESPOON BUTTER

Reduce *sauce espagnole* in a thick-bottomed saucepan to half the original quantity. Add Madeira and bring slowly to the boil, stirring occasionally. Take off heat and stir in finely-diced truffles and truffle liquor. Add butter to the sauce, melting it in by moving the saucepan in a circular motion until butter is completely absorbed.

Serve with baked eggs, eggs *en cocotte*, beef, chicken and veal.

TOMATO SAUCE

1 SPANISH ONION, FINELY CHOPPED
2 CLOVES GARLIC, FINELY CHOPPED
2 TABLESPOONS BUTTER
4 TABLESPOONS OLIVE OIL
6 TABLESPOONS ITALIAN TOMATO CONCENTRATE
1 LARGE TIN ITALIAN PEELED TOMATOES
2 BAY LEAVES
2 TABLESPOONS FINELY-CHOPPED PARSLEY
¼ TABLESPOON OREGANO
1 SMALL STRIP LEMON PEEL
6 TABLESPOONS DRY WHITE WINE
6 TABLESPOONS WATER
SALT AND FRESHLY-GROUND BLACK PEPPER
1 TABLESPOON WORCESTERSHIRE SAUCE

Sauté finely-chopped onion and garlic in butter and olive oil in a large, thick-bottomed frying pan until transparent and soft, but not coloured. Stir in tomato concentrate and continue to cook for a minute or two, stirring constantly. Pour in Italian peeled tomatoes; add bay leaves, parsley, *oregano* and a small strip of lemon peel. Add dry white wine and an equal quantity of water, and salt and freshly-ground black pepper, to taste, and simmer gently, stirring from time to time, for 1 to 2 hours. Just before serving, stir in Worcestershire sauce. Good for *pasta*, meat, poultry and veal.

Emulsion Sauces

SAUCE BÉARNAISE

2 SPRIGS TARRAGON
3 SPRIGS CHERVIL
1 TABLESPOON CHOPPED SHALLOTS
2 CRUSHED PEPPERCORNS
2 TABLESPOONS TARRAGON VINEGAR
¼ PINT DRY WHITE WINE
3 EGG YOLKS
1 TABLESPOON WATER
½ POUND SOFT BUTTER
SALT AND CAYENNE PEPPER

Chop leaves and stems of tarragon and chervil coarsely and combine with shallots, peppercorns, vinegar and white wine in a saucepan. Cook over a hot fire until liquid is reduced to two-thirds of its original quantity.

Place egg yolks, herb and wine mixture, and water in the top of a double saucepan over hot, but not boiling, water and stir briskly with a wire whisk until light and fluffy. Never let water in bottom of saucepan begin to boil, or sauce will not 'take'. Add butter gradually to egg mixture, stirring briskly all the time, as sauce begins to thicken. Continue adding butter and stirring until sauce is thick. Season to taste with salt and a little cayenne pepper, strain through a fine sieve and serve.

SAUCE HOLLANDAISE

1 TEASPOON LEMON JUICE
1 TABLESPOON COLD WATER
SALT AND WHITE PEPPER
½ POUND SOFT BUTTER
4 EGG YOLKS
LEMON JUICE

Combine lemon juice, water, salt and white pepper in the top of a double saucepan or *bain-marie*. Divide butter into 4 equal pieces. Add the egg yolks and a quarter of the butter to the liquid in the saucepan and stir the mixture rapidly and constantly with a wire whisk over hot, but not boiling, water until the butter is melted and the mixture begins to thicken. Add the second piece of butter and continue whisking. As the mixture thickens and the second piece of butter melts, add the third piece of butter, stirring from the bottom of the pan until it is melted. Be careful not to allow the water over which the sauce is cooking to boil at any time. Add rest of butter, beating until it melts and is incorporated in the sauce.

Now remove top part of the saucepan from the heat and continue to beat the sauce for 2 to 3 minutes longer. Replace saucepan over hot, but not boiling, water for 2 minutes more, beating constantly. By this time the emulsion should have formed and your sauce will be rich and creamy. 'Finish' sauce with a few drops of lemon juice, strain and serve.

If at any time in the operation the mixture should curdle, beat in 1 or 2 tablespoons cold water to rebind the emulsion.

MAYONNAISE

2 EGG YOLKS
SALT AND FRESHLY-GROUND BLACK PEPPER
¼ TEASPOON MUSTARD
LEMON JUICE
½ PINT OLIVE OIL

Place egg yolks (make sure gelatinous thread of the egg is removed), salt, pepper and mustard in a bowl. Use a wire whisk, fork or wooden spoon, and beat the yolks to a smooth paste. Add a little lemon juice (the acid helps the emulsion) and, drop by drop, beat in about a quarter of the oil. Add a little more lemon juice to the mixture and next, a little more quickly now, add more oil, beating all the while. Continue adding oil and beating until the sauce is of a good thick consistency. Correct seasoning (more salt, pepper and lemon juice) as desired. If you are going to make the mayonnaise a day before using, stir in 1 tablespoon boiling water when it is of the desired consistency. This will keep it from turning or separating.

Note: If the mayonnaise should curdle, break another egg yolk into a clean bowl and gradually beat the curdled mayonnaise into it. Your mayonnaise will begin to 'take' immediately.

SAUCE LOUIS

½ PINT WELL-FLAVOURED MAYONNAISE
2 TABLESPOONS CHILI SAUCE
3 TABLESPOONS OLIVE OIL
1 TABLESPOON WINE VINEGAR
2 LEVEL TABLESPOONS FINELY-GRATED ONION
2 TABLESPOONS FINELY-CHOPPED PARSLEY
6 TABLESPOONS DOUBLE CREAM, WHIPPED
SALT, FRESHLY-GROUND BLACK PEPPER AND CAYENNE
1–2 TABLESPOONS CHOPPED STUFFED OR RIPE OLIVES

Blend together mayonnaise, chili sauce, olive oil, wine vinegar, finely-grated onion, finely-chopped parsley and whipped cream. Season to taste with salt, pepper and a dash of cayenne. Stir in chopped stuffed or ripe olives and chill for 1 or 2 hours before serving. Delicious for seafood cocktails and a 'must' for crab Louis.

SAUCE VERTE

½ PINT WELL-FLAVOURED MAYONNAISE
1 TABLESPOON FINELY-CHOPPED WATERCRESS LEAVES
1 TABLESPOON FINELY-CHOPPED CHERVIL
2 TABLESPOONS FINELY-CHOPPED PARSLEY
1 TABLESPOON FINELY-CHOPPED TARRAGON LEAVES
LEMON JUICE
SALT AND FRESHLY-GROUND BLACK PEPPER

Whirl mayonnaise, chopped watercress and herbs in an electric blender, or blend well with a whisk, and add lemon juice, salt and freshly-ground pepper, to taste. Serve this sauce with fish and shellfish, poached and grilled salmon, or fish mousse.

SAUCE RÉMOULADE

½ PINT WELL-FLAVOURED MAYONNAISE
1 TABLESPOON FINELY-CHOPPED FRESH TARRAGON, BASIL OR CHERVIL
1 TABLESPOON FINELY-CHOPPED PARSLEY
1 CLOVE GARLIC, FINELY CHOPPED
1 LEVEL TEASPOON DRY MUSTARD
1 TEASPOON CAPERS
2 SMALL PICKLES, FINELY CHOPPED

Combine ingredients; chill and serve with grilled fish, prawns and lobster. Excellent with cold pork chops.

GREEK GARLIC SAUCE (SKORDALIA)

2–4 CLOVES GARLIC, CHOPPED
2 TABLESPOONS FINELY-CHOPPED PARSLEY
1 LARGE BOILED POTATO OR AN EQUAL QUANTITY OF MOIST FRESH BREADCRUMBS
2 OUNCES BLANCHED AND CRUSHED ALMONDS
OLIVE OIL
2–4 TABLESPOONS WINE VINEGAR
SALT AND FRESHLY-GROUND BLACK PEPPER

Pound chopped garlic, finely-chopped parsley, boiled potato (or moist breadcrumbs) and blanched, crushed almonds in a mortar. Add olive oil and vinegar little by little, pounding mixture until it is a smooth paste. Add salt and freshly-ground black pepper, to taste, and continue adding olive oil, beating briskly, until sauce is of the desired consistency.

SAUCE GRIBICHE

3 HARD-BOILED EGGS
1 LEVEL TABLESPOON DIJON MUSTARD
1 TABLESPOON FINELY-CHOPPED PARSLEY, CHIVES AND CHERVIL
¼ PINT OLIVE OIL
VINEGAR OR LEMON JUICE
SALT AND FRESHLY-GROUND BLACK PEPPER

Pound egg yolks with mustard and *fines herbes* in a mortar until smooth. Add olive oil little by little, stirring all the time as for a mayonnaise. Season to taste with vinegar or lemon juice and salt and freshly-ground black pepper. Chop egg whites finely and add to sauce. Stir just before serving.

ROUILLE

- 2 FAT CLOVES GARLIC
- 1 LEVEL TABLESPOON PAPRIKA
- 1 SLICE WHITE BREAD, TRIMMED OF CRUSTS
- 2 TABLESPOONS OLIVE OIL
- 2 TABLESPOONS MAYONNAISE

Pound garlic and paprika (or crushed red peppers) in a mortar with bread which you have dipped in water and then squeezed dry. Add olive oil and mayonnaise little by little and blend to a smooth paste.

PROVENÇAL TAPÉNADE

- 2 OUNCES STONED RIPE OLIVES
- 1 OUNCE ANCHOVY FILLETS
- 1 OUNCE TUNA FISH
- DIJON MUSTARD
- 2 OUNCES CAPERS
- 2 FLUID OUNCES OLIVE OIL
- COGNAC
- FRESHLY-GROUND BLACK PEPPER

Pound stoned ripe olives, anchovy fillets and tuna fish to a smooth paste in a mortar with Dijon mustard and capers, adding olive oil bit by bit as you would for a mayonnaise. Season to taste with cognac and freshly-ground black pepper and force mixture through a fine sieve. The *tapénade* mixture keeps well in a jar, and is excellent with hard-boiled eggs or as a highly-flavoured *canapé* spread.

Butters

BEURRE NOISETTE

- ¼ POUND BUTTER
- JUICE OF ½ LEMON

Melt butter and cook to a light hazelnut colour. Add lemon juice. Serve with eggs, brains and boiled vegetables.

GARLIC BUTTER

- ¼ POUND BUTTER
- 2–4 CLOVES GARLIC, CRUSHED
- 1 TABLESPOON FINELY-CHOPPED PARSLEY
- 1–2 TABLESPOONS LEMON JUICE
- SALT AND FRESHLY-GROUND BLACK PEPPER

Cream butter with crushed garlic and finely-chopped parsley. Season to taste with lemon juice, salt and freshly-ground black pepper. Chill. Serve with grilled steak.

CRAYFISH BUTTER

- 2 TABLESPOONS BUTTER
- 1 SMALL ONION, FINELY CHOPPED
- 1 BAY LEAF
- PINCH THYME
- CRUSHED CRAYFISH SHELLS
- ¼ POUND BUTTER

Sauté finely-chopped onion with bay leaf, thyme and crushed crayfish shells (which you have dried in the oven for a few minutes) for 20 to 30 minutes. Cool. Add butter and pound in mortar until creamy. Rub mixture through a fine sieve and use as required in fish or shellfish soups, *bisques* and sauces.

SHRIMP OR PRAWN BUTTER

As above, but use shrimp or prawn shells.

LOBSTER BUTTER

As above, but use shells and coral of lobster.

Sweet Sauces

APRICOT SAUCE

½ PINT APRICOT JAM
¼ PINT WATER
2 TABLESPOONS KIRSCH

Combine apricot jam and water in a saucepan and bring to the boil. Lower heat and simmer gently, stirring from time to time, for 5 to 10 minutes. Strain through a fine sieve and stir in Kirsch.

VANILLA CUSTARD SAUCE

¾ PINT MILK
½ TEASPOON VANILLA ESSENCE
4 TABLESPOONS SUGAR
4 EGG YOLKS
¼ TEASPOON SALT

Simmer milk for 5 minutes; stir in vanilla essence. Combine sugar, egg yolks and salt and beat until fluffy and lemon-coloured. Pour a little of the hot milk into the egg and sugar mixture; blend well; then stir into the hot milk. Heat slowly in the top of a double saucepan, stirring constantly, until the mixture coats a spoon. Serve warm over cake, sweet soufflé or ice cream.

ZABAGLIONE SAUCE

3 EGG YOLKS
1 OUNCE GRANULATED SUGAR
3–4 TABLESPOONS MARSALA OR SHERRY
1½ TABLESPOONS BRANDY

Combine egg yolks with sugar and Marsala or sherry in the top of a double saucepan. Whisk mixture over hot, but not boiling, water until sauce coats the back of a spoon. Stir in Marsala (or sherry) and brandy, and serve immediately. For cakes, puddings, sweet soufflés and ice cream.

CRÈME PÂTISSIÈRE

4 EGG YOLKS
2 OUNCES SUGAR
2 TEASPOONS FLOUR
½ PINT WARM MILK
¼ TEASPOON VANILLA ESSENCE

Beat yolks and sugar together until mixture is fluffy and lemon-coloured. Mix in flour, then add milk and vanilla and mix thoroughly. Place mixture in top of a double saucepan and cook over water, stirring constantly, until it reaches boiling point. Boil for 2 minutes; remove from heat; put through sieve and allow to cool.

RUM SAUCE

2 EGG YOLKS
2 TABLESPOONS SUGAR
½ PINT DOUBLE CREAM
2 FLUID OUNCES RUM
½ TEASPOON VANILLA ESSENCE
SUGAR

Beat egg yolks with 2 tablespoons sugar until fluffy and lemon-coloured. Whip cream until stiff; add rum and vanilla essence and whip until stiff again. Add more sugar to taste. Fold beaten egg yolks into whipped cream.

CHAPTER 4

EGGS

It was in France that I first learned to treat eggs with the respect that they deserve. Until then, I had always considered them as just another breakfast food or late-night snack. But in France, where an omelette can be a thing of fragile beauty and where the soufflé soars to gastronomic heights of gossamer distinction, the egg really comes into its own as gourmet fare for any occasion.

France also taught me to appreciate the egg in its hard-boiled state – eggs mayonnaise as the refreshing beginning to a meal on a sun-dappled terrace; eggs *en tonneaux*, whole hard-boiled eggs filled with anchovies and made to look like little caper-filled barrels; and stuffed and dressed eggs of every variety.

Eggs are good mixers. They go well with any meat, fish or sauce, are one of the most versatile of foods, and can be prepared in almost endless ways. To my mind, no single food is more essential to good cooking than the egg.

The most important thing to remember in cooking eggs is to use low heat. The making of an omelette is the outstanding exception, and here the higher heat is nullified by the short time the eggs are subjected to it.

Always store eggs in the refrigerator. Keep eggs broad end up and away from smells (the porous nature of the shell makes the contents particularly receptive to odours). Do not store them near highly-flavoured cheeses or onions. For best cooking results, bring eggs to room temperature (about 45 minutes) before using them. Whites will beat up faster and to a larger volume and shells will not crack when you boil them. If they have just come from the refrigerator, run warm water over them for a minute or so to bring them to room temperature.

BOILED EGGS

This is a misnomer. Eggs should never be boiled. Doing so produces an unpalatable tough white and a yolk which is dull yellow and rubbery. For the best results, eggs in the shell should be cooked in water which is barely simmering.

Fill a pan with enough water to cover the eggs thoroughly. Bring the water to a rolling boil and lower the eggs into it gently, using a spoon. Then lower heat until the water is just barely bubbling; otherwise the eggs will bang against the side of the pan and the shells may break. And eggs boiled more gently seem to taste better, too.

The classic soft-boiled egg – the white coagulated but still on the soft side and the golden yolk runny – is cooked for 3 to 4½ minutes. A 6-minute egg (*œuf mollet*) has a firm white and runny yolk. A true hard-boiled egg is cooked in simmering water for about 10 minutes.

Remove eggs from the water at once or they will go on cooking. Rinse them under cold water for a brief second to make handling easier.

POACHED EGGS

For the best results it is essential to use fresh eggs, preferably not more than three or four days old. I always find that the whites of older eggs tend to go stringy and the yolks are much more apt to break than those of fresh ones. A large wide pan is a necessity, too, if you intend to poach more than one egg at a time. And be sure it is deep enough to allow at least an inch of water over the eggs to prevent them from sticking to the bottom of the pan.

Fill the pan with water; bring it to the boil and add 1 tablespoon of vinegar and a little salt to help eggs keep their shape. Have your eggs ready, each broken into a separate cup. Holding a cup in each hand, tip the eggs into the rapidly boiling water. Remove pan from the heat; as the whites begin to set, turn eggs once or twice with a perforated spoon to give them a proper shape; cover pan and allow eggs to simmer gently, still off the heat, for about 3 minutes. Lift eggs out with a perforated spoon and, if you are not going to serve them immediately, slide them into a bowl of warm water. If you are, put them in cold water for a minute to stop cooking and to remove all taste of acidity; drain them dry on a clean towel and trim straggly bits of white with a pair of scissors.

ŒUFS MOLLETS

Poached eggs are not easy, by any standards, to make successfully. I often prefer to use *œufs mollets* in recipes that call for poached eggs. An *œuf mollet* is the French culinary term for a shelled soft-boiled egg with the white delicately firm and the yolk deliciously runny. Cook *œufs mollets* as boiled eggs, but for 6 minutes only. Shell carefully under cold water.

Any French chef will tell you that certain egg dishes served with a special sauce or garniture require a poached egg, and that there are others which require an *œuf mollet*. As a matter of fact, these are practically interchangeable. So if, as I do, you find difficulty in preparing poached eggs, then by all means use shelled soft-boiled eggs instead.

BAKED EGGS

Butter individual baking dishes or soufflé dishes with a teaspoon of butter. Slide 1 or 2 eggs into each, being careful not to break the yolks. Sprinkle the top with pepper and salt to taste and add a small dab of butter. Place baking dishes in a pan of hot water and bake in a pre-heated moderate oven (325° to 350°F. Mark 2 to 3) for about 8 minutes, or a little longer if a firmer egg is desired. And be sure to remove eggs from the oven before they are completely cooked. They will continue cooking from the heat of the baking dish.

BAKED EGGS WITH CREAM

¼ PINT CREAM
2 TABLESPOONS GRATED GRUYÈRE
2 TABLESPOONS LEMON JUICE
2 TABLESPOONS DRY WHITE WINE
1–2 TEASPOONS PREPARED MUSTARD
SALT AND FRESHLY-GROUND BLACK PEPPER
8 EGGS
BUTTERED BREADCRUMBS

Mix together cream, grated cheese, lemon juice and dry white wine; add mustard and salt and pepper, to taste. Break eggs into individual buttered ramekins or casseroles, 2 eggs in each. Cover the eggs with the sauce and sprinkle buttered breadcrumbs over the top. Place ramekins in a pan of hot water and bake in a moderate oven (375°F. Mark 4) for about 15 minutes. Serves 4.

BAKED EGGS EN SOUFFLÉ

4 EGGS
SALT AND WHITE PEPPER
BUTTER
4 TABLESPOONS DOUBLE CREAM
4 TABLESPOONS GRATED PARMESAN CHEESE

Separate eggs. Beat the whites until very stiff and season generously with salt and white pepper. Butter individual ramekins or casseroles and spoon egg whites into each. Use rather large ramekins as egg whites tend to rise like a soufflé. Make a depression with the back of your spoon for each egg yolk. Place yolks in hollows (1 to each ramekin); cover each yolk with 1 tablespoon cream and sprinkle with grated cheese. Bake in a hot oven (450°F. Mark 7) for 8 to 10 minutes. Serves 4.

EGGS EN CASSEROLE

4 HARD-BOILED EGGS
1 TABLESPOON PREPARED MUSTARD
1 TABLESPOON OLIVE OIL
2 TABLESPOONS FINELY-CHOPPED PARSLEY
SALT AND FRESHLY-GROUND BLACK PEPPER
4 TABLESPOONS FRESHLY-GRATED PARMESAN
2 SLICES BREAD, CRUSTS REMOVED
2 TABLESPOONS BUTTER
½ PINT WELL-FLAVOURED TOMATO SAUCE
1 TEASPOON GRATED ONION
1–2 TABLESPOONS CHOPPED STUFFED OLIVES

Cut eggs in half crosswise and remove yolks carefully. Mash yolks and mix with mustard, olive oil and 1 tablespoon finely-chopped parsley. Season to taste with salt, pepper and half the cheese. Stuff egg cavities with this mixture.

Dice bread and sauté in butter until crisp and golden. Place diced toast at the bottom of individual oven-proof baking dishes and arrange stuffed eggs on top. Cover with tomato sauce to which you have added remaining chopped parsley, grated onion and finely-chopped stuffed olives. Sprinkle with remaining cheese and heat through in a moderate oven (375°F. Mark 4) for 15 minutes. Serve alone as hot first course, or with rice as a luncheon dish. Serves 4.

DEEP-FRIED STUFFED EGGS

6 HARD-BOILED EGGS
1 TIN SARDINES
1 TEASPOON FRENCH MUSTARD
JUICE OF 1 LEMON
WORCESTERSHIRE SAUCE
SALT AND FRESHLY-GROUND BLACK PEPPER
1–2 TABLESPOONS MAYONNAISE
FLOUR, EGG AND BREADCRUMBS FOR COATING
CORN OR OLIVE OIL FOR FRYING

Cut the eggs in half lengthwise and remove the yolks. Sieve the yolks; mash the sardines and mix well together. Add the seasonings and sufficient mayonnaise to make a firm paste.

Mound each half of egg with the filling and form into shape of whole egg. Dip in flour and then coat with egg and breadcrumbs. Fry about 2 minutes or until a golden-brown colour in deep hot oil.

ŒUFS FARCIS AUX ANCHOIS

4 HARD-BOILED EGGS
4–6 ANCHOVY FILLETS
4–6 CAPERS
1 TABLESPOON FINELY-CHOPPED PARSLEY
¼ PINT THICK BÉCHAMEL SAUCE
SALT AND FRESHLY-GROUND BLACK PEPPER
BREADCRUMBS
BUTTER

Remove shells and cut each egg in half lengthwise. Remove yolks and mash to a smooth paste in a mortar with anchovies, capers and parsley. Add thick béchamel sauce to this mixture and season to taste with salt and pepper. Blend well together. Take each half egg and mound mixture on to it to re-form egg into a whole.

Place the re-formed eggs in a well-buttered baking dish, stuffing side on top. Sprinkle with breadcrumbs. Dot each egg with butter and heat through in a moderate oven (375°F. Mark 4) for 10 minutes. Serves 4.

ŒUFS À LA TAPÉNADE

2 OUNCES STONED RIPE OLIVES
1 OUNCE ANCHOVY FILLETS
1 OUNCE TUNA FISH
1 TEASPOON MUSTARD
1 OUNCE CAPERS
4–6 TABLESPOONS OLIVE OIL
1 TABLESPOON COGNAC
FRESHLY-GROUND BLACK PEPPER
4 HARD-BOILED EGGS
LETTUCE, TO GARNISH

Pound stoned ripe olives, anchovy fillets and tuna fish to a smooth paste in a mortar with mustard and capers (called *tapéno* in Provençal, from which this dish gets its name) When the mixture has been blended to a smooth paste, put it through a fine sieve and whisk olive oil into it. Add cognac and black pepper to taste.

To make *œufs à la tapénade:* cut hard-boiled eggs in half lengthwise and remove yolks. Blend yolks with *tapénade* mixture, adding a little more olive oil if necessary; fill egg cavities, and serve on a bed of lettuce. The *tapénade* mixture keeps well in a covered jar, and is excellent as a *canapé* spread.

EGGS AND MUSHROOMS AU GRATIN

8 EGGS
½ POUND MUSHROOMS
2 TABLESPOONS BUTTER
½ PINT WELL-FLAVOURED BÉCHAMEL SAUCE
4 TABLESPOONS GRATED PARMESAN

Boil eggs gently for about 6 minutes so that the yolk is still soft and the white not yet cooked hard. Shell carefully and chop coarsely. Add sliced mushrooms, sautéed in butter, to a well-flavoured béchamel. Stir in egg pieces and spoon the mixture into individual casseroles or soufflé dishes. Sprinkle with grated cheese and brown under the grill. Serve immediately. Serves 4.

BOUILLABAISSE D'ŒUFS

6 TABLESPOONS OLIVE OIL
2 LEEKS, WHITES ONLY, FINELY CHOPPED
1 SPANISH ONION, FINELY CHOPPED
3 TOMATOES, COARSELY CHOPPED
4 CLOVES GARLIC, MASHED
A LITTLE FENNEL, IF AVAILABLE
1 BOUQUET GARNI
1 PIECE OF ORANGE PEEL
6 POTATOES, THINLY SLICED
SAFFRON
SALT AND FRESHLY-GROUND BLACK PEPPER
WATER, OR WATER AND STOCK, TO COVER
1 EGG PER PERSON
1 PIECE OF BREAD PER PERSON

Sauté chopped leeks and onion in olive oil until they are transparent. Add chopped tomatoes, mashed garlic, fennel, *bouquet garni*, orange peel, potatoes and saffron, to taste, and generous amounts of salt and pepper. Cover with water, or water and stock, and boil as for a *bouillabaisse*. When potatoes are cooked, poach eggs in the *bouillon*. To serve, pour *bouillon* over pieces of bread in individual soup plates. Serve the potatoes and eggs on a hot serving platter.

BAKED EGGS LORRAINE

4 EGGS
4 SLICES BACON
BUTTER
2 THIN SLICES SWISS CHEESE, DICED
SALT AND WHITE PEPPER
8 TABLESPOONS DOUBLE CREAM

Poach bacon in boiling water for 5 minutes. Drain and dry. Dice and sauté in butter until golden. Place diced bacon in the bottom of 4 individual baking dishes. Cover bacon with a layer of diced cheese. Break 1 egg into each dish; season to taste with salt and pepper and cover with cream. Bake in a moderately hot oven (400°F. Mark 5) for 20 minutes, or until whites are set. Serve immediately. Serves 4.

STUFFED EGGS MORNAY

8 HARD-BOILED EGGS
¼ POUND COOKED FISH
16 CAPERS, FINELY CHOPPED
1–2 TABLESPOONS OLIVE OIL
SALT AND FRESHLY-GROUND BLACK PEPPER
½ PINT HOT MORNAY SAUCE

Cut eggs in half lengthwise. Remove yolks and combine in a bowl with the cooked fish and capers and enough olive oil to make a smooth paste. Season mixture to taste with salt and freshly-ground black pepper.

Fill egg whites with mixture, cover with hot well-flavoured Mornay sauce and brown under the grill. Serves 8.

ŒUFS AU FOIE GRAS LOUIS OLIVER

4 THIN SLICES PÂTÉ DE FOIE GRAS
SALT AND FRESHLY-GROUND BLACK PEPPER
CAYENNE PEPPER
BUTTER
8 FRESH EGGS
MADEIRA SAUCE

Cut 4 thin slices of *pâté de foie gras*; pepper them lightly with freshly-ground black pepper and a little cayenne, and sauté gently in butter. Place in 4 buttered egg dishes and break 2 eggs per person into separate cups. Season to taste with salt and pepper and pour eggs into egg dishes. Cook gently on a low heat or on an asbestos mat until eggs set.

When the eggs are cooked, pour a little hot Madeira sauce over them and serve very hot. Serves 4.

ŒUFS EN MEURETTE

¼ POUND DICED GREEN BACON
1 TABLESPOON OLIVE OIL
1 MEDIUM ONION, FINELY CHOPPED
1 CLOVE GARLIC, FINELY CHOPPED
1 TABLESPOON FLOUR
¼ PINT HOT BEEF STOCK
¼ PINT RED WINE
SALT AND FRESHLY-GROUND BLACK PEPPER
1 PINCH MARJORAM
1 PINCH THYME
1 BAY LEAF
1 TABLESPOON LEMON JUICE
2 TABLESPOONS FINELY-CHOPPED PARSLEY
3 TABLESPOONS BUTTER
4 EGGS
LEMON JUICE OR VINEGAR
4 TRIANGLES OR ROUNDS OF WHITE BREAD

Sauté diced green bacon in olive oil until golden. Remove bacon bits and reserve. Sauté finely-chopped onion and garlic in the resulting fat until transparent; sprinkle with flour and blend well. Add hot beef stock and wine alternately, stirring all the time, and simmer until sauce is thick and smooth. Add salt and freshly-ground black pepper to taste, marjoram, thyme and a bay leaf, and simmer, uncovered, over a low flame for 20 minutes.

Strain the sauce through a fine sieve; stir in bacon bits, lemon juice, parsley and 1 tablespoon butter, and keep warm.

Poach eggs in water to which you have added a little lemon juice or vinegar; drain. Sauté triangles or rounds of bread in remaining butter until golden. Place 1 poached egg on each slice of bread; pour sauce over all and serve. Serves 4.

ŒUFS FLORENTINE

8 EGGS
SALT AND LEMON JUICE
1 POUND COOKED SPINACH, FINELY CHOPPED AND SEASONED WITH BUTTER
GRATED NUTMEG
½ PINT MORNAY SAUCE
GRATED PARMESAN CHEESE

Poach eggs in salted water containing a little lemon juice for added flavour and to help hold eggs together. Butter ramekins or individual baking dishes large enough to hold 2 eggs and spread a good layer of seasoned spinach in each. Sprinkle with grated nutmeg and a little lemon juice and place 2 poached eggs in each. Cover with Mornay sauce; dust with grated Parmesan and place under grill for a few moments until nicely browned. Serve hot. Serves 4.

ŒUFS À LA TRIPE

6 EGGS
4 ONIONS
2 TABLESPOONS BUTTER
½ PINT HOT BÉCHAMEL SAUCE
SALT AND FRESHLY-GROUND BLACK PEPPER

Hard-boil the eggs for 15 minutes in boiling water. Remove shells and slice. Slice onions and sauté them in butter until they are soft and golden; do not let them brown. Add onions and butter to hot béchamel sauce; stir well; fold in the egg slices and add salt and pepper, to taste. Heat through in an oven-proof casserole and serve hot. Serves 4.

STUFFED EGG AND TOMATO SALAD

1 SMALL TIN TUNA FISH
6 HARD-BOILED EGGS
4–6 TABLESPOONS MAYONNAISE
JUICE OF ½ LEMON
SALT AND FRESHLY-GROUND BLACK PEPPER
6 TOMATOES, SLICED
FRENCH DRESSING
2 TABLESPOONS FINELY-CHOPPED PARSLEY

Pound fish in mortar until smooth. Shell eggs and halve lengthwise. Remove yolks, mash them and add to fish mixture. Stir in mayonnaise, lemon juice, salt and pepper, and mix well. Taste and correct seasoning. Add more mayonnaise or lemon juice if mixture is too thick. Stuff eggs with this mixture and serve on a bed of sliced tomatoes dressed with French dressing. Garnish dish with finely-chopped parsley. Serves 4.

Scrambled Eggs

Use plenty of butter in the pan. It should be hot when the eggs are added, but not smoking or browned.

Allow 2 eggs per person and add an extra one for the pan. Mix eggs slightly; but do not beat them. Add 1 tablespoon water or cream for each egg. Water will make exceedingly fluffy eggs; cream gives a richer, smoother mixture.

Butter a small saucepan generously; pour in the eggs and cook over hot, but not boiling, water.

For fluffy or creamy scrambled eggs, allow the eggs to set slightly after you put them in the pan and then stir constantly with a wooden spoon, being certain to run the edge of the spoon around the edges and into the centre of the pan. Good scrambled eggs need constant and careful attention.

You may add seasonings when mixing the eggs or while they are cooking, or you may prepare seasonings first, pour the eggs over them and scramble with the pre-cooked seasonings. Serve immediately on hot plates.

SCRAMBLED EGGS WITH HERBS: Use fresh herbs; prepared herb mixtures for eggs are usually dry and tasteless. The most agreeable herbs are parsley, chives, chervil and tarragon, chopped fine and added to the egg mixture either before or during cooking. I like to sprinkle extra herbs over the eggs just before serving for added flavour.

SCRAMBLED EGGS WITH SMOKED SALMON: Cut thin slices of smoked salmon *en julienne* and heat for a moment in butter. Add eggs (2 for each person, 1 for the pan), slightly beaten with a little water or cream. Scramble. Add freshly-ground black pepper and salt, to taste. Cook as above. Just before removing from the fire, add a few drops of lemon juice and a little chopped parsley.

RUMBLED EGGS: Beat eggs; melt butter in a saucepan; add pepper and salt, to taste. When butter is hot, pour in the eggs and stir over a gentle heat until soft and creamy. The moment the eggs cream, scoop out on to hot buttered toast spread with anchovy paste.

SCRAMBLED EGGS WITH OYSTERS

2 TABLESPOONS BUTTER
1 TEASPOON ANCHOVY PASTE
6 EGGS
DASH OF TABASCO
12 OYSTERS
SALT AND FRESHLY-GROUND BLACK PEPPER
1 TABLESPOON FINELY-CHOPPED PARSLEY
CROÛTONS OF FRIED BREAD

Melt butter with anchovy paste. Whisk eggs with a dash of Tabasco.

Pour into hot anchovy butter and scramble as usual. When eggs are just beginning to set, toss in 12 oysters, chopped and drained, and finish scrambling. Season to taste with salt and freshly-ground black pepper. Sprinkle with finely-chopped parsley and serve with *croûtons* of bread fried in butter and olive oil. Serves 4.

SCRAMBLED EGGS WITH WHITE TRUFFLES

6 EGGS
½ CLOVE GARLIC
SALT AND WHITE PEPPER
3 TABLESPOONS BUTTER
1 WHITE TRUFFLE, THINLY SLICED
6 TABLESPOONS FRESH CREAM

Rub bowl in which you are going to beat the eggs with half a clove of garlic. Beat eggs lightly, just enough to mix the whites and the yolks; add salt and white pepper, to taste.

Melt butter in a thick-bottomed saucepan, and as soon as it is hot, add sliced truffle and sauté in butter for 2 minutes. Add beaten eggs and cook over a low heat so that the eggs do not set too quickly. When the eggs just begin to set and are still quite liquid, stir in cream and continue stirring until eggs are creamy. Serve immediately. Serves 4.

The Omelette

So much has been said as well as written about the omelette's capricious nature that otherwise daring cooks often refuse to attempt it. In actual fact, most of omelette-making is easier to do than to explain.

Omelettes can be infinitely varied in flavour, for no other dish so lends itself to the inventiveness of the cook. And once you learn to make a basic omelette, its countless variations – *paysanne*, *provençale*, *parisienne*, *Parmentier*, *caviare*, *fines herbes* – become child's play. An omelette is perfectly easy to make and yet so easy to spoil. One false move and the dish is ruined. You might as well throw it away. It takes talent to make it right and you must be on the job every moment it is in preparation, for speed and efficiency count above all. Every omelette must be made to measure – let your guests wait for the omelette, never let the omelette wait for the guests.

THE BASIC OMELETTE

Small omelettes are much easier to make than big ones. Four eggs make an easily-handled omelette for two to three people. If you have more guests, it is best to make several omelettes, for they then come hotter to the table and have a much better consistency.

For each small omelette, break 4 eggs into a bowl and season to taste with salt and pepper. Add, if desired, 1 tablespoon of water, milk or cream.

Heat the omelette pan gradually on a medium flame until it is hot enough to make butter sizzle on contact. Beat eggs with a fork or wire whisk just enough to mix yolks and whites (about 30 seconds). Add 1 tablespoon of butter to heated pan and shake so butter coats bottom evenly. When butter is sizzling, but before it has turned colour, pour in the beaten eggs, all at once.

Quickly stir eggs for a second or two in the pan to assure even cooking just as you would for scrambled eggs. Then, as eggs start to set, lift edges with your fork so that the liquid can run under. Repeat until liquid is all used up but the eggs are still moist and soft. You can keep eggs 'slipping-free' by shaking pan during the above operation. Now, remove eggs from flame and with one movement press the handle of the pan downwards and slide the omelette towards the handle. When a third of the omelette has slid up the rounded edge of the pan, fold this quickly toward the centre with a knife. Then raise the handle of the pan, and slide opposite edge of omelette one-third up the side farthest away from the handle. Hold a heated serving dish under it and, as the rim of the omelette touches the dish, raise the handle more and more until the pan is turned upside down and your oval-shaped, lightly-browned omelette rests on the dish. Rapidly 'finish' the omelette by piercing a piece of butter with the tip of a knife and skimming the surface lightly to leave a glistening trail. Garnish with fresh parsley and serve immediately.

THE OMELETTE PAN

Although some cooks claim that an omelette can be made in any pan, I keep a pan exclusively for eggs. It is a pan expressly designed for omelettes alone – one of good weight, with rounded sides so the eggs can slide easily on to the plate when cooked. And unless you want your omelette to stick, never wash the pan. Instead, just rub it clean with paper and a few drops of oil.

If the pan is new, you must 'season' it before using by slowly heating oil in it; then leave the oil to soak into the pan for at least 12 hours.

Your pan must not be too small or too large for the number of eggs used in the omelette. A pan 7 or 8 inches in diameter is just about right for a 4-egg omelette.

VARIATIONS ON THE THEME

Practice makes perfect and once you have mastered the basic omelette to your satisfaction you are ready to try some of the many exciting variations on the omelette theme. Some of the most delicious are the easiest to prepare; but always remember to make the omelette filling before you make the actual omelette itself. In this way your omelettes can come to the table crisply cased with a wonderfully moist interior and filling.

CHEESE OMELETTE

Perhaps the easiest version of all. Make your omelette as above and, just as eggs begin to set, add 2 tablespoons finely-grated Parmesan cheese and, if you like, 2 tablespoons fresh cream.

WATERCRESS OMELETTE

Add 2 tablespoons finely-chopped watercress to the egg mixture, cook as above, and serve omelette surrounded with fresh watercress.

OMELETTE FLORENTINE

Warm 4 tablespoons freshly-cooked, well-drained spinach in butter. Rub omelette pan lightly with garlic and make omelette as above. When eggs are just set, spread spinach in centre, fold and serve. Another version of this recipe chops the spinach and adds it to the egg mixture before cooking. In either case, make sure spinach is well drained before using.

OMELETTE AUX FINES HERBES

Chop finely equal quantities of fresh parsley, chervil, tarragon and chives (optional), enough to fill 2 to 3 tablespoons. Add half of this mixture to your beaten eggs and proceed to make omelette as above. Mix remainder of chopped herbs with 1 tablespoon of melted butter and pour over finished omelette before serving.

Originally, the term '*fines herbes*' included some finely-chopped mushrooms and truffles, sautéed lightly in butter, an excellent refinement to a delicious dish.

MUSHROOM OMELETTE

Marinate ¼ pound sliced mushrooms in 1 tablespoon brandy for 15 minutes. Add a tablespoon butter and stir over heat until liquid evaporates. Add 2 to 4 tablespoons cream, salt and pepper to taste, and keep warm while you make omelettes as above. As omelette sets, spread with this mixture, fold and serve.

OMELETTE PARMENTIER

Brown 4 tablespoons diced boiled potatoes in butter. Add ½ teaspoon each of finely-chopped parsley and chives to egg mixture and, just before pouring into pan, add lightly-browned potatoes. Prepare omelette as above.

FRENCH COUNTRY OMELETTE

2 TABLESPOONS DICED SALT PORK OR GREEN BACON
2 TABLESPOONS BUTTER
4 TABLESPOONS DICED BOILED POTATOES
4 EGGS, LIGHTLY BEATEN
FINELY-CHOPPED PARSLEY
FINELY-CHOPPED CHIVES
SALT AND FRESHLY-GROUND BLACK PEPPER

Parboil diced salt pork or green bacon in water for a few minutes. Drain and sauté in butter. When meat is browned, remove from pan and keep warm. Sauté diced boiled potatoes in the fat until they are golden. Combine lightly-beaten eggs with meat, finely-chopped parsley and chives; add salt and pepper to taste and pour over potatoes in the pan.

Cook as for basic omelette above, and when the first odour of browning is evident, turn the omelette and brown it slightly on the other side. Slide it on to a hot platter and serve.

LA PIPÉRADE DU PAYS BASQUE

1 GREEN PEPPER, SLICED
PORK FAT OR OLIVE OIL
4 RIPE TOMATOES, PEELED AND SEEDED
1 ONION, SLICED
½ CLOVE GARLIC, CRUSHED
2–4 TABLESPOONS DICED JAMBON DE BAYONNE OR COOKED HAM
SALT AND FRESHLY-GROUND BLACK PEPPER
1 TABLESPOON BUTTER
4 EGGS

Sauté sliced green pepper very gently in pork fat or olive oil. Add peeled and seeded tomatoes, finely chopped, with sliced onion, crushed garlic and diced ham, and season to taste with salt and pepper. Add butter and simmer mixture slowly for about 30 minutes or until the vegetables turn into a rather soft purée.

Beat 4 eggs slightly with salt and pepper, and stir gently into the hot vegetable mixture. Be sure not to let them overcook, for this Basque omelette should be soft and wet, with almost the consistency of scrambled eggs. Serves 2.

MADAME PRUNET'S OMELETTE

3 TABLESPOONS CASTOR SUGAR
⅔ PINT MILK
3 TABLESPOONS FLOUR
3 EGGS
RUM
PEANUT OIL
BUTTER
SUGAR

Mix sugar with ½ glass milk. Add flour and eggs and blend well. Pour in remaining milk and flavour with rum to taste. Mixture should be smooth and rather light.

Heat a large thick-bottomed frying pan and oil it lightly. Pour a ladle of the omelette mixture into the pan and cook as you would a pancake. When it is cooked, roll it tightly and push to the edge of the pan. Oil pan again and continue cooking as above until mixture is used up. Place the rolled omelettes in a buttered baking tin and cook in a hot oven (470°F. Mark 7) for 10 minutes. The omelettes will swell and become crisp. Sprinkle with sugar; flame with rum and serve immediately. Serves 4 to 6.

L'OMELETTE DU PÈRE JOSEPH

6–8 EGGS
6 TABLESPOONS CREAM
SALT AND FRESHLY-GROUND BLACK PEPPER
¼ POUND BUTTER
¼ POUND DICED PÂTÉ DE FOIE GRAS
1–2 SMALL TRUFFLES, DICED
1–2 TABLESPOONS DRY SHERRY
6 TABLESPOONS WARM CREAM
TRUFFLES, CUT IN THIN STRIPS
COOKED TONGUE, CUT IN THIN STRIPS

Combine eggs and cream in a bowl; add salt and freshly-ground black pepper to taste, and whisk until mixture is frothy. Make omelette in usual way, using ¼ pound butter.

Just before rolling omelette, stuff it with diced *foie gras* and diced truffles which you have heated in a little dry sherry. Pour slightly warmed cream over omelette and sprinkle with slivered truffles and tongue. Serves 4.

Illustration on facing page

Italian Minestrone

– basically a mixture of beans and fresh vegetables, simmered in bean broth and rich beef stock or water, with meats, herbs, olive oil, *pasta* and freshly-grated cheese – is one of the great peasant dishes of the world. I like it so thick that a spoon will almost stand up in it. (Recipe on page 92.)

Illustration on following two pages

Casserolettes de Filets de Sole 'Lasserre'

Gaining a third star for a restaurant is like winning the *Grand Prix* doubled with the *Legion d' Honneur*. There are only a dozen restaurants in France to which this high accolade has been given, and of these, only Lasserre and La Tour d'Argent – a famous name in France's culinary annals since the sixteenth century – have the added distinction of being awarded the maximum Michelin rating of five knives and forks for comfort, three stars for the excellence of cuisine, with the whole printed in red, a sign to the discerning that the decorations and setting are particularly worthy of notice.

In addition to Lasserre's menu – (twenty-seven hot and cold *hors-d'oeuvre*, seventeen fish dishes, twenty-five *entrées* and twenty-one sweets), its impressive wine list, its décor, its comfort and its twenty chefs – the famous *Club de la Casserole* (every one of the 15,000 members has his own gold watch chain with a diminutive casserole pillbox which entitles him to the first round of drinks on the house) adds to the general charm and pleasures offered by René Lasserre on the Avenue Franklin D. Roosevelt.

One of my special dishes at Lasserre is *Casserolettes de Filets de Sole 'Lasserre'* (tiny pastry cases filled with poached fillets of sole, covered with a rich *sauce bechamel* and glazed under the grill or broiler). (Recipe on page 147.)

OMELETTE SURPRISE 'VALBERG'

8 EGGS
SUGAR
2 TABLESPOONS BUTTER
1 TABLESPOON PEANUT OIL
2–4 TABLESPOONS COINTREAU OR GRAND MARNIER
ORANGE OR BANANA SLICES, OR DICED PINEAPPLE
BUTTER
1–2 TEASPOONS SUGAR
4 TABLESPOONS COGNAC, ARMAGNAC OR RUM

Separate eggs; whisk yolks until frothy; whisk whites until very stiff. Fold yolks into beaten whites and add sugar to taste.

Heat butter and oil in omelette pan and, when very hot, pour in omelette mixture. Spoon over Cointreau or Grand Marnier and cook until omelette is done but still moist.

Place slices of orange, banana or pincapple, which you have heated in a little butter, in centre of egg mixture. Fold over. Place on a hot platter. Sprinkle with sugar and glaze under a hot grill. Flame with cognac, Armagnac or rum and serve immediately. Serves 4 to 6.

ITALIAN FRITTATA

½ SPANISH ONION, FINELY CHOPPED
2 TABLESPOONS OLIVE OIL
6–8 EGGS
1 TABLESPOON EACH FINELY-CHOPPED FRESH PARSLEY, MINT AND BASIL
SALT AND FRESHLY-GROUND BLACK PEPPER
BUTTER
OLIVE OIL

Sauté finely-chopped onion in olive oil until soft and transparent. Combine in a bowl with beaten eggs, finely-chopped parsley, mint and basil. Add salt and freshly-ground black pepper, to taste, and mix well.

Cook slowly on one side in butter and olive oil until brown; add a little more butter before turning to cook other side. Serves 4.

Illustration on facing page

The Egg

– one of the great basics of all cookery – was held in a kind of sacred veneration by the ancients. To them it represented the world and the elements: the shell, earth; the white, water; the yolk, fire; even air was contained in this perfect package.

FIFINE'S PIPÉRADE

8–10 EGGS
4 TABLESPOONS OLIVE OIL
½ SPANISH ONION, COARSELY SLICED
4 PEPPERS (GREEN, YELLOW AND RED), COARSELY SLICED
4 TOMATOES
SALT AND FRESHLY-GROUND BLACK PEPPER
2 TABLESPOONS FRESHLY-GRATED GRUYÈRE
2 TABLESPOONS FRESHLY-GRATED PARMESAN
2 TABLESPOONS BUTTER

Heat olive oil in frying pan; add sliced onion and sauté, stirring from time to time, until onion is transparent. Add sliced and seeded peppers and cook over a low flame, stirring from time to time, until peppers are soft but not mushy. Turn flame higher and stir in skinned and seeded tomatoes. Season generously with salt and pepper.

Break eggs into a bowl and beat with a whisk until foamy. Pour eggs over vegetables, allow to set for a moment, then stir with a wooden spoon or spatula as you would for scrambled eggs. Sprinkle with finely-grated cheese (Gruyère and Parmesan mixed) to bind mixture, and fold omelette into shape. Slide butter under omelette to add flavour, turn out on to a hot serving dish and serve immediately. Serves 4 to 6.

The Savoury Soufflé

The soufflé – to many people one of the most awe-inspiring creations of French *haute cuisine* – is, in reality, nothing more than a simple airy mixture of eggs, butter, flour and a purée of vegetables, meat, fish or fowl. And the last-mentioned – unexciting and unpretentious as the case may be – are very often left-overs.

Try the soufflé as a perfect beginning to a meal, whether it be a simple cheese affair (try a combination of Gruyère and Parmesan), a concoction of fish or shellfish, or one made with a well-seasoned base of puréed vegetables (endive, onion, or mushroom and cheese).

Savoury soufflés also make light-as-air entrées of distinction for luncheon or supper parties. And there you can always let your imagination run riot. What do you risk? The basic soufflé mixture stays just the same. Add a breakfast-cupful of diced, grilled kippers to your basic soufflé mixture for an after-theatre supper for four. Spike a béchamel sauce with Parmesan cheese and a little cream; stir in beaten egg yolks; fold in beaten egg whites. Spoon half the mixture into your soufflé dish; add 4 poached eggs and cover with the rest of the soufflé mixture and you have the famous *œufs mollets en soufflé* created by Marcel Boulestin. Or take the same basic mixture (béchamel sauce, grated Parmesan, a little cream, beaten egg yolks and whites), flavour with a hint of cognac, and instead of poached eggs, bury a surprise catch of diced lobster meat which you have first flamed in cognac, or in a more sophisticated moment, in Pernod. It's as easy as that!

You will find that soufflés are quite easy to make if a few basic rules are followed. First and foremost: a soufflé must be eaten when ready. A soufflé will not wait for your guests: your guests must wait for this delicate and sometimes temperamental dish. A rich, smooth sauce is the base of all soufflés. Many French soufflé recipes simply require a thick, well-flavoured *sauce béchamel*.

The egg yolks and egg whites must be beaten separately; the yolks until thick and lemon-coloured, the whites until stiff but not dry. In separating the eggs, be sure that there is no speck of yolk left in the whites. Otherwise you will not be able to beat your whites stiff. Use an unbuttered soufflé dish for your first attempts so that the soufflé can cling to the sides of the dish and rise to its full height. For added flavour – when you butter the dish sprinkle the buttered surface with fresh breadcrumbs or a little finely-grated Parmesan cheese.

A slow to medium oven (325° to 350°F. Mark 2 to 3) is essential. If your oven is too hot, the soufflé will be well cooked on top and undercooked inside. As long as it remains in a warm oven a soufflé is pretty sturdy. The best way to determine when a soufflé is done is to open the door after 20 or 25 minutes and to give the dish a slight shove. If the top crust moves only very slightly, the soufflé is done. However, if it really trembles, leave it in a few minutes more.

BASIC SAVOURY SOUFFLÉ

2 TABLESPOONS BUTTER
2 TABLESPOONS FLOUR
½ PINT HOT MILK
5 EGG YOLKS
4–6 OUNCES GRATED CHEESE
SALT AND FRESHLY-GROUND BLACK PEPPER
6 EGG WHITES

Melt butter; add flour gradually and mix to a smooth paste, stirring constantly. Add hot milk and cook in double saucepan until sauce is smooth and thick. Remove from fire and add egg yolks, one by one, alternately with a mixture of grated Gruyère and grated Parmesan. Mix well and return to fire. Cook until cheese melts. Add generous amounts of salt and pepper, remove from fire and allow to cool slightly.

Beat egg whites till they are stiff and fold into the warm cheese mixture. Pile mixture in a buttered soufflé dish or casserole. Bake in a pre-heated oven (350°F. Mark 3) for 35 to 40 minutes, or until soufflé is golden. Serve immediately. Serves 4.

CRAB SOUFFLÉ

4 TABLESPOONS BUTTER
3 TABLESPOONS FLOUR
½ PINT HOT MILK
8 TABLESPOONS GRATED PARMESAN
6 OUNCES COOKED CRABMEAT
SALT AND CAYENNE
4 EGG YOLKS
5 EGG WHITES

Melt butter in the top of a double saucepan; add flour and stir until well blended. Add milk and continue cooking, stirring continuously, until the sauce has thickened. Stir in grated cheese and heat until cheese has melted into the mixture. Add well-boned, shredded crabmeat (fresh or canned) and heat through. Season to taste with salt and cayenne pepper.

Beat egg yolks slightly and add hot sauce to them. Whisk egg whites stiffly and gently fold mixture into them, a little at a time. Pour into a buttered and floured casserole and set in a pan of hot water. Bake in a slow (350°F. Mark 3) oven for 25 to 30 minutes. Serve at once. Serves 4 to 6.

SUPPER SOUFFLÉ

2 TABLESPOONS BUTTER
2 TABLESPOONS FLOUR
½ PINT HOT MILK
1 TABLESPOON GRATED ONION
2 TABLESPOONS GRATED PARMESAN
SALT AND FRESHLY-GROUND BLACK PEPPER
MUSTARD
½ POUND POACHED FILLETS OF SOLE
4 EGGS

Melt butter in the top of a double saucepan; add flour and stir until smooth. Add hot milk and stir over low heat until thick. Remove from heat. Add grated onion, Parmesan and salt, pepper and mustard, to taste. Flake poached fish fillets (sole, turbot, etc.) and stir into soufflé mixture. Allow to cool.

Separate eggs; beat yolks lightly and stir into sauce. Beat whites until they are stiff, but not dry, and fold into sauce. Pour into an 8-inch soufflé dish around which you have tied greaseproof paper to make a high 'collar'. Pre-heat oven to 350°F. (Mark 3) and bake for 45 minutes. Serve immediately. Serves 4.

CHICKEN SOUFFLÉ

2 TABLESPOONS BUTTER
2 TABLESPOONS FLOUR
½ PINT HOT MILK
PINCH DRY MUSTARD
5 EGG YOLKS
½ POUND CHICKEN, MINCED
2 TABLESPOONS COGNAC
SALT AND FRESHLY-GROUND WHITE PEPPER
6 EGG WHITES, BEATEN STIFF

Melt butter in a saucepan. Blend in flour. Add hot milk and stir over fire until mixture comes to the boil. Remove from fire and add cognac. Season with salt, white pepper and a pinch of dry mustard. Beat in egg yolks, one at a time. Add purée of cooked chicken. Fold the beaten egg whites into chicken mixture.

Butter an 8-inch soufflé dish and tie a band of buttered greaseproof paper around the outside. Fill about three-quarters full with soufflé mixture and bake for about 40 minutes in a pre-heated oven (350°F. Mark 3) or until top is slightly browned and soufflé feels firm to the touch. Remove from oven, take off paper and serve immediately. Serves 4.

MUSHROOM SOUFFLÉ

2 TABLESPOONS BUTTER
2 TABLESPOONS FLOUR
½ PINT HOT MILK
2 TABLESPOONS GRATED PARMESAN
SALT AND CAYENNE PEPPER
PINCH GRATED NUTMEG
1–2 SHALLOTS, FINELY CHOPPED
6–8 OUNCES THINLY-SLICED MUSHROOMS
2 TABLESPOONS BUTTER
4 EGG YOLKS
5 EGG WHITES

Melt butter in the top of a double saucepan; add flour and cook until the flour just starts to turn golden. Add milk and cook, stirring constantly with a wire whisk, until the sauce is thick and smooth. Add grated Parmesan and salt, cayenne pepper and grated nutmeg, to taste.

Sauté finely-chopped shallot in butter until shallot is transparent; add sliced mushrooms and cook until all the moisture has evaporated. Add mushrooms to hot sauce mixture. Beat egg yolks until frothy. Fold into sauce mixture. Beat egg whites until they are stiff, but not dry, and fold into mixture. Fill a buttered baking dish about three-quarters full and bake in a pre-heated oven (350°F. Mark 3) for about 40 minutes. Serves 4.

CHEESE SOUFFLÉ WITH GARLIC CROÛTONS

2 TABLESPOONS BUTTER
2 TABLESPOONS FLOUR
½ PINT HOT MILK
5 EGG YOLKS
4–6 OUNCES GRATED CHEESE
SALT AND FRESHLY-GROUND BLACK PEPPER
2 TABLESPOONS BUTTER OR OLIVE OIL
1 CLOVE GARLIC, MINCED
1 SLICE BREAD, CUBED
6 EGG WHITES

Melt butter; add flour gradually and mix to a smooth paste, stirring constantly. Add hot milk and cook in double saucepan until smooth and thick. Remove from fire and add egg yolks, one by one, alternately with grated cheese. Mix well and return to fire. Cook until cheese melts. Add generous amounts of salt and pepper. Allow to cool slightly.

Melt butter or oil in another pan; add garlic and bread cubes and sauté until golden. Remove from fire and drain.

Beat egg whites until stiff and then fold in warm cheese mixture. Fold in garlic *croûtons* and pile mixture in a buttered soufflé dish or casserole. Bake in a pre-heated oven (350°F. Mark 3) for 35 to 40 minutes, or until soufflé is golden. Serve immediately.

The Sweet Soufflé

BASIC SWEET SOUFFLÉ

2 TABLESPOONS BUTTER
2 TABLESPOONS FLOUR
½ PINT HOT MILK
PINCH SALT
5 EGG YOLKS
4 TABLESPOONS SUGAR
½ TEASPOON VANILLA ESSENCE
6 EGG WHITES

Step 1. Melt butter in the top of a double saucepan; add flour and cook, stirring, until well blended. Add hot milk and salt. Cook the sauce, stirring constantly, until smooth and thick and continue cooking, stirring constantly, for a few more minutes. Let sauce cool slightly.

Step 2. Beat egg yolks well with sugar and vanilla essence and mix well with batter. Beat egg whites until they are stiff, but not dry, and fold gently into the batter mixture. Pour the batter into a buttered and lightly sugared soufflé mould and bake in a slow oven (350°F. Mark 3) for 35 to 45 minutes, or until the soufflé is puffed and golden. Serve at once. Serves 4.

LEMON SOUFFLÉ

2 TABLESPOONS BUTTER
2 TABLESPOONS FLOUR
½ PINT HOT MILK
PINCH SALT
GRATED RIND OF 1 LEMON
3 TABLESPOONS LEMON JUICE
5 EGG YOLKS
3 TABLESPOONS SUGAR
6 EGG WHITES

Step 1 as for *Basic Sweet Soufflé*. Then stir in grated peel and lemon juice.

Beat egg yolks well with sugar and combine them with batter. Beat egg whites until they are stiff, but not dry, and fold into the mixture. Pour the batter into a buttered and lightly sugared soufflé mould and bake in a slow oven (350°F. Mark 3) for 35 to 45 minutes, or until the soufflé is puffed and golden. Serve at once.

SOUFFLÉ AU GRAND MARNIER

2 TABLESPOONS BUTTER
2 TABLESPOONS FLOUR
½ PINT HOT MILK
PINCH SALT
5 EGG YOLKS
4 TABLESPOONS SUGAR
½ TEASPOON VANILLA ESSENCE
2 TABLESPOONS GRAND MARNIER
HALVED SPONGE FINGERS (OPTIONAL)
2 TABLESPOONS COGNAC (OPTIONAL)
6 EGG WHITES

Step 1 as for *Basic Sweet Soufflé*.

Beat egg yolks with sugar and vanilla essence and mix well with batter. Stir in Grand Marnier.

Pre-heat oven to 350°F. (Mark 3). Line a buttered soufflé dish with halved sponge fingers sprinkled with cognac. Beat the egg whites until stiff, but not dry, and fold into the cooled batter mixture. Pour into prepared soufflé dish. Bake 35 minutes or until soufflé is puffed and golden. Serve with apricot or rich vanilla sauce. Serves 4.

GREAT DISHES OF THE WORLD

CHAPTER 5

FISH

Poached Salmon in Aspic

Cooks in Britain seem to regard fish as mainly something to fry. They seem afraid of its other propensities – why, I wonder, when there is such a variety of ways which exist for their preparation.

'*C'est la sauce qui fait manger le poisson*' is the adage in France, and French culinary history is full of delicious recipes for grilled, poached and baked fish of all kinds, served with delicately-flavoured sauces. Grilled fillets of sole or flounder with a shrimp sauce or a Hollandaise; turbot simmered in a *court-bouillon* and served with green butter; sole, flounder and turbot, marinated in a white wine marinade and simmered *en casserole* in their own juices; turbot cooked in red wine – these are but a few of the delights that French fish cookery can offer us.

The art of cooking with wine is made easier for us these days by the wonderful array of imported vintages at our disposal. Keep a good stock of Burgundies, both white and red. Yes, fish can be cooked in red wine – *rosé*, too, for that matter. This legend of white for fish and red for meat is just so much old-fashioned nonsense! There are no rules for this sort of thing and, indeed, anything goes. So add dry sherry and vermouth to your cooking cellar. Experiment with port and Madeira.

Of course, even the most superb wine sauce cannot transform fish that is stale or overcooked. Always buy fish with firm skin and scales and bright eyes. And cook it carefully to the point when the moist, opaque flesh can be easily flaked with a fork. More crimes are committed in fish cookery by plain, simple overcooking than by any other means.

Fish should be firm and moist, not an overboiled mush of watery tastelessness.

GRILLED FISH

In Provence, I learned to like my fish grilled on an outdoor fire that had been fed with aromatic herbs. Many are the midnight beach picnics enjoyed on the vast expanses of Pampelonne, at which barbecued fish, freshly caught from the gulf of Pampelonne, played the starring role, preceded by a cool salad of Mediterranean vegetables and cold *ratatouille*, a Provençal vegetable stew of tomatoes, aubergines and *courgettes*, served cold with a *vinaigrette* dressing, the fish accompanied by melted tarragon butter and plain boiled potatoes, and washed down by liberal quantities of chilled *vin blanc du Var*.

Basil, tarragon, parsley and rosemary have natural affinities for fish. Their fragrant perfume and the odorous smoke from the wood fire make fish a dish fit for a king. Try this on your own barbecue as the weather gets warmer. But be sure you use a hinged grill so that you can turn your fish easily without danger of breaking its tender flesh. Flour and oil all fish lightly before grilling, and if you are using fish steaks or fish fillets, be sure to baste them frequently with olive oil during cooking time. Whole fish, with skins intact, require less attention. I like to stuff cavities of fish with herbs before grilling them – a selection of fennel, parsley and thyme – and then baste them with olive oil as they grill, often using a switch of bay leaves as a basting brush to give added flavour.

FLAMED FISH

Along the coast from Marseilles to St. Tropez, in the little sea towns on the way, it has long been the custom to serve grilled fish in a jacket of flaming herbs. This is a delicious way of dealing with any fresh fish. First grill your fish as above and remove it to a heated serving dish which has been covered with rosemary, fennel, parsley and thyme. The fish is then topped with additional herbs; 2 or 3 tablespoons of hot cognac are poured over it and ignited. The burning herbs give the fish a subtle flavour which, once you have tasted it, is irresistible.

FISH COURT-BOUILLONS AND FUMETS

When fish is to be served cold with a fish sauce, *vinaigrette* sauce or mayonnaise, or, for a special occasion, in a cool coat of shimmering aspic, it is always best to cook it in a well-flavoured fish *court-bouillon* to give it the utmost in flavour. A fish *court-bouillon* does for fish what a good chicken stock does for poached chicken.

FISH COURT-BOUILLON

- 2 small carrots
- 2 stalks celery
- 1 large Spanish onion, sliced
- 3 tablespoons butter
- 3 tablespoons olive oil
- 1 pint water
- 1 pint dry white wine
- 2 pounds fish trimmings (haddock, halibut, cod)
- 1 bouquet garni (celery, thyme and parsley)
- 2 bay leaves
- 6 bruised peppercorns
- 2 cloves
- 1 teaspoon salt

Sauté carrots, celery and onion, all finely chopped, in butter and olive oil, until onion is transparent but not brown. Add water, white wine and fish trimmings and bring to the boil. Skim froth from liquid; add *bouquet garni*, bay leaves, peppercorns, cloves and salt; cover the saucepan and simmer for 30 minutes. Strain and use as required. Fish *court-bouillon* will keep, covered, in a refrigerator for 2 to 3 days. Halve recipe for small quantities.

LIGHT FISH COURT-BOUILLON

- 3 pints water
- 1 bottle dry white wine
- 1 large Spanish onion, sliced
- 4 carrots, sliced
- 2 stalks celery, sliced
- 2 bay leaves
- 1 bouquet garni (celery, thyme and parsley)

Combine ingredients in a kettle or saucepan large enough to hold fish to be poached; bring to the boil; skim; lower heat and simmer for 30 minutes. Strain and use as required.

FISH FUMET

- ½ pound whiting, hake or fresh cod
- 2 pints cold water
- ¼ pint dry white wine
- 2 carrots, sliced
- 1 leek, sliced
- 1 Spanish onion, sliced
- 6 whole peppercorns
- 1 bouquet garni (parsley, bay leaf, thyme)
- 1 clove garlic
- Salt

Combine ingredients in a saucepan; cover and cook gently for 30 minutes.

CONCENTRATED FISH FUMET

- 1 pound bones and trimmings of sole
- 1 carrot, chopped
- 1 onion, chopped
- 4 tablespoons chopped parsley
- 4 tablespoons butter
- ¾ pint water
- ½ pint dry white wine
- 3 bruised peppercorns
- Salt

Melt butter in a saucepan and sauté fishbones and trimmings with chopped carrot, onion and parsley in a covered casserole for 10 minutes. Add water, white wine, peppercorns and salt, and allow to simmer gently, covered, for 30 minutes. Strain the *fumet* and use as required. Makes 1½ pints.

FISH ASPIC

Add ¼ pound any white fish, finely chopped, and the white part of 1 leek, finely chopped, 1 egg white and 1 crushed egg shell, to 1½ pints fish *fumet*. Bring to the boil, stirring constantly, and simmer, uncovered, for 20 minutes. Strain through a fine sieve. Soften 1 tablespoon gelatine in 4 tablespoons dry white wine and stir it into the hot stock.

For moulds or glazing, use fish aspic as soon as it is cool, but before it starts to set.

SALMON POACHED IN COURT-BOUILLON

1 WHOLE SALMON (ABOUT 6 POUNDS)
LEMON SLICES
CUCUMBER SLICES
FRESH WATERCRESS OR PARSLEY

COURT-BOUILLON:
3 PINTS WATER
1 BOTTLE DRY WHITE WINE
1 LARGE SPANISH ONION, SLICED
4 CARROTS, SLICED
2 STALKS CELERY, SLICED
2 BAY LEAVES
1 BOUQUET GARNI

Combine elements of *court-bouillon* in a kettle large enough to hold salmon; bring to the boil; skim; lower heat and simmer for 30 minutes. Let *court-bouillon* cool slightly; then lower the salmon, wrapped in muslin, into it. Add more liquid if necessary. Simmer gently for 45 to 60 minutes or until the fish flakes easily with a fork.

Remove fish carefully from the *court-bouillon* with the help of the muslin and carefully remove the skin. Arrange the salmon on a hot platter and garnish with lemon slices, cucumber slices, and watercress or parsley. Serve with a *sauce mousseline*, *sauce Choron* or a *sauce verte*.

POACHED SALMON IN ASPIC

1 SALMON POACHED IN COURT-BOUILLON
1 EGG WHITE AND SHELL
2¼ TABLESPOONS GELATINE
¼ PINT COLD WATER

Poach salmon as above; remove carefully from *court-bouillon* to a large board or platter and let it cool. Remove the skin carefully, cutting it at the tail and stripping it to the head.

Reduce *court-bouillon* to 2 pints. Clarify it with the crushed shell and the white of an egg and strain it through a clean cloth. Dissolve gelatine in water and prepare an aspic using the hot *court-bouillon*. Brush salmon with cooled aspic. Decorate and brush with aspic again.

Serve with mayonnaise or *sauce verte*.

SALMON KEDGEREE

3 OUNCES RICE
1 POUND POACHED SALMON
4 TABLESPOONS BUTTER
1 TEASPOON CURRY POWDER
2 HARD-BOILED EGGS
SALT AND FRESHLY-GROUND BLACK PEPPER
½ PINT HOT CREAM SAUCE

Cook rice in boiling salted water until tender, but not mushy. Drain and keep warm.

Dice or flake salmon, removing any bones and skin. Melt butter in saucepan; blend in curry powder; add fish and sauté gently.

Combine finely-chopped whites of hard-boiled eggs with rice and fish. Season to taste with salt and freshly-ground black pepper. Fold in hot cream sauce. Serve on platter with yolks of hard-boiled eggs, pressed through a sieve or finely chopped, over the top. Serves 4.

GRILLED SALMON STEAKS

4 LARGE SALMON STEAKS
SALT AND FRESHLY-GROUND BLACK PEPPER
4 TABLESPOONS MELTED BUTTER
LEMON AND PARSLEY BUTTER
LEMON WEDGES

Season both sides of salmon steaks with salt and freshly-ground black pepper, to taste, and leave at room temperature for 15 minutes.

Place steaks on a buttered, pre-heated baking tin; brush with melted butter and grill 3 to 5 minutes about 3 inches from heat. Turn steaks, brush with remaining butter and grill until fish flakes easily with a fork (3 to 5 minutes). Serve with lemon and parsley butter and lemon wedges. Serves 4.

To make lemon and parsley butter: Pound 4 ounces slightly-softened butter in a mortar with 2 tablespoons finely-chopped parsley and lemon juice, salt and pepper, to taste.

FRENCH SALMON TOURTE

SHORTCRUST PASTRY FOR 2-CRUST PIE
¾ POUND RAW FRESH SALMON, THINLY SLICED
¼ POUND MUSHROOM CAPS
6 OUNCES BUTTER
4 FLUID OUNCES CREAM
4 FLUID OUNCES DRY WHITE WINE
SALT AND FRESHLY-GROUND BLACK PEPPER
NUTMEG
2 EGG WHITES

LEMON BUTTER SAUCE:
4 TABLESPOONS MELTED BUTTER
1 TEASPOON CHOPPED TARRAGON
1 TEASPOON CHOPPED PARSLEY
1 TEASPOON CHOPPED CHIVES
JUICE OF ½ LEMON

Skin and bone ½ pound raw fresh salmon, reserving rest. Pound to a smooth paste in a mortar with button mushroom caps, butter, cream and white wine. Season to taste with salt, pepper and nutmeg. Fold in beaten whites of two eggs.

Line a pie dish with short pastry. Half-fill with salmon paste; cover with a thin layer of raw salmon and season lightly with salt and pepper. Add remainder of salmon paste and cover with a second layer of pastry. Make a hole in the centre of pastry crust and bake in a hot oven for 30 to 40 minutes. Just before serving, pour lemon butter sauce (made by combining melted butter, herbs and lemon juice) through hole in top crust.

BARBECUED FISH WITH TARRAGON

2 SEA BASS OR GREY MULLET
HERBS: ROSEMARY, FENNEL, SAGE, BAY LEAF
4 TABLESPOONS DRY WHITE WINE
6 TABLESPOONS MELTED BUTTER
SALT AND FRESHLY-GROUND BLACK PEPPER

SERVING SAUCE:
¼ POUND MELTED BUTTER
JUICE OF 1 LEMON
4 TABLESPOONS FRESH TARRAGON, FINELY CHOPPED

Stuff cleaned and scaled fish with herbs (rosemary, fennel, sage, bay leaf).

Secure fish to the spit with thin wire or wet cord; combine wine and butter, season to taste with generous amounts of salt and freshly-ground black pepper and grill over rather hot coals for 20 to 25 minutes, depending on size. Brush from time to time with wine-butter sauce. When fish is done, it flakes easily when tested with a fork.

Serve with plenty of lemon and melted butter flavoured with finely-chopped fresh tarragon. Serves 4.

Note: Fish may be cooked in oven or under the grill.

Matelote à la Bourguignonne

Fish and wine have always seemed to me to have natural affinities . . . ever since the memorable summer of '31 when I was eight, my favourite brother was fourteen, and we lived on the banks of the Hudson River just twenty-five miles from New York. It was Prohibition – a zany period in American political history, when to indulge in a quiet drink between friends was punishable by law – and my brother and I spent the summer 'fishing' along with other members of the local citizenry for cases of champagne and caviare hastily thrown overboard one evening by a boatload of bootleggers temporarily at grips with the law.

Introduced to the illicit pleasures of fish and wine at such a tender age, it is small wonder that today I prefer fish and shellfish served in generous quantities of my favourite potions.

And I am not alone. The art of cooking fish in wine is as old as the art of gastronomy. The Rhône valley was probably the first to have its forests cleared and planted with vines by the early Romans when they conquered Gaul. Vines still flourish practically all along the Rhône today, coming into greater prominence below Lyons in the wine-growing districts of Châteauneuf du Pape, Hermitage and Côte Rôtie. Some of the most exciting little restaurants in France are to be found in this region; small bistros and unknown cafés where the food-conscious traveller is sure to find some of the best wine-simmered dishes in the country; simple little places with sawdust-strewn floors, where the chef is known to make the finest *matelote* in the region. The *matelote*, like the *pochouse bourguignonne*, combines the delicate meats of carp, pike, eel, and other local fish, flamed in brandy, and then simmered in a rich, smooth sauce of red or white wine, according to the tastes of house or region.

One of the best *matelote* recipes I know is that of Pierre Lefrank, genial French *antiquaire* and *bon vivant* of the rue Bonaparte, who used to entertain us so lavishly in Paris just after the war. Henri Sauguet, Christian Berard, Victor Grandpierre, Dior's decorator, and Prince Sturza were among those who enjoyed this famous dish.

MATELOTE À LA BOURGUIGNONNE

1 POUND EEL
1½–2 POUNDS CARP
1½–2 POUNDS PIKE
2 TABLESPOONS OLIVE OIL
2 TABLESPOONS BUTTER
4 OUNCES DICED SALT PORK
1 SPANISH ONION, CHOPPED
4 CARROTS, CHOPPED
8 SHALLOTS, CHOPPED
4 CLOVES GARLIC, MASHED
4 TABLESPOONS WARM COGNAC
½ BOTTLE GOOD RED BURGUNDY
SALT AND FRESHLY-GROUND BLACK PEPPER
1 BOUQUET GARNI (THYME, BAY LEAF, PARSLEY, CELERY, ROSEMARY)
1 STRIP LEMON PEEL
¼ TEASPOON DRIED BASIL
4 TABLESPOONS BUTTER
2 TABLESPOONS FLOUR
12 BUTTON ONIONS
12 BUTTON MUSHROOMS
BUTTER, LEMON JUICE, PARSLEY
FRIED CROÛTONS

Clean and skin eel and cut into thick serving pieces (your fishmonger, from whom you will have to order in advance, can do this for you); cut carp and pike into serving pieces; sauté them in equal parts olive oil and butter with diced salt pork, chopped onion, chopped carrots, finely-chopped shallots and mashed garlic. When the fish pieces begin to turn gold in colour, flame them in cognac. Shake pan gently until the flames die down and add Châteauneuf du Pape and enough water to cover. Add salt and pepper to taste, *bouquet garni*, twist of lemon peel and dried basil. Cook fish slowly in this mixture until tender.

Melt 4 tablespoons butter in a porcelain or enamel saucepan and make a *roux* by adding 2 tablespoons of flour; cook *roux* for a few minutes without allowing it to take colour; add the strained liquid from fish and cook over low heat, stirring from time to time to make a slightly thickened sauce. Add fish pieces and pork bits, and garnish with button onions simmered in *court-bouillon*, and button mushrooms cooked in butter and lemon juice. To finish dish, stir in 2 tablespoons butter and serve very hot with fried *croûtons* and chopped fresh parsley. Serves 6 to 8.

MATELOTE DE BROCHET AU VIN ROSÉ

2 FRESH PIKE (1½ POUNDS EACH)
4 TABLESPOONS BUTTER
2 TABLESPOONS OLIVE OIL
1 GLASS (2 OUNCES) MIRABELLE
4 SHALLOTS, FINELY CHOPPED
SALT AND FRESHLY-GROUND BLACK PEPPER
½ BOTTLE VIN ROSÉ
1 BOUQUET GARNI (THYME, BAY LEAF, PARSLEY, CELERY, ROSEMARY)
2 TABLESPOONS BUTTER
2 TABLESPOONS FLOUR
¼ PINT FRESH CREAM
¼ POUND BUTTON MUSHROOMS, SLICED
FRIED CROÛTONS

Clean pike, cut into thick serving pieces and sauté in butter and olive oil until golden. Pour 1 glass Mirabelle over fish pieces and flame. Add finely-chopped shallots and pepper and salt, to taste. Cover and allow to 'sweat' over a low flame for a few minutes; add dry *vin rosé*, *bouquet garni* and enough water or fish stock to cover. Allow to cook gently in an open pan until fish flakes easily with a fork. Remove fish pieces carefully from stock and keep warm.

In another pan, make a pale *roux* with 2 tablespoons butter and 2 tablespoons flour; add the fish stock, strained, and cook for about 15 minutes until thick. Just before serving, add fresh cream to the sauce; place fish pieces delicately in a heated serving dish. Pour hot sauce over them; and garnish with finely-sliced mushrooms sautéed in butter, and fried *croûtons*. Serves 4 to 6.

TURBOT IN WHITE WINE WITH GREEN BUTTER

3 POUNDS TURBOT, CUT IN SERVING PORTIONS
1 SPANISH ONION, THINLY SLICED
2–4 CARROTS, THINLY SLICED
1 BOUQUET GARNI (THYME, BAY LEAF, PARSLEY, CELERY, ROSEMARY)
DRY WHITE WINE
SALT AND FRESHLY-GROUND BLACK PEPPER

GREEN BUTTER:
½ POUND SOFTENED BUTTER
2 SIEVED HARD-BOILED EGGS

2 TABLESPOONS OLIVE OIL
1 CLOVE GARLIC, MASHED
6 SPINACH LEAVES
6 LETTUCE LEAVES
6 SPRIGS WATERCRESS
6 SPRIGS PARSLEY
2 SHALLOTS, CHOPPED
2 TABLESPOONS CAPERS
½ LEVEL TEASPOON FRENCH MUSTARD
LEMON JUICE
SALT AND FRESHLY-GROUND BLACK PEPPER

Wipe turbot with a damp cloth and place in a shallow well-buttered baking pan. Add sliced onion, carrot and *bouquet garni*. Cover fish with dry white wine and water in equal quantities, and add salt and pepper, to taste. Poach gently for 30 minutes or until the flesh of fish flakes easily with a fork. When done, drain well, place on a heated serving dish and garnish each portion with a slice of green butter.

To make green butter: Place soft butter, sieved hard-boiled eggs, olive oil and mashed garlic in an electric blender and blend until creamy. Add more oil if mixture is too dry.

Blanch 6 spinach leaves with stems removed, green lettuce leaves, watercress, parsley and chopped shallots. Drain well, chop and add to butter mixture with 2 tablespoons capers and ½ teaspoon French mustard. When well blended, add lemon juice and salt and pepper, to taste, and chill until you are ready to serve. This is also delicious with grilled salmon. Serves 4 to 6.

TURBOT AU CHAMPAGNE

4 TURBOT FILLETS, BONED AND SKINNED
¼ POUND BUTTER
2 TABLESPOONS OLIVE OIL
2 SHALLOTS, FINELY CHOPPED
¼ POUND BUTTON MUSHROOMS, SLICED
6 TABLESPOONS FISH STOCK MADE FROM FISH TRIMMINGS
½ QUARTER BOTTLE OF CHAMPAGNE
SALT AND WHITE PEPPER
¼ PINT DOUBLE CREAM
1 LEVEL TABLESPOON CORNFLOUR

Melt half the butter in a large shallow saucepan with olive oil; sauté finely-chopped shallots until transparent; add sliced mushrooms and continue cooking until tender.

Remove; add remaining butter and sauté turbot fillets until lightly coloured. Add sautéed mushrooms and onions, fish stock and half the champagne, adding more if necessary barely to cover the turbot fillets. Season to taste with salt and white pepper and simmer very slowly for a few minutes until tender.

Remove turbot fillets to a serving dish and keep warm. Add cream to the liquid in the pan; let simmer without boiling until cream is warm. Mix cornflour with a small amount of water, add to the sauce and cook, stirring constantly, over a very low heat, until sauce is smooth and rich.

When ready to serve, pour in remaining champagne, stir and mix with the sauce until warm. If you prefer a thicker sauce, use less champagne. Pour over turbot fillets and serve immediately. Serves 4.

TURBOT À LA MARINIÈRE

4 TURBOT FILLETS (ABOUT ½ POUND EACH)
4 CARROTS, SLICED
1 SPANISH ONION, SLICED
2 TABLESPOONS FINELY-CHOPPED PARSLEY
2 BAY LEAVES
1 PINCH CINNAMON
1 PINCH THYME
SALT AND FRESHLY-GROUND BLACK PEPPER
¼ PINT DRY WHITE WINE
¼ PINT CHICKEN STOCK
¼ PINT WATER
4 TABLESPOONS OLIVE OIL
1 POUND POTATOES, SLICED
MELTED BUTTER

Combine carrots, onion, parsley, bay leaves, cinnamon, thyme, salt and pepper. Add dry white wine, chicken stock, water, olive oil and sliced potatoes, and cook over a high flame for 25 minutes.

Place turbot fillets carefully in the *court-bouillon* and cook over a high flame until fish flakes easily with a fork (about 20 minutes). Serve fish and potatoes with *court-bouillon* and a little melted butter. Serves 4.

BAKED FISH ALBERT

2 SEA BASS (OR 5–6 POUNDS TURBOT OR HALIBUT)
6 MEDIUM-SIZED ONIONS, FINELY CHOPPED
4 CLOVES GARLIC, FINELY CHOPPED
4 TABLESPOONS EACH FINELY-CHOPPED PARSLEY, CHERVIL AND TARRAGON
¼ PINT DRY WHITE WINE
¼ PINT WATER
2 TABLESPOONS PERNOD
4 TABLESPOONS OLIVE OIL
1 LARGE LEMON, THINLY SLICED
¼ POUND BUTTER, DICED
SALT AND FRESHLY-GROUND BLACK PEPPER

Combine finely-chopped onions, garlic, parsley, chervil, tarragon, dry white wine, water and Pernod.

Place fish (2 large sea bass or the equivalent weight of turbot or halibut) in a large baking dish and moisten with olive oil. Pour over wine and herb mixture; cover with thin slices of lemon; dot with butter and season to taste with salt and freshly-ground black pepper. Bake fish in a hot oven (450°F. Mark 7) for 30 to 40 minutes, or until fish flakes easily with a fork, basting from time to time. If fish becomes too dry, add a little water and wine. Serves 6 to 8.

SUPRÊME OF RED MULLET NIÇOISE

4 FRESH RED MULLET, FILLETED
SALT AND CAYENNE PEPPER
DRY WHITE WINE
FISH FUMET
WHITE OF 1 LEEK, CUT IN THIN STRIPS

2 TABLESPOONS BUTTER
½ PINT DOUBLE CREAM
4 TOMATOES
BUTTER
SAFFRON

Put fillets in a well-buttered oven-proof dish; add salt and a pinch of cayenne; add equal parts dry white wine and fish *fumet* to cover, and bake in a slow oven (350°F. Mark 3) for 10 to 15 minutes. When fish is flaky but still moist, keep warm in several spoonfuls of the stock.

Reduce the rest of the liquid to half its original quantity with a fine *julienne* of white of leek cooked in butter. Add cream and tomatoes which have been skinned, seeded, chopped and reduced to a purée in a little butter. When this mixture forms a smooth creamy emulsion just thick enough to coat the back of a spoon, stir in 2 tablespoons butter mixed with a pinch of saffron. Heat well; place fillets on a serving dish and mask with the sauce. Serves 4.

Fish Soups

BOUILLABAISSE FOR NORTHERN SEAS

4 CARROTS, SLICED
2 SPANISH ONIONS, SLICED
4 CLOVES GARLIC, BRUISED
2 LEEKS, SLICED
¼ PINT OLIVE OIL
4–6 TOMATOES
1 BOUQUET GARNI (THYME, BAY LEAF, PARSLEY, CELERY, ROSEMARY)
1 POUND EEL, CUT IN 2-INCH LENGTHS
2 POUNDS FISH (COD, HADDOCK, SEA BASS, ETC.), CUT IN 2-INCH LENGTHS
4–6 POTATOES, CUT IN SLICES
1 PINT FISH STOCK (MADE FROM FISH TRIMMINGS)
½ LEVEL TEASPOON POWDERED SAFFRON
SALT AND FRESHLY-GROUND BLACK PEPPER
CAYENNE
24 MUSSELS
1 OR 2 SMALL LOBSTERS

Place carrots, onions, garlic, leeks and oil in a large, thick-bottomed, fire-proof casserole and sauté until golden brown. Seed and chop the tomatoes coarsely; add to vegetables with *bouquet garni* and sliced eel, fish and potatoes and cook about 6 minutes, stirring gently from time to time. Add fish stock and just enough water to cover fish; season to taste with saffron, salt, freshly-ground black pepper and cayenne, and bring to the boil. Cook for 15 minutes. Add mussels and lobsters and continue cooking until mussels open.

Serve this wonderful dish in two courses: the amber-tinted soup first in a deep soup tureen, accompanied by garlic-flavoured *croûtons* and *rouille*, and the fish and potatoes immediately after the soup. Serves 6 to 8.

SOUPE AIGO-SAU (PROVENÇAL FISH SOUP WITH ROUILLE)

2 POUNDS ANY FIRM WHITE FISH
1 LEEK, CHOPPED
1 SPANISH ONION, CHOPPED
4 TOMATOES, CHOPPED
6 POTATOES, CUT IN THICK SLICES
SALT AND FRESHLY-GROUND BLACK PEPPER
2 CLOVES GARLIC, CRUSHED
2 SPRIGS PARSLEY
1 SPRIG FENNEL
1 BAY LEAF
1 PIECE OF LEMON PEEL
BOILING WATER, TO COVER
SLICED FRENCH BREAD
OLIVE OIL
ROUILLE

Cut white fish of assorted kinds into pieces of the same size. Place in a large saucepan with leek, onions, tomatoes and potatoes. Season generously with salt and freshly-ground pepper; add garlic, parsley, fennel, bay leaf and lemon peel. Cover with boiling water and cook over a high flame for 20 minutes.

To serve: place slices of French bread in a soup tureen; sprinkle with olive oil and pepper. Strain fish *bouillon* over and serve separately. Fish pieces and potatoes should be served together with a *rouille*. Serves 4 to 6.

To make *rouille*: pound 2 fat cloves of garlic and 2 hot red peppers in a mortar with ¼ slice white bread with crusts cut off, which you have dipped in water and then squeezed dry. Blend to a smooth paste with 2 tablespoons olive oil, and then thin this *pommade* to the consistency of heavy cream with about ¼ pint of hot fish *bouillon*. This is often served with *bouillabaisse*. (You will find another recipe for *rouille* on page 104.)

COTRIADE

3 POUNDS FIRM FISH
4 LARGE POTATOES, SLICED
2 SPANISH ONIONS, SLICED
1 BOUQUET GARNI (THYME, BAY LEAF, PARSLEY, CELERY, ROSEMARY)
¼ TEASPOON DRIED MARJORAM
2½ PINTS FISH STOCK (MADE FROM FISH TRIMMINGS)
SALT AND FRESHLY-GROUND BLACK PEPPER

Make fish stock with fish heads, bones and trimmings. Strain. Cook sliced potatoes and onions with *bouquet garni*, marjoram, and salt and pepper to taste, in fish stock for 20 minutes. Add fish – cod, haddock, fresh sardines, grey mullet, mackerel, sea bass, etc., cut in 2-inch lengths – and enough water, if necessary, just to cover fish; cook over a high flame until potatoes are tender and the fish flakes easily with a fork (10 to 15 minutes).

Serve soup in one bowl with garlic-flavoured *croûtons*; fish and vegetables in another. Serve olive oil and vinegar with fish. Serves 6 to 8.

CREOLE CRAB GUMBO

2 TABLESPOONS BUTTER
2 TABLESPOONS OLIVE OIL
1 SPANISH ONION, CHOPPED
1 SMALL GREEN PEPPER, CHOPPED
2 TABLESPOONS FLOUR
SALT AND FRESHLY-GROUND BLACK PEPPER
1 BOUQUET GARNI (CELERY, PARSLEY, THYME)
1 CLOVE GARLIC, FINELY CHOPPED
1 SMALL THIN STRIP LEMON PEEL
DASH TABASCO SAUCE
¾ POUND CRABMEAT, FLAKED
12 LARGE COOKED PRAWNS, SLICED
1 TIN (8 OUNCES) OKRA WITH LIQUOR
1 LARGE TIN ITALIAN PEELED TOMATOES
½ PINT MILK
¼ PINT CREAM

Combine butter and olive oil in a saucepan and heat until butter has melted. Add chopped onion and green pepper and sauté until tender. Blend in flour and cook, stirring continuously, until smooth and thickened. Add salt and freshly-ground black pepper, to taste, *bouquet garni*, garlic, lemon peel and Tabasco sauce. Stir in crabmeat, sliced prawns, okra and tomatoes, and heat to boiling point. Cover saucepan and simmer for 20 to 25 minutes. Gradually stir in milk and cream; cook a few minutes more over medium heat, stirring occasionally, until heated through. Correct seasoning, remove *bouquet garni* and serve immediately. Serves 4 to 6.

SEAFOOD BISQUE

6 TABLESPOONS BUTTER
6 TABLESPOONS FLOUR
1½ PINTS HOT MILK
4 TABLESPOONS FINELY-CHOPPED SHALLOTS
1 TEASPOON CURRY POWDER
1 COOKED LOBSTER
¼ POUND FROZEN PRAWNS
1 TIN MINCED CLAMS
3 TABLESPOONS OLIVE OIL
¼ PINT DRY WHITE WINE
SALT AND FRESHLY-GROUND BLACK PEPPER
2 TABLESPOONS FINELY-CHOPPED PARSLEY

Melt butter in the top of a double saucepan; add flour and cook over water until *roux* is well blended. Gradually add hot milk, stirring continuously. Then add finely-chopped shallots and curry powder and simmer, stirring from time to time, until sauce is thick and well blended.

Shell lobster and dice meat; thaw prawns; drain minced clams, reserving liquid. Sauté shellfish in olive oil until golden. Pour over reserved clam juice; add to milk mixture and cook over a low heat, stirring constantly, until well heated. Just before serving, add dry white wine and salt and pepper, to taste, and sprinkle with finely-chopped parsley. Serves 4.

NEW ENGLAND OYSTER STEW

¾ PINT OYSTER LIQUOR
1 QUART OYSTERS
¾ PINT MILK
4 TABLESPOONS BUTTER
¼ PINT CREAM
SALT AND FRESHLY-GROUND BLACK PEPPER
CAYENNE PEPPER

Strain oyster liquor (approximately ¾ pint) into a large saucepan. Wash oysters thoroughly and add to liquor. Simmer over low heat for 5 minutes. Add milk, and heat thoroughly, but do not allow it to boil. Stir in butter and cream; add salt and pepper, to taste, and a dash of cayenne pepper. Serves 4.

ZUPPA DI PESCE

1 LARGE ONION, THINLY SLICED
6 TABLESPOONS OLIVE OIL
2 TABLESPOONS BUTTER
2 POUNDS TOMATOES, PEELED AND DICED
2 TABLESPOONS TOMATO CONCENTRATE DILUTED IN ¼ PINT WATER
1 CLOVE GARLIC, CHOPPED
4 TABLESPOONS CHOPPED PARSLEY
3 POUNDS MIXED FISH (SOLE, MULLET, MACKEREL, WHITING), CLEANED
1 SMALL EEL, CUT IN PIECES
2 SMALL SQUID, CUT IN PIECES (OPTIONAL)
BOILING WATER
¼ PINT DRY WHITE WINE
1 TABLESPOON WINE VINEGAR
SALT AND FRESHLY-GROUND BLACK PEPPER

Sauté onion in oil and butter until soft, then add tomatoes, diluted tomato concentrate, garlic and parsley. Simmer uncovered for 15 to 20 minutes, then add fish, enough boiling water to cover, and let it come to the boil. Add the white wine and wine vinegar and cook over a low flame for 15 minutes. Season to taste. Serves 6 to 8.

HAWAIIAN FISH CHOWDER

¼ POUND SALT PORK, DICED
2 TABLESPOONS OLIVE OIL
1 SPANISH ONION, FINELY CHOPPED
1 POUND COD, DICED
1 POUND NEW POTATOES, SLICED
4 RIPE TOMATOES, SLICED
¾ PINT BOILING WATER
½ PINT MILK
SALT AND FRESHLY-GROUND BLACK PEPPER

Sauté salt pork in olive oil until golden. Remove. Add finely-chopped onion and sauté in resulting fat until transparent. Add diced fish, sliced potatoes and tomatoes, and sauté for a minute or two more. Then add water and simmer for ½ hour, or until potatoes are tender. Add the milk and simmer 5 minutes more. Season to taste with salt and freshly-ground black pepper. Serves 6 to 8.

Provençal Aïoli

A strange, soaring elation always grips me as I drive along the winding coastal road from St. Raphael and first catch sight of the pink-shaded towers of St. Tropez across the glittering bay. There are certain places in the world for each of us – magic places where we immediately feel at home at first meeting – as if somehow, sometime, we had been there before. St. Tropez holds this magic for me.

Sheer good luck – unearned and unadorned – is as satisfying as it is exciting. Newton sitting under an apple tree, for instance; or the owner of the left-bank café, Les Deux Magots, awaking one morning to find his corner the most famous rendezvous in France.

St. Tropez is a case in point. I have watched its legend grow since the war and have often pondered on the pure chance that made virtual millionaires out of the simple folk I had come to know so well during the years that I owned a house there, the café-owners on the port, the fishermen-turned-restaurateurs, the shopkeepers and the hoteliers of the town on whom this providential manna had fallen.

Today, summer visitors flock to St. Tropez like migratory birds. How many of them realise, I wonder, that one of the best cooks in Provence can be found practically within arm's reach of the port?

Chez Fifine is a tiny restaurant on rue Suffren, with a kitchen and one small room containing five tables on the ground floor, a slightly larger dining room upstairs, and a few tables placed strategically outside for the inevitable overflow. Fifine does all the cooking herself, aided by a kitchen staff of one; the service is carried out by family and friends – Josef, ex-fisherman and famous local *pétanque* champion, directs the activities of a team of personable young 'cousins' who wait on table. For those who demand *la grand cuisine*, an impressive décor and impeccable service, my advice is to stay away. For here the service is friendly but often erratic; there is no *cave* of select vintage wines; no flaming *spécialités de la maison*, no fuss, no bother; but the simple rustic dishes of Provence, lovingly prepared by Fifine, are sublime. All Provence is her domaine: fennel comes from the mountains behind the coast, wild thyme and rosemary from the neighbouring hills; the town's best fishermen arrive at her door several times a day with their latest catch; tomatoes are selected with care from one special *vendeuse* in the open-air vegetable market, fresh *basilic* from another.

Eggs and vegetables are delivered daily from a nearby farm.

Fifine loves and excels in the rustic dishes of Provence and the fruits of her private sea, the Gulf of St. Tropez. It was she who taught me the pleasures of the unknown local wines; the special richness of the pure olive oil of Provence; what fish to put into *bouillabaisse*; how to make an *aïoli*, a *rouille*, a *tapénade*.

Aïoli, sometimes referred to as *le beurre de Provence*, was originally a sauce made of olive oil and crushed garlic, thickened with fresh breadcrumbs and mashed boiled potato. Today, the *liaison* of this famous sauce is almost always made with raw egg yolk, and modern *aïoli* is really a mayonnaise with a pungent garlic base.

Chez Fifine, *aïoli*, served *sur commande* only and a masterpiece of presentation and high savour, features salt codfish, tiny octopus and a medley of boiled vegetables – carrots, new potatoes, sweet potatoes, baby marrows, onions, runner beans – also hard-boiled eggs, raw tomatoes and fresh basil and parsley, served with a strong *aïoli* sauce from which the dish gets its name.

FIFINE'S AÏOLI

1 POUND SALT CODFISH
6 POTATOES IN THEIR JACKETS
6 SWEET POTATOES
6 BABY MARROWS
1 POUND SMALL CARROTS
1 POUND FRENCH BEANS
6 HARD-BOILED EGGS
6 RIPE TOMATOES
LETTUCE, FRESH HERBS (PARSLEY AND BASIL, ETC.) TO DECORATE SERVING DISHES

SAUCE:
4 FAT CLOVES OF GARLIC PER PERSON
1 EGG YOLK FOR EACH TWO PERSONS
OLIVE OIL
SALT AND FRESHLY-GROUND BLACK PEPPER
LEMON JUICE

Soak codfish overnight in cold water. Boil fish and vegetables – white and sweet potatoes in their jackets, whole baby marrows and carrots and French beans – separately. All vegetables should be tender but still quite firm, and on no account overcooked. Serve hot vegetables, hard-boiled eggs in their shells and raw tomatoes on large serving dishes decorated with lettuce and sprigs of fresh herbs. Place fish in centre. For best effect, group well-drained vegetables by colour. Serve with *aïoli* sauce, from which this famous dish gets its name. Serves 4 to 6.

To make sauce: Take 4 fat cloves of garlic per person and 1 egg yolk for each 2 persons. Crush garlic to a smooth paste in a mortar with a little salt; blend in egg yolks until mixture is a smooth homogeneous mass. Now take olive oil and proceed (drop by drop at first, a thin fine trickle later) to whisk the mixture as you would for a mayonnaise. The *aïoli* will thicken gradually until it reaches the proper stiff, firm consistency. The exact quantity of oil is, of course, determined by the number of egg yolks used. Season to taste with additional salt, a little pepper and lemon juice. This sauce is served chilled in a bowl. Guests help themselves.

PORTUGUESE CODFISH

1 POUND SALT COD FILLETS
6 TABLESPOONS OLIVE OIL
4 TABLESPOONS WINE VINEGAR

DRESSING:
1 SPANISH ONION, FINELY CHOPPED
4 TABLESPOONS FINELY-CHOPPED PARSLEY
6 TABLESPOONS OLIVE OIL
2 TABLESPOONS LEMON JUICE
SALT AND FRESHLY-GROUND BLACK PEPPER

Soak cod in water overnight. Drain and place in a saucepan; cover with cold water and bring slowly to the boil. Remove from heat and allow to steep for 10 minutes.

Drain fish fillets and sauté gently in olive oil until golden. Remove from heat; pour vinegar over and allow to stand for 5 minutes. Transfer fish to a warm serving dish and pour onion dressing over it.

To make onion dressing: Combine finely-chopped onion and parsley with olive oil, lemon juice, and salt and freshly-ground black pepper, to taste. Whisk with blender until well blended. Serves 6.

BRANDADE DE MORUE

1 POUND SALT COD FILLETS
2 CLOVES GARLIC, CRUSHED
6 TABLESPOONS DOUBLE CREAM
¼ PINT OLIVE OIL
JUICE AND GRATED PEEL OF ½ LEMON
FRESHLY-GROUND BLACK PEPPER
TOAST TRIANGLES FRIED IN OLIVE OIL OR BUTTER

Soak cod fillets in cold water for at least 12 hours, changing the water often. Place drained cod fillets in a saucepan, cover with cold water and bring to the boil. Remove from the fire, cover saucepan and let cod simmer gently in water for 10 minutes. Strain cod, remove bones and skin, and flake fish with a fork.

Place cod flakes in electric blender with crushed garlic, 2 tablespoons cream and 4 tablespoons olive oil and blend, adding remainder of cream and olive oil alternately from time to time until the oil and cream are completely absorbed and the *brandade* has the consistency of mashed potatoes. When ready to serve, simmer mixture in a *bain-marie*, or in a saucepan over water; stir in lemon juice and grated peel and add seasoning to taste. *Brandade de morue* may be served hot or cold. If hot, place in a mound on a warm serving dish and surround with toast triangles fried in olive oil or butter. If *brandade* is too salty, blend in 1 or 2 boiled potatoes.

DÉLICES DE SOLE LUCAS CARTON

3 SOLE (1–1¼ POUNDS EACH)
6 OUNCES BUTTER
½ MEDIUM SPANISH ONION, FINELY CHOPPED
1 SPRIG PARSLEY
6–8 TABLESPOONS DRY WHITE WINE
SALT AND FRESHLY-GROUND BLACK PEPPER
2–4 VERY RIPE TOMATOES
2 OUNCES VERY WHITE BUTTON MUSHROOMS
6–8 TABLESPOONS DOUBLE CREAM

Have fishmonger fillet the sole, but ask him for the bones, head and fish trimmings to make a fish *fumet*. Soak fillets and bones in cold water for 1 hour.

To make fish *fumet:* cut bones in 4 or 5 pieces and simmer gently in a covered saucepan for 6 to 8 minutes with chopped onion, parsley and 2 tablespoons butter. Moisten with dry white wine and 6 to 8 tablespoons water. Bring to the boil, skim scum from surface and simmer for 10 to 12 minutes.

Butter a long oven-proof dish and place the fillets of sole in it. Season well with salt and pepper, to taste. Peel, seed and chop tomatoes and scatter over fish fillets with mushrooms which you have cut into slivers. Pour over the *fumet*; cover with buttered paper and bring to the boil. Cook for 7 to 8 minutes.

Pour the liquid into a saucepan; stir in the cream and reduce over a high flame until the sauce is of the desired consistency. Place sauce in the top of a double saucepan and gradually add remaining butter in little pieces, whisking sauce constantly as you would for a *sauce hollandaise*, without letting water under the pan come to the boil. Cover the fillets with this sauce and glaze under the grill for a few seconds. Serve immediately. Serves 6.

FILETS DE SOLE BONNE FEMME

2 SOLE (ABOUT 1 POUND EACH)
SALT AND FRESHLY-GROUND BLACK PEPPER
2 TABLESPOONS FINELY-CHOPPED SHALLOTS
2 TABLESPOONS FINELY-CHOPPED MUSHROOMS
¼ PINT DRY WHITE WINE
FISH STOCK (MADE FROM FISH TRIMMINGS)
1 BOUQUET GARNI (BAY LEAF, THYME, 4 SPRIGS PARSLEY)
12 BUTTON MUSHROOM CAPS
2 TABLESPOONS BUTTER
1 TABLESPOON LEMON JUICE
FLOUR
BUTTER

Ask your fishmonger to fillet sole; keep heads, bones and trimmings for stock. Season fillets generously with salt and freshly-ground black pepper and put them in the bottom of a buttered earthenware baking dish. Sprinkle with finely-chopped shallots and mushrooms and add $\frac{1}{8}$ pint dry white wine and just enough fish stock to cover fish. Add *bouquet garni*; bring to the boil; cover with a buttered paper and bake in a moderate oven (375°F. Mark 4) for 10 minutes. Sauté mushroom caps in butter and lemon juice until tender.

Arrange poached fillets on a heated serving dish; put fish liquor into a small saucepan; add remaining dry white wine and reduce over a brisk flame to two-thirds of the original quantity. Thicken the sauce if necessary with a *beurre manié* (made by kneading equal quantities of butter and flour to a smooth paste). Bring sauce to the boil and cook until it has the consistency of cream.

Place 3 mushroom caps on each portion of sole; pour sauce over and glaze for a minute or two under grill before serving. Serves 4.

CASSEROLETTES DE FILETS DE SOLE 'LASSERRE'

2 SOLE (ABOUT 1 POUND EACH)
BUTTER
2 SHALLOTS, FINELY CHOPPED
4 MUSHROOM STALKS, FINELY CHOPPED
SALT AND FRESHLY-GROUND BLACK PEPPER
4 INDIVIDUAL BAKED PASTRY SHELLS
8 BUTTON MUSHROOMS, FINELY CHOPPED
16 ASPARAGUS TIPS
BÉCHAMEL SAUCE
1 EGG YOLK
4 SLICES TRUFFLE (OPTIONAL)
PARSLEY

Remove fillets from sole and cut each fillet into 3 equal pieces; arrange in a well-buttered gratin dish. Sprinkle with chopped shallots and mushroom stalks, add salt and pepper to taste, and cover with fish bones. Cover with buttered paper and poach in a hot oven (450°F. Mark 7) for 10 minutes.

In the meantime, garnish the bottom of each baked pastry shell with finely-chopped mushrooms and 4 asparagus tips, sautéed in butter.

Arrange poached fish in the pastry shells. Reduce cooking liquid from the sole and add it to a well-flavoured *sauce béchamel* with the yolk of 1 egg and a knob of butter. Fill pastry shells with this sauce and glaze under grill until golden.

Lasserre tops each *casserolette* with a glazed slice of truffle; sprinkles dish with parsley and fixes a small pastry 'handle' to each tart to form a *casserolette*, or little casserole. Serves 4.

TROUT AMANDINE

4–6 FRESH TROUT
SALT AND FRESHLY-GROUND BLACK PEPPER
MILK
FLOUR
¼ POUND BUTTER
1 TABLESPOON OLIVE OIL
4–6 TABLESPOONS BLANCHED SLIVERED ALMONDS
JUICE OF ½ LEMON
2–4 TABLESPOONS FINELY-CHOPPED PARSLEY

Season cleaned trout with salt and a little pepper; dip them in milk and then in flour, and sauté fish in half the butter and 1 tablespoon oil until golden brown on both sides. Drain the fat from the pan and melt remaining butter. Add blanched slivered almonds and cook, shaking pan continuously, until the almonds are golden brown. Add lemon juice and finely-chopped parsley and pour the sauce over trout on a heated platter. Serves 4 to 6.

TROUT PÈRE LOUIS

4 FRESH TROUT
4 TABLESPOONS BUTTER
6–8 TABLESPOONS DOUBLE CREAM
2 TABLESPOONS GRAND MARNIER
2 TABLESPOONS COGNAC
SALT AND FRESHLY-GROUND BLACK PEPPER
2–4 TABLESPOONS SLICED TOASTED ALMONDS

Melt butter in a thick-bottomed frying pan and sauté trout until tender. Heat cream, without letting it come to the boil, in a saucepan. Stir in Grand Marnier and cognac and add salt and freshly-ground black pepper to taste. Place trout on a heated serving dish; pour over the sauce and sprinkle with sliced toasted almonds. Serve immediately. Serves 4.

CREAMED FINNAN HADDIE

2 POUNDS SMOKED HADDOCK
MILK AND WATER, TO COVER
3 TABLESPOONS BUTTER
3 TABLESPOONS FLOUR
¾ PINT CREAM
FRESHLY-GROUND BLACK PEPPER AND NUTMEG
TRIANGLES OF BREAD
BUTTER

Soak haddock in water for 2 hours. Drain haddock; put it in a saucepan; cover with equal amounts of water and milk and bring to a fast boil. Remove from heat and allow to stand for 15 minutes. Drain haddock, reserving stock.

Melt butter in the top of a double saucepan; stir in flour and cook over water for 3 minutes, stirring continuously until smooth. Add cream and ½ pint haddock stock and continue to cook, stirring from time to time. Season to taste with freshly-ground black pepper and a little grated nutmeg.

Remove skin and bones from haddock and break into pieces. Fold haddock pieces into sauce and simmer gently until ready to use. Serve in a shallow casserole, surrounded by triangles of bread which you have sautéed in butter. Serves 4 to 6.

FISH FINGERS IN FOIL

2 TABLESPOONS FINELY-CHOPPED ONION
½ POUND BUTTON MUSHROOMS, FINELY CHOPPED
2 TABLESPOONS FINELY-CHOPPED PARSLEY
6 TABLESPOONS BUTTER
2 LEVEL TABLESPOONS FLOUR
SALT AND FRESHLY-GROUND BLACK PEPPER
¼ PINT MILK
6 TABLESPOONS DOUBLE CREAM
8–12 FROZEN FISH FINGERS

Sauté finely-chopped onion, mushrooms and parsley in 2 tablespoons butter until onion is transparent. Blend in flour, and salt and pepper, to taste. Combine milk and cream and stir into vegetable mixture gradually. Bring to the boil; then simmer, stirring from time to time, until sauce is thick.

Season fish fillets to taste with salt and pepper and sauté in remaining butter until browned on both sides.

Cut 4 pieces of aluminium foil, approximately 8½ inches by 11 inches; fold in half and cut into heart shape. Open foil; brush with oil and spread vegetable mixture on one half; place 2 fish fillets on vegetables and top with remaining vegetable mixture. Fold the foil shapes over and seal edges well by crimping them together. Place on a baking sheet and bake in a moderately hot oven (400°F. Mark 5) for 10 minutes. Arrange on a serving platter; slit edges of foil, roll back and serve. Serves 4 to 6.

TRUITE MARINÉE ÉTOILE

6 MEDIUM-SIZED TROUT
6 TABLESPOONS OLIVE OIL
MALT VINEGAR (JUST ENOUGH TO COVER TROUT)
MARJORAM
SALT AND FRESHLY-GROUND BLACK PEPPER
ESCOFFIER'S SAUCE DIABLE
CHILI SAUCE
¼ POUND BUTTON ONIONS
VINEGAR

Clean and trim trout and sauté gently in olive oil until fish flakes with a fork. Place trout in a porcelain bowl and allow to cool.

Combine malt vinegar, just enough to cover trout, with marjoram, salt and pepper, to taste, and bring to the boil; pour marinade mixture over the trout and allow to marinate for 24 hours.

Place trout on a serving dish. Add a little *Sauce Diable* and chili sauce to strengthen the marinade and pour over the trout. Add whole button onions which you have boiled lightly and then soaked in vinegar. Serves 6.

CHINESE STEAMED FISH

- 2 WHITING (ABOUT ¾ POUND EACH)
- ½ POUND BUTTON MUSHROOMS
- 1 CLOVE GARLIC, FINELY-CHOPPED
- 2 CHOPPED SPRING ONIONS (OR 2 TABLESPOONS COARSELY-CHOPPED ONION OR SHALLOTS)
- 4 TABLESPOONS OLIVE OIL
- 2 TABLESPOONS SOY SAUCE
- 1 LEVEL TEASPOON CORNFLOUR
- 2 TABLESPOONS DRY WHITE WINE
- SALT AND FRESHLY-GROUND BLACK PEPPER

Place cleaned fish in a flat dish large enough to hold them. Slice mushrooms thinly and add to dish. Combine finely-chopped garlic and coarsely-chopped spring onion, or onion or shallots, with olive oil, soy sauce, cornflour, dry white wine and salt and black pepper, to taste. Mix well and pour over fish.

Place dish in a large steamer, or on a rack in a large saucepan wide enough to hold it, with about 2 inches of rapidly boiling water. Cover and steam for 15 minutes. Remove to a hot platter and serve immediately. Steamed rice or steamed sliced carrots, new potatoes and green beans should accompany this dish. Serves 2.

TRUITE AU VIN ROSÉ

- 4 GOOD-SIZED TROUT
- VIN ROSÉ, TO COVER
- 4 SHALLOTS, FINELY CHOPPED
- ¼ PINT THICK HOLLANDAISE SAUCE
- 4 TABLESPOONS DOUBLE CREAM
- SALT AND FRESHLY-GROUND BLACK PEPPER
- 8 TRIANGLES WHITE BREAD
- 2 TABLESPOONS BUTTER
- CHOPPED PARSLEY

Place trout in a well-buttered baking dish. Pour in *vin rosé* to cover; add shallots, very finely chopped, and cover the dish with buttered paper. Poach the fish in a slow oven (300°F. Mark 1) for about 20 minutes, or until they are cooked through but still firm. Lay trout on a dry cloth and carefully remove skins.

Reduce the liquid in which the fish were poached until there remains only a small amount of slightly-thickened sauce. Cool the sauce, strain it, and add about ¼ pint thick Hollandaise mixed with 4 tablespoons double cream. Add salt and pepper, to taste.

Arrange the trout on a warm platter; spoon the sauce over the fish and serve garnished with triangles of bread sautéed in butter.

GREAT DISHES OF THE WORLD

CHAPTER 6

SHELLFISH

Lobster a l'Amèricaine

They are fishing the Mediterranean dry. Voracious hordes of tourists are taking their toll on the sea itself, as well as despoiling the coastline of Southern France. This year, even in the fishing ports, local fish cost more than those brought overland a thousand miles from the Atlantic.

At the end of the war the rocky coves of the Riviera were filled with lobsters. But year by year the French have had to go farther afield to catch them, until now they have virtually deserted the shores of Metropolitan France and are to be found in great numbers only off the coasts of Corsica.

I think the reason the French are eating up their sources of lobster so quickly is that they are not content just to boil them and serve them with mayonnaise or a *sauce verte* as we do in this country. The English have a fixation about the perfection of their raw materials which makes them shy of masking their true flavours. But even the most perfect raw material can be enhanced by skilful blending with other flavours that will develop its subtleties and draw out its delicacy. It is this that the French have done with lobster *à l'américaine*, one of the truly great dishes of the world – or, if you prefer it, lobster *à l'armoricaine*, as it is sometimes described on menus throughout France.

For there are two schools of thought on the lobster argument: certain food snobs claim that the spelling is *à l'armoricaine*, because *armor* was the old Breton name for sea and Brittany was at one time called *Armorica*; according to them, there was no other part of France where you could get better lobsters and so France's greatest lobster dish was at once baptised *à l'armoricaine*. Any other version of this name, they decided, was only a mistake in spelling. The other school of purists claim that this dish could not be Breton because of its use of garlic, tomatoes and cognac in the recipe and that it most nearly resembled lobster cooked in the Provençal manner of Southern France.

They called the dish lobster *à l'américaine*, not because the dish was of American extraction, but because it was created by Pierre Graisse, a Parisian chef recently returned from America, who, following the current vogue for all things American, called his restaurant Peter's and named this dish, his creation, lobster *à l'américaine*.

Legend has it that one evening when the dinner hour was well and truly over and Pierre-Peter was getting ready to close up for the night, a party of guests entered his restaurant and insisted that he serve them dinner. The chef decided that if they had soup and *hors-d'œuvre*, he would just have time to prepare a fish dish for them. But on looking into the depleted stores of the restaurant, he discovered that there was no fish left, just some live lobsters ready for the following morning. He chopped some onions, garlic and shallots, sautéed them gently in butter and olive oil, added tomatoes, fish stock and some dry white wine, and when the sauce was bubbling, cut up the lobsters and cooked them in the highly-spiced sauce. The result surpassed all expectations and one of the world's most famous dishes was born . . . the product of a moment of necessity and the inspiration of a great cook.

LOBSTER À L'AMÉRICAINE

2 LIVE LOBSTERS (2 POUNDS EACH)
¼ POUND BUTTER
¼ PINT OLIVE OIL
1 CARROT, FINELY CHOPPED
1 SMALL ONION, FINELY CHOPPED
2 SHALLOTS, FINELY CHOPPED
2 CLOVES GARLIC, FINELY CHOPPED
½ PINT DRY WHITE WINE
4 TABLESPOONS COGNAC
1 PINT TINNED TOMATOES
2 TABLESPOONS TOMATO PURÉE
1 BAY LEAF
¼ PINT FISH STOCK OR DRY WHITE WINE
SALT AND FRESHLY-GROUND BLACK PEPPER
1 TABLESPOON FLOUR
1 TABLESPOON BUTTER
LEMON JUICE
PINCH CAYENNE PEPPER
FINELY-CHOPPED FRESH PARSLEY, CHIVES AND TARRAGON

Order live lobsters from your fishmonger; drop into warm water and bring to the boil so that they lose consciousness and die painlessly. Remove from the heat. Working over a shallow bowl to catch juices, break off and crack claws. Cut each lobster tail into thick slices. Cut body shells in half; remove and discard the intestinal tube which is exposed when the body of the lobster is cut open; reserve coral and all the juices left in the bowl.

Combine 3 tablespoons butter and 3 tablespoons olive oil in a thick-bottomed frying pan; add lobster pieces and sauté for 5 minutes, stirring occasionally. Reserve.

Heat remaining butter and olive oil in another pan and sauté finely-chopped carrot, onion, shallots and garlic until onion is transparent. Place lobster pieces on a bed of vegetables; pour over white wine and simmer for 3 minutes. Add warmed brandy and flame. Add tomatoes, tomato purée, bay leaf, lobster liquids, fish stock and salt and pepper, to taste. Cover the pan and simmer for 15 minutes.

Remove lobster; keep warm. Simmer tomato sauce, uncovered, until slightly reduced. Blend in the coral, creamed with 1 tablespoon each flour and butter, and simmer until thickened; strain sauce and flavour to taste with lemon juice, salt, pepper and cayenne. Add lobster pieces and juice from pan in which lobsters were cooked and heat through.

Just before serving, sprinkle with finely-chopped parsley, chives and tarragon. Serve hot with boiled rice or pilaff. Serves 4 to 6.

BOILED LOBSTER

One of the best ways to appreciate a sweet, firm lobster, full of the clean taste of the sea, is to eat it freshly boiled. So if a fresh, live lobster comes your way, the best method of cooking is to plunge him into a simple *court-bouillon* (water, salt, freshly-ground pepper, bay leaf and thyme) and poach him for 5 minutes for the first pound and 5 minutes more for each additional pound. Remember, the most common error in preparing lobster (and all fish, for that matter) is overcooking.

When the lobster is cooked, allow it to cool in the *court-bouillon*; then remove it, place it on its back on a chopping block and split it lengthwise down the middle with a heavy French knife or kitchen cleaver. Give the knife or cleaver a quick blow with a hammer or mallet so that the shell and meat are severed at the same time; remove the stomach, intestines and the dark vein that runs through the body at the centre. But do not throw away the greyish-green liver or coral-coloured roe; they are delicacies. Crack the claws so that the meat can be easily extracted and serve the lobster hot with melted butter and lemon wedges, or cold with freshly-made mayonnaise. Allow 1 to 1½ pounds of lobster per portion.

GRILLED LOBSTER

Grilling a lobster takes a delicate touch. Its succulence depends on many things: the freshness of the lobster, its size, the heat of the grill and, of course, above all on your own judgment. Split the live lobster down through the middle of the body and the tail; remove the roe (black when it is uncooked) and the dark vein that runs through the tail. Grill it for 8 to 10 minutes on the shell side; turn it over, spread with softened butter and grill for 6 to 8 minutes on the flesh side.

Garnish with paprika and melted butter to which a little lemon juice has been added. Serve additional melted butter with each lobster. Allow 1 small lobster per portion.

GRILLED LOBSTER WITH SHERRY

2 LIVE LOBSTERS (1½–2 POUNDS EACH)
SALT AND FRESHLY-GROUND BLACK PEPPER
6 TABLESPOONS BUTTER
2–4 TABLESPOONS DRY SHERRY
CAYENNE PEPPER
PAPRIKA

Plunge lobsters in warm water to which you have added salt and a generous amount of pepper, and bring gently to the boil. Boil for 1 minute. Drain and halve lengthwise. Keep warm.

Melt butter lightly in a saucepan, add dry sherry and season to taste with cayenne pepper and paprika. Pour over lobster and grill until golden. Serves 4.

LOBSTER NEWBURG

4 SMALL COOKED LOBSTERS
4 TABLESPOONS BUTTER
4 TABLESPOONS HEATED COGNAC
½ PINT DOUBLE CREAM
2 EGG YOLKS, BEATEN
SALT AND FRESHLY-GROUND BLACK PEPPER
CAYENNE AND PAPRIKA

Cut lobsters in half lengthwise. Crack claws. Remove lobster meat from the shells and cut into large cubes. Sauté lobster pieces in butter for a few minutes. Add heated cognac and flame.

Combine beaten egg yolks and cream in the top of a double saucepan and cook over water, stirring continuously, until the mixture coats the spoon. Add lobster meat and pan juices and heat through, taking care that the sauce does not curdle. Add salt, pepper, cayenne and paprika, to taste. Serve on a bed of rice or in individual *vol-au-vent* cases. Serves 4 to 6.

QUICK LOBSTER THERMIDOR

4 SMALL COOKED LOBSTERS
¾ PINT RICH CREAM SAUCE
DRY SHERRY
1 LEVEL TEASPOON DRY MUSTARD
PINCH CAYENNE
WORCESTERSHIRE SAUCE
SALT AND FRESHLY-GROUND BLACK PEPPER
4 TABLESPOONS GRATED PARMESAN
PAPRIKA
BUTTER

Cut lobsters in half lengthwise. Crack claws. Remove lobster meat from the shells and cut into large cubes. Reserve shells. Heat cream sauce; season to taste with a little dry sherry, dry mustard, cayenne pepper, Worcestershire sauce, salt and pepper. Simmer gently for 2 minutes; add diced lobster meat and heat through.

Fill lobster shells with mixture; sprinkle grated Parmesan over top; dust with paprika; dot with butter and brown under grill. Serves 4.

GREEN LOBSTER SALAD

3 RIPE AVOCADO PEARS
1 LOBSTER, COOKED IN COURT-BOUILLON
¼ PINT WELL-FLAVOURED MAYONNAISE
6 TABLESPOONS PURÉED SPINACH
SALT, FRESHLY-GROUND BLACK PEPPER AND CAYENNE
JUICE OF 2 LEMONS
½ CUCUMBER, PEELED, SEEDED AND DICED
2 HARD-BOILED EGGS, DICED
FINELY-CHOPPED TARRAGON, CHIVES AND PARSLEY, TO GARNISH

Make a *sauce verte* by combining well-flavoured mayonnaise with puréed spinach. Season to taste with salt, pepper, cayenne and a little lemon juice, and pass green mayonnaise through a fine sieve.

Dice lobster meat; prepare cucumber and hard-boiled eggs. Slice ripe avocado pears in half; score the flesh with a sharp knife in even-sized segments about ¼ inch square, cutting down to the skin. Be careful not to pierce skin with knife while doing so. Remove avocado segments carefully with a spoon; dice segments and marinate in lemon juice. Brush inside of avocado shells with lemon juice and reserve.

Combine drained diced avocado, cucumber, lobster and eggs in a bowl. Add *sauce verte*; toss carefully and fill avocado shells with this mixture. Chill, and just before serving sprinkle with finely-chopped tarragon, chives and parsley. Serves 6.

AMERICAN CRAB SALAD – I

¼ PINT CREAM, WHIPPED
2 TABLESPOONS TOMATO KETCHUP OR CHILI SAUCE
1 TABLESPOON GRATED ONION
2 TABLESPOONS FINELY-CHOPPED GREEN PEPPER
2 TABLESPOONS FINELY-CHOPPED GREEN OLIVES
1 TABLESPOON FINELY-CHOPPED PARSLEY
1 TABLESPOON LEMON JUICE
1 POUND COOKED CRABMEAT, FLAKED
SALT AND FRESHLY-GROUND BLACK PEPPER
4 LARGE TOMATOES
LETTUCE AND SLICED HARD-BOILED EGGS, TO GARNISH

Combine first seven ingredients in a bowl. Add flaked crabmeat; season to taste with salt and freshly-ground black pepper and mix well.

Slice tomatoes in half; place on individual plates; pile crab salad on tomatoes and garnish with lettuce and sliced hard-boiled eggs. Serves 4.

AMERICAN CRAB SALAD – II

- 1 POUND COOKED CRABMEAT
- ¼ POUND CELERY, FINELY CHOPPED
- 1 TABLESPOON FINELY-CHOPPED PIMENTO
- JUICE OF 1 LEMON
- DRY MUSTARD
- SALT, FRESHLY-GROUND BLACK PEPPER AND CAYENNE
- ¼ PINT MAYONNAISE
- LETTUCE
- 4 TOMATOES
- 2 HARD-BOILED EGGS
- 8 RIPE OLIVES
- FINELY-CHOPPED PARSLEY

Combine lightly the cold, cooked crabmeat with finely-chopped celery and pimento. Season with lemon juice, dry mustard, salt, pepper and cayenne, to taste.

Bind the salad with well-flavoured mayonnaise and serve on lettuce leaves. Garnish with quartered tomatoes and hard-boiled eggs and with ripe olives. Top with a little mayonnaise and dust with finely-chopped parsley.

BAKED AVOCADO WITH CRAB AURORE

- 1 PINT THICK BÉCHAMEL SAUCE
- 2 TABLESPOONS TOMATO PURÉE
- 1 TABLESPOON GRATED ONION
- 1 TABLESPOON BUTTER
- 1 TABLESPOON CURRY POWDER
- 1 POUND COOKED CRABMEAT
- 2 RIPE AVOCADO PEARS
- SALT
- JUICE OF 1 LEMON

To 1 pint thick béchamel sauce add 2 tablespoons of tomato purée and 1 tablespoon each of grated onion, butter and curry powder. Fold in flaked crabmeat and heat mixture just to boiling point, but do not let it boil.

Halve 2 avocado pears lengthwise; remove the stones and score flesh with a knife; sprinkle with salt and lemon juice to preserve colour. Pile avocado halves high with crabmeat mixture and arrange in a baking dish; add 1 inch boiling water and cover dish with aluminium foil. Bake in a slow oven (350°F. Mark 3) for about 30 minutes.

AVOCADO CRAB SALAD

- 1 POUND COOKED CRABMEAT
- ¼ PINT MAYONNAISE
- ¼ PINT CREAM, WHIPPED
- 1 TABLESPOON GRATED ONION
- 4–6 TABLESPOONS CHILI SAUCE (OR KETCHUP)
- SALT AND FRESHLY-GROUND BLACK PEPPER
- 2 RIPE AVOCADO PEARS
- LEMON JUICE

Remove tendons and bits of shell from cooked crab; flake and combine with well-flavoured (home-made) mayonnaise, whipped cream, grated onion, chili sauce (ketchup will do) and salt and freshly-ground black pepper to taste. Chill.

Slice ripe avocado pears in half; remove the stones and score the flesh with a sharp knife in even-sized segments about ¼ inch square, cutting down to the skin. Be careful not to pierce skin with knife while doing so. Remove avocado segments carefully with a spoon; dice segments and marinate in lemon juice. Brush inside of avocado shells with lemon juice to preserve colour. Reserve.

Combine crabmeat salad with diced avocado segments; if necessary add more mayonnaise or lemon juice. Correct seasoning and fill avocado shells with this mixture. Serves 4.

LOBSTER AU GRATIN

2 LIVE LOBSTERS (ABOUT 1½–2 POUNDS EACH)
2 TABLESPOONS BUTTER
2 TABLESPOONS OLIVE OIL
1 CARROT, 1 ONION, 1 STALK CELERY
BUTTER
1 BAY LEAF, 1 PINCH THYME
SALT AND FRESHLY-GROUND BLACK PEPPER
6 TABLESPOONS COGNAC
¼ PINT DRY WHITE WINE
GENEROUS PINCH CAYENNE
½ POUND BUTTON MUSHROOMS, SLICED
1 LARGE TRUFFLE, DICED
¼ PINT DOUBLE CREAM
½ PINT BÉCHAMEL SAUCE
2 TABLESPOONS FINELY-GRATED GRUYÈRE
KNOBS OF BUTTER
CRESCENTS OF FLAKY PASTRY

Cut lobsters in two and removes and sacks and intestinal tubes. Reserve. Heat butter and olive oil in a thick-bottomed frying pan and sauté lobster halves for 3 minutes on each side. Remove from pan; place finely-chopped carrot, onion and celery, which you have softened in a little butter, with bay leaf, thyme, salt and pepper, in pan. Place lobster halves on top of this mixture and sauté for 1 minute. Flame with cognac; when flames die out, pour over the dry white wine. Season to taste with salt, freshly-ground black pepper and cayenne; cover pan and simmer gently for 20 minutes.

When cooked, remove lobster meat from shells and dice coarsely. Slice mushrooms, dice truffle and add to vegetable mixture. Stir in cream and simmer over the lowest heat possible until well blended.

Combine rich béchamel sauce with diced lobster mixture; season generously and bring to the boil. Remove from fire; combine with creamed vegetable mixture and pour into a well-buttered gratin dish. Sprinkle with grated Gruyère and little knobs of butter and heat under the grill until golden. Serve very hot, garnished with crescents of flaky pastry. Serves 4.

DEVILLED CRAB

1 POUND COOKED CRABMEAT
4 TABLESPOONS BUTTER
4 TABLESPOONS FLOUR
¾ PINT HOT MILK
4 HARD-BOILED EGGS, CHOPPED
1 TABLESPOON DIJON MUSTARD
1 LEVEL TEASPOON DRY MUSTARD
1–2 TABLESPOONS WORCESTERSHIRE SAUCE
2 TABLESPOONS FINELY-CHOPPED PARSLEY
1 TABLESPOON FINELY-CHOPPED ONION
1 TABLESPOON FINELY-CHOPPED GREEN PEPPER
SALT AND FRESHLY-GROUND BLACK PEPPER
CAYENNE PEPPER
2–4 TABLESPOONS FRESHLY-GRATED PARMESAN

Melt butter in the top of a double saucepan; add flour and cook over water, stirring continuously until *roux* is well blended. Add hot milk gradually, stirring continuously until sauce begins to thicken. Stir in chopped hard-boiled eggs, mustards, Worcestershire sauce, finely-chopped parsley, onion and green pepper. Simmer sauce, stirring from time to time, until thick.

Flake crabmeat and add to sauce, stirring gently so as not to break meat. Add salt, cayenne and freshly-ground black pepper, to taste, and fill crab shells or individual casseroles with mixture. Sprinkle top with freshly-grated Parmesan and bake in a hot oven (450°F. Mark 7) for 20 minutes.

CRAB TART

SHORTCRUST PASTRY FOR 8-INCH PIE TIN
BEATEN EGG
½ POUND COOKED CRABMEAT
2 TABLESPOONS FINELY-CHOPPED PARSLEY
2 TABLESPOONS BUTTER
2 TABLESPOONS DRY SHERRY
4 EGG YOLKS
½ PINT SINGLE CREAM
SALT AND FRESHLY-GROUND BLACK PEPPER
GRATED NUTMEG

Line pie tin with shortcrust pastry. Prick bottom with a fork; chill for at least an hour; brush with a little beaten egg and bake 'blind' for 15 minutes.

Sauté crabmeat and parsley in butter; sprinkle with sherry and fill pastry shell with crabmeat.

Whisk egg yolks in a bowl; add cream and whisk until thick and lemon-coloured. Flavour to taste with salt, pepper and freshly-grated nutmeg, and pour over the crabmeat mixture.

Bake in a moderate oven (375°F. Mark 4) for about 30 minutes, or until custard is set. Serves 4 to 6.

CURRIED CRAB PANCAKES

PANCAKES:
4 OUNCES FLOUR
1 LEVEL TABLESPOON SUGAR
1 GENEROUS PINCH SALT

2 EGG YOLKS
$\frac{3}{4}$ PINT MILK
2 EGGS
2 TABLESPOONS MELTED BUTTER
2 TABLESPOONS COGNAC
BUTTER, FOR FRYING

Sift together flour, sugar and salt. Beat together whole eggs and egg yolks and add them to the dry ingredients. Mix in the milk, melted butter and cognac smoothly. Strain through a fine sieve and let batter stand for at least 2 hours before cooking the pancakes. Batter should be as thin as cream.

For each pancake, melt 1 teaspoon butter in a small, thick-bottomed frying pan (6 to 8 inches in diameter); add about 2 tablespoons batter, swirling pan to allow batter to cover entire bottom of pan thinly; brush a piece of butter around edge of hot pan with the point of a knife and cook over a medium heat until just golden, not brown (about 1 minute each side). Makes 20 to 24 thin golden pancakes.

CRAB FILLING:
1 APPLE, PEELED, CORED AND SLICED
4 SHALLOTS, FINELY CHOPPED
$\frac{1}{4}$ POUND BUTTER
1 TABLESPOON CURRY POWDER
1 TEASPOON CRUSHED CORIANDER
1 TABLESPOON FLOUR
MILK
$\frac{3}{4}$ PINT WELL-FLAVOURED BÉCHAMEL SAUCE
LEMON JUICE
SALT AND FRESHLY-GROUND BLACK PEPPER
1 POUND COOKED CRABMEAT
BUTTER
GRATED PARMESAN

Bake the pancakes as above, using either an electric griddle or a thick-bottomed frying pan.
To make filling: Sauté sliced apple and chopped shallots in butter until they are soft. Add curry powder, crushed coriander and flour, and mix well. Add just enough milk to make a thick paste. Stir well-flavoured béchamel sauce into mixture and add lemon juice and seasoning to taste. Add crabmeat and heat through. Fill pancakes with mixture and place in a buttered baking dish; dot with butter and a little grated Parmesan and glaze in the oven. Serves 8.

Oysters

The Roman Emperor Tiberius is said to have lived on oysters practically all of his life. Now I am not suggesting you follow suit, but a plate of fresh oysters from Colchester or Whitstable, served on ice with freshly-ground black pepper and a wedge or two of lemon, is hard to beat.

It is very easy to tell a good oyster from a bad one. The shells of live oysters are tightly closed; those of dead oysters are usually, though not always, a little open. If tapping the shell produces a hollow sound within, it is very likely dead.

Oysters are a fine choice for a late-night supper party, either served on ice with piping hot tiny sausages as they do in Northern France; deep-fried in hot oil and butter and served with wedges of lemon, or, if you must, a little *sauce tartare*; or, perhaps my favourite of all, the New Orleans recipe for oysters Rockefeller, so named because they are 'as rich as Rockefeller'.

OYSTERS ROCKEFELLER

- 4 TABLESPOONS FINELY-CHOPPED SHALLOTS
- ½ POUND BUTTER
- 4 TABLESPOONS FINE BREADCRUMBS
- 1 BUNCH WATERCRESS
- 4 TABLESPOONS CHOPPED CELERY LEAVES
- 4 TABLESPOONS CHOPPED PARSLEY
- 1 TEASPOON FINELY-CHOPPED CHERVIL
- 1 TEASPOON FINELY-CHOPPED TARRAGON
- 4 TABLESPOONS PERNOD
- SALT, FRESHLY-GROUND BLACK PEPPER AND CAYENNE
- ROCK SALT
- 24 FRESHLY-OPENED OYSTERS

Sauté shallots in 4 tablespoons of the butter until transparent; add breadcrumbs and stir over a low heat until lightly browned.

Chop finely watercress leaves, separated from their stems, celery and parsley. Combine shallot and breadcrumb mixture with minced greens in a large bowl or mortar; add finely-chopped chervil and tarragon, Pernod, and salt, pepper and cayenne pepper, to taste. Add the remaining butter and pound to a smooth paste. Keep cool until ready to use.

Place a bed of rock salt in a baking tin large enough to hold the oysters comfortably, or in 4 small tins; damp salt slightly and place oysters, opened, on this bed. Place 1 tablespoon of green herb butter on each oyster and bake in a hot oven (450°F. Mark 7) for 4 to 5 minutes, or until butter has melted and oysters are heated through. Serve immediately. Serves 4.

FRIED OYSTERS

- 2–3 DOZEN OYSTERS
- 2 EGGS, BEATEN
- 4 TABLESPOONS DOUBLE CREAM
- SALT AND FRESHLY-GROUND BLACK PEPPER
- CORNMEAL, BISCUIT CRUMBS OR FRESH BREADCRUMBS
- ¼ POUND BUTTER
- ¼ PINT OLIVE OIL
- LEMON WEDGES

Shell oysters. Combine beaten eggs and cream in a bowl. Add salt and freshly-ground black pepper, to taste. Dip oysters in egg mixture, then in cornmeal or crumbs, and allow to set on aluminium foil for about 5 minutes before cooking.

Melt butter in a large, thick-bottomed frying pan or deep-fryer. Add olive oil; bring to frying temperature and cook oysters in fat until they are golden brown. Serve immediately with wedges of lemon. Serves 4 to 6.

OLD ENGLISH STEW'D OYSTERS

1 PINT OYSTERS AND LIQUOR
1 BAY LEAF
4 TABLESPOONS BUTTER
1 TEASPOON WORCESTERSHIRE SAUCE
SALT AND CAYENNE
¼ LEVEL TEASPOON PAPRIKA
½ PINT HOT MILK
½ PINT HOT CREAM
2–4 TABLESPOONS DRY SHERRY
FRESHLY-GRATED NUTMEG

Place oysters and their liquor in a saucepan with bay leaf, butter, Worcestershire sauce, salt, cayenne and paprika, and simmer gently until oyster edges begin to curl.

Remove bay leaf; add milk and cream, which you have previously heated. Stir once, bring to simmering point again; add sherry; correct seasoning and pour into individual serving bowls. Just before serving, dust with a little freshly-grated nutmeg. Serves 4.

Moules Marinière

I have never seen a mussel growing on the Mediterranean coast, yet I can hardly remember a restaurant there that does not make a speciality of some delicious manner of serving mussels. There are vast quantities of mussels along the cliffs of Cornwall; but how many of the local restaurants serve even the simplest mussel dish?

Moules marinière – one of the world's great dishes – makes the most of mussels, simmered for a few minutes only in dry white wine with a few finely-chopped shallots or a small onion or two and a little parsley and thyme. Make this simple and inexpensive dish your own. And then, using this same basic recipe, prepare mussels in any number of ways for a delicious first course or for a light luncheon or supper dish.

Try mussels *en brochette*, first simmered in dry white wine with aromatics, then stripped of their shells, rolled in egg yolk and breadcrumbs, slipped on metal skewers alternately with cubes of fat green bacon, and grilled in the oven until delicately brown. Or, more simply, fry egg-and-breadcrumbed mussels which you have prepared in this way in deep fat until golden, and serve with lemon wedges or *sauce tartare*. I like mussels, too, prepared as above and folded into a creamy omelette; as the sea-rich savour of an Italian spaghetti sauce; or served in the half-shell with a cheese or garlic butter dressing.

TO CLEAN MUSSELS: Place mussels in a bowl and wash well under running water. Scrape each shell with a knife, removing all traces of mud, seaweed and barnacles. Discard any mussels with cracked, broken or opened shells; they are dangerous. Rinse again in running water and remove 'beards'.
TO KEEP COOKED MUSSELS: Wrap mussels in a damp towel and put them on one of the lower shelves of your refrigerator. Strained mussel liquor can also be kept in the refrigerator to use the following day for a *sauce velouté* or a *soupe aux moules*.

MOULES MARINIÈRE

48 MUSSELS
4 SHALLOTS, FINELY CHOPPED
1 TABLESPOON BUTTER
½ PINT DRY WHITE WINE
2–3 TABLESPOONS FINELY-CHOPPED PARSLEY
2 SPRIGS THYME
1 BAY LEAF
FRESHLY-GROUND BLACK PEPPER
2 TABLESPOONS BUTTER
1 TABLESPOON FLOUR

1. Sauté finely-chopped shallots in butter until transparent but not coloured. Add dry white wine, parsley, thyme, bay leaf and freshly-ground black pepper, to taste, and simmer gently for 10 minutes.
2. Wash, scrape and beard mussels; add to wine and herb mixture; cover saucepan and steam, shaking constantly, until shells open. Remove top shells from mussels and arrange mussels in a large, deep, heated serving platter. Keep warm.
3. Reduce the cooking liquor to half its original volume and thicken by adding a *beurre manié*, made by creaming together 2 tablespoons butter and 1 tablespoon flour. Correct seasoning and pour sauce over mussels. Sprinkle with a little finely-chopped parsley and serve immediately.

Ring the changes on this basic mussel recipe for any of the following recipes by simply following Steps 1 and 2 and reducing the quantity of wine by half.

MUSSELS À L'AIL

Prepare mussels as above. Place in a shallow baking pan or gratin dish. Chop 1 shallot and 4 cloves of garlic finely and sauté vegetables in 2 ounces butter until soft. Do not let butter take on colour. Add 2 tablespoons finely-chopped parsley and spoon mixture over mussels. Allow to cool; sprinkle with fresh breadcrumbs and bake in a moderately hot oven (400°F. Mark 5) until the sauce is melted and delicately browned. Serve at once. Serves 4.

MOUCLADE

Prepare mussels as above. Remove shells completely and place mussels in a shallow oven-proof dish. Strain mussel liquor and reduce over a high heat for 2 to 3 minutes. Add ¼ pint cream and simmer for 10 to 15 minutes, stirring from time to time. Pour over mussels; sprinkle lightly with fresh breadcrumbs and bake in a 400°F. oven (Mark 5) until heated through. Serve at once. Serves 4.

MUSSELS MAYONNAISE

Prepare mussels as above. Remove shells completely and allow to drain in a colander. Make a thick mayonnaise and flavour with 2 tablespoons strained mussel liquor. Combine with mussels in a serving dish; sprinkle with finely-chopped parsley and chill. Serves 4.

SALADE DE MOULES

48 MUSSELS
2 TABLESPOONS CHOPPED SHALLOTS
2 SPRIGS THYME
2 SPRIGS PARSLEY
1 BAY LEAF
SALT
¼ PINT VERY DRY WHITE WINE
WINE VINEGAR
OLIVE OIL
FRESHLY-GROUND BLACK PEPPER
4 TABLESPOONS CHOPPED PARSLEY

Scrape, beard and wash mussels. Place in a saucepan together with chopped shallots, thyme, parsley and a bay leaf.

Season lightly with salt and moisten with dry white wine. Simmer until the mussels are well opened. Remove them from their shells.

Prepare a dressing made of one part liquid in which the mussels were cooked, one part wine vinegar and one part olive oil. Add salt and freshly-ground black pepper, to taste; and pour over mussels while they are still warm. Sprinkle with chopped parsley. Mussels should be moist, but without excess dressing. Serve cold as *hors-d'œuvre*. Serves 4.

STEAMED MUSSELS IN CROCK 'FOUR SEASONS'

48 MUSSELS
3 SHALLOTS, FINELY CHOPPED
½ OUNCE BUTTER
6 FLUID OUNCES WHITE WINE
4 FLUID OUNCES CLAM JUICE
4 SPRIGS PARSLEY, FINELY CHOPPED
¼ PINT DOUBLE CREAM
SALT AND FRESHLY-GROUND BLACK PEPPER
LEMON JUICE

Scrape and beard mussels and place in a fire-proof crock with shallots, butter, white wine, clam juice and finely-chopped parsley. Cover and steam for 5 minutes or until mussels are all open. Add cream, salt, pepper and lemon juice, to taste. Bring to boil again and serve. Serves 4.

DEEP-FRIED MUSSELS BÉARNAISE

48 LARGE MUSSELS
2 TABLESPOONS CHOPPED SHALLOTS
2 SPRIGS THYME
2 SPRIGS PARSLEY
1 BAY LEAF
SALT
¼ PINT DRY WHITE WINE
½ POUND GREEN BACON (IN ONE PIECE)
FRESHLY-GROUND BLACK PEPPER
FLOUR
BEATEN EGG
BREADCRUMBS
BÉARNAISE SAUCE

Scrape, beard and wash mussels and place in a saucepan with finely-chopped shallots, thyme, parsley and a bay leaf.

Season lightly with salt and moisten with dry white wine. Cover saucepan and steam 4 to 5 minutes, or until shells are well opened.

Remove mussels from their shells; dice green bacon and place mussels on small skewers with squares of bacon between them. Season to taste with freshly-ground black pepper. Roll in flour; dip in beaten egg and then in dry breadcrumbs. Thread skewers on a piece of string and fry in deep fat until golden. Serve with Béarnaise sauce. Serves 4.

MUSSELS VICTORIA

48 MUSSELS
2 TABLESPOONS CHOPPED SHALLOTS
2 SPRIGS THYME
2 SPRIGS PARSLEY
1 BAY LEAF
SALT
¼ PINT DRY WHITE WINE
½ POUND BUTTER
3 CLOVES GARLIC, FINELY CHOPPED
¾ CUP FINELY-CHOPPED PARSLEY
¼ CUP FINELY-CHOPPED CHIVES

Choose fine fat mussels and scrape, beard and wash them. Place in a saucepan together with finely-chopped shallots, thyme, parsley and a bay leaf.

Season lightly with salt and moisten with dry white wine. Steam for 4 to 5 minutes, or until the shells are well opened. Remove 1 half-shell from each; butter mussels copiously with *beurre d'escargots*; and place mussels in their half-shells in 4 individual oven-proof dishes. Bake in hot oven (450°F. Mark 7) for 2 to 3 minutes. Serves 4.

To make *beurre d'escargots*: knead together butter, finely-chopped garlic, parsley and chives. If chives are unavailable, add more parsley. Chill butter before using.

GRILLED SCALLOPS

8 SCALLOPS
BUTTER
SALT AND FRESHLY-GROUND BLACK PEPPER
4 SLICES HOT BUTTERED TOAST
1 TABLESPOON FINELY-CHOPPED PARSLEY
LEMON JUICE

Wash and trim scallops; dry carefully. Place on a buttered baking tin. Dot with butter; season to taste with salt and freshly-ground black pepper. Pre-heat grill; place scallops about 3 inches from heat and grill for 4 to 6 minutes, or until scallops become delicately browned.

To serve: place on hot buttered toast and sprinkle with finely-chopped parsley and lemon juice. Serves 4.

FRIED SCALLOPS

8 SCALLOPS
2 EGGS, BEATEN
4 TABLESPOONS DOUBLE CREAM
SALT AND FRESHLY-GROUND BLACK PEPPER
CORNMEAL, BISCUIT CRUMBS OR FRESH BREADCRUMBS
¼ POUND BUTTER
¼ PINT OIL
LEMON WEDGES

Wash and trim scallops; slice in half. Combine beaten eggs and cream in a bowl. Add salt and freshly-ground black pepper, to taste. Dip scallops in egg mixture, then in cornmeal or crumbs, and allow to set on aluminium foil for about 5 minutes before cooking.

Melt butter in a thick-bottomed frying pan or deep-fryer. Add oil; bring to frying temperature and cook scallops in fat until they are golden brown.

Serve immediately with wedges of lemon. Serves 4.

BASIC POACHED SCALLOPS

8–10 SCALLOPS
½ PINT DRY WHITE WINE
WATER, TO COVER
½ ONION, CHOPPED
1 BOUQUET GARNI (PARSLEY, THYME, BAY LEAF)
SALT AND FRESHLY-GROUND BLACK PEPPER

Wash and trim scallops. Drain. Place in a saucepan with dry white wine and enough water barely to cover scallops. Add chopped onion and *bouquet garni* and season with salt and freshly-ground black pepper, to taste. Bring slowly to the boil and simmer gently for 5 minutes or until tender. Drain the scallops, straining and reserving the liquor. Slice scallops if they are large and use as directed in any of the following recipes. Serves 4.

BAKED SCALLOPS PROVENÇAL

BASIC POACHED SCALLOPS
2 TABLESPOONS BUTTER
2 TABLESPOONS OLIVE OIL
1 CLOVE GARLIC, FINELY CH PPED
2 TABLESPOONS FRESHLY-GRATED BREADCRUMBS
SALT AND FRESHLY-GROUND BLACK PEPPER
2 TABLESPOONS FINELY-CHOPPED PARSLEY

Prepare scallops as above. Heat butter and olive oil in a heat-proof baking dish until butter sizzles. Slice scallops thickly and toss in dish with finely-chopped garlic, parsley and grated breadcrumbs. Season to taste with salt and freshly-ground black pepper, and bake under the grill until scallops are golden. Serves 4.

SCALLOP SALAD

BASIC POACHED SCALLOPS
3 TABLESPOONS OLIVE OIL
1 TABLESPOON WINE VINEGAR
SALT AND FRESHLY-GROUND BLACK PEPPER
WELL-FLAVOURED MAYONNAISE
LETTUCE LEAVES

Prepare scallops as above. Drain, slice and, while still warm, toss in a bowl with olive oil, vinegar, salt and freshly-ground black pepper, to taste.

Chill. Just before serving, add mayonnaise and toss. Serve in a lettuce-lined bowl. Serves 4.

CURRIED SCALLOPS

BASIC POACHED SCALLOPS
2 TABLESPOONS BUTTER
2 TABLESPOONS FLOUR
¼–½ LEVEL TEASPOON CURRY POWDER
4–6 TABLESPOONS DOUBLE CREAM
SALT AND FRESHLY-GROUND BLACK PEPPER
FINELY-CHOPPED PARSLEY

Prepare scallops as above. Melt butter in the top of a double saucepan; stir in flour and curry powder and cook over water, stirring continuously, until *roux* is well blended. Add enough scallop liquor (about ½ pint) to make a smooth, rich sauce. Add cream, sliced scallops and salt and freshly-ground black pepper, to taste.

Fill scallop shells or individual casseroles with this mixture and sprinkle with parsley. Serves 4.

SCALLOPS MORNAY

BASIC POACHED SCALLOPS
2 TABLESPOONS BUTTER
2 TABLESPOONS FLOUR
¼ PINT CREAM
4 TABLESPOONS GRATED GRUYÈRE
FRESHLY-GRATED BREADCRUMBS
FRESHLY-GRATED CHEESE
BUTTER

Prepare scallops as above. Melt butter in the top of a double saucepan; stir in flour and cook over water, stirring continuously, until *roux* is well blended. Add cream and enough scallop liquor (about ¼ pint) to make a smooth, rich sauce. Stir in grated Gruyère cheese and poached sliced scallops and heat through.

Fill scallop shells or individual casseroles with this mixture. Sprinkle with breadcrumbs and cheese; dot with butter and heat under grill for a few minutes to glaze top.

SCALLOPS AND MUSHROOMS IN WHITE WINE

- BASIC POACHED SCALLOPS
- 12 BUTTON MUSHROOMS, THINLY SLICED
- 4 SHALLOTS, FINELY CHOPPED
- 2 TABLESPOONS FINELY-CHOPPED PARSLEY
- 4 TABLESPOONS BUTTER
- 2 TABLESPOONS FLOUR
- 4 TABLESPOONS DOUBLE CREAM
- FRESH BREADCRUMBS
- BUTTER

Prepare scallops as above. Sauté sliced mushrooms, finely-chopped shallots and parsley in butter until golden. Blend in 2 tablespoons flour and add the reserved stock very slowly, stirring constantly. Stir in cream and combine scallops with the sauce in a baking dish. Sprinkle scallops with bread-crumbs, dot with butter and brown under the grill. Serves 4.

SCALLOPS AU GRATIN

- 8–10 SCALLOPS
- ½ PINT DRY WHITE WINE
- 2 TABLESPOONS FINELY-CHOPPED SHALLOTS
- SALT AND FRESHLY-GROUND BLACK PEPPER
- 4 TABLESPOONS DOUBLE CREAM
- 2 TEASPOONS BUTTER
- 2 TEASPOONS FLOUR
- 2 TABLESPOONS SAUCE HOLLANDAISE, OR 1 EGG YOLK
- 4 BUTTON MUSHROOMS, SLICED AND SIMMERED IN ACIDULATED WATER

Wash scallops well in cold water. Separate coral from scallops and remove any membranes still attached.

Combine scallops and coral in a saucepan with dry white wine, shallots, cream, and salt and pepper, to taste. Cover pan and simmer for 5 minutes.

Remove meats; add *beurre manié*, made by combining flour and butter until smooth, and simmer sauce until it is well blended and reduced a little. To finish sauce, stir in 2 tablespoons *sauce hollandaise*, or if this is not available, egg yolk.

Garnish scallop shells or individual heat-proof dishes with sliced scallops and coral; add a few slices of simmered mushroom.

Pour sauce over and put under the grill until brown. Serve immediately. Serves 4.

SCALLOP KEBABS

16 SCALLOPS
¼ POUND MELTED BUTTER
4 TABLESPOONS DRY BREADCRUMBS
FINELY-CHOPPED PARSLEY
¼ TEASPOON DRIED MARJORAM
GRATED RIND OF ½ LEMON
SALT AND FRESHLY-GROUND BLACK PEPPER
4–8 RASHERS GREEN BACON
MELTED BUTTER
FINELY-CHOPPED PARSLEY
LEMON JUICE

Dip washed and dried scallops in melted butter and then in dry breadcrumbs mixed with finely-chopped parsley, marjoram and grated lemon rind. Season to taste with salt and freshly-ground black pepper. Arrange 4 scallops on each skewer with 1 or 2 rashers of green bacon, weaving the bacon slice back and forth between the scallops.

Grill scallops lightly over charcoal or under the grill, basting with melted butter and turning the skewers frequently during cooking time. Serve with melted butter seasoned with lemon juice and parsley. Serves 4.

COUPE 'CAPRICE'

1 SMALL MELON
1 8-OUNCE PACKET OF PRAWNS
½ PINT WELL-FLAVOURED MAYONNAISE
1 TABLESPOON TOMATO KETCHUP
4 TABLESPOONS DOUBLE CREAM
1 TABLESPOON FINELY-CHOPPED GREEN PEPPER
1 TABLESPOON FINELY-CHOPPED RED PEPPER
SALT AND FRESHLY-GROUND BLACK PEPPER
DASH OF TABASCO
1 TABLESPOON FINELY-CHOPPED FRESH TARRAGON

Chill melon and prawns. Combine mayonnaise, ketchup and cream; stir in peppers and season to taste with salt and pepper and a dash of Tabasco. Chill. Peel, seed and dice melon and combine with prawns and sauce. Spoon into individual salad bowls. Sprinkle with tarragon and serve immediately. Serves 4.

Illustration on facing page

Saumon en Gelée à l'Estragon

– fresh poached salmon garnished with tarragon aspic – is one of the great dishes served at Maxim's, Paris. The photograph was taken against the elegant décor of this famous restaurant. (Recipe on page 132.)

Illustration on following page

Lobster à l'Américaine

Whether you term it *à l'américaine* or *à l'armoricaine*, this is a world-famous dish guaranteed to make your name as cook-cum-host or hostess. Our photograph shows the main protagonists of this culinary drama. (Recipe on page 152–3.)

PRAWNS IN WHISKY

1 POUND FROZEN PRAWNS
4 TABLESPOONS BUTTER
4 TABLESPOONS OLIVE OIL
2 TABLESPOONS FINELY-CHOPPED SHALLOTS (OR ONION)
1 CLOVE GARLIC, FINELY CHOPPED
2 TOMATOES, PEELED, SEEDED AND CHOPPED
SALT AND FRESHLY-GROUND BLACK PEPPER
CAYENNE PEPPER
6 TABLESPOONS WHISKY
6 TABLESPOONS DRY WHITE WINE
1 TEASPOON CORNFLOUR
4 TABLESPOONS DOUBLE CREAM
1 PINCH DRIED TARRAGON
1 EGG YOLK
BOILED RICE

Combine butter and olive oil in a frying pan; add finely-chopped shallots (or onion) and garlic, and sauté until vegetables are transparent. Add prawns, chopped tomatoes and salt, pepper and cayenne pepper, to taste; sauté gently for a few minutes. Pour over 4 tablespoons whisky and flame.

Add dry white wine and simmer for 5 minutes. Remove prawns and keep warm. Combine remaining whisky, cornflour and fresh cream; add to sauce and beat vigorously over a high flame until sauce comes to the boil. Boil for 1 minute; remove from heat; add dried tarragon and pour a little hot sauce over egg yolk. Mix well and then stir egg mixture into sauce. Pour over prawns and serve immediately with rice. Serves 4.

Illustration on previous page

Beef of Old England

To the Englishman nothing can compare with a roast of English beef, charred on the outside, moistly tender within, served with King Edward potatoes baked in their jackets. Other traditional English dishes pictured: Beefsteak and Kidney Pie, Beefsteak and Kidney Pudding, Beef Olives, and a foaming tankard of draught Guinness. (Recipe on page 172–3.)

Illustration on facing page

Boeuf à la Bourguignonne

Tender nuggets of beef bathed in a wine-rich sauce, with crisp *lardons* of green bacon or fat salt pork, tiny white onions parboiled to *al dente* tenderness, and button mushrooms sautéed in butter and lemon juice, make this dish as delicious to eat as it is easy to prepare. (Recipe on page 181–2.)

HAWAIIAN PRAWNS WITH PINEAPPLE

- 24 LARGE FROZEN PRAWNS
- 1 TABLESPOON CORNFLOUR
- ¼ PINT PINEAPPLE JUICE
- 2 TABLESPOONS SOY SAUCE
- 1 TABLESPOON HONEY
- 1 TABLESPOON VINEGAR
- ¼ LEVEL TEASPOON POWDERED GINGER
- 1 SMALL TIN PINEAPPLE CHUNKS

Blend cornflour with a little pineapple juice, then combine with remaining juice, soy sauce, honey, vinegar and ginger. Cook over low heat, stirring constantly, until thickened.

Thread prawns and pineapple chunks alternately on individual skewers and dip in sauce. Grill until delicately browned on all sides. Serves 4.

Quartered button mushrooms, squares of green pepper, etc., can be threaded alternately with prawns and pineapple chunks, if desired.

CHINESE STEAMED PRAWNS

- 1½ POUNDS LARGE FROZEN PRAWNS
- CORNFLOUR
- 4 SHALLOTS, FINELY CHOPPED
- 4 OUNCES MUSHROOMS, FINELY SLICED
- 2 OUNCES CUCUMBER, FINELY SLICED
- 4 TABLESPOONS SOY SAUCE
- 4 TABLESPOONS DRY WHITE WINE
- FRESHLY-GROUND BLACK PEPPER
- RICE
- TOMATOES

Defrost prawns; roll in cornflour and place on a platter in steamer with finely-chopped shallots, sliced mushrooms and cucumber, soy sauce and white wine. Season with a little freshly-ground pepper; and cook over 2 inches of fast-boiling water, covered so that the platter is entirely confined in steam, until tender.

Serve hot from the steamer on a bed of rice, garnished with fresh tomatoes. Serves 4.

GREAT DISHES OF THE WORLD
CHAPTER 7

BEEF

The Roast Beef of England

When Erasmus described, more than four hundred years ago, the things upon which various nations of the world prided themselves – the Scots their nobility and logical sense, the French their breeding – he said of the English that they 'particularly challenge to themselves Beauty, Music and Feasting'. The excellence of English food had been a byword for centuries before Erasmus wrote, perhaps because the penalties for slapdash cooking were so severe, for Edward I once ordered all the cooks of the inns on the road between London and York to be executed because their dishes were not to his taste.

But even as early as the seventeenth century the English were looking back nostalgically to the good old days when 'poor boyes did turn the spitts and lick't the dripping-pan, and grew to be huge, lusty knaves'. The meat they were roasting, the meat of meats for the English, was Beef. The roast was brought to the table on a spit, a servant holding it while the guest cut off a piece, which was eaten with the fingers and often without a plate. Indeed, medieval directions for setting a table often referred to 'trencher pieces' of bread on which guests could lay down their portion of meat.

Nothing can compare with roast beef, charred on the outside, moistly tender within, served with King Edward potatoes baked in their jackets and a melting Yorkshire pudding, happy recipient of the noble juices of the roast.

Accompany this perfection with freshly-grated horseradish beaten into whipped cream – a modern touch to an ancient recipe – and a green vegetable: topped and tailed green beans, a purée of green peas or new-born Brussels sprouts swathed in delicately browned, buttered breadcrumbs.

Beef contains the highest form of protein for human consumption in the most palatable, stimulating and digestible form. Its juiciness is due to the presence of a certain proportion of fat both outside and inside the meat. It is the slow melting of this inside fat – the 'marbling', and its penetration into every cell of the roast – that is responsible for its savouriness.

FIVE TIPS FOR ROASTING BEEF

1. Only tender pieces of beef make good roasts.
2. A sirloin or rib roast, like all large pieces of meat, should stand for an hour or two at room temperature before roasting. So, if your beef has been stored in the refrigerator, be sure to take it out at least two hours before roasting.
3. Do not salt beef before putting it in the oven; the salt forms a crust which prevents meat from colouring uniformly. I like to prepare mine by rubbing it generously with fresh dripping or butter and then dusting it lightly with a mixture of dry mustard, freshly-ground black pepper and a little browned flour, before leaving it to absorb these flavours for an hour or two at room temperature.
4. Remember to heat the serving dish and, especially, the sauceboat.
5. Do not put sliced beef to warm in the oven; it will dry out and become grey in colour.

ROAST BEEF

1 SIRLOIN OR RIB ROAST OF BEEF (5–8 POUNDS)
4–6 TABLESPOONS DRIPPING OR BUTTER
1 LEVEL TABLESPOON DRY MUSTARD
FRESHLY-GROUND BLACK PEPPER
2 TABLESPOONS LIGHTLY-BROWNED FLOUR
1 FLATTENED PIECE BEEF SUET, TO COVER
4–6 TABLESPOONS WATER OR RED WINE
SALT

Spread beef with dripping or butter and sprinkle with a mixture of dry mustard, pepper and flour which you have lightly browned in a frying pan or in the oven. Tie a flattened layer of beef suet over the top.

When ready to roast, place the meat on a rack over a roasting pan and brown in a pre-heated, fairly hot oven (425°F. Mark 6) for 15 minutes. Reduce oven to 325°F. (Mark 2); add warmed red wine or water to the pan and continue to roast, basting frequently, allowing 15 to 18 minutes per pound if you like your beef rare, 20 to 24 minutes per pound for medium, and 25 to 30 minutes per pound if you prefer it well done.

When meat is cooked to your liking, season to taste with salt and additional pepper; remove to a warm serving platter and let it stand for 15 to 20 minutes at the edge of the open oven before carving. During this time the beef sets, the cooking subsides and the roast is ready for carving. In the meantime, pour off the fat in the roasting pan and use the pink juices that pour from the roast as it sets; stir all the crusty bits into it to make a clear sauce. I sometimes add a little wine, a knob or two of butter and a dash of Worcestershire sauce. Bring to the boil, reduce heat and simmer for 1 or 2 minutes. Strain and serve in a sauceboat with roast. This recipe serves 8 to 10.

SLICED BEEF IN ASPIC

8 SLICES RARE ROAST BEEF
½ TEASPOON THYME
½ TEASPOON BASIL
SALT AND FRESHLY-GROUND BLACK PEPPER
CARROT SLICES, COOKED
BUTTON ONIONS, BOILED
LEAVES OF CHERVIL, TARRAGON OR PARSLEY
1 PINT MADEIRA ASPIC
1 TEASPOON WORCESTERSHIRE SAUCE
CAYENNE PEPPER

Arrange overlapping slices of cold rare beef in a shallow serving dish. Sprinkle with thyme, basil, salt and pepper. Garnish with rows of carrot slices and button onions; decorate with leaves of chervil, tarragon or parsley.

Heat Madeira aspic; add Worcestershire sauce and a few grains of cayenne pepper; cool until the aspic is syrupy. Pour aspic over the beef slices and chill in the refrigerator for at least 2 hours, or until the aspic has set. Serves 4.

SUMMER BEEF SALAD

1 POUND COLD ROAST BEEF
2 EATING APPLES
2 STALKS CELERY
4 SHALLOTS, FINELY CHOPPED
1 SMALL CLOVE GARLIC, FINELY CHOPPED
4 TABLESPOONS FINELY-CHOPPED PARSLEY
6–8 TABLESPOONS OLIVE OIL
2–3 TABLESPOONS WINE VINEGAR
SALT AND FRESHLY-GROUND BLACK PEPPER

Trim and dice roast beef. Peel, core and dice apples. Clean and dice celery. Combine diced beef, apples and celery with shallots, garlic and parsley in a salad bowl. Season to taste with olive oil, vinegar, salt and freshly-ground black pepper, and chill. Makes an *hors-d'œuvre* salad for 4 to 6.

GRILLED STEAK

1 RUMP STEAK (ABOUT 1½ INCHES THICK)
FRESHLY-GROUND BLACK PEPPER
2–4 TABLESPOONS SOFTENED BUTTER
SALT

Remove steak from refrigerator at least 30 minutes before cooking and slit fat in several places around side to prevent meat from curling during cooking. Pre-heat grill for 15 to 20 minutes. Sprinkle both sides of steak with freshly-ground black pepper and spread with butter.

Rub hot grill with a piece of suet; place steak on grid and grill for 8 minutes on each side for a rare steak; grill a few more minutes if you prefer steak to be medium rare. Sprinkle with salt to taste. Serves 4.

STEAK À LA BORDELAISE

Prepare steak as above.

Finely chop ½ Spanish onion and 2 shallots; add 2 tablespoons finely-chopped parsley and sauté mixture in 2 tablespoons olive oil until onion is transparent. Stir in 1 level tablespoon flour; add ¼ pint red wine and cook over a high flame, stirring continuously, until wine bubbles. Then lower flame and simmer, stirring continuously, until sauce thickens a little. Poach some beef marrow for 1 minute in hot water; slice and add to sauce. Pour sauce over steak and serve immediately.

STEAK ALLA PIZZAIOLA

Prepare steak as above and serve with *pizzaiola* sauce.

Sauté 1 sliced clove garlic in 2 tablespoons olive oil until transparent. Add 1 medium tin Italian peeled tomatoes and salt and pepper, to taste, and cook over a high flame for 15 minutes. Stir in 1 tablespoon finely-chopped parsley and ¼ teaspoon dried *oregano*, and pour sauce over steak. Serve immediately.

BEEFSTEAK AU ROQUEFORT

1 FINE RUMP STEAK (2 INCHES THICK)
2 TABLESPOONS MELTED BUTTER
SALT AND FRESHLY-GROUND BLACK PEPPER
1 OUNCE ROQUEFORT CHEESE
2 OUNCES BUTTER
JUICE OF ½ LEMON
2 TABLESPOONS FINELY-CHOPPED PARSLEY, CHERVIL OR CHIVES

Trim excess fat from steak. Brush with melted butter and place on a very hot grill. Grill until cooked to your liking. Add salt and freshly-ground black pepper, to taste.

While steak is grilling, cream Roquefort and butter with lemon juice, finely-chopped herbs and a little salt and pepper. Serve steak immediately, topped with Roquefort butter. Serves 4 to 6.

ENTRECÔTE À LA MIRABEAU

1 THICK STEAK
2 TABLESPOONS BUTTER
1 TABLESPOON FLOUR
1 LEVEL TEASPOON ANCHOVY PASTE
FRESHLY-GROUND BLACK PEPPER
ANCHOVY FILLETS
SLICED STUFFED OLIVES
OLIVE OIL
BUTTER

Mash butter and flour to a smooth paste; add anchovy paste and blend well. Spread anchovy mixture over steak; season to taste with freshly-ground black pepper and grill on one side in usual manner. Remove steak; turn it over and make a lattice-work of anchovy fillets on the uncooked side. Fill each square with a slice of olive; brush with melted butter or olive oil and grill until done. Serve with melted butter. Serves 4 to 6.

STEAK AU POIVRE

2 POUNDS RUMP STEAK
1 TABLESPOON PEPPERCORNS
SALT
PARSLEY OR GARLIC BUTTER
WATERCRESS

Crush peppercorns coarsely with a rolling pin or with a mortar and pestle. Sprinkle one side of steak with half the pepper, pressing it into the meat with the flat of your hand. Repeat with other side. Let steak stand at room temperature for at least 30 minutes to absorb flavours.

Pre-heat grill. Cook steak 3 to 4 inches from grill until brown; turn and cook other side 5 more minutes for a very rare steak. Grill slightly longer for medium rare.

Transfer steak to a hot serving dish; sprinkle with salt to taste and dot with parsley or garlic butter. Garnish with watercress. Serves 4.

TOURNEDOS

4 TOURNEDOS
FRESHLY-GROUND BLACK PEPPER
2 TABLESPOONS BUTTER
2 TABLESPOONS OLIVE OIL
4 ROUNDS OF BREAD
BUTTER
LEMON JUICE
SALT

Ask your butcher to prepare 4 *tournedos* for you – slices cut from fillet, usually encased in a thin layer of fat. Season with freshly-ground black pepper, to taste, and sauté in butter and olive oil until well browned (2 to 3 minutes on each side) but still pink and moist in the centre. Remove from pan and keep warm. Sauté 4 rounds of bread in butter; sprinkle lightly with lemon juice; place a *tournedos* on each slice; season to taste with salt and serve with one of the following garnishes or sauces. Serves 4.

TOURNEDOS À LA BÉARNAISE

Cook as above and spoon 2 tablespoons Béarnaise sauce on each *tournedos*.

TOURNEDOS BEAUHARNAIS

Cook as above and set a small cooked artichoke heart filled with Béarnaise sauce on each *tournedos*. Sprinkle with finely-chopped parsley and tarragon. Pour Madeira sauce around *tournedos*.

TOURNEDOS ROSSINI

Cook as above, but place a slice of *pâté de foie gras* on each fried *croûton* before topping with *tournedos*. Pour Madeira sauce around *tournedos*.

BŒUF STROGANOFF – I

- 2 POUNDS RUMP OR FILLET OF BEEF
- FRESHLY-GROUND BLACK PEPPER
- 2 TABLESPOONS FINELY-CHOPPED ONION
- 4 TABLESPOONS BUTTER
- ½ POUND BUTTON MUSHROOM CAPS, SLICED
- SALT, NUTMEG AND MACE
- ½ PINT SOUR CREAM

Cut steak across the grain into slices ½ inch thick. Season to taste with freshly-ground black pepper and flatten each slice with a wooden mallet.

Sauté onion in half the butter until it just begins to turn colour; add sliced beef and sauté for about 5 minutes, turning pieces so that all sides are browned. Remove from pan and keep warm.

Add remaining butter to pan and sauté sliced mushroom caps. Return beef to pan. Season to taste with salt, nutmeg and mace; add sour cream and heat through. Serves 4 to 6.

BŒUF STROGANOFF – II

As above, but simmer beef after browning, for 15 minutes in a sauce made of ½ pint well-flavoured beef stock mixed with 1 or 2 tablespoons tomato concentrate, and thickened with a *roux* made of 2 level tablespoons each of flour and butter.

SWISS STEAK

- 2 POUNDS BEEF (RUMP, ROUND OR CHUCK)
- SALT AND FRESHLY-GROUND BLACK PEPPER
- 4 TABLESPOONS FLOUR
- ½ SPANISH ONION, FINELY CHOPPED
- 4 TABLESPOONS OLIVE OIL
- 1 MEDIUM TIN TOMATOES

Season beef with salt and freshly-ground black pepper, to taste. Rub well with flour.

Sauté finely-chopped onion in olive oil in a thick-bottomed, fire-proof casserole until soft and transparent. Add meat and brown well on both sides. Pour in tomatoes; cover casserole and cook very slowly on top of the stove until the meat is tender (about 2 hours), adding a little water from time to time if necessary. Serves 4 to 6.

CARBONADE DE BŒUF

2 POUNDS RAW BEEF STEAK
SALT AND FRESHLY-GROUND BLACK PEPPER
2 TABLESPOONS OLIVE OIL
2 TABLESPOONS BUTTER
4 ONIONS
1 TABLESPOON FLOUR
1 BOTTLE GUINNESS

Heat olive oil in a thick-bottomed frying pan. Season beef to taste with salt and freshly-ground black pepper and brown meat on both sides in heated oil. Place meat in a small oven-proof casserole.

Add butter to frying pan; slice onions thinly and brown. Sprinkle with flour and add onion to meat in casserole. Add Guinness to cover; place lid on casserole and cook over a low flame for about 2 hours, or until beef is tender. Correct seasoning.

Serve with a potato purée or *spaetzle* (thick egg noodles). Serves 4.

FILLET OF BEEF 'EN CHEMISE'

1 FILLET OF BEEF (APPROXIMATELY 2½ POUNDS)
BRANDY
¼ POUND MUSHROOMS, FINELY CHOPPED
½ SPANISH ONION, FINELY CHOPPED
2 TABLESPOONS BUTTER
4 TABLESPOONS PÂTÉ DE FOIE GRAS
4 TABLESPOONS SOFTENED BUTTER
SALT AND FRESHLY-GROUND BLACK PEPPER
PUFF PASTRY
1 EGG YOLK, SLIGHTLY BEATEN

Brush fillet of beef with brandy; trim it neatly, removing ends, and let stand at room temperature for at least 30 minutes. Sauté finely-chopped mushrooms and onion in butter until soft.

Roast fillet in a moderate oven (375°F. Mark 4) for 15 to 20 minutes, or until half cooked. Allow fillet to cool slightly; remove skewers, cords and fat; spread with a mixture of *foie gras* and butter, seasoned to taste with salt and freshly-ground black pepper. Spread thinly with mushroom and onion mixture.

Roll out puff pastry into a thin sheet and wrap the fillet in it, securing it neatly. Place on a baking tin; brush pastry with cold water and bake in a hot oven (450°F. Mark 7) for 12 to 15 minutes. Brush pastry with slightly beaten egg yolk and continue baking until the crust is browned.

FILLET OF BEEF 'EN COCHONAILLES'

1 FILLET OF BEEF (APPROXIMATELY 2½ POUNDS)
BRANDY
11 SLICES COOKED HAM OR BOILED BACON
½ POUND MUSHROOMS, FINELY CHOPPED
1 SPANISH ONION, FINELY CHOPPED
4–6 TABLESPOONS BUTTER
SOFTENED BUTTER
SALT AND FRESHLY-GROUND BLACK PEPPER
PUFF PASTRY
1 EGG YOLK, SLIGHTLY BEATEN
BÉARNAISE SAUCE

Brush fillet of beef with brandy; trim it neatly, removing ends, and slice into 12 equal parts without completely separating the slices. Place a thin slice of cooked ham or boiled bacon, cut to fit the fillet, between each slice and spread with finely-chopped mushrooms and onions, seasoned to taste and sautéed until soft in butter.

Re-form the fillet; fasten with metal skewers and roast it in a moderate oven (375°F. Mark 4) for 15 to 20 minutes, or until half cooked.

Allow fillet to cool slightly; remove skewers, cords and fat; spread with softened butter; season to taste with salt and freshly-ground black pepper and spread thinly with remaining mushroom and onion mixture.

Roll out puff pastry into a thin sheet and wrap the fillet in it, securing it neatly. Place on a baking tin; brush pastry with cold water and bake in a hot oven (450°F. Mark 7) for 12 to 15 minutes. Brush the pastry with slightly beaten egg yolk and continue baking until the crust is browned. Serve with Béarnaise sauce.

BEEF STEAK AND KIDNEY PIE

2 POUNDS THICK BEEF STEAK, CUT INTO LARGE BITE-SIZE PIECES
¾ POUND CALF'S KIDNEY
2 TABLESPOONS FLOUR
1 LEVEL TEASPOON SALT
½ LEVEL TEASPOON FRESHLY-GROUND BLACK PEPPER
4 TABLESPOONS BUTTER, OR SUET IN EQUAL QUANTITY
4 SHALLOTS, FINELY CHOPPED
½ PINT RICH BEEF STOCK
¼ TEASPOON FRESHLY-GROUND BLACK PEPPER
1 BAY LEAF
1 TEASPOON CHOPPED PARSLEY
PINCH EACH POWDERED CLOVE, MARJORAM
FLAKY PASTRY, TO COVER
1 TABLESPOON DRY SHERRY
1 TEASPOON WORCESTERSHIRE SAUCE

Clean kidney, split, remove fat and large tubes and soak in salted water for 1 hour. Dry kidney and cut into ¼-inch slices. Mix flour, salt and pepper, and roll beef and kidney in this mixture.

Melt butter or suet in a thick-bottomed saucepan or iron casserole and sauté finely-chopped shallots until golden. When shallots have taken on a little colour, add the beef and kidneys and brown them thoroughly, stirring almost constantly. Moisten with beef stock, add pepper, bay leaf, chopped parsley, powdered clove and marjoram; stir; cover, and simmer over a low flame for 1 to 1¼ hours or until meat is tender. If liquid is too thin, thicken with a little flour mixed to a smooth paste with water.

Grease a deep baking dish, place a pie funnel in centre of dish, add meats and liquid, and allow to cool. In the meantime, make flaky pastry crust and place over meat, moistening and pinching edges to dish. Make vents in the pastry to allow steam to escape and bake in a hot oven (450°F. Mark 7) for 10 minutes. Lower heat to moderate (375°F. Mark 4) and continue baking 15 minutes, or until pastry crust is golden brown. Just before serving the pie, insert a small funnel into centre vent and pour in a mixture of 1 tablespoon of dry sherry and 1 teaspoon of Worcestershire sauce. Serves 4 to 6.

STEAK AND KIDNEY PUDDING

1½–2 POUNDS STEAK, CUT INTO SMALL PIECES
½ POUND CALF'S KIDNEY
2 TABLESPOONS FLOUR
½ LEVEL TEASPOON FRESHLY-GROUND BLACK PEPPER
½ LEVEL TEASPOON SALT
12 OUNCES SELF-RAISING FLOUR
SALT AND FRESHLY-GROUND BLACK PEPPER
6 OUNCES FRESHLY-GRATED OR PACKAGED SUET
DRIPPING
4 TABLESPOONS FINELY-CHOPPED SHALLOT OR ONION
¼ PINT RICH BEEF STOCK
¼ PINT PORT WINE
2 TEASPOONS SOY SAUCE
GRATED RIND OF ½ LEMON

Cut steak and kidney into rather small pieces and shake well in a bowl containing flour, pepper and salt, until all the pieces are well coated.

Combine finely-chopped suet with flour, adding pepper and salt to taste, to make a light suet crust.

Grease a basin with dripping, line it with the crust, put in the seasoned meat and finely-chopped shallot or onion. Combine stock, port wine, soy sauce and lemon rind, and fill up the basin with this mixture to near the top; put on the pastry lid, making sure that the edges are well sealed to keep in the steam. Cover the whole pudding with a floured cloth and simmer or steam for 3 to 4 hours. Crust should be rather damp. Serves 4 to 6.

BEEF OLIVES

4 OUNCES FRESH BREADCRUMBS
2 OUNCES SUET
4 TABLESPOONS FINELY-CHOPPED PARSLEY
1 TEASPOON DRIED MARJORAM, THYME OR WINTER SAVORY
½ LEVEL TEASPOON GRATED LEMON RIND
2 EGGS
GRATED NUTMEG
SALT AND FRESHLY-GROUND BLACK PEPPER
WATER OR WHITE WINE, TO MIX
2 POUNDS TOP SIDE OF BEEF CUT INTO THIN SLICES (APPROXIMATELY 3 INCHES BY 4 INCHES)
1 SPANISH ONION, FINELY CHOPPED
¼ POUND MUSHROOMS, FINELY CHOPPED
4 TABLESPOONS BUTTER OR OIL
¾ PINT BEEF STOCK
1 TABLESPOON FLOUR
1 TABLESPOON BUTTER

To prepare forcemeat stuffing: mix breadcrumbs, freshly-grated suet, fresh parsley, dried herbs, lemon rind and eggs. Season generously with grated nutmeg, salt and freshly-ground black pepper. If mixture seems too dry, add a little water or dry white wine.

Trim thin slices of beef into rectangles approximately 3 inches by 4 inches and beat meat well with a rolling pin to flatten and tenderise it. Spread forcemeat mixture on each piece of meat; roll up and secure with very fine string.

Sauté finely-chopped onion and mushrooms in butter or olive oil in a flame-proof casserole until onion is transparent. Add beef olives and brown on all sides. Pour over stock; cover and simmer until tender, 1½ to 2 hours.

Just before serving, remove strings and thicken gravy by stirring in knobs of butter mixed to a smooth paste with flour. Correct seasoning and serve immediately. Makes 12 beef olives. Serves 4 to 6.

Bœuf à la Bourguignonne

If one gave stars to the regions of France – as well as to their better restaurants – for the excellence of their cooking, Burgundy would have an unchallenged 'three'. The high quality of its native beef and poultry, allied to the fame of its vintages, makes this one of the most distinctive – if one of the richest – cuisines of France.

Most Burgundian dishes are of the long, slow-cooking variety – superb casseroles of meat, fish and game – guaranteed to make even the least expensive cuts of meat taste delicious. Indeed, food and wine are so closely linked together in Burgundy that it is a toss-up whether it is the famous vintages of the region or *bœuf à la bourguignonne* that has brought Burgundy the greater international fame. For *bœuf à la bourguignonne* – or *bœuf bourguignon* as it is sometimes more simply called – is one of the truly great dishes of the world. Combining tender nuggets of beef bathed in a rich wine-flavoured sauce with crisp *lardons* of green bacon or fat salt pork, tiny white onions parboiled to *al dente* tenderness, and button mushrooms sautéed in butter and lemon juice, this dish is as delicious to eat as it is easy to prepare.

Like many wine-based dishes, *bœuf à la bourguignonne* is better when re-heated and served on the following day. Make this world-famous casserole one of your regular party dishes, preceded by a hot clear soup or a cold or hot *hors-d'œuvre* and followed by a crisp green salad, cheese or fruit. Nothing could be simpler or more delicious.

BŒUF À LA BOURGUIGNONNE

3 POUNDS TOP SIDE OR TOP RUMP OF BEEF
FLOUR
4 TABLESPOONS OLIVE OIL
4 TABLESPOONS BUTTER
¼ POUND SALT PORK, DICED
SALT AND FRESHLY-GROUND BLACK PEPPER
4 TABLESPOONS COGNAC, WARMED
2 CARROTS
1 LEEK
4 SHALLOTS
1 SPANISH ONION
1 CLOVE GARLIC
1 CALF'S FOOT, SPLIT (OPTIONAL)
1 BOUQUET GARNI (1 SPRIG THYME, 1 BAY LEAF, 1 STALK CELERY, 2 SPRIGS PARSLEY)
½ BOTTLE GOOD RED BURGUNDY
BEEF STOCK OR WATER, TO COVER
1 TABLESPOON FLOUR
1 TABLESPOON BUTTER
18 BUTTON ONIONS
12 BUTTON MUSHROOMS
SUGAR
LEMON JUICE
CHOPPED PARSLEY

Cut beef into large cubes; remove fat and roll cubes in flour. Heat 2 tablespoons olive oil and 2 tablespoons butter in a large frying pan and sauté diced salt pork until crisp and brown. Remove pork from pan and transfer to a large earthenware casserole. Brown meat well on all sides in remaining fat, season to taste with salt and pepper and moisten with warmed cognac. Ignite cognac; let the flame burn away and add meat to casserole.

Coarsely chop carrots, leek, shallots, onion and garlic, and cook vegetables in fat remaining in frying pan, stirring occasionally, until they are lightly browned, adding a little more butter and olive oil, if necessary.

Transfer vegetables to the casserole with the meat; add the calf's foot and *bouquet garni*. Pour over all but 4 tablespoons of the wine, and just enough hot water or good beef stock to cover contents of the casserole. Cover and cook in a very slow oven (280°F. to 300°F. Mark 1) for 1½ to 2 hours.

Remove fat from sauce; stir in, bit by bit, 1 tablespoon butter worked with 1 tablespoon flour; cover; continue to cook gently in the oven for about 2 hours or longer.

Brown onions in 1 tablespoon butter in a saucepan with a little sugar. Add 4 tablespoons red wine, cover and cook over low flame until onions are almost tender. Keep warm. Sauté mushroom caps in remaining oil and butter and a little lemon juice. Keep warm.

When meat is tender, remove calf's foot and *bouquet garni*; correct seasoning; add onions and mushroom caps and sprinkle lavishly with finely-chopped parsley. Serves 4 to 6.

BŒUF À LA MODE

1 BONED JOINT OF BEEF (ABOUT 4–5 POUNDS)
SALT AND FRESHLY-GROUND BLACK PEPPER
½ PINT RED OR WHITE WINE
1 SPANISH ONION, SLICED
2 LARGE CARROTS, SLICED
1 CLOVE GARLIC
2 STALKS CELERY, SLICED
2 BAY LEAVES
4 SPRIGS PARSLEY
4 TABLESPOONS COGNAC
PINCH OF THYME
2 TABLESPOONS LARD OR DRIPPING
2 TABLESPOONS BUTTER
2 TABLESPOONS FLOUR
½ PINT BEEF OR VEAL STOCK
1 OR 2 BEEF OR VEAL BONES
1 SMALL TIN TOMATOES
6 CARROTS
24 BUTTON ONIONS
BUTTER
SUGAR

Have your butcher lard beef (silverside or top rump of beef is best) with strips of larding pork. Season it with salt and pepper and put in a porcelain or earthenware bowl (not metal) with red or white wine, sliced onion, carrots, garlic, celery, bay leaves and parsley. Add cognac and a pinch of thyme. Let the meat marinate in a cold place in this mixture for 6 hours or more, turning the meat over several times to allow it to absorb the wine.

Remove meat from the marinade; drain and dry the piece thoroughly. Melt lard or dripping in a heat-proof casserole just large enough to hold beef; add meat and brown it on all sides. Pour off excess fat.

Melt butter in a large saucepan; stir in flour and cook the *roux*, stirring constantly, until it is browned. Gradually stir in the marinade followed by beef or veal stock. Bring the sauce to the boil, stirring constantly, and pour it over the meat. Add beef or veal bones and tinned tomatoes.

Cover casserole closely and braise on top of the stove or in a very slow oven (280°F. to 300°F. Mark 1) for 2 hours.

Cut carrots into pieces and blanch; glaze onions in a little butter and sugar. Remove meat from gravy and skim off all fat. Clean pan and put back meat with glazed carrots and onions and strained gravy. Bring back to the boil; reduce heat and simmer 1½ to 2 hours longer, or until the meat is tender. Correct seasoning of the gravy, which should have reduced to about half the original quantity. If it has not done so, reduce by boiling it separately over a high heat until you are left with the correct quantity. Skim off any remaining fat.

Slice the meat thinly across the grain so that the larding will show. Serve sauce separately. Serves 8 to 10.

BŒUF EN DAUBE À LA PROVENÇALE

4 POUNDS LEAN BEEF
2 ONIONS, SLICED
2 CARROTS, SLICED
1 BOUQUET GARNI (THYME, PARSLEY AND BAY LEAF)
SALT AND FRESHLY-GROUND BLACK PEPPER
½ PINT RED WINE
4 TABLESPOONS COGNAC
4 TABLESPOONS OLIVE OIL
½ POUND LEAN BACON, DICED
1 SPANISH ONION, CUT IN QUARTERS
4 CLOVES GARLIC
1 PIECE ORANGE PEEL
½ PINT HOT STOCK OR WATER
¼ POUND STONED RIPE OLIVES

Cut the meat in 1-inch cubes and place in a large bowl or earthenware casserole with sliced onions and carrots, a *bouquet garni*, salt, freshly-ground black pepper, red wine and cognac, and marinate in this mixture for 5 to 6 hours, stirring occasionally.

Heat oil in a frying pan; melt diced bacon in it and brown onion quarters in the fat. Drain meat, reserving juices of marinade, and sauté meat with bacon bits and onions until browned, shaking the pan from time to time. Add garlic cloves and orange peel; then moisten with the marinade which has been reduced to half the original quantity. Pour over ½ pint hot stock or, failing this, hot water. Cover the pot with greaseproof paper and the lid, and cook in a very slow oven (280° to 300°F. Mark 1) for 3 to 4 hours. Remove from the oven; skim fat from the surface; add stoned olives and correct seasoning. Cook for another 30 minutes. Serve in the casserole. Serves 6 to 8.

ESTOUFFADE DE BŒUF

½ POUND LEAN BACON
2 TABLESPOONS BUTTER
2 TABLESPOONS OLIVE OIL
3 POUNDS LEAN BEEF
2 TABLESPOONS FLOUR
6 MEDIUM-SIZED ONIONS, QUARTERED
SALT AND FRESHLY-GROUND BLACK PEPPER
1 BOTTLE RED WINE
WELL-FLAVOURED BEEF STOCK, TO COVER
2 CLOVES GARLIC, CRUSHED
1 BOUQUET GARNI (THYME, BAY LEAF, PARSLEY AND CELERY)
½ POUND MUSHROOMS, SLICED
BUTTER

Dice lean bacon, blanch in boiling water and sauté in butter and olive oil until golden. Remove from pan. Cut lean beef into good-sized chunks; sprinkle with flour and brown in the same amalgamation of fats. Add quartered onions to meat chunks and cook, stirring constantly, until they are well browned. Season with salt and freshly-ground black pepper. Add red wine and beef stock to cover, crushed garlic and a *bouquet garni*. Bring to the boil; cover and cook in a very slow oven (280° to 300°F. Mark 1) for 2½ to 3 hours.

Drain the *ragoût* on a fine sieve placed over a terrine. Place beef chunks and bacon cubes in a clean casserole. Sauté mushrooms in a little butter and add to the meat. Skim fat from the sauce; reduce over a high flame to the desired consistency and strain it over the meat and garniture. Simmer gently, covered, for 30 minutes or until tender, and serve in the casserole. Serves 4.

OXTAIL RAGOÛT

1 MEDIUM-SIZED OXTAIL
FLOUR
SALT AND FRESHLY-GROUND BLACK PEPPER
2 TABLESPOONS BUTTER
2 TABLESPOONS OLIVE OIL
4 OUNCES FAT BACON, DICED
2 SPANISH ONIONS, STUCK WITH CLOVES
1 GENEROUS BOUQUET GARNI
2 FAT CLOVES GARLIC
8 CARROTS
¾ PINT TOMATO JUICE
¾ PINT BEEF STOCK
4 TURNIPS
4 LEEKS
4 STALKS CELERY

Get your butcher to cut oxtail into serving pieces. Soak in cold water for 3 to 4 hours. Put them in fresh water and bring to the boil, skimming regularly. Drain, and dry with a clean cloth.

Put some flour, seasoned with salt and pepper, into a large paper bag; add blanched oxtail pieces and shake well to coat evenly with seasoned flour mixture. Heat butter and olive oil in a large flame-proof casserole; add bacon pieces and sauté until golden. Remove bacon and brown oxtail sections in resulting fat. Then return bacon bits; add onions stuck with cloves, *bouquet garni*, garlic, 4 of the carrots, thickly sliced, and salt and pepper, to taste. Combine tomato juice and beef stock; add to the meat and vegetables and bring slowly to the boil. Cover the casserole; transfer to a very slow oven (280° to 300°F. Mark 1) and cook gently for 3 to 4 hours. Cool and skim off fat.

Forty-five minutes before serving: scrape the remaining carrots and cut them in half lengthwise; scrape and quarter turnips; clean leeks and celery carefully. Add vegetables to the *ragoût* and continue cooking gently until tender. Serves 4 to 6.

ITALIAN BEEF STEW

1 TABLESPOON LARD
1 TABLESPOON OLIVE OIL
½ POUND FAT SALT PORK, DICED
1 ONION, SLICED
2 CLOVES GARLIC, CHOPPED
2½ POUNDS LEAN BEEF, CUT INTO BITE-SIZED PIECES
SALT AND FRESHLY-GROUND BLACK PEPPER
1 GENEROUS PINCH MARJORAM
¼ PINT DRY RED WINE
4 TABLESPOONS TOMATO CONCENTRATE, DILUTED IN WATER

Combine lard and olive oil in a thick pan or flame-proof casserole; when fat begins to bubble, add diced salt pork, sliced onion and garlic and sauté until golden. Add pieces of meat seasoned with salt, pepper and marjoram, and cook, stirring frequently, until meat is well browned on all sides. Now add dry red wine (one of the rougher Italian ones) and continue cooking until the wine has been reduced to half the original quantity. Add diluted tomato purée and enough boiling water to cover the meat. Cover the pan and simmer slowly for about 2 hours, or until the meat is tender and the savoury sauce is thick and richly coloured. A tablespoon or two of red wine just before serving will add extra *bouquet* to this dish, which should be served directly from the casserole. Serves 4 to 6.

SAUERBRATEN

4 POUNDS TOP ROUND OF BEEF
¾ PINT DRY RED WINE
¼ PINT WINE VINEGAR
1 TEASPOON SALT
1 TEASPOON CRUSHED BLACK PEPPERCORNS
2 LARGE ONIONS, SLICED
2 LARGE CARROTS, SLICED
2 STALKS CELERY, CHOPPED
½ LEMON, SLICED
2 BAY LEAVES
4 SPRIGS PARSLEY
4 ALLSPICE BERRIES
4 CLOVES
6 TABLESPOONS BUTTER
4 TABLESPOONS FLOUR
1 TABLESPOON BROWN SUGAR
DUMPLINGS OR BUTTERED NOODLES

Get your butcher to roll the meat and tie it into a round. Wipe with a damp cloth and place in a deep bowl. Make a marinade by combining wine and wine vinegar with salt, peppercorns, onions, carrots, celery, lemon, bay leaves, parsley, allspice and cloves. Bring to the boil and pour over the meat; cover and place in the refrigerator for 3 days, turning it once a day.

Remove meat from marinade and wipe dry. Heat the marinade. Meanwhile, melt 4 tablespoons butter in a deep pot and sear the meat; sprinkle with 2 tablespoons flour and brown on all sides. Pour the hot marinade over it and cover tightly; lower the heat and simmer gently for 2½ to 3 hours, or until the meat is tender. Pour the liquid off the meat to cool, and set the pot with meat aside. Skim fat from liquid; strain broth. Melt remaining butter in a saucepan and blend in 2 tablespoons of the flour and the sugar; cook slowly until slightly browned. Gradually add the strained marinade and continue cooking, stirring constantly, until thick and smooth. Pour sauce over meat, cover, and simmer for 30 minutes. Serve with dumplings or buttered noodles. Serves 4 to 6.

The American Meat Loaf

Among the great dishes of the world, many American specialities take pride of place – New England boiled dinner, clam chowder and Boston baked beans, Southern fried chicken, prawn and chicken gumbo, Caesar salad, San Francisco's '*cioppino*', Philadelphia's 'pepper pot', lobster Newburg and oysters Rockefeller – to name just a few. But none has captured the heart of the American people so completely as the all-American meat loaf . . . an easy-to-cook, easy-to-serve Sunday night supper that is famous the length and breadth of the land.

Try this interesting meat loaf pâté – first cousin of the hamburger – the next time you want an informal supper dish for the family. It will become a fast favourite, I know.

Shape your meat loaf into a loaf or round to bake on a flat baking tray, or press it into a loaf tin or ring mould and cook in the same fashion.

Ring the changes on the basic recipe. Cut ingredients by half for a 'young family' loaf. Use just beef, or pork and veal, or just veal in the basic recipe. Make a loaf of tinned corned beef or a combination of calf's liver and sausage meat. Try poached chicken, finely ground and blended with a spicy, curry-flavoured béchamel sauce before baking.

Change the flavours at will. Almost anything goes in the world of the American meat loaf. Try dry mustard, Worcestershire sauce and finely-chopped savory for a different flavour accent. Give your meat loaf body and softness with fresh breadcrumbs, diced white bread and even cornflakes. For a chunky texture, stir in finely-chopped green pepper, celery, crisp bacon or water chestnuts. Onions, garlic, herbs and spices lend flavour. Red wine, dry white wine, brandy, lemon juice, tomato, chili and Worcestershire sauces give dash and accent. Eggs are used to bind the mixture together.

Serve with tomato sauce, chili sauce, chilled sour cream, hot curry sauce or red wine sauce *à la bordelaise*.

AMERICAN MEAT LOAF

- 1 POUND FINELY-GROUND BEEF
- ½ POUND FINELY-GROUND VEAL
- ½ POUND FINELY-GROUND PORK
- 6 TABLESPOONS FINELY-CHOPPED ONION
- 6 TABLESPOONS FINELY-CHOPPED CELERY
- 2 CLOVES GARLIC, FINELY CHOPPED
- 2 TABLESPOONS OLIVE OIL
- 2 TABLESPOONS BUTTER
- ¼ PINT RED WINE
- 2–4 SLICES BREAD
- 1 LEVEL TEASPOON SALT
- ½ LEVEL TEASPOON FRESHLY-GROUND BLACK PEPPER
- GROUND ALLSPICE
- ½ TEASPOON RUBBED THYME
- 2 BAY LEAVES, CRUSHED
- 2 EGGS, WELL BEATEN
- TOMATO OR CHILI SAUCE

Sauté finely-chopped onion, celery and garlic in olive oil and butter until transparent. Add red wine and simmer gently for 5 minutes.

Trim crusts from bread; dice; add to wine mixture and pour mixture over ground meats. Mix well and season with salt, pepper, allspice, thyme and bay leaves. The seasoning should be rather sharp.

Stir in the beaten eggs and put in a well-greased baking dish, or pat into loaf shape on a greased baking tin or oiled board, and bake in a slow oven (325°F. Mark 2). Baste from time to time with a few tablespoons of heated wine. Cooking time: a minimum of 1 hour. Serve with tomato or chili sauce. Serves 8.

EASY BLENDER LOAF

- 2 EGGS
- 6 TABLESPOONS RED WINE
- 1 ONION, SLICED
- 1 CLOVE GARLIC
- 6 SPRIGS PARSLEY, COARSELY CHOPPED
- 1½ POUNDS FINELY-GROUND BEEF
- ½ POUND FINELY-GROUND PORK
- 1 LEVEL TEASPOON SALT
- FRESHLY-GROUND BLACK PEPPER
- POWDERED SAGE OR THYME

Place eggs, red wine, sliced onion, garlic and coarsely-chopped parsley in container of electric blender. Blend until vegetables are finely chopped; mix well with ground meats and season to taste with salt, pepper and sage or thyme. Seasoning should be rather sharp.

Pack loaf mixture into an oiled loaf tin and bake for 1 to 1¼ hours in a slow oven (325°F. Mark 2). Serves 8.

GRILLED BEEFBURGERS

- 2 POUNDS CHOPPED FRESH LEAN BEEF
- 4 TABLESPOONS CHOPPED BEEF MARROW
- 4 TABLESPOONS THICK CREAM OR COLD WATER
- 4 TABLESPOONS FINELY-CHOPPED ONION
- SALT AND FRESHLY-GROUND BLACK PEPPER
- 2 TABLESPOONS MELTED BUTTER

Combine first four ingredients; add salt and freshly-ground black pepper to taste and form into 8 patties. Brush patties with melted butter and grill for 4 to 5 minutes on each side. Serves 4.

SHEPHERD'S PIE

1 SPANISH ONION, FINELY CHOPPED
2 TABLESPOONS OLIVE OIL
1 POUND COOKED ROAST BEEF, MINCED
½ PINT RICH BEEF GRAVY OR SAUCE ESPAGNOLE
2 TEASPOONS WORCESTERSHIRE SAUCE
1 TABLESPOON FINELY-CHOPPED PARSLEY
¼ TEASPOON MIXED HERBS
SALT AND FRESHLY-GROUND BLACK PEPPER
6 TABLESPOONS DOUBLE CREAM
3 TABLESPOONS MELTED BUTTER
1 EGG, LIGHTLY BEATEN
MASHED POTATOES

Sauté onion in olive oil until transparent and soft; add minced cooked beef, gravy (or *sauce espagnole*), Worcestershire sauce, finely-chopped parsley, mixed herbs and salt and freshly-ground black pepper, to taste. Keep warm.

Add cream, 2 tablespoons melted butter and beaten egg to hot mashed potatoes and season to taste with salt and pepper.

Place the meat mixture in the bottom of a deep, well-buttered, oven-proof baking dish. Top with mashed potatoes; brush with remaining melted butter and bake for 15 to 20 minutes in a moderately hot oven (400°F. Mark 5) or until potatoes are golden brown. Serves 6.

MEAT BALLS IN TOMATO SAUCE

1 POUND MINCED BEEF
½ SPANISH ONION, FINELY CHOPPED
1 CLOVE GARLIC, FINELY CHOPPED
2 TABLESPOONS FINELY-CHOPPED PARSLEY
2 TABLESPOONS FINELY-GRATED PARMESAN
4 SLICES WHITE BREAD
MILK
2 EGGS
DRY WHITE WINE
SALT AND FRESHLY-GROUND BLACK PEPPER
2 TABLESPOONS BUTTER
2 TABLESPOONS OLIVE OIL
TOMATO SAUCE

Combine beef, finely-chopped onion, garlic, parsley and grated Parmesan in a bowl and mix thoroughly. Trim crusts from bread, soak in milk, squeeze dry and shred into mixture. Add eggs and mix well to a smooth paste. Add a little dry white wine and salt and freshly-ground black pepper, to taste. Form the mixture into small balls and sauté until golden in butter and olive oil. Simmer in tomato sauce for 1 to 2 hours. Serve with spaghetti. Serves 4 to 6.

CHILI CON CARNE

2 POUNDS LEAN BEEF
1 POUND FRESH PORK
1 SPANISH ONION, FINELY CHOPPED
4 CLOVES GARLIC, CHOPPED
2 TABLESPOONS BACON FAT
1 PINT GOOD BEEF STOCK
4 TABLESPOONS CHILI POWDER
1 TABLESPOON FLOUR
2 BAY LEAVES
½ TEASPOON POWDERED CUMIN
½ TEASPOON OREGANO
SALT AND FRESHLY-GROUND BLACK PEPPER
BOILED RED BEANS
RICE

Cut beef and pork into bite-sized cubes, trimming fat as you go. Brown meat, chopped onion and chopped garlic in bacon fat in a thick-bottomed, flame-proof casserole.

Cover meat with boiling beef stock; bring again to the boil; cover casserole and simmer gently for about 1 hour.

Blend chili powder with flour in a little of the hot pan juices and add to the casserole at the same time as bay leaves, cumin, *oregano* and freshly-ground black pepper and salt, to taste.

Simmer over low heat until meat is tender. Check seasoning and serve with boiled red beans and rice. Serves 4 to 6.

New England Boiled Dinner

New England, the group of Eastern states that formed the Federal Union – with New York, Pennsylvania and Virginia – in the days when the American flag had only thirteen stars, has given us many great dishes.

The Irish cooks of the great New England first families whose fortunes came from the four-masted sailing ships which plied the seven seas prided themselves on their plain, good, substantial and nourishing fare. And this love of hearty food, with no frills or furbelows, has come down to us to this very day.

I like New England clam chowder made with native clams (quahaugs) so fresh that the salty tang of the sea is still with them, combined with crisp bits of bacon, potatoes and onions simmered to pale gold, and bathed in a rich soup of milk, cream and butter; Saturday night suppers of Boston baked beans, cooked with tender salt pork and a touch of dry mustard, sweet with dark molasses and brown sugar, sometimes laced with Jamaican rum. This unctuous dish, Puritan cousin of the French *cassoulet*, is at its succulent best when served with its traditional partner, steamed Boston brown bread, rich and moist.

I like Sunday breakfasts of deep-fried codfish cakes; grilled Maine lobsters with drawn butter; the fabulous outdoor feast that is the New England clam bake, a misnomer really, for clams make up only one item of this outdoor dinner and 'bake' is a relative term, for the clams and their companions – corn on the cob, lobsters, sausages, frankfurters and sweet and white potatoes – are actually steamed between layers of fresh seaweed, heated on a base of white-hot stones.

But best of all, in my estimation, is the New England boiled dinner. There is no misnomer here, for this is indeed a complete meal, a transatlantic echo of the great country dish that has found its way into the cuisine of every great nation – the hot pot of cock and beef of old England, the *pot-au-feu royale* of France, the *olla podrida* of Spain, and the *bollito misto* of Italy. The New England boiled dinner is an earthy concoction of corned brisket of beef, plump boiling fowl and fat salt pork, simmered until fork-tender with a quartered cabbage, carrots, turnips, onions and potatoes, and served with boiled beetroot, horse-radish sauce and pickles.

To make this country dish, ask your butcher to 'corn' or 'salt' a brisket of beef in brine and saltpetre for seven days. Silverside, too, makes for very good eating.

NEW ENGLAND BOILED DINNER

4–5 POUNDS CORNED BRISKET OF BEEF
1 POUND SALT PORK
2 BAY LEAVES
6 PEPPERCORNS
1 BOILING CHICKEN
6 LARGE CARROTS, SCRAPED
6 MEDIUM ONIONS, PEELED
6 LARGE POTATOES, PEELED
2 MEDIUM TURNIPS, PEELED AND QUARTERED
1 MEDIUM HEAD CABBAGE, QUARTERED
2 MEDIUM BEETROOT, QUARTERED
HORSE-RADISH SAUCE
PICKLES

Wipe corned beef with a damp cloth; tie into shape and put into a large stock-pot or heavy-bottomed saucepan. Add enough cold water to cover and bring to the boil. Drain and rinse beef. Repeat this operation.

Cover brisket with boiling water; add salt pork, bay leaves and peppercorns; cover and simmer over low heat for 3 to 4 hours, or until meat is tender, adding chicken after first hour.

Cool slightly; skim excess fat and add carrots, onions, potatoes and turnips. Cook for about 20 minutes, then add cabbage wedges; cook until cabbage and vegetables are crisp and tender.

Serve the beef on a platter garnished with vegetables and with cooked beetroot. Accompany with horse-radish sauce and pickles. Serves 8 to 10.

BOILED BEEF AND CARROTS

4–5 POUNDS ROUND OF BEEF
2 QUARTS WATER
24 LARGE CARROTS
2 TURNIPS
2 SPANISH ONIONS
2 STALKS CELERY
8 PEPPERCORNS
SALT
2 CLOVES
1 BOUQUET GARNI (BAY LEAF, 2 SPRIGS CELERY TOPS, 4 SPRIGS PARSLEY)

Wash and prepare vegetables; tie beef securely; cover with water and bring to the boil. Lower heat so that the water barely simmers; cover casserole and simmer for 20 minutes. Skim; add peppercorns, salt to taste, cloves and *bouquet garni*; cover and simmer gently for 3 to 4 hours or until the meat is just tender and the vegetables are soft.

To serve: remove meat from broth; untie it and place on a heated serving dish; serve the vegetables on another dish. Accompany with onion sauce, dumplings or buttered noodles.

CHINESE STEAMED BEEF

2 POUNDS RUMP STEAK
½ POUND BUTTON MUSHROOMS
2–4 TABLESPOONS COARSELY-CHOPPED ONION
2 TABLESPOONS SOY SAUCE
4 TABLESPOONS OLIVE OIL
1 LEVEL TABLESPOON CORNFLOUR
2 TABLESPOONS DRY WHITE WINE
FRESHLY-GROUND BLACK PEPPER
STEAMED RICE

Slice rump steak thinly across the grain. Wash mushrooms and slicc thinly. Chop onion coarscly. Put mcat and vcgctables in a shallow heat-proof dish. Combine soy sauce, olive oil, cornflour and dry white wine and pour over meat and vegetables. Season to taste with freshly-ground black pepper and place dish in steamer or on a rack in a large saucepan with about 2 inches of rapidly boiling water.

Cover and steam for 15 minutes.

Serve hot from steamer, accompanied by steamed rice. Serves 4 to 6.

GREAT DISHES OF THE WORLD

CHAPTER 8

LAMB

Middle East Kebabs

Kebab (*kabab* or *kabob*) means 'to grill or broil' in most of the languages in which it appears. *Shish* (Turkish and Middle Eastern) or *sikh* or *seekh* (Indian) means 'skewer'. So that any food skewered and grilled is a *shish* or *sikh kebab.* In Britain, *kebab* commonly means skewered bits of meat, or meat and vegetables. grilled over charcoal, or under a gas or electric grill.

On a recent trip to Morocco, I was fascinated by the little stalls in the streets, where cooks grilled small *brochettes* of meat – tiny cubes of beef, lamb or liver – over portable charcoal braziers in the open market-places. The tantalising aroma of these grilled meats with their pungent sauces and spices made my mouth water in every city I visited. The famous *saté* of Java is a similar version of this dish. Made of beef, pork, lamb or chicken, the *saté* consists of nothing but meat, marinated in soy sauce and spices, grilled on thin skewers of bamboo.

But of all the skewered meat dishes in the world, by far the best known – and the most easily translatable in our kitchens – is Turkish *shish kebab.* I like to serve this dish with a rice pilaff or on a bed of shredded lettuce lightly dressed with oil and lemon juice, or with skewered vegetables. Or combine the two for a *shish kebab* with vegetables. Green pepper, tomatoes, poached onions, sliced baby marrow or aubergines and button mushrooms all lend their flavours and textures to this magnificent dish.

First marinate your meat – the Turks like lamb, cut from the leg; others prefer beef. Let it remain in this mixture for at least 4 hours, or overnight. Then thread the cubed meat on long skewers alternately with the vegetables of your choice.

Do not push the pieces of meat and vegetables too closely together. Grill about 4 inches from charcoal, or gas or electricity, until the meat is medium brown, basting with marinade juices from time to time.

Nothing beats a rotating spit for *kebabs*. This method ensures the even cooking and self-basting of precious juices. And if the weather is too cool for outdoor cookery, *kebabs* can be grilled indoors with ease. Electric or gas-fired grills or 'rotisserie' spits equipped with skewers approximate the outdoor fire. Or simply arrange the skewers under the grill and brown the meat, fish, vegetables or fruit as you would a steak or chops.

When cooking on a skewer, be careful not to let the skewered meat touch the metal grill. If you do, some of the meat will stick to the hot metal. And when you attempt to turn the skewer, the meat or vegetables may stick to the grid and some pieces may fall into the fire. It is much wiser to suspend the skewers above the flames and away from the hot metal grid. When cooking outdoors, for instance, I usually place a brick on each end of the grid and place the ends of the skewers on the bricks so that they can be turned easily.

TURKISH LAMB KEBABS

2 POUNDS LAMB, CUT FROM LEG
4 SMALL GREEN PEPPERS, CAPS AND SEEDS REMOVED
4 TOMATOES
4 SMALL ONIONS, POACHED
2 BABY MARROWS, SLICED THICKLY
4 MUSHROOM CAPS
4 METAL SKEWERS

MARINADE SAUCE:
6 TABLESPOONS OLIVE OIL
4 TABLESPOONS SHERRY
1–2 CLOVES GARLIC, FINELY CHOPPED
¼ SPANISH ONION, FINELY CHOPPED
2 TABLESPOONS FINELY-CHOPPED PARSLEY
1 LEVEL TEASPOON OREGANO
SALT AND FRESHLY-GROUND BLACK PEPPER

Combine marinade ingredients in a mixing bowl. Cut meat into 1½-inch squares and place in marinade mixture, making sure each piece of meat is properly covered. Cover bowl with a plate and refrigerate for 12 to 24 hours. Turn meat several times during marinating period.

When ready to cook, place meat on large skewers alternately with green pepper, tomato, poached onion, sliced baby marrow and mushroom caps.

Brush meat and vegetables with marinade sauce and cook over charcoal or under grill until done, turning skewers frequently and basting several times during cooking. Serve kebabs with rice pilaff. Serves 4.

MOROCCAN SKEWERED LAMB

¾ POUND LAMB
¾ POUND LAMB FAT
1 LEEK
½ SPANISH ONION
1 TABLESPOON CHOPPED CHERVIL
1 LEVEL TEASPOON SALT
1 LEVEL TEASPOON EACH OF POWDERED CUMIN AND GINGER, AND CRUSHED BLACK PEPPER
CAYENNE PEPPER AND PAPRIKA
2 TABLESPOONS OLIVE OIL

Cut lamb and fat into equal-sized cubes about ¾ inch square and place in a large bowl. Pound white part of leek, onion, chervil and salt in a mortar; add to meat and sprinkle with powdered cumin, ginger, crushed black pepper, cayenne and paprika, and oil. Mix well and let meat marinate in this mixture for at least 2 hours. Cook as above. Serves 4.

RUSSIAN SKEWERED LAMB

1½ POUNDS BONED LAMB
½ POUND GREEN BACON (1 PIECE)
½ POUND RAW GAMMON (1 PIECE)
SALT AND FRESHLY-GROUND BLACK PEPPER
OLIVE OIL
¾ POUND RICE
2 TABLESPOONS FINELY-CHOPPED PARSLEY

Cut lamb, bacon and gammon into bite-sized pieces. Blanch bacon and gammon; drain.

Place lamb, bacon and gammon on skewers alternately. Season to taste with salt and freshly-ground black pepper; brush with olive oil and cook over charcoal or under grill for 10 to 15 minutes, or until done.

Cook rice in usual way. Serve skewers on bed of rice. Sprinkle with finely-chopped parsley. Serves 4 to 6.

MOUSSAKA

1 SPANISH ONION, FINELY CHOPPED
1–2 CLOVES GARLIC, FINELY CHOPPED
4 TABLESPOONS OLIVE OIL
1 POUND COOKED LAMB, DICED, CHOPPED FINELY OR MINCED
½ POUND MUSHROOMS, CHOPPED
4–6 TOMATOES, PEELED, SEEDED AND CHOPPED
2 TABLESPOONS PARSLEY, FINELY CHOPPED
SALT AND FRESHLY-GROUND BLACK PEPPER
1–2 TABLESPOONS TOMATO CONCENTRATE
4–6 TABLESPOONS RICH BEEF OR VEAL STOCK
4–6 AUBERGINES, UNPEELED
FLOUR
OLIVE OIL
4–6 TABLESPOONS GRATED PARMESAN

Sauté onion and garlic in olive oil until transparent. Add finely-chopped lamb and continue cooking, stirring from time to time, until brown. Add chopped mushrooms, peeled, seeded and chopped tomatoes, parsley and salt and pepper, to taste, and cook until onion is tender.

Dilute tomato concentrate in stock – beef or veal – add to meat and vegetable mixture and simmer for 10 minutes.

Slice aubergines, unpeeled, lengthwise in thin slices; dust

with flour and fry on both sides in hot olive oil. Drain aubergine slices on absorbent paper. Line a baking dish with slices of aubergine; spread a layer of stuffing mixture on them; sprinkle lightly with grated Parmesan; cover with a layer of aubergines and continue this process until baking dish is full, ending with a layer of aubergines. Sprinkle with grated Parmesan and bake in a moderate oven (375°F. Mark 4) until the top has browned nicely. Serve hot, or it is also very good cold and can be successfully re-heated.

MOUSSAKA VARIATIONS

1. Add grated Parmesan and freshly-grated breadcrumbs to meat and vegetable mixture and proceed as above.
2. Add grated Parmesan and freshly-grated breadcrumbs to meat and vegetable mixture. Fill aubergine-lined baking dish with mixture; pour over a well-flavoured white sauce; top with aubergine slices and grated cheese; bake as above.
3. Beat 2 eggs; blend in 2 tablespoons flour; add 1 jar yoghourt and whisk to a creamy sauce. Pour this sauce over meat and vegetable mixture and proceed as above.
4. Dice 1 aubergine; dust with flour; sauté in oil and combine with meat and vegetable mixture in original recipe or in any of the variations above.

MOROCCAN KEFTA

1½ POUNDS LAMB, TAKEN FROM THE LEG
½ POUND LAMB FAT, OR MADE UP TO THIS AMOUNT WITH BEEF SUET
½ SPANISH ONION, FINELY CHOPPED
6–8 MINT LEAVES, FINELY CHOPPED
6–8 SPRIGS PARSLEY, FINELY CHOPPED
½ TEASPOON DRIED MARJORAM
SALT AND FRESHLY-GROUND BLACK PEPPER
¼ TEASPOON EACH POWDERED CUMIN, CAYENNE PEPPER AND PAPRIKA
1 GENEROUS PINCH OF 2 OR MORE OF THE FOLLOWING: POWDERED NUTMEG, CINNAMON, CLOVES, GINGER AND CARDAMOM
BUTTER

Put lamb, fat and Spanish onion through the finest blade of your mincer 3 times. Combine in a large mixing bowl with finely-chopped mint leaves, parsley, marjoram, salt, pepper and spices, to taste. Mix well. The *kefta* mixture should be very highly flavoured.

Form into little balls the size of a marble and poach gently in water for 10 minutes. Then sauté gently in butter until lightly browned.

Finally, simmer in *kefta* sauce for at least 10 minutes before serving. Serve in sauce or on a bed of rice with sauce apart. Serves 6 to 8.

KEFTA SAUCE

1 POUND TOMATOES, PEELED, SEEDED AND COARSELY CHOPPED
½ SPANISH ONION, FINELY CHOPPED
2 TABLESPOONS FINELY-CHOPPED PARSLEY
1 CLOVE GARLIC, FINELY CHOPPED
4 TABLESPOONS OLIVE OIL
½ PINT WATER
PAPRIKA AND CAYENNE PEPPER
SALT

Combine ingredients (sauce should be very highly flavoured) and simmer for 1 hour, uncovered.

ROAST SADDLE OF LAMB

1 SADDLE OF LAMB
SALT AND FRESHLY-GROUND BLACK PEPPER
SOFTENED BUTTER
CRUSHED ROSEMARY
¼ PINT WATER
¾ PINT BEEF STOCK
1 TABLESPOON BUTTER
1 TABLESPOON FLOUR

Spread saddle of lamb with softened butter and sprinkle with salt, freshly-ground black pepper and crushed rosemary, to taste.

Place saddle in a moderately hot oven (400°F. Mark 5); pour water into roasting pan and roast lamb for about 1 hour, basting frequently.

Remove roast from oven; discard fat from pan; add well-flavoured beef stock and a *beurre manié* (1 tablespoon butter kneaded to a smooth paste with 1 tablespoon flour); and cook over a high flame, stirring all crusty bits from sides of pan into sauce, until sauce is smooth and thick. Strain and keep warm. Serve saddle of lamb with puréed potatoes and peas. Serve gravy separately.

ROAST SADDLE OF LAMB À L'ARLÉSIENNE

1 SADDLE OF LAMB
SOFTENED BUTTER
SALT AND FRESHLY-GROUND BLACK PEPPER
CRUSHED ROSEMARY
¼ PINT WATER
¾ PINT HOT BEEF STOCK
1 TABLESPOON BUTTER
1 TABLESPOON FLOUR
6 MEDIUM-SIZED BABY MARROWS
6 TOMATOES, SLICED
1 SPANISH ONION, FINELY CHOPPED
SPRIGS OF THYME
CLOVES OF GARLIC, UNPEELED
OLIVE OIL

GARNISH:
24 NEW POTATOES, BOILED AND SAUTÉED IN BUTTER
6 TABLESPOONS FINELY-CHOPPED MUSHROOMS AND 2 TABLESPOONS EACH FINELY-CHOPPED PARSLEY AND TRUFFLES, SAUTÉED IN BUTTER
WATERCRESS

Spread saddle of lamb with softened butter and sprinkle with salt, pepper and crushed rosemary, to taste.

Place saddle in a moderately hot oven (400°F. Mark 5); pour water into roasting pan and roast lamb for 1 hour, basting frequently.

Remove roast from oven; discard fat from pan; add well-flavoured beef stock and a *beurre manié* (1 tablespoon butter kneaded to a smooth paste with 1 tablespoon flour) and cook over a high flame, stirring all crusty bits from sides of pan into sauce, until sauce is smooth and thick. Strain and keep warm.

Slice each baby marrow lengthwise into 4 or 5 slices, without cutting all the way through, to make a fan shape. Place a thin slice of tomato in each opening. Place partially roasted saddle of lamb in an oiled baking tin on which you have scattered finely-chopped onion, sprigs of thyme, garlic and salt and freshly-ground black pepper, to taste. Surround with stuffed marrows; sprinkle with a little olive oil and continue to roast for about 45 minutes, or until meat is tender (allow about 15 minutes per pound in all).

To serve: place lamb on a large heated serving dish; place stuffed baby marrows at one end of the dish and sautéed potatoes at the other. Sprinkle vegetables with finely-chopped mushrooms, parsley and truffles, which you have sautéed in butter. Garnish with watercress. Serve gravy separately.

BARBECUED SADDLE OF LAMB

1 SADDLE OF LAMB
2 CLOVES GARLIC, FINELY CHOPPED
4 TABLESPOONS OLIVE OIL
4 TABLESPOONS SOY SAUCE
2 TABLESPOONS DRY WHITE WINE
SALT AND FRESHLY-GROUND BLACK PEPPER

Rub saddle of lamb with a damp cloth. Combine finely-chopped garlic, olive oil, soy sauce, dry white wine and salt and freshly-ground black pepper, to taste, in a bowl.

Rub this mixture well into whole saddle of lamb and allow the flavour to penetrate for at least 1 hour. Just before cooking, rub more of the mixture into the lamb, reserving some for basting.

Place the saddle in a slow oven (325°F. Mark 2) and roast for 15 to 20 minutes per pound, basting from time to time, or until roast is pink and rare.

ROAST SHOULDER OF LAMB WITH HERBS

1 SHOULDER OF LAMB
2 TABLESPOONS OLIVE OIL
SALT AND FRESHLY-GROUND BLACK PEPPER
6 SPRIGS EACH THYME, BAY LEAVES, ROSEMARY

Have your butcher bone and trim a shoulder of lamb ready for rolling. Do not have him roll it.

Lay lamb out flat; brush with olive oil and sprinkle with salt and freshly-ground black pepper, to taste. Place 2 sprigs each thyme, bay leaves and rosemary on lamb; roll up neatly and tie securely. Place 4 sprigs each thyme, bay leaves and rosemary around lamb and tie securely. Brush with olive oil and roast in a hot oven (450°F. Mark 7) for 20 minutes; lower heat to moderate (375°F. Mark 4) and cook until tender.

BARBECUED LAMB PROVENÇAL

1 LEG OF LAMB (6–7 POUNDS)
6 CLOVES GARLIC, FINELY CHOPPED
6 TABLESPOONS FRESH BREADCRUMBS
6 TABLESPOONS FINELY-CHOPPED PARSLEY
6 TABLESPOONS SOFTENED BUTTER
JUICE OF 1 LEMON
SALT AND FRESHLY-GROUND BLACK PEPPER

Make a smooth paste of finely-chopped garlic, parsley, fresh breadcrumbs, butter and lemon juice, and season to taste with salt and freshly-ground black pepper. Wipe lamb with a damp cloth and spread with this paste, pressing it well in so seasonings do not fall off during the cooking. Allow the flavour to penetrate for at least 1 hour. Start fire at least an hour before cooking time to have a bed of ash-grey coals to cook over. Balance lamb on the spit, inserting the spit in line with the bone so it can rotate freely and easily. Roast for 1½ to 2 hours for a leg of lamb as pink and juicy as I like it, longer if you like it less rare. Allow the meat to rest on the spit for 10 minutes to retain juices before removing spit. Serves 6 to 8.
Note: A leg of lamb may be roasted on a rack in a roasting pan in a slow oven (325° to 350°F. Mark 2 to 3) for 15 to 20 minutes per pound Provençal dressing will give same wonderful flavour.

CHUMP CHOPS STUFFED WITH CHICKEN LIVERS

4 CHUMP LAMB CHOPS
4 CHICKEN LIVERS, CHOPPED
2 SHALLOTS, FINELY CHOPPED
3 TABLESPOONS BUTTER
1 TABLESPOON LEMON JUICE
SALT AND FRESHLY-GROUND BLACK PEPPER
1 PINCH CURRY POWDER
4 LARGE MUSHROOM CAPS
WATERCRESS

Trim fat from thick chump chops and slit a pocket in each. Sauté chicken livers and shallots in 2 tablespoons butter until livers are cooked.

Mash livers to a smooth paste with lemon juice and season to taste with salt, pepper and curry powder. Stuff chops with this mixture and grill in usual manner.

Sauté mushroom caps until tender in remaining butter. To serve: place stuffed chops on heated platter; set 1 mushroom on each chop and garnish with fresh watercress. Serves 4.

ROAST LEG OF LAMB PROVENÇAL

1 LEG OF LAMB (ABOUT 6 POUNDS)
1 TABLESPOON BUTTER
6 CLOVES GARLIC
1½ POUNDS POTATOES, PEELED AND SLICED
SALT AND FRESHLY-GROUND BLACK PEPPER
4–6 TABLESPOONS FINELY-CHOPPED PARSLEY
½ PINT RICH CHICKEN STOCK

Have your butcher trim and tie a leg of lamb. Butter a shallow fire-proof casserole or gratin dish just large enough to hold leg of lamb comfortably and rub it lightly with a cut clove of garlic. Peel and cut potatoes in thick slices and arrange in the bottom of the dish in overlapping rows. Salt and pepper the potatoes generously. Chop remaining garlic finely and sprinkle over potatoes with finely-chopped parsley. Place the raw lamb on the potatoes and moisten with rich chicken stock.

Roast in a slow oven (325°F. Mark 2) for 1¼ to 1½ hours, or until lamb is pink and tender. If you prefer lamb less pink, increase cooking time. Serve as it is. Serves 8.

MOROCCAN STEAMED LAMB

5 POUNDS LAMB (CUT FROM SHOULDER)
1 LEVEL TABLESPOON COARSE SALT
⅛ LEVEL TEASPOON POWDERED SAFFRON
¼ LEVEL TEASPOON POWDERED CUMIN
FRESHLY-GROUND BLACK PEPPER
4 TABLESPOONS BUTTER
RICE
POWDERED CUMIN
SALT

Combine salt, powdered saffron and cumin, and rub lamb with this mixture. Season to taste with freshly-ground black pepper.

Wrap meat in a clean kitchen towel and place in the top section of a large double steamer over boiling water. (Bottom section of steamer should be three-quarters full.)

Close steamer hermetically with damp towels and steam lamb over a high flame for 3 hours without lifting cover.

Just before serving, sauté lamb in butter until golden. Serve with rice, powdered cumin and salt. Serves 6 to 8.

LAMB CHOPS 'EN CUIRASSE'

6 LAMB CHOPS
6 TABLESPOONS BUTTER
½ POUND MUSHROOMS, FINELY CHOPPED
1 SPANISH ONION, FINELY CHOPPED
2 SLICES HAM, FINELY CHOPPED
SALT AND FRESHLY-GROUND BLACK PEPPER
FLAKY PASTRY
1 EGG, BEATEN
TOMATO SAUCE

Trim lamb chops and sauté in a little butter until golden. Remove and allow to cool. Add remaining butter to pan and sauté finely-chopped mushrooms, onion and ham until vegetables are soft. Season to taste with salt and freshly-ground black pepper. Cool.

Spread mushroom mixture on both sides of each chop. Roll out pastry into 6 circles (big enough to encase chops); place 1 chop on each; wrap in pastry, leaving bone out; moisten join with water and seal securely.

Place pastry-wrapped chops on baking sheet, join side down; brush with beaten egg and bake in a hot oven (450°F. Mark 7) for 15 to 20 minutes. Serve with tomato sauce. Serves 6.

ITALIAN BREADED LAMB CHOPS

- 4–6 BABY LAMB CHOPS
- 1 TABLESPOON OLIVE OIL
- SALT AND FRESHLY-GROUND BLACK PEPPER
- FLOUR
- 1 EGG, BEATEN
- DRY BREADCRUMBS
- 4–6 TABLESPOONS BUTTER
- 4–6 TABLESPOONS OLIVE OIL
- WATERCRESS

Brush lamb chops with olive oil and season to taste with salt and freshly-ground black pepper. Dust chops with flour; dip in beaten egg and roll in dry breadcrumbs.

When ready to serve, sauté in butter and olive oil until golden brown. Garnish with watercress. Serves 4 to 6.

GRILLED MARINATED LAMB CHOPS – I

- 8–10 LOIN LAMB CHOPS
- SALT AND FRESHLY-GROUND BLACK PEPPER
- 2 BAY LEAVES, CRUMBLED
- 2 CLOVES GARLIC, FINELY CHOPPED
- 6 TABLESPOONS OLIVE OIL
- 6 TABLESPOONS DRY WHITE WINE

Have your butcher trim a loin of baby lamb into 8 or 10 chops. Arrange them in a large, flat dish and season to taste with salt and freshly-ground black pepper. Add crumbled bay leaves, finely-chopped garlic, olive oil and dry white wine, and marinate chops in this mixture, turning them once or twice, for at least 2 hours.

Pre-heat grill for 15 to 20 minutes; rub grid with pieces of suet; place chops on it and grill for 2 to 3 minutes on each side. Serve immediately. Serves 4 to 6.

GRILLED MARINATED LAMB CHOPS – II

- 6 LAMB CHOPS
- SALT AND FRESHLY-GROUND BLACK PEPPER
- ¼ PINT LEMON JUICE
- ¼ PINT OLIVE OIL OR CORN OIL
- 4 TEASPOONS FINELY-CHOPPED MINT
- 1 TEASPOON GRATED LEMON RIND
- 1 CLOVE GARLIC, CHOPPED FINELY

Salt and pepper the chops on both sides. Combine remaining ingredients in a small bowl and blend well. Place lamb chops in a flat dish just large enough to hold them and pour marinade mixture over them. Marinate chops for 2 to 4 hours, turning occasionally. When ready to serve, grill over charcoal for 5 minutes; turn and grill 5 minutes longer, or until chops are cooked through. Brush chops with marinade mixture during cooking time. Serves 6.

ROGNONS FLAMBÉS 'LASSERRE'

4 LAMB KIDNEYS
4 TABLESPOONS BUTTER
1–2 TEASPOONS DIJON MUSTARD
SALT AND FRESHLY-GROUND BLACK PEPPER
2–4 TABLESPOONS PORT
ARMAGNAC
2–4 TABLESPOONS PÂTÉ DE FOIE GRAS
1–2 TABLESPOONS LEMON JUICE
BOILED NEW POTATOES

Skin kidneys and sauté quickly in half the butter to allow them to 'stiffen' and brown while still remaining practically raw.

Dice kidneys; melt remaining butter in a thick-bottomed frying pan and add diced kidneys, Dijon mustard and salt and freshly-ground black pepper, to taste, and stir well over a high flame for a minute or two before adding port.

Sprinkle kidneys with Armagnac and ignite, allowing flames to die down and alcohol to disappear, stirring continuously.

Mash *pâté de foie gras* with a fork until well blended; stir into sauce; and cook for a minute or two more until sauce is unctuous and kidneys are tender. Do not allow sauce to boil at any time during its preparation. Just before serving, stir in lemon juice to taste. Serve with boiled new potatoes. Serves 4.

Navarin de Mouton

I first became interested in French casserole cookery when I lived in Paris and Naomi came from her native Burgundy in answer to my advertisement for a housekeeper in the daily press. As soon as I saw her I knew that hire her I must. She was a trim, white-haired, little old lady with fat rosy cheeks, dressed in a strict blue suit and cream flannel blouse, with a narrow black tie that exactly matched the ribbon on her pince-nez.

Naomi had been a *cordon bleu* cook to a famous Marquis and as such was qualified for the highest of positions, but age and recurrent attacks of migraine had taught her to avoid the heavy responsibilities of *haute cuisine* and hire herself out as cook and maid of all work. I engaged her on the spot and for the five long years that I remained in Paris I never regretted the day. For Naomi proved to be a treasure such as I have rarely known, a superb cook, a wonderful housekeeper and a true friend.

Most of Naomi's dishes were of the long, slow-cooking variety – the superb casseroles of meat, fish and game for which France is so famous. And she was an expert in the art of making even the least desirable cuts of meat taste delicious. Sometimes she would marinate the meat in wine, olive oil and herbs to tenderise it before it was cooked. Other times she would 'seize' it in a little butter or olive oil, flavour it with aromatic herbs and a touch of garlic, and then simmer it for hours in a sauce made rich with stock, wine or cream.

I soon learned, however, that long cooking alone cannot ensure perfect results. Naomi taught me to watch the pot to make certain it cooked so gently that it hardly bubbled, for it was only in this way that meat could be kept from going stringy and tough; to add crisp *lardons* of streaky bacon or fat salt pork, along with tiny white onions parboiled to *al dente* tenderness, and button mushrooms sautéed in butter and lemon juice, to lend contrast in texture and flavour to my dishes. And she taught me to give casserole dinners. For Naomi had one failing only – a hangover from her days in the household of the Marquis – she disliked waiting at table, preferring the anonymity of her kitchen to facing the battery of guests in the dining-room. So together we evolved the perfect plan for easy entertaining: one superb casserole dish cooked to perfection, preceded by a cold or hot *hors-d'œuvre*, and followed by a crisp green salad, cheese and fruit. Nothing could be simpler or more delicious. And nothing moved my circle of Paris friends to more heartfelt thanks than one of Naomi's casseroles.

Navarin de mouton was one of her favourites – and to anyone who once tasted Naomi's version of this famous dish, no ordinary lamb stew would ever be the same again. A boned shoulder or breast of young lamb was the secret here, browned in butter and lard with a quartered onion, and simmered in a tomato-flavoured stock with a few quartered turnips.

Naomi always added glazed button onions, sautéed button mushrooms, crisp, golden bacon bits and tiny new potatoes or fresh peas to her *navarin* after the first hour of gentle cooking so that the vegetables and diced bacon would offer texture and flavour contrast to the meltingly tender lamb.

NAVARIN DE MOUTON

2½ POUNDS BONED SHOULDER OR BREAST OF LAMB
2 TABLESPOONS BUTTER
2 TABLESPOONS LARD
1 SPANISH ONION, QUARTERED
2 TABLESPOONS FLOUR
1 PINCH GRANULATED SUGAR
SALT AND FRESHLY-GROUND BLACK PEPPER
1 CLOVE GARLIC, CHOPPED
4 SMALL TURNIPS, QUARTERED
1 BOUQUET GARNI
½ PINT LIGHT STOCK
4 TABLESPOONS TOMATO CONCENTRATE
12 SMALL WHITE ONIONS
4 OUNCES GREEN BACON, DICED
12 SMALL POTATOES, PEELED
¼ POUND FRESH PEAS
2 TABLESPOONS CHOPPED PARSLEY

Cut lamb into cubes and brown in butter and lard with quartered onion. Remove some of the fat; blend in flour, stirring over low heat until butter is slightly thickened; sprinkle with a generous pinch of granulated sugar to give a deeper colour to the sauce and season to taste with salt and freshly-ground black pepper.

Add the finely-chopped garlic, quartered turnips and a *bouquet garni*. Stir in stock and tomato concentrate diluted with a little water. Simmer, covered, in a slow oven (350°F. Mark 3) for 1 hour.

Drain the pieces of lamb in a sieve, removing bits of skin and small bones which have separated from meat during cooking. Allow sauce to cool; skim fat from surface and strain into a clean casserole. Add pieces of lamb. Then glaze button onions; blanch and sauté diced green bacon; peel potatoes; shell peas and add these to the stew. Bring to the boil, and cook, covered, in a slow oven (350°F. Mark 3) for 30 to 40 minutes or until vegetables are cooked and lamb is tender. Sprinkle with chopped parsley just before serving. Serves 4 to 6.

ITALIAN LAMB STEW

1 TABLESPOON LARD
1 TABLESPOON OLIVE OIL
½ POUND FAT SALT PORK, DICED
1 SPANISH ONION, SLICED
2 CLOVES GARLIC, CHOPPED
2½ POUNDS BONED LAMB, CUT INTO BITE-SIZED PIECES
SALT AND FRESHLY-GROUND BLACK PEPPER
1 GENEROUS PINCH MARJORAM
1 GENEROUS PINCH ROSEMARY
¼ PINT DRY RED WINE
4 TABLESPOONS CONCENTRATED TOMATO PURÉE, DILUTED IN WATER

Combine lard and olive oil in a thick pan or flame-proof casserole; when fat begins to bubble, add diced salt pork, sliced onion and garlic and sauté until golden. Add pieces of meat seasoned with salt, pepper, marjoram and rosemary and cook, stirring frequently, until meat is well browned on all sides. Now add dry red wine (one of the rougher Italian ones) and continue cooking until the wine has reduced to half the original quantity. Add diluted tomato purée and enough boiling water to cover the meat. Cover the pan and simmer slowly for about 2 hours, or until the meat is tender. A tablespoon or two of red wine just before serving will add extra *bouquet* to this dish, which should be served directly from the casserole. Serves 4 to 6.

SCOTS HOTCH POTCH

3 POUNDS NECK OF LAMB
2 QUARTS WATER OR STOCK
2 SPANISH ONIONS, COARSELY CHOPPED
SALT AND FRESHLY-GROUND BLACK PEPPER
CELERY SALT
1 POUND PEAS
½ POUND BROAD BEANS
4–6 YOUNG CARROTS
4–6 YOUNG TURNIPS
1 SMALL CAULIFLOWER
4 TABLESPOONS FINELY-CHOPPED PARSLEY

Place neck of lamb in a saucepan with water or stock, coarsely-chopped onion and salt, pepper and celery salt, to taste. Bring slowly to the boil and skim carefully. Add half the quantity of peas with beans and diced carrots and turnips. Bring to the boil again; skim carefully; lower heat and simmer slowly, covered, for 3 hours.

Wash cauliflower well and separate into flowerets. Half an hour before serving, add prepared cauliflower and remaining peas and continue cooking until vegetables are tender. Just before serving, remove lamb; cut into serving pieces and add with finely-chopped parsley. Correct seasoning. Serves 4 to 6.

IRISH STEW

3 POUNDS SHOULDER OF MUTTON
1 POUND ONIONS
2 POUNDS POTATOES
2 STALKS CELERY
½ POUND CARROTS
SALT AND FRESHLY-GROUND BLACK PEPPER
WATER OR LIGHT STOCK, TO COVER
2–3 TABLESPOONS CHOPPED PARSLEY

Cut mutton in 2½-inch cubes; peel and slice onions and potatoes thickly. Trim and slice celery; peel and slice carrots. Place a layer of sliced onions, celery and carrots on the bottom of a heat-proof casserole; cover with a layer of meat, and then a layer of potatoes, and continue filling casserole in alternate layers, finishing with potatoes. Season each layer to taste with salt and freshly-ground black pepper. Add water or light stock to cover; bring to the boil; skim; lower heat and simmer, covered, until tender (almost 3 hours). Just before serving, sprinkle with chopped parsley. Serves 4 to 6.

BLANQUETTE D'AGNEAU

- 2½ POUNDS SHOULDER OR BREAST OF LAMB
- 1 QUART VEAL STOCK (OR STOCK AND WATER)
- 1 TEASPOON SALT
- FRESHLY-GROUND BLACK PEPPER
- 1 SPANISH ONION, STUDDED WITH A CLOVE
- 2 CARROTS
- 1 LEEK
- 1 BOUQUET GARNI (2 OR 3 SPRIGS PARSLEY, 1 SPRIG THYME, 1 BAY LEAF, 1 STALK CELERY)
- 12 BUTTON ONIONS
- 12 BUTTON MUSHROOMS, SIMMERED IN BUTTER AND LEMON JUICE
- 2 TABLESPOONS BUTTER
- 2 TABLESPOONS FLOUR
- 2 EGG YOLKS
- 4 OUNCES CREAM
- LEMON JUICE
- FRESHLY-GRATED NUTMEG

Cut shoulder or breast of lamb, or a combination of the two, into small pieces, and let soak for 12 hours in cold water with a little lemon juice. Change water 2 or 3 times.

Place blanched lamb pieces in a deep flame-proof casserole with enough light veal stock (or stock and water) to cover, add salt and freshly-ground black pepper and bring to the boil. Remove any scum that forms on the surface with a perforated spoon as you would for a *pot-au-feu.*

Add onion studded with clove, carrots, leek and *bouquet garni.* Cover casserole and simmer gently over a very low flame or in a low oven for 1½ hours, or until tender.

Cook button onions in a little water until just firm. Drain and keep warm. Simmer mushroom caps in a little butter and lemon juice and keep warm.

Make a white *roux* by combining 2 tablespoons butter and 2 tablespoons flour in a saucepan. Add 1 pint of stock from the lamb and stir well over a high flame until sauce is smooth and creamy. Lower flame and simmer for 15 minutes, stirring from time to time. Remove saucepan from heat and 'finish' sauce by stirring in egg yolks, cream and the juice of half a lemon.

Drain lamb pieces from the remaining stock (removing bits of bone and fat which have separated from meat in cooking). Cleanse casserole; return lamb pieces to it and strain sauce through a fine sieve over the meat. Stir mushroom caps and onions carefully into the *blanquette*; season with a little grated nutmeg and keep warm in oven with casserole covered until ready to serve. A little more fresh cream and a squeeze of lemon may be added just before serving. Serves 4 to 6.

CARIBBEAN LAMB

3 POUNDS SHOULDER OF LAMB
4 TABLESPOONS BUTTER
2 TABLESPOONS OLIVE OIL
1 TABLESPOON CURRY POWDER
½ LEVEL TEASPOON TURMERIC
⅛ LEVEL TEASPOON POWDERED GINGER
¼ LEVEL TEASPOON CAYENNE PEPPER
SALT AND FRESHLY-GROUND BLACK PEPPER
2 TABLESPOONS LEMON JUICE
½ PINT WELL-FLAVOURED STOCK

GARNISH:
RICE, FRIED BANANAS, CHUTNEYS

Cut lamb in 2½-inch cubes and sauté in butter and olive oil until golden. Combine curry powder, turmeric, ginger, cayenne, and coarse salt and freshly-ground black pepper, to taste, and stir into meat. Sprinkle with lemon juice; stir again and then add well-flavoured stock and enough water barely to cover meat.

Cover casserole and simmer for 30 minutes, or until lamb is tender and sauce is reduced to proper consistency. Serve curry with boiled rice, fried bananas and an assortment of chutneys. Serves 4 to 6.

DAUBE DE MOUTON

3 POUNDS BONED SHOULDER OF MUTTON
THIN STRIPS PORK FAT
THIN STRIPS GREEN BACON
2 ONIONS, SLICED
4 CARROTS, SLICED
1 BOUQUET GARNI (THYME, PARSLEY AND BAY LEAF)
SALT AND FRESHLY-GROUND BLACK PEPPER
1 PINT RED WINE
4 TABLESPOONS OLIVE OIL
¼ POUND GREEN BACON, DICED
1 SPANISH ONION, SLICED
1 CLOVE GARLIC, FINELY CHOPPED
1 PINT HOT STOCK
2–4 TABLESPOONS TOMATO CONCENTRATE
2 TABLESPOONS FINELY-CHOPPED PARSLEY

Cut mutton into 2½-inch cubes; lard each piece with thin strips of pork fat and green bacon and place in a large bowl or earthenware casserole with sliced onions and carrots, a *bouquet garni*, salt and freshly-ground black pepper and red wine. Marinate meat in this mixture for 5 or 6 hours, stirring occasionally.

Remove lamb from marinade; drain. Heat olive oil in a frying pan; sauté diced green bacon and sliced Spanish onion until onion is transparent. Add lamb and sauté with bacon and onion until browned, shaking the pan from time to time. Add chopped garlic; moisten with the marinade which has been reduced to half the original quantity. Pour over 1 pint hot stock mixed with tomato concentrate.

Cover casserole with greaseproof paper and the lid, and cook in a slow oven (325°F. Mark 2) for 3 to 4 hours. Remove from the oven; skim fat from the surface, sprinkle with finely-chopped parsley and serve in the casserole.

CURRIED LAMB LOAF

2 POUNDS BONED LAMB, MINCED
1 TABLESPOON CURRY POWDER
¼ LEVEL TEASPOON EACH GINGER, TURMERIC AND CORIANDER
⅛ LEVEL TEASPOON EACH PAPRIKA AND CAYENNE
1 TABLESPOON FLOUR
COARSE SALT
FRESHLY-GROUND BLACK PEPPER
1 EGG, LIGHTLY BEATEN

COURT-BOUILLON:
1½ PINTS WATER
1 LEVEL TABLESPOON CORIANDER
GENEROUS PINCH THYME

SAUCE:
½ SPANISH ONION, FINELY CHOPPED
BUTTER
SALT AND FRESHLY-GROUND BLACK PEPPER
¼ LEVEL TEASPOON PAPRIKA
¼ LEVEL TEASPOON CORIANDER
¼ PINT YOGHOURT

Combine minced lamb, curry powder, ginger, turmeric, coriander, paprika, cayenne, flour, and salt and pepper, to taste. Add 1 egg; mix well and form meat mixture into a loaf.

Place loaf in a buttered gratin dish just large enough to hold it.

To steam loaf: combine water, coriander and thyme; bring to the boil, place gratin dish in the top of a steamer and steam loaf for 20 to 30 minutes.

To make sauce: Sauté onion in butter until soft; sprinkle with salt, pepper, paprika and coriander, to taste; pour in juices from loaf; stir in yoghourt and heat through. Pour over loaf. Serves 4 to 6.

LAMB CURRY

2½ POUNDS BONED LAMB
4 TABLESPOONS BUTTER
2 TABLESPOONS OLIVE OIL
1 LARGE SPANISH ONION, FINELY CHOPPED
1 CLOVE GARLIC, FINELY CHOPPED
1 GREEN PEPPER, FINELY CHOPPED
2 STALKS CELERY, FINELY CHOPPED
¼ PINT COCONUT MILK (DRIED COCONUT, MILK, BUTTER)
½ PINT WELL-FLAVOURED STOCK
2 OUNCES SEEDLESS RAISINS
4 TABLESPOONS YOGHOURT
RICE
CURRY CONDIMENTS

KARI BLEND:
2 TABLESPOONS CURRY POWDER
½ LEVEL TEASPOON EACH GINGER AND TURMERIC
¼ LEVEL TEASPOON EACH PAPRIKA AND CAYENNE
1 TABLESPOON FLOUR
COARSE SALT
FRESHLY-GROUND BLACK PEPPER

Cut lamb into cubes 1½ inches in diameter and sauté in butter, turning with a wooden spoon to preserve juices, until golden. Remove meat from pan; add olive oil and sauté finely-chopped onion, garlic, green pepper and celery until vegetables are soft.

Mix *kari* blend thoroughly in a bowl and stir into vegetable mixture. (*Note:* if this is your first curry, stir in half the mixture; check flavour of sauce after you have added coconut milk and stock, and add more *kari* until the sauce is of desired pungency.)

Make coconut milk by simmering a handful of dried coconut in ¼ pint milk with 1 tablespoon butter. Press this mixture through a fine sieve; combine with stock and add to vegetables and spices. Cover and simmer for 15 minutes. Add meat and raisins and continue cooking over a low heat until meat is tender, stirring occasionally.

Remove from heat, stir in yoghourt; correct seasoning and serve with boiled rice, *pappadoms*, and traditional curry condiments: mango chutney, apple chutney, preserved *kumquats*, chopped cooked bacon, etc. Serves 4 to 6.

CHAPTER 9

Veal

Osso Buco

Why can't restaurants write menus that really help? First of all, most menus are too full. To offer a choice of seventy different dishes is not really helpful to the diner. Nobody's taste could be so jaded that they could not select a meal they want from a dozen or so alternatives. This *embarras du choix*, in fact, defeats all but the most practised, for the majority of people if faced by too wide a selection (and this is proved by statistics) embarrassedly plump for shrimp cocktail and steak.

I cannot see why at least some of the main dishes on each menu cannot be described in some detail. The White Tower in London and the Forum of the Twelve Caesars in New York have made quite a thing out of their poetic descriptions of the day's specialities. But even a straightforward description of what is in a dish and how it is cooked would prove invaluable. So many people seem to be nervous of betraying their ignorance of what something is, particularly when they are young, that they stick to the same dreary things they have had before every time they eat out. And yet everyone has to eat every dish for the first time some time.

I remember seeing a much travelled sixty-year-old American – knowledgeable beyond belief about the intricacies of Russian and Chinese cooking – tripped by *osso buco*. Much to the scorn of the waiter, she left the marrow. To me it seems that it was the waiter who showed his ignorance in not telling her that the marrow was the climax of the dish, instead of just whisking it away with a distinct sneer.

Because I am always trying something new, some dish I have only heard of before, I am never shy about asking. I discuss constantly with waiters what they mean by the international phrases they use so loosely (and to most waiters, remember, French is as foreign a language as it is to us). They never seem to mind this cross-examination; in fact, they seem rather to like it – at least you are showing an interest in their work and, as Dale Carnegie never tires of pointing out, there is no better way to win friends, etc.

But back to *osso buco*: what other dish hides its most

succulent treats so secretly? How on earth, if you had not had it explained to you, could you be expected to know how to enjoy it? I like to serve *osso buco* accompanied by saffron rice as the main course for a summer luncheon with an Italian flavour. It is a sturdy country dish – rich and full-bodied – that fairly cries out to be eaten in the sun. This is definitely not a dish for dieters; it should be savoured to the very last mouthful.

Serve the lightest of *antipasti* before it and follow with a tossed green salad and a choice of cheeses – Italian, of course – or perhaps a fresh fruit salad macerated in Chianti. Chianti or Bardolo Rosso is the perfect liquid accompaniment.

OSSO BUCO

4 THICK SLICES SHIN OF VEAL
FLOUR
SALT AND FRESHLY-GROUND BLACK PEPPER
2 TABLESPOONS OLIVE OIL
2 TABLESPOONS BUTTER
2 CLOVES GARLIC, FINELY CHOPPED
½ SPANISH ONION, FINELY CHOPPED
¼ PINT BOILING WATER OR LIGHT STOCK
¼ PINT DRY WHITE WINE
2–4 TABLESPOONS TOMATO CONCENTRATE
1 ANCHOVY FILLET, FINELY CHOPPED
4 TABLESPOONS CHOPPED PARSLEY
GRATED RIND OF ½ LEMON
SAFFRON RICE

Choose shin of veal with plenty of meat and have it sawn into pieces 2 inches thick. Dredge pieces with flour; season with salt and freshly-ground black pepper and brown them in olive oil and butter. Add 1 clove of garlic and ½ Spanish onion, finely chopped; pour over boiling water or light stock, white wine and tomato concentrate; cover the pan and simmer for 1½ hours. Then add the anchovy fillet and the remaining garlic clove, both finely chopped. Blend thoroughly, heat through and serve sprinkled with chopped parsley and grated lemon rind, and accompanied by saffron rice. Serves 4.

BLANQUETTE DE VEAU

3 POUNDS SHOULDER OR BREAST OF VEAL
1 QUART VEAL STOCK (OR STOCK AND WATER)
1 TEASPOON SALT
FRESHLY-GROUND BLACK PEPPER
1 SPANISH ONION, STUDDED WITH A CLOVE
2 CARROTS
1 LEEK
1 BOUQUET GARNI (2 OR 3 SPRIGS PARSLEY, 1 SPRIG THYME, 1 BAY LEAF, 1 STALK CELERY)
12 BUTTON ONIONS
12 BUTTON MUSHROOMS SIMMERED IN BUTTER AND LEMON JUICE
2 TABLESPOONS BUTTER
2 TABLESPOONS FLOUR
2 EGG YOLKS
¼ PINT DOUBLE CREAM
LEMON JUICE
FRESHLY-GRATED NUTMEG

Cut shoulder or breast of veal, or a combination of the two, into small pieces and let soak for 12 hours in cold water with a little lemon juice. Change water 2 or 3 times.

Place blanched veal pieces in a deep flame-proof casserole with enough light veal stock (or stock and water) to cover; add salt and freshly-ground pepper and bring to the boil. Remove any scum that forms on the surface with a perforated spoon as you would for a *pot-au-feu.*

Add onion studded with clove, carrots, leek and *bouquet garni.* Cover casserole and simmer gently over a very low flame, or in a very slow oven, for 1½ hours, or until tender.

Cook button onions in a little water until just firm. Drain and keep warm. Simmer mushroom caps in a little butter and lemon juice and keep warm.

Make a white *roux* by combining 2 tablespoons butter and 2 tablespoons flour in a saucepan. Add 1 pint of stock from the veal and stir well over a high flame until sauce is smooth and creamy. Lower flame and simmer for 15 minutes, stirring from time to time. Remove saucepan from heat and 'finish' sauce by stirring in egg yolks, cream and the juice of half a lemon.

Drain veal pieces from the remaining stock (removing bits of bone and fat which have separated from meat in cooking). Cleanse casserole; return veal pieces to it and strain sauce through a fine sieve over the meat. Stir mushroom caps and onions carefully into the *blanquette*; season with a little grated nutmeg and keep warm in oven with casserole covered until ready to serve. A little more fresh cream and a squeeze of lemon may be added just before serving. Serves 4 to 6.

ZÉPHIRES DE RIS DE VEAU 'PLANSON'

3 PAIRS SWEETBREADS
DRY WHITE WINE
WATER
1 POUND FILLET OF VEAL, DICED
SALT AND FRESHLY-GROUND BLACK PEPPER
4 EGG WHITES
1 PINT DOUBLE CREAM
SAUCE BÉARNAISE

Soak sweetbreads in iced water and parboil for 15 minutes in dry white wine and water to cover. Drain; cool and slice them slantwise in 2 or 3 rather thick slices and arrange them in the centre of a veal mousse made in the following manner.

Put diced veal through the finest blade of your mincer; then force through a fine sieve. Add salt and freshly-ground black pepper, to taste. Place the meat in a bowl set in a bowl of ice; stir in egg whites, little by little; then add double cream to this mixture, little by little, beating with a wooden spoon until mixture is light and smooth.

Butter a ring mould and line it with veal mousse. Lay slices of sweetbread in mould, filling up any empty spots with mousse, and top with remaining mousse mixture. Cover with buttered paper. Set the mould in a pan of water and bake in a slow oven (350°F. Mark 3) for 20 to 30 minutes, or until firm. Unmould and serve with *sauce béarnaise*.

MAÎTRE PAUL'S 'BLANQUETTE DE VEAU MENOIGÈRE'

3 POUNDS SHOULDER OR BREAST OF VEAL
2–4 TABLESPOONS BUTTER
12 SMALL ONIONS
1 TABLESPOON FLOUR
WATER
1 BOUQUET GARNI
SALT AND FRESHLY-GROUND BLACK PEPPER
2 EGG YOLKS
JUICE OF ½ LEMON
2 TABLESPOONS DOUBLE CREAM
RICE OR STEAMED NEW POTATOES

Cut veal into 2-inch squares and sauté until golden in butter with 12 small onions in a thick-bottomed, fire-proof casserole. Sprinkle with flour and add just enough water to cover the meat. Add a *bouquet garni* and salt and pepper, to taste.

Simmer veal gently for about 1½ hours; cool for a few minutes. Then remove meat pieces and onions to a hot serving bowl or shallow casserole. Keep warm.

Thicken the sauce in the following manner: whisk egg yolks, lemon juicc and cream in a bowl. Whisking vigorously, add a ladle of boiling sauce from the veal. Pour this *liaison* into the sauce and bring it to the boil, whisking well until thick and creamy. Pass sauce through a fine sieve over the meat and onions and serve immediately, accompanied by rice or steamed new potatoes. Serves 4 to 6.

GOURMANDISE 'BRILLAT SAVARIN' LASSERRE

4 SLICES FILLET OF VEAL (ABOUT 4 OUNCES EACH)
4 TABLESPOONS BUTTER
SALT AND FRESHLY-GROUND BLACK PEPPER
12 BUTTON MUSHROOMS, SLICED VERY THINLY
2 TEASPOONS VERY FINELY CHOPPED SHALLOTS
3–4 TABLESPOONS DRY SHERRY
4 THIN PANCAKES (6–8 INCHES IN DIAMETER)
BUTTER
2–4 TABLESPOONS GRATED GRUYÈRE

Sauté slices of veal fillet in butter until well coloured and three-quarters cooked. Season to taste with salt and pepper. Remove veal and keep warm.

Sauté sliced mushrooms quickly in the butter which you have used for cooking the veal fillet, together with chopped shallots. Add dry sherry, salt and pepper, to taste, and cook, stirring constantly, until sherry is reduced.

Spoon an eighth of mushroom-shallot mixture on one side of each thin pancake; place a nearly-cooked fillet on top, and cover with remaining mushroom-shallot mixture.

Close the pancake as if folding a package and place on a buttered dish; put a knob of butter on top of each and sprinkle with a little freshly-grated Gruyère.

Place in a hot oven (450°F. Mark 7) for 5 minutes and serve immediately.

CÔTE DE VEAU NORMANDE 'BOCAGE FLEURI'

4 VEAL CHOPS
SALT AND FRESHLY-GROUND BLACK PEPPER
2 TABLESPOONS BUTTER
¼ POUND MUSHROOMS, SLICED
4 TABLESPOONS CALVADOS
3 TABLESPOONS FRESH CREAM PER CHOP
2 TART EATING APPLES, PEELED AND QUARTERED
BUTTER

Season veal chops with salt and freshly-ground black pepper and sauté in butter until golden on both sides. Add sliced mushrooms and simmer gently for 10 minutes. Add Calvados; flame; stir in cream. Reduce sauce, stirring continuously, until the sauce is smooth and thick.

Serve veal chops in cream, garnished with quartered apples which you have sautéed in butter. Serves 4.

ESCALOPES 'VISCAYENNES'

1 SPANISH ONION, FINELY CHOPPED
6 CLOVES GARLIC, FINELY CHOPPED
2 TABLESPOONS BUTTER
2 TABLESPOONS OLIVE OIL
4 GREEN PEPPERS, SLICED
8 TOMATOES, COARSELY CHOPPED
PINCH SUGAR
SALT AND FRESHLY-GROUND BLACK PEPPER
4 VEAL ESCALOPES
BUTTER
4–6 TABLESPOONS DRY WHITE WINE
¼ PINT DOUBLE CREAM
BUTTER
FINELY-CHOPPED FRESH PARSLEY

Sauté finely-chopped onion and garlic in butter and oil until transparent. Add sliced green pepper, then the coarsely-chopped tomatoes and cook, stirring continuously, for a minute or two. Season to taste with sugar, salt and pepper, and simmer for 30 minutes.

Sauté veal escalopes in a little butter in a frying pan until cooked through. Arrange on a hot serving platter and keep warm. Stir dry white wine into pan juices and cook over a high flame until sauce is reduced by half. Add cooked tomato, pepper and onion mixture; pour in cream and simmer sauce gently for 5 minutes. Whip butter into the sauce and pour over escalopes. Sprinkle with parsley and serve immediately. Serves 4.

ESCALOPES DE VEAU À LA VALLÉE D'AUGE

4 VEAL ESCALOPES
SALT AND FRESHLY-GROUND BLACK PEPPER
2–4 TABLESPOONS BUTTER
2–4 TABLESPOONS CALVADOS
2 TABLESPOONS DRY WHITE WINE
6 OUNCES SLICED BUTTON MUSHROOMS, SAUTÉED IN BUTTER
¼ PINT DOUBLE CREAM

Season escalopes to taste with salt and freshly-ground black pepper and sauté in butter until tender. Pour over warmed Calvados and flame. Remove from pan and keep warm. Add dry white wine to pan juices. Cook over a high flame, stirring in all the crusty bits from sides of pan. Add sautéed mushrooms and cream. Season to taste with salt and freshly-ground black pepper. Simmer for 2 or 3 minutes; return escalopes to pan and heat through in sauce. Serve immediately. Serves 4.

CÔTE DE VEAU COUPOLE

4 VEAL CHOPS
SALT AND FRESHLY-GROUND BLACK PEPPER
4 TABLESPOONS BUTTER
2 LEVEL TEASPOONS FINELY-CHOPPED SHALLOTS
6 TABLESPOONS CREAM
4 TABLESPOONS PORT
12–16 BUTTON MUSHROOMS, SLICED
4 TABLESPOONS FINELY-CHOPPED HAM
SAUTÉED POTATOES

Season veal chops to taste with salt and freshly-ground black pepper and sauté in butter; when cooked, sprinkle with finely-chopped shallots. Remove from pan and keep warm under grill. Stir cream and port into juices in pan; add sliced mushrooms; heat through and pour sauce over veal.

Sprinkle with finely-chopped ham. Serve with sautéed potatoes. Serves 4.

Illustration on facing page

Lamb

– both cooked and raw – is pictured at Oustao de Baumanière, the elegant three-star French restaurant hidden at the base of the great white cliffs of Les Baux-de-Provence in Southern France. Under the direction of Raymond Thuilier, Beaumanière is one of the great temples of French gastronomy. (Recipe on page 197–8.)

Illustration on following two pages

New England Boiled Dinner

Many great dishes come to us from the rocky shores of New England: Boston Baked Beans, Boston Brown Bread, Boston Cream Pie, New England Clam Chowder and the world-famous New England Clam Bake; but none can compare, to my mind, with New England Boiled Dinner.

VEAL CHOPS 'EN PAPILLOTE'

4 VEAL CHOPS, ½ INCH THICK
SALT AND FRESHLY-GROUND BLACK PEPPER
6 TABLESPOONS BUTTER
2 TABLESPOONS CHOPPED SHALLOTS
½ POUND MUSHROOMS, FINELY-CHOPPED
1 TABLESPOON LEMON JUICE
1 CLOVE GARLIC, CRUSHED
¼ PINT DRY WHITE WINE
2 TABLESPOONS TOMATO PURÉE
2 TABLESPOONS GRATED BREADCRUMBS
2 TABLESPOONS CHOPPED PARSLEY
8 THIN SLICES PROSCIUTTO

Season veal chops with salt and pepper and sauté gently in 4 tablespoons butter until they are golden on both sides (5 to 10 minutes). Remove and keep warm. Prepare a mushroom *duxelles* sauce as follows: add remaining butter to the pan and cook finely-chopped shallots and mushrooms gently in the frying pan with lemon juice and crushed garlic. Add dry white wine, tomato purée, salt and pepper, to taste, grated breadcrumbs and chopped parsley, and cook until a soft paste results.

Cut 8 sheets of white paper into heart shapes big enough to enclose chops; oil them, and place hearts on table in pairs. Place a slice of *prosciutto* in centre of each of 4 sheets. Coat this with the *duxelles* paste. Place veal chop on this; coat with paste and cover with another piece of *prosciutto*. Cover with the other paper hearts, oiled sides down, and roll and pinch the edges together very firmly. Fry these *papillotes* in hot oil until they swell up like balloons; transfer to a baking sheet and bake in a moderately hot oven (400°F. Mark 5) until the meat is tender (about 20 to 25 minutes). Serves 4.

AÏLLADE DE VEAU

2 POUNDS LEAN VEAL
4 TABLESPOONS OLIVE OIL
2 TABLESPOONS FRESH BREADCRUMBS
10 FAT CLOVES GARLIC
4 TABLESPOONS TOMATO CONCENTRATE
SALT AND FRESHLY-GROUND BLACK PEPPER
4 FLUID OUNCES DRY WHITE WINE
2 FLUID OUNCES WATER
RICE

Cut veal into pieces 1 inch square and sauté them in olive oil until golden; add breadcrumbs, garlic and tomato concentrate. Cook over gentle heat, stirring continuously, for 5 to 7 minutes. Season to taste with salt and freshly-ground black pepper. Moisten with dry white wine and water and simmer gently for 1 hour. Serve with rice.

Illustration on facing page

Choucroute Garnie

This is one of the greatest, most extrovert, man-sized party dishes in the world, perfect for informal entertaining.
Choucroute Garnie is a magnificent combination of sauerkraut, pork, sausages and ham, spiked with dry white wine, onion, garlic, herbs and spices. (Recipe on page 228.)

VEAU AU VIN BLANC

1 SHOULDER OR LOIN OF VEAL (3–5 POUNDS)
2 SPANISH ONIONS
4 LARGE CARROTS
4 TOMATOES
¼ POUND BUTTER
SALT AND FRESHLY-GROUND BLACK PEPPER
2 BAY LEAVES
1 LARGE CLOVE GARLIC
4 LARGE SPRIGS PARSLEY
½ PINT DRY WHITE WINE

Ask your butcher to bone, roll and tie your roast. Peel onions and carrots and slice thinly. Skin and seed tomatoes and chop coarsely. Sauté sliced vegetables in half quantity of butter for about 3 minutes. Remove vegetables from pan and brown veal on all sides in pan juices and remaining butter until golden on all sides. Season thoroughly with salt and pepper.

Return vegetables to casserole, making them into a bed for the veal. Add bay leaves, garlic and parsley. Place veal on this bed; moisten with warmed dry white wine; cover casserole and roast in a 280°F. to 300°F. oven (Mark 1) for 2½ to 3 hours, or until tender.

Remove vegetables; keep veal warm; skim fat from pan juices. Moisten vegetables with a little pan juice and purée vegetables in an electric blender. Add and stir into the vegetables enough of the remaining pan juices to make a gravy of the consistency you require.

SALTIMBOCCA ALLA ROMANA

8 THIN SLICES OF VEAL
8 FRESH SAGE LEAVES OR ½ TEASPOON RUBBED SAGE
FRESHLY-GROUND BLACK PEPPER
8 THIN SLICES PROSCIUTTO
BUTTER
2 TABLESPOONS MARSALA OR DRY WHITE WINE
GREEN BEANS, PEAS OR CROÛTONS OF FRIED BREAD

Flatten veal into thin pieces about 4 by 5 inches; place 1 sage leaf (or pinch of rubbed sage) on each slice, and add freshly-ground black pepper to taste (no salt, the *prosciutto* will flavour meat). Cover each slice of veal with *prosciutto* cut to the same size; make each into a small roll and secure with a toothpick. Cook these little rolls in melted butter until they are golden on all sides, and then add Marsala or white wine. Let them cook for a moment, then cover the pan and simmer gently until the veal and ham rolls are quite tender. Remove toothpicks and transfer to a hot dish, surrounded by green beans, fresh peas in butter, or simply with *croûtons* of fried bread. Serves 4.

Vitello Tonnato

It is almost impossible to eat badly in Rome. Italians have always regarded cooking as an art and you have only to visit a Roman street market in mid-morning to see some of the most beautiful raw foods in existence. Great platters of fish in all the colours of the rainbow; fruits and vegetables spilling from the stalls almost to the pavement; golden yellow cheeses; minute purple artichokes; milk-fed lambs and young kid no bigger than hares; tender young leaves of spinach, cabbage and red cabbage, picked when they are hardly more than sprouts, just right to be included raw, along with crisp pink radishes, in the salads so appreciated by the Romans.

Italian fishermen bring back a great variety of excellent fish and shellfish from the nearby sea. Fresh trout comes from the neighbouring hillside streams. And even the wines from the Alban hills – the famous *castelli romani*, which are not castles at all, but little mountain villages – even the wines are young.

You, like every visitor, will soon have your favourite little *trattoria* where on Fridays they make the most delicious *zuppa di pesce* in the world – one of these intimate little places where the inexpensive local wine has the warmth and colour of the sun – and where the company is as good as the food. These restaurants, scattered throughout the city, are for the most part quite cheap: 600 lire to 2,000 lire for lunch, including a bottle of *vino locale* from the hills behind Rome. They are small and usually crowded. The décor with few exceptions is modest, sometimes non-existent. But the food is uniformly excellent.

There are many Italian specialities that are particularly Roman in origin. Begin your meal with the famous *fettucine all' uove*, freshly-made thin egg noodles served with country butter and finely-grated Parmesan cheese; or try *lasagne alla romana*, wide ribbons of *pasta* dough arranged in alternate layers with *ricotta* and *mozzarella* cheese, minced pork and veal, and slices of hard-boiled egg, the whole bathed with two unctuous sauces – a rich *béchamel* and a special *ragù alla romana.*

Then there are the spaghettis: *alla carrettiera*, cooked *al dente* and served with an aromatic sauce of tuna fish, mushrooms and herbs; *alla matriciana*, with a sauce flavoured with chopped bacon and onions; *all' arrabbiata*, a special sauce made hot with chillies and flavoured with herbs and tomatoes; and *alla carbonara*, spaghetti or macaroni served with fried bacon or ham and a sauce of finely-grated Parmesan, butter and the yolks of eggs.

Carciofi alla romana – fresh young artichokes cooked in Roman style – are also on the list of specialities not to be missed. They are utterly delicious in Rome, where they pick them early in the season when they are not much bigger than a baby's fist. The sharp tips of the leaves are cut off, the centre is opened and the whole is baked in oil and herbs. There's no need to remove the 'choke' in the Italian artichoke; all of the plant may be eaten, including the stem.

Romans are not, as a rule, overfond of roasts, steaks or chops. But Rome's own *abbacchio* – milk-fed lamb – is an exception. *Abbacchio* is wonderfully tender and delicate in flavour whether it is cooked *al forno*, in the oven, with a breath of rosemary, or *alla cacciatora*, hunter's style, with tomatoes, peppers, garlic, wine and herbs. *Saltimbocca alla romana* is a perfect way of giving much needed flavour to veal. Here the Roman çook combines thin pieces of tender veal with slices of *prosciutto*, flavours them with sage and fries them in butter.

One of my favourite Italian summer dishes is *vitello tonnato*, lightly poached veal bathed in a rich tuna fish and anchovy sauce. Try Italian 'tunnied veal' as the cold first course for a company dinner, or as the refreshing main course for an outdoor luncheon in the sun. Serve a chilled white wine with it and follow with a crisp green salad.

VITELLO TONNATO

1 LEG OF VEAL (2½–3 POUNDS WHEN BONED AND TRIMMED)
6 ANCHOVY FILLETS
SEVERAL BAY LEAVES
1 SPANISH ONION, SLICED
2 CARROTS, SLICED
2 STALKS CELERY, SLICED
2 SPRIGS PARSLEY
2 CLOVES
SALT AND FRESHLY-GROUND BLACK PEPPER
½ PINT DRY WHITE WINE (OPTIONAL)

TUNA FISH SAUCE:
¾ PINT WELL-FLAVOURED MAYONNAISE
6 OUNCES TUNA FISH
6 ANCHOVY FILLETS
1 TEASPOON CAPERS
2 TABLESPOONS LEMON JUICE
FRESHLY-GROUND BLACK PEPPER
LEMON SLICES

Have your butcher bone and tie a piece of leg of veal (2½ to 3 pounds when boned and trimmed). Cut anchovy fillets into small pieces; pierce holes in surface of meat and insert pieces of anchovy fillet into holes. Top roast with bay leaves. Then place rolled meat in a flame-proof casserole with sliced onion, carrots, celery, parsley, cloves and salt and pepper, to taste.

Pour in dry white wine and add just enough water to cover meat (or use water only); bring it slowly to the boil, turn down heat, cover casserole, and simmer veal for 1½ to 2 hours. When veal is tender, remove cord and skewers and allow it to cool in the stock.

When cold, drain well and place in a bowl, and cover with tuna fish sauce; cover bowl and let the meat marinate in the sauce overnight.

Three hours before serving, remove veal from sauce; slice

thinly; arrange slices on a serving dish and cover with sauce which you have thinned with a little veal stock or olive oil. I blend mine in the electric blender. Refrigerate until ready to serve. Serve with sliced lemon.

To make tuna sauce: Make a thick mayonnaise. Pound tuna fish, anchovy fillets and capers with lemon juice and freshly-ground black pepper until smooth. Combine with mayonnaise in electric blender and blend (adding a little veal stock if too thick) until the sauce is smooth and creamy.

Note: Remainder of veal stock can be used as the base for a delicious vegetable soup.

MAYONNAISE:

2 EGG YOLKS
¼ LEVEL TEASPOON DRY MUSTARD
SALT AND FRESHLY-GROUND BLACK PEPPER
LEMON JUICE
½ PINT OLIVE OIL

Combine egg yolks with mustard, salt and pepper in a bowl; mix well; then add olive oil slowly, drop by drop, whisking all the time with a fork or rotary beater until mayonnaise is of a good thick consistency. Add lemon juice and more salt and pepper to taste. This will make a more than sufficient quantity for the above recipe.

HUNGARIAN VEAL GULYAS

2 SPANISH ONIONS, FINELY CHOPPED
2 CLOVES GARLIC, FINELY CHOPPED
2 TABLESPOONS LARD
2½ POUNDS BONED VEAL
2 LEVEL TABLESPOONS PAPRIKA
¼ LEVEL TEASPOON CARAWAY SEED
1 BAY LEAF
1 GENEROUS PINCH EACH MARJORAM AND THYME
SALT AND FRESHLY-GROUND BLACK PEPPER
1 POUND BUTTON MUSHROOMS, SLICED
2 RED PEPPERS, DICED
2 GREEN PEPPERS, DICED
1 TIN ITALIAN PEELED TOMATOES
½ PINT SOUR CREAM

Sauté finely-chopped onions and garlic in lard in a large flame-proof casserole until transparent. Cut veal into 2-inch cubes; add to casserole and sauté until golden on all sides. Sprinkle with paprika and caraway seed; add bay leaf and herbs and simmer gently for 10 minutes.

Season to taste with salt and freshly-ground black pepper. Top with sliced mushrooms, diced peppers and peeled tomatoes. Cover casserole; bring gently to the boil and simmer gently in a very slow oven (290°F. Mark 1) for at least 2 hours, or until tender. Serve with sour cream. Serves 6 to 8.

ROAST LOIN OF VEAL

1 LOIN OF VEAL
SALT AND FRESHLY-GROUND BLACK PEPPER
CRUSHED ROSEMARY
2–4 TABLESPOONS SOFTENED BUTTER
¼ PINT DRY WHITE WINE

Have butcher bone and trim loin of veal. Season to taste with salt, freshly-ground pepper and crushed rosemary. Spread with softened butter and roast the meat in a moderate oven (375°F. Mark 4) for about 18 to 20 minutes per pound, or until it is well done, basting frequently. Add a little hot water if fat tends to scorch during cooking. Remove veal from oven; add dry white wine to roasting pan and make a thin sauce in the usual manner.

ROAST BREAST OF VEAL

3–4 POUNDS BREAST OF VEAL
LEMON JUICE
SALT AND FRESHLY-GROUND BLACK PEPPER
½ POUND SAUSAGE MEAT
½ SPANISH ONION, FINELY CHOPPED
2 TABLESPOONS BUTTER
1 TABLESPOON FINELY-CHOPPED PARSLEY
1 BEATEN EGG
½ POUND SPINACH, CHOPPED AND SAUTÉED IN BUTTER
SALT, PEPPER AND SPICES
FLOUR
2 TABLESPOONS BUTTER
2 TABLESPOONS OLIVE OIL

Wipe veal on both sides with a damp cloth; sprinkle with lemon juice and season to taste with salt and freshly-ground black pepper.

Combine the following ingredients in a large mixing bowl: sausage meat, finely-chopped onion which you have sautéed in butter until transparent, finely-chopped parsley, beaten egg, sautéed spinach, and salt, pepper and spices, to taste. Mix well. Lay this stuffing in the centre of the veal; make into a neat roll and sew up with fine string.

Dust the veal roll with flour; place it in a roasting pan with 2 tablespoons each butter and olive oil and roast it in a slow oven (325°F. Mark 2) for about 1½ to 2 hours, basting frequently with fat.

POACHED BREAST OF VEAL

1 BREAST OF VEAL, STUFFED AS ABOVE
2 SPANISH ONIONS
6 SMALL LEEKS
6 CARROTS
6 SMALL TURNIPS
1 BOUQUET GARNI
WATER OR LIGHT STOCK

Stuff breast of veal as in recipe above; combine with prepared vegetables – onions, leeks, carrots and turnips – and poach gently with *bouquet garni* in salted water or a light stock until tender. Serve surrounded by vegetables.

VEAL PARMIGIANA

4 THIN VEAL ESCALOPES
1 BEATEN EGG
2 OUNCES BREADCRUMBS
3 TABLESPOONS GRATED PARMESAN
SALT AND FRESHLY-GROUND BLACK PEPPER
2 TABLESPOONS OLIVE OIL
BUTTER
½ PINT HOT TOMATO SAUCE
MOZZARELLA CHEESE

Dip escalopes in beaten egg, then in breadcrumbs mixed with grated Parmesan cheese and seasoned to taste with salt and freshly-ground black pepper. Let breaded escalopes stand for 10 minutes.

Sauté escalopes in olive oil until cooked through; then place them in a shallow, well-buttered gratin dish. Pour over tomato sauce; top with thin strips *mozzarella* cheese and bake in a moderate oven (375°F. Mark 4) for 10 to 15 minutes, or until cheese melts and browns.

SAUTÉED VEAL PATTIES

1 POUND RAW VEAL
2 OUNCES COOKED HAM
2 OUNCES SAUSAGE MEAT
½ SPANISH ONION, FINELY CHOPPED
1 CLOVE GARLIC, FINELY CHOPPED
2 TABLESPOONS BUTTER
½ LEVEL TEASPOON THYME
2 TABLESPOONS FINELY-CHOPPED PARSLEY
SALT AND FRESHLY-GROUND BLACK PEPPER
1 CUP STALE BREADCRUMBS
¼ PINT MILK
1 BEATEN EGG
FLOUR
OLIVE OIL
BUTTER
DRY WHITE WINE OR STOCK

Put raw veal, cooked ham and sausage meat through finest blade of your mincer 3 times. Sauté finely-chopped onion and garlic in butter until transparent. Combine minced meats and sautéed vegetables in a large mixing bowl; add thyme, parsley, and salt and pepper, to taste.

Soak breadcrumbs in milk for 5 minutes; press out as much of the milk as you can and add crumbs to meat mixture. Stir in beaten egg and mix well.

Form patties of the veal; dredge with flour and sauté in olive oil and butter for 2 to 3 minutes on each side. Pour off excess fat; cover pan and simmer gently for 15 minutes, turning the patties from time to time. Serve with pan juices to which you have added a little dry white wine or stock.

SAUTÉ DE VEAU

3 POUNDS BONED SHOULDER OF VEAL
FLOUR
SALT AND FRESHLY-GROUND BLACK PEPPER
1 LEVEL TEASPOON PAPRIKA
2 TABLESPOONS BUTTER
2 TABLESPOONS OLIVE OIL
2 ONIONS, FINELY CHOPPED
1 CLOVE GARLIC
1 BOUQUET GARNI
½ PINT VEAL STOCK
¼ PINT DRY WHITE WINE
12 SMALL WHITE ONIONS
4 SMALL CARROTS, SLICED
1 TABLESPOON BUTTER
1 TABLESPOON FLOUR
2 TABLESPOONS CHOPPED PARSLEY
BUTTERED NOODLES OR BOILED NEW POTATOES

Cut boned veal into 2-inch squares; dredge meat with flour; season with salt, pepper and paprika and sauté in hot butter and olive oil until pieces are browned on all sides. Add finely-chopped onions and garlic; allow to cook a little; then add *bouquet garni*, veal stock and white wine. Cover the pan and simmer gently for 45 minutes.

Add small onions and sliced carrots; cover the pan and simmer until the vegetables are tender and the meat cooked through. Remove the herbs, and if you like the sauce to be a little thick, add a *beurre manié* (1 tablespoon flour and 1 tablespoon butter kneaded together and stirred, bit by bit, into the stew until liquid is thick and smooth). Sprinkle with freshly-chopped parsley and serve with buttered noodles or boiled new potatoes. Serves 4 to 6.

SAUTÉ DE VEAU MARENGO

3 POUNDS BONED SHOULDER OF VEAL
FLOUR
SALT AND FRESHLY-GROUND BLACK PEPPER
2 TABLESPOONS BUTTER
2 TABLESPOONS OLIVE OIL
2 ONIONS, FINELY CHOPPED
1 CLOVE GARLIC, FINELY CHOPPED
½ PINT VEAL STOCK
1 STRIP ORANGE PEEL
1 BOUQUET GARNI
2–3 TABLESPOONS TOMATO CONCENTRATE
¼ PINT DRY WHITE WINE
1 TABLESPOON FLOUR
1 TABLESPOON BUTTER
2 TABLESPOONS FINELY-CHOPPED PARSLEY

Cut boned veal into 2-inch squares; dredge meat with flour; season to taste with salt and freshly-ground black pepper. Sauté veal in hot butter and olive oil until pieces are browned on all sides. Add finely-chopped onions and garlic; simmer for a few minutes.

Bring veal stock to the boil; add orange peel, *bouquet garni*, tomato concentrate and dry white wine, and pour over veal pieces; cover the pan and simmer until the meat is cooked through. Remove the herbs, and stir in a *beurre manié* (1 tablespoon flour and 1 tablespoon butter, kneaded together and stirred, bit by bit, into the stew until liquid is thick and smooth). Sprinkle with finely-chopped parsley. Serves 4 to 6.

MOROCCAN BROCHETTES

1 POUND CALF'S LIVER
½ POUND BEEF FAT
SALT AND FRESHLY-GROUND BLACK PEPPER
POWDERED CUMIN
CAYENNE PEPPER

Cut liver into cubes about ¾ inch square; cut fat into slightly smaller cubes. Thread meat and fat on skewers alternately. Just before grilling over charcoal or under the grill, sprinkle with salt, freshly-ground black pepper, powdered cumin and cayenne pepper, to taste. Turn skewers frequently during cooking time. Serves 4.

RIS DE VEAU TRUFFÉ À LA CRÈME

2 PAIRS CALF'S SWEETBREADS
JUICE OF ½ LEMON
COURT-BOUILLON (WHITE WINE, VEAL STOCK AND WATER)
½ PINT BÉCHAMEL SAUCE
1 TABLESPOON FINELY-CHOPPED TRUFFLE
1–2 TABLESPOONS MADEIRA
SALT AND FRESHLY-GROUND BLACK PEPPER
RICE OR VOL-AU-VENT CASES

Soak sweetbreads in acidulated cold water (water and juice of ½ lemon) for 1 hour, changing water when it becomes tinged with pink. Blanch them for 15 minutes in a simmering *court-bouillon* of dry white wine, veal stock and water in equal quantities. When cool, trim and cut into slices 2 inches thick. Add sweetbreads to ½ pint hot *sauce béchamel* and heat thoroughly without letting the sauce boil. Add 1 tablespoon finely-chopped truffle and a little Madeira to the sauce; season to taste with salt and freshly-ground black pepper and serve in a ring of rice or in individual *vol-au-vent* cases.

GREAT DISHES OF THE WORLD

CHAPTER 10

Pork

Choucroute Garnie

Choucroute garnie is the beginning and end of all party meals: perfect for informal parties, beer gatherings and any other hospitable occasion when appetites are keen. Do not attempt to make this dish unless you know seven hearty trenchermen to share it with you. For *choucroute* (sauerkraut) *garnie* (with all the trimmings) is not for the timid, for the wary or for the ubiquitous watchers of weight. This great country dish from Alsace is definitely for those who like to eat and prefer to wash down their hearty fare with generous quantities of chilled lager or dry white wine.

To me, making *choucroute garnie* is as enjoyable as eating it. For when you cook sauerkraut you do not just lump it into a pot. You cook it in a low oven or over a gentle, slow fire, tossing it from time to time with a long fork until it is soft.

For flavour embellishments, you add a little sliced onion, garlic and apple, perhaps a little grated potato, a few caraway seeds, or juniper berries if you have them, and instead of water, stock or dry white wine.

All sorts of changes can be rung upon the accessories cooked with or added to *choucroute* just before serving. Build your *choucroute garnie* on a flavoursome base of sauerkraut, and add your choice of the following: salt pork, smoked ham, a wing or two of goose or partridge, a loin of pork or pork chops, and a combination of every type of sausage you can get your hands on . . . *Bratwurst*, *Knockwurst*, Frankfurt or Vienna sausages, *saucisses de Toulouse* or just plain 'bangers'. In France, a hot, spicy Lorraine sausage is one of the highlights of the feast. I often add a *cotechino* sausage stripped of its casing, cooked with the sauerkraut, and then cut into fat slices just before serving.

Serve your sauerkraut on your largest platter and dress it with cooked meats and sausages, ham and floury boiled potatoes. Serve with mustard, pickles and lashings of chilled lager. *Choucroute garnie* is a party feast you will long remember.

CHOUCROUTE GARNIE

- PORK FAT, THINLY SLICED
- 2 SPANISH ONIONS, SLICED
- 2 COOKING APPLES, CORED AND SLICED
- 4 CLOVES GARLIC, COARSELY CHOPPED
- 4 POUNDS SAUERKRAUT, WELL WASHED
- ½–¾ POUND SALT PORK
- FRESHLY-GROUND BLACK PEPPER
- 6–8 JUNIPER BERRIES, CRUSHED
- DRY WHITE WINE, TO COVER
- 1 BONED LOIN OF PORK
- 1 LARGE GARLIC SAUSAGE
- 8–16 SAUSAGES (BRATWURST, TOULOUSE, KNOCKWURST OR FRANKFURTERS)
- 8 BOILED POTATOES
- 8 SLICES COOKED HAM (OPTIONAL)

Line a deep earthenware casserole or stock-pot with thinly-sliced pork fat; add half the sliced onions, apples and chopped garlic. Place a thick layer of well-washed and drained sauerkraut on top with a piece of salt pork. Grind plenty of black pepper over it; sprinkle with juniper berries and add remaining onions, apples and garlic. Cover with remaining sauerkraut and add just enough dry white wine to cover the sauerkraut. Cover and cook in a 300°F. (Mark 1) oven for 4 to 6 hours. The longer it cooks the better.

A loin of pork, fresh or smoked, is excellent with *choucroute*. Add it to the *choucroute* about 2½ hours before serving. Half an hour later add a large garlic sausage and a selection of small sausages as available. To serve, heap the *choucroute* in the middle of a platter and arrange slices of meat, sliced garlic sausage and other sausages around it.

Serve with boiled potatoes and, if desired, slices of cooked ham. Serves 8 royally.

Bauernschmaus

In cooking, sometimes the simple things are best. When at home, Henri Soulé, the celebrated owner of New York's Pavillon and Côte Basque restaurants, loves to serve *brandade de morue*, a delicious purée of salt cod. Mario Gallati, the guiding light behind three famous London restaurants, the Caprice, the Empress and the Écu de France, like nothing better than a huge plate of chicken wing-tips. René Hure, proprietor of the Hostellerie de la Poste in Avallon, one of France's greatest restaurants, prefers to serve an earthy *pot-au-feu* of beef, pork and chicken, simmered in beef stock, when he entertains special guests.

One of my favourite peasant dishes (worthy, I think, to take its place among the great dishes of the world) is *Bauernschmaus* (a delectable concoction of boiled meats and sauerkraut, graced by the magisterial presence of a huge dumpling), an Austrian speciality famous from Salzburg to Vienna.

It was at the Vienna Culinary Festival held at the Carlton Tower that I renewed my happy acquaintance with this homely dish. Master chef Karl Duch and his team of Viennese experts prepared many delicious meals for us during his stay here: *Leberknödelsuppe* (strong consommé with calf's liver dumplings), *Tafelspitz 'alt Wiener Art* (the specially cut, slow-simmered beef so beloved by the Viennese) served with a chive and horse-radish sauce and a beetroot salad, and *Paprikahuhn 'Franz Lehar'* (poached chicken in a paprika cream sauce) served with *spaetzle* (home-made Viennese egg noodles). But it was the *Bauernschmaus* that I returned to sample time and time again.

Bauernschmaus is very simple to make in our English kitchens and very simple to serve. You will need a loin of pork, a piece of back bacon, sauerkraut, fresh or tinned, and some delicious bread dumplings flavoured with parsley and nutmeg.

BAUERNSCHMAUS

1 LOIN OF PORK (CUT INTO CHOPS)
2 POUNDS SAUERKRAUT, WITH JUICES
BEER OR WATER, TO COVER
1 LEVEL TEASPOON CUMIN (OR CARAWAY) SEED
1–2 CLOVES GARLIC
SALT AND FRESHLY-GROUND BLACK PEPPER
2 LARGE RAW POTATOES, GRATED
2 SPANISH ONIONS, SLICED
2 OUNCES LARD
1 PIECE BACK BACON (SLICED)
12 FRANKFURTER SAUSAGES

Simmer pork with sauerkraut, beer, cumin seed (or caraway), garlic, and salt and freshly-ground black pepper, to taste, for 1½ hours. Stir in grated raw potatoes, moistened with a little cold water. Cook for 2 to 3 minutes more.

Sauté sliced onions in lard until transparent; add to sauerkraut with back bacon and frankfurters, and simmer for 1 hour longer, adding water or more beer if necessary.

To serve: drain the sauerkraut, reserving juices, and pile on a large wooden platter. Surround with 3 kinds of meat; garnish platter with large dumplings and serve the gravy separately, seasoned to taste. Serves 6.

Continued on page 230

DUMPLINGS:
6 ROLLS
¼ PINT MILK
2 EGGS, BEATEN
2 TABLESPOONS FINELY-CHOPPED PARSLEY
SALT, FRESHLY-GROUND BLACK PEPPER AND NUTMEG
1½ OUNCES SIFTED FLOUR

Break up rolls into small pieces and soak in milk. Add eggs, parsley, and salt, pepper and nutmeg, to taste. Then add flour and work mixture into a dough with your hands, adding more flour if the dough is too moist to handle.

Shape dough into 6 balls and drop them into a large saucepan of boiling salted water. Boil for 12 to 15 minutes, uncovered, until dumplings rise to the surface. Skim dumplings from water and drain well. Serves 6.

SAUERKRAUT AND FRANKFURTERS

4 TABLESPOONS BUTTER
2 MEDIUM-SIZED SPANISH ONIONS, SLICED
1 CLOVE GARLIC, FINELY CHOPPED
1 LARGE CAN UNDRAINED SAUERKRAUT
½ PINT BEER
2 TABLESPOONS BROWN SUGAR
1 BAY LEAF
½ TEASPOON CELERY (OR CARAWAY) SEED
SALT AND FRESHLY-GROUND BLACK PEPPER
8 FRANKFURTERS
PAPRIKA
MUSTARD

Melt 2 tablespoons butter in a thick-bottomed frying pan and sauté finely-sliced onion and garlic until lightly browned. Add undrained sauerkraut, beer, sugar, bay leaf, celery (or caraway) seed, and salt and freshly-ground black pepper, to taste.

Stir well, cover and simmer for about ¾ hour, stirring from time to time.

Slash frankfurters diagonally to prevent bursting; dust with paprika and brown in remaining butter. Serve with sauerkraut and mustard. Serves 4.

Eliza Acton's Sucking Pig

'After the pig has been scalded and prepared for the spit, wipe it as dry as possible, and put into the body about half a pint of fine breadcrumbs, mixed with three heaped teaspoonsful of sage, minced very small, three ounces of good butter, a large saltspoonful of salt, and two-thirds as much of pepper or some cayenne. Sew it up with soft, but strong cotton; truss it as a hare, with the forelegs skewered back, and the hind ones forward; lay it to a strong clear fire, but keep it at a moderate distance, as it would quickly blister or scorch if placed too near. So soon as it has become warm, rub it with a bit of butter tied in a fold of muslin or of thin cloth, and repeat this process constantly while it is roasting. When the gravy begins to drop from it, put basins or small deep tureens under to catch it in. [A deep oblong dish of suitable size seems better adapted to this purpose.] As soon as the pig is of a fine light amber brown and the steam draws strongly towards the fire, wipe it quite dry with a clean cloth, and rub a bit of cold butter over it. When it is half done, a pig iron, or in lieu of this, a large flat iron should be hung in the centre of the grate, or the middle of the pig will be done long before the ends. When it is ready for table lay it into a very hot dish, and before the spit is withdrawn, take off and open the head and split the body in two; chop together quickly the stuffing and the brains, put them into half a pint of good veal gravy ready thickened, add a glass of Madeira or of sherry, and the gravy which has dropped from the pig; pour a small portion of this under the roast and serve the remainder as hot as possible in a tureen: a little pounded mace and cayenne with a squeeze of lemon juice, may be added, should the flavour require heightening. Fine bread sauce, and plain gravy should likewise be served with it. Some persons still prefer the old fashioned currant sauce to any other and many have the brains and stuffing stirred into rich melted butter, instead of gravy; but the receipt which we have given has usually been so much approved, that we can recommend it with some confidence, as it stands.' (1859)

ROAST SUCKLING PIG

1 SUCKLING PIG
OLIVE OIL
SALT AND FRESHLY-GROUND BLACK PEPPER
4 TABLESPOONS OLIVE OIL
4 TABLESPOONS BUTTER
4 TABLESPOONS LEMON JUICE
CRUSHED THYME

GARNISH:
1 SMALL RED APPLE
SPRIGS OF WATERCRESS OR PARSLEY
BÉARNAISE SAUCE

Scald and prepare suckling pig for roasting: brush pig inside and out with olive oil. Season interior generously with salt and freshly-ground black pepper. Roast in a hot oven (450°F. Mark 7) for 1½ to 2 hours, basting frequently with a mixture of olive oil, butter and lemon juice. If skin starts to bubble, prick bubbles immediately. Fifteen minutes before end of cooking time season well with salt, freshly-ground black pepper and crushed thyme. When cooked, remove from oven; sprinkle with lemon juice; place a small red apple in its mouth; garnish its ears with sprigs of watercress or parsley and place it on a bed of watercress. Serve with Béarnaise sauce.

ROAST LOIN OF PORK

1 LOIN OF PORK (7–8 CUTLETS)
4 TABLESPOONS SOFTENED BUTTER
CRUMBLED THYME AND BAY LEAF
DIJON MUSTARD
SALT AND FRESHLY-GROUND BLACK PEPPER
FLOUR
BUTTER
WATERCRESS
PURÉED POTATOES

Have your butcher remove rind from loin without removing fat. Mix softened butter, crumbled thyme, bay leaf and mustard to a smooth paste and rub well into pork several hours before roasting. Sprinkle to taste with salt and freshly-ground black pepper and let stand at room temperature to absorb flavours. Arrange the meat, fat side up, and brown in a hot oven (450°F. Mark 7) for 15 minutes. Reduce the heat to slow (350°F. Mark 3) and continue to roast until the meat is done, about 1¼ to 1½ hours.

Remove excess fat from the pan and thicken pan drippings with a little flour kneaded with an equal amount of butter. Garnish with sprigs of watercress and serve with puréed potatoes. Serves 6 to 8.

COLD LOIN OF PORK

1 COOKED LOIN OF PORK
COLD POTATO SALAD
RED CABBAGE SALAD
APPLE SAUCE OR MAYONNAISE

Cut cold loin of pork into chops. Serve with potato salad, red cabbage salad and apple sauce or mayonnaise. Serves 6 to 8.

CARRÉ DE PORC À LA BONNE FEMME

1 LOIN OF PORK (7–8 CUTLETS)
4 TABLESPOONS SOFTENED BUTTER
CRUMBLED THYME AND BAY LEAF
SALT AND FRESHLY-GROUND BLACK PEPPER
2 TABLESPOONS OLIVE OIL
18 PEELED SMALL NEW POTATOES
18 GLAZED BUTTON ONIONS
18 SAUTÉED MUSHROOM CAPS
1 BOUQUET GARNI
2 TABLESPOONS FINELY-CHOPPED PARSLEY

Have butcher remove the rind from loin, leaving the fat. Mix softened butter, crumbled thyme and bay leaf to a smooth paste and rub well into pork several hours before roasting. Sprinkle to taste with salt and pepper, and let stand at room temperature to absorb flavours.

Place pork, fat side up, in an oven-proof casserole; add olive oil and roast in a slow oven (350°F. Mark 3) for 1 hour or until half cooked. Place peeled new potatoes, glazed button onions and sautéed mushroom caps around pork; add a *bouquet garni*, and continue cooking, basting frequently, until tender. Sprinkle with finely-chopped parsley and serve from casserole. Serves 6 to 8.

BOILED SALT PORK WITH PEASE PUDDING

1 SHOULDER OR BREAST OF SALT PORK
6 LARGE CARROTS
2 SPANISH ONIONS, STUCK WITH 2 CLOVES
6 SMALL LEEKS
6 PARSNIPS

PEASE PUDDING:
1 POUND SPLIT PEAS
1 SPANISH ONION, THINLY SLICED
¼ POUND BUTTER
3 EGGS, BEATEN
SALT, FRESHLY-GROUND BLACK PEPPER AND GRATED NUTMEG

Place salt pork in water; bring to the boil; skim; add vegetables; bring to the boil and skim again. Then lower heat and simmer pork and vegetables gently until tender. Place the pork on a heated serving dish; surround with accompanying vegetables and serve with pease pudding.
To make pease pudding: Soak peas in cold water overnight. Place in a saucepan with sliced onion; cover with water and simmer gently for 2 to 4 hours, or until cooked. Purée. Combine purée of split peas, butter and beaten eggs, and season to taste with salt, freshly-ground pepper and grated nutmeg. Mix well, put into a buttered pudding basin and cook in the oven, in water, until done; or place in a scalded, buttered and floured cloth, tie up and cook in the pot with the pork. Serves 6 to 8.

CARRÉ DE PORC À LA PROVENÇALE

1 LOIN OF PORK (7–8 CUTLETS)
8–12 SAGE LEAVES
SALT AND FRESHLY-GROUND BLACK PEPPER
CRUMBLED THYME AND BAY LEAF
OLIVE OIL
6 TABLESPOONS WATER
6 TABLESPOONS DRY WHITE WINE
6 TABLESPOONS OLIVE OIL
2–3 CLOVES GARLIC

Have butcher bone and tie loin of pork. Pierce with the point of a sharp knife and insert sage leaves into pork. Season to taste with salt, freshly-ground black pepper, crumbled thyme and bay leaf. Sprinkle with a little olive oil and allow to stand for at least 12 hours to absorb flavours.

Place pork in an oven-proof casserole; add water, dry white wine and olive oil; crush garlic cloves with the flat of your hand and add them to cooking liquid. Roast pork in a slow oven (350°F. Mark 3) until tender, about 35 to 40 minutes per pound. Serves 6 to 8.

PORK CHOPS À LA CHARCUTIÈRE

4 THICK PORK CHOPS
2–4 TABLESPOONS MELTED BUTTER
BREADCRUMBS
SALT AND FRESHLY-GROUND BLACK PEPPER
PURÉED POTATOES

CHARCUTIÈRE SAUCE:
¼ SPANISH ONION, FINELY CHOPPED
1 TABLESPOON BUTTER
2 FLUID OUNCES DRY WHITE WINE
1 TABLESPOON WINE VINEGAR
½ PINT BROWN SAUCE
1 TABLESPOON TOMATO CONCENTRATE
MUSTARD
1 TABLESPOON FINELY-CHOPPED PICKLES
1 TABLESPOON FINELY-CHOPPED PARSLEY

Trim excess fat from 4 good-sized pork chops; brush with melted butter; dip in breadcrumbs, pressing them well in, and season to taste with salt and freshly-ground black pepper. Grill chops until they are tender and cooked through. Serve with puréed potatoes and a *charcutière* sauce. Serves 4.

To make charcutière sauce: Sauté finely-chopped onion in butter until golden. Add wine and vinegar and cook until sauce is reduced to half its original quantity. Add brown sauce; stir in tomato concentrate and simmer, uncovered, stirring from time to time, for 15 minutes. When ready to serve, stir in mustard, to taste, and finely-chopped pickles and parsley.

PORK CHOPS BAKED IN CREAM

4 THICK PORK CHOPS
2 TABLESPOONS BUTTER
½ POUND FINELY-CHOPPED MUSHROOMS
1 TABLESPOON LEMON JUICE
1 TABLESPOON FLOUR
SALT AND FRESHLY-GROUND BLACK PEPPER
THYME OR OREGANO
4 TABLESPOONS DOUBLE CREAM
FINELY-CHOPPED PARSLEY

Trim excess fat from 4 good-sized pork chops, and sauté in butter until golden on both sides. Remove.

Spoon off all but 2 tablespoons fat from the pan and sauté finely-chopped mushrooms in remaining fat until soft; stir in lemon juice; sprinkle with flour and cook until slightly thickened and almost dry. Season with salt and freshly-ground black pepper.

Rub chops with a little dried thyme or *oregano*, and season to taste with salt and pepper.

Cut 4 pieces of aluminium foil into heart shapes large enough to wrap a pork chop completely. Brush hearts with oil; place chop on one half; cover chops with mushroom mixture and pour 1 tablespoon cream over each chop. Sprinkle with parsley; fold the foil shape over and seal edges well by crimping them together. Place foil shapes on a baking sheet and bake in a slow oven (325°F. Mark 2) until the chops are tender, 45 to 60 minutes. Serves 4.

PORK CHOPS 'ARDENNAISE'

4 THICK PORK CHOPS
SALT AND FRESHLY-GROUND BLACK PEPPER
2 TABLESPOONS BUTTER
1 TABLESPOON LARD
6 TABLESPOONS DRY WHITE WINE
2–3 CRUSHED JUNIPER BERRIES
6 TABLESPOONS BEEF STOCK
1 TABLESPOON BUTTER
1 TABLESPOON FLOUR
SAUTÉED POTATOES MIXED WITH BACON BITS AND FINELY-CHOPPED ONION SAUTÉED IN BUTTER

Trim excess fat from 4 good-sized pork chops; season and sauté in butter and lard until they are tender. Remove chops and keep warm.

Skim excess fat from the pan and add wine, stirring crusty bits from sides of pan into sauce. Add crushed juniper berries, beef stock and a *beurre manié* (made by kneading butter and flour to a smooth paste). Bring to the boil; boil for a few minutes; correct seasoning and pour over chops. Serve with sautéed potatoes mixed with bacon bits and finely-chopped onion sautéed in butter. Serves 4.

CÔTELETTES DE PORC AU SAUGE

4 THICK PORK CHOPS
1 TEASPOON FINELY-CHOPPED ONION
1 TEASPOON FINELY-CHOPPED PARSLEY
GENEROUS PINCH CRUMBLED SAGE (ABOUT 2 LEAVES)
1 EGG
SALT AND FRESHLY-GROUND BLACK PEPPER
FRESH BREADCRUMBS
OLIVE OIL OR LARD, FOR FRYING
SAUTÉED SLICED APPLES
SAUTÉED SLICED POTATOES

Combine finely-chopped onion, parsley, crumbled sage and egg in a bowl. Beat well; season to taste with salt and freshly-ground black pepper. Trim excess fat from 4 good-sized pork chops and dip in this mixture several times. Drain well and dip in fresh breadcrumbs, pressing them well in. Allow to stand for 30 minutes. Fry breaded chops in oil or lard. Serve immediately with sautéed apples and potatoes. Serves 4.

PORK CHOPS IN WINE – I

4 THICK PORK CHOPS
SIFTED FLOUR
2 TABLESPOONS BUTTER
1 TABLESPOON OLIVE OIL
SALT AND FRESHLY-GROUND BLACK PEPPER
1 TABLESPOON FINELY-CHOPPED SHALLOTS
¼ PINT DRY WHITE WINE
2 TABLESPOONS FINELY-CHOPPED PARSLEY

Trim excess fat from 4 good-sized pork chops and blanch in boiling water for 1 minute. Drain; dry well and dust with sifted flour. Sauté chops in butter and olive oil in a thick-bottomed frying pan until golden on both sides. Season to taste with salt and freshly-ground black pepper. Add finely-chopped shallots; then pour over wine and simmer until wine is reduced and chops are tender.

Place pork chops on a heated serving dish; pour over sauce and sprinkle with finely-chopped parsley. Serves 4.

PORK CHOPS IN WINE – II

4 THICK PORK CHOPS
2 TABLESPOONS BUTTER
1 TEASPOON COARSE SALT
¼ LEVEL TEASPOON FRESHLY-GROUND BLACK PEPPER
½ LEVEL TEASPOON DRY MUSTARD
1 SPANISH ONION, FINELY CHOPPED
4 TABLESPOONS BUTTER
¼ PINT DRY WHITE WINE
2 TABLESPOONS FINELY-CHOPPED PARSLEY

Trim excess fat from 4 good-sized pork chops. Pound butter, salt, pepper and mustard to a smooth paste and spread on both sides of each chop.

Sauté finely-chopped onion in butter until transparent; add chops and sauté until golden brown on both sides. Pour over dry white wine and simmer gently, covered, until tender, about 45 minutes. Correct seasoning; sprinkle with parsley and serve. Serves 4.

PORK CHOPS 'AUBERGE DU GRAND SAINT PIERRE'

4 THICK PORK CHOPS
1 TABLESPOON OLIVE OIL
1 TABLESPOON BUTTER
SALT AND FRESHLY-GROUND BLACK PEPPER
¼ POUND GRUYÈRE CHEESE, FINELY GRATED
1–2 LEVEL TEASPOONS STRONG MUSTARD
DOUBLE CREAM

Trim excess fat from 4 good-sized pork chops and sauté them gently with a little oil and butter in a thick-bottomed frying pan; season to taste with salt and pepper.

When cooked, spread with a *pommade* made of finely-grated Gruyère (about 6 tablespoons) mixed with mustard and just enough cream to make a smooth mixture of spreading consistency.

Spread chops generously with cheese *pommade* and glaze quickly under the grill until sauce is golden. Serve immediately. Serves 4.

COLD GAMMON OF BACON

1 GAMMON OF BACON (10–12 POUNDS)
2 SPANISH ONIONS, STUCK WITH CLOVES
4 LARGE CARROTS
2 LEEKS
2 TURNIPS, QUARTERED
2 BAY LEAVES
6 PEPPERCORNS
TOASTED BREADCRUMBS
Optionals: CLOVES, BROWN SUGAR, DRY MUSTARD AND CIDER OR FRUIT JUICE

Wash gammon well; do not take off rind; soak for 24 to 48 hours to remove salt, changing water several times.

Cover gammon completely with cold water and bring slowly to the boil.

Change water; add vegetables, bay leaves and peppercorns and bring slowly to boiling point again; reduce heat immediately. Cover pan and simmer until cooking is complete, about 20 minutes per pound for an average-sized gammon.

Allow gammon to cool in water in which it was cooked. Do not remove rind until well set if you are going to serve it cold. I leave mine overnight. Then remove skin and sprinkle fat with toasted breadcrumbs; or, if you prefer, score fat criss-cross; stud with cloves; sprinkle with brown sugar and a little dry mustard and brown in the oven for 20 to 30 minutes, basting from time to time with cider or fruit juice.

HAM AND MUSHROOM PANCAKES

½ BASIC CRÊPES MIXTURE
2 OUNCES BUTTER
¼ POUND MUSHROOMS, COARSELY CHOPPED
JUICE OF ½ LEMON
1 SMALL ONION, FINELY CHOPPED
1 OUNCE FLOUR
½ PINT MILK
¼ POUND COOKED HAM, DICED
2 TABLESPOONS FINELY-CHOPPED PARSLEY
SALT AND FRESHLY-GROUND BLACK PEPPER

For the filling: Heat 1 ounce butter in a frying pan. Add coarsely-chopped mushrooms and lemon juice, and cook for a minute or two.

Heat remaining butter in a frying pan. Add finely-chopped onion and sauté until golden. Stir in flour and mix well. Add milk and cook for 2 or 3 minutes, stirring constantly, until sauce is thick and smooth.

Fold in mushrooms and juices. Add diced ham and chopped parsley; and season to taste with salt and freshly-ground black pepper. Fill pancakes. Serves 4.

JAMBON CHAUD MODE D'ICI

4 shallots, finely chopped
¼ pint dry white Chablis
4 tarragon leaves, finely chopped
¼ pint rich beef stock
4 tablespoons tomato concentrate
¼ pint double cream
2 tablespoons butter
4 thick ham slices

Makes a good *sauce piquante* with a reduction of finely-chopped shallots, dry white Chablis and a few tarragon leaves. Moisten with rich beef stock. Add tomato concentrate; cover and simmer gently for an hour on a very low heat.

Add an equal quantity of cream to this sauce and simmer for 10 minutes more. Pass through a fine sieve; add butter and serve on hot ham slices. Serve very hot. Serves 4.

JAMBON CHAUD À LA CHABLISIENNE 'HOSTELLERIE DE LA POSTE'

1 York ham (about 10 pounds)
4 large carrots
2 Spanish onions
1 bouquet garni (celery, thyme, bay leaf, parsley)
2 onions
2 large carrots
4 shallots
butter
2 sprigs thyme
2 bay leaves
2 sprigs parsley
½ bottle dry white Chablis
water

SAUCE:
2–3 sprigs fresh tarragon, finely chopped
1¼ pints well-flavoured veal stock
3 tablespoons tomato concentrate
salt and freshly-ground black pepper
¾ pint double cream

Soak ham in cold water overnight. Simmer gently for 2½ to 3 hours in water with 4 large carrots, 2 Spanish onions and a *bouquet garni.*

Allow to cool in its own liquid; take off skin and some of the fat.

To braise ham: Chop the onions, carrots and shallots coarsely, and sauté in butter until golden. Spread vegetables in the bottom of a roasting pan just large enough to hold ham; add thyme, bay leaves and parsley, place ham on vegetables, moisten with equal quantities of dry white Chablis and water and braise in a slow oven (350°F. Mark 3) until ham is tender.

To make sauce: Remove herbs and reduce the braising liquids over a high flame until almost dry. Add finely-chopped fresh tarragon, veal stock and tomato concentrate, season to taste with salt and pepper, and simmer sauce for 1 hour, skimming from time to time. Strain sauce; add cream, correct seasoning and heat through.

To serve: Slice braised ham; arrange on a heated platter and serve sauce separately. Ham prepared in this way is delicious served cold or used in any number of other recipes.

Chinese Pork and Lobster Balls in Sweet and Sour Sauce

Just how far back good cooking actually goes in China is hard to determine, but the Chinese were early discoverers of fire, and have been farmers for well over four thousand years. In the course of their long history they have evolved a high sense of harmony in the delicate blending of tastes and textures.

Some cooks believe that Chinese food is too exotic to be attempted in the home kitchen, but nothing could be further from the truth, for no special utensils are needed and the few special extras – soy sauce, bean sprouts, bamboo shoots and water chestnuts – can now be bought, bottled or tinned, throughout the country.

Chinese dishes are inexpensive, quick to prepare and fun to cook. Using an electric frying pan, or a more traditional chafing dish, you can even cook Chinese food right in the dining-room in front of your guests. A Chinese dinner served in true Oriental fashion assures a gay evening. And for those who like an authentic atmosphere, Chinese serving dishes and chopsticks are inexpensive and easily obtainable.

SERVING A CHINESE MEAL

Rice is the staple food of the Chinese but it is a mistake to think that the Chinese eat nothing but rice. Rice is the centre, the focal point, but ringed with a dozen different dishes, each blending perfectly with it and with each other. According to Chinese food authority Kenneth H. C. Low, an average Chinese meal consists of one or two soups – vegetable soup and a chicken or beef-based soup – one or two meat dishes, an egg or fish dish, and one or two vegetable dishes, served in conjunction with the rice. In wealthier families, when up to a dozen separate dishes are served during each meal, rice merely acts as a 'buffer' to the rich and tasty dishes, which may be served course by course or all at the same time.

The one supreme meat for the Chinese is pork. Those Chinese who can afford it eat it almost every day, poorer Chinese dream about it, and even the poorest try to save up a few coins to buy some with which to celebrate the New Year.

Sweet and sour conveys the Orient to our Western palates. Here are two classic recipes for serving pork and lobster balls with this favourite sauce. In our picture, crisp leaves of paper-thin pastry, deep-fried Chinese fashion, form a nest for golden batter balls of pork or lobster in sweet and sour sauce.

PORK IN SWEET AND SOUR SAUCE

1¼ POUNDS MINCED PORK
1 SMALL CLOVE GARLIC, MINCED
1 LEVEL TEASPOON SALT
1 TABLESPOON DRY SHERRY
1 TABLESPOON SOY SAUCE
BUTTER
OIL FOR FRYING

Combine minced pork and garlic. Season with salt, sherry and soy sauce and form into small balls the size of a walnut. Roll in butter and sauté in hot oil for about 5 minutes on each side. Remove pork balls to a serving dish and keep hot.

LOBSTER IN SWEET AND SOUR SAUCE

1 POUND LOBSTER (OR SHRIMPS, PRAWNS OR FISH)
¼ POUND PORK, NOT TOO LEAN
1 LEVEL DESSERTSPOON CORNFLOUR
1 TABLESPOON DRY SHERRY
1 TABLESPOON SOY SAUCE
¼ TEASPOON SALT
1 TEASPOON SUGAR
2 TABLESPOONS WATER
OIL FOR FRYING

Shell and clean lobster, shrimps or prawns (or skin and bone fish), and mince finely. Mince pork. Pound fish and meat to a smooth paste in a large mixing bowl with cornflour, sherry, soy sauce, salt, sugar and water. Make the paste into balls the size of large walnuts.

Heat the oil in a thick-bottomed frying pan until very hot. Then reduce heat; dip balls in batter and place in hot oil. Fry for about 5 minutes, turning from time to time so they are cooked to a golden brown on all sides.

This dish is best when served hot from the pan, but may be put in an oven to crisp for 5 minutes before serving.

BATTER:

1 EGG
8 TABLESPOONS ICE-COLD WATER
8 LEVEL TEASPOONS SIEVED FLOUR

Stir 1 egg in a small bowl, but do not whip or beat. Add ice-cold water and mix well; then sprinkle with sieved flour. Do not beat, just stir lightly to mix the ingredients. Do not worry about lumps in batter. If you stir too much, the batter becomes sticky and will not react properly.

SWEET AND SOUR SAUCE

1 SMALL TIN PINEAPPLE CHUNKS
2 SMALL CARROTS
1 GREEN PEPPER
1 LEVEL TABLESPOON CORNFLOUR
1 TABLESPOON BROWN SUGAR
2–3 TEASPOONS SOY SAUCE
2 TABLESPOONS OLIVE OIL
2–3 TABLESPOONS VINEGAR
3–4 SWEET PICKLES, SLICED

Drain the pineapple chunks. Reserve juice. Peel and slice carrots thinly; slice green pepper. Simmer vegetables gently in pineapple juice for 5 minutes, or until tender. Mix cornflour, brown sugar, soy sauce, oil and vinegar together smoothly and stir into the stock. Cook for 3 minutes. Add pineapple chunks and sliced pickles and add to the sauce. Pour over pork and lobster balls and serve hot.

CHINESE SWEET AND SOUR PORK

2 POUNDS BONED PORK, CUT IN 1-INCH CUBES
1 TABLESPOON SOY SAUCE
2 TABLESPOONS CORNFLOUR
1 TABLESPOON SAKE (OR DRY SHERRY)
FAT FOR DEEP-FRYING
1 CLOVE GARLIC, FINELY CHOPPED
1 ONION, FINELY SLICED
1 GREEN PEPPER, CUT IN THIN STRIPS
2 SMALL CARROTS, FINELY SLICED
½ TABLESPOON THINLY-SLICED GINGER ROOT
1 TABLESPOON BROWN SUGAR
3 TABLESPOONS VINEGAR
6 TABLESPOONS WATER
1 LEVEL TABLESPOON CORNFLOUR
SALT

Combine soy sauce, cornflour and *sake* (or dry sherry); add diced pork and mix well. Let stand for 10 minutes. Fry pork in deep fat until golden brown (about 10 minutes). Drain.

Heat 2 tablespoons fat in a frying pan and sauté finely-chopped garlic, onion, thinly-sliced green pepper, carrots and ginger root for 2 minutes. Mix sugar, vinegar, water, cornflour and salt, to taste. Add to the vegetables, stirring steadily until the mixture comes to the boil. Add pork. Cook over a low heat for 3 minutes. Serves 4.

CHINESE BRAISED PORK

2 POUNDS BONED PORK, CUT IN 1-INCH CUBES
2–4 TABLESPOONS LARD
6 TABLESPOONS SOY SAUCE
3 TABLESPOONS SAKE (OR DRY SHERRY)
6 TABLESPOONS WATER
1 TEASPOON FINELY-CHOPPED GINGER
1 CLOVE GARLIC, FINELY CHOPPED
1 GENEROUS PINCH SUGAR
FRESHLY-GROUND BLACK PEPPER
2 TABLESPOONS OIL
1 POUND SPINACH

Heat lard in a deep frying pan; add pork and sauté, stirring constantly, until golden brown. Combine soy sauce, *sake* (or dry sherry), water, finely-chopped ginger, garlic, sugar and pepper, to taste, and pour over pork. Bring mixture to the boil; cover and simmer gently for 1 hour.

Heat oil in a saucepan; add washed and drained spinach and cook, stirring constantly, for 5 minutes. Drain well and serve with pork. Serves 6 to 8.

Italian Sausage

The humble sausage – esteemed worthy meat only for a country breakfast or a family supper of 'bangers and mash' in Britain today – was considered a great delicacy by the early Greeks and Romans.

The very word sausage comes from the Latin *salsus*, salty proof indeed that the sausage was a method of preserving as well as a type of food, a very necessary adjunct to good living in the days before refrigerators. And Italians today are as fond of the sausage as they were in Pliny's time.

A well-known Italian sausage, now so popular throughout the world that it is also produced in Germany, Hungary and the United States, is *salame*, generally made of lean pork, fat pork and beef, finely ground and highly seasoned, coloured with red wine and pickled in brine before it is air-dried. There is seemingly no end to the varieties of *salame* to be found in Italy today. Some are highly flavoured with garlic, others are mild; some are eaten fresh and others are considered to be at their best when they are most mature. A visit to any busy, crowded little *salumeria* in Rome – pungent-smelling shops with sausages of all sorts piled high in the windows and hung in stacks like church candles from the ceiling – will give you an immediate idea of the immense variety of *salame*, smoked and raw hams and sausages available.

Perhaps the most familiar to us in this country are the *crespone* or *salame de Milano*, about 2½ inches in diameter, red-hued and granite-grained, with a very spicy flavour, and the *salame de Cremona*, a larger, slightly coarser-grained version of the Milan sausage. Try, too, the *salame casalinga*, a rough-marbled sausage with a more distinctive flavour; look for the deep cherry-red of the meat and the white waxiness of the fat which indicate that it is fresh.

Salame fiorentian – and its anise-flavoured brother, *salame finocchiona* – I have only had in Italy, but I am assured that they are available in this country from time to time. Both these sausages, specialities of Tuscany, are larger than the Milan sausage and made of pure lean pork and fat.

Good, too, for the *antipasti* platter are the silver-wrapped *cacciatora* and *turisto* sausages on sale here. They both keep well and are to be recommended for travellers and for picnics.

One of my favourite Italian sausages is the large, round, rosy-fleshed *mortadella*, a smooth-tasting sausage studded with square white chunks of fat. *Mortadella* is made in Florence and Bologna from the flesh of pigs which feed on the chestnuts and acorns in the surrounding forests. Seasoned with wine, garlic and spices, it is very good for cooking.

The best sausages for culinary purposes are, of course, the ones specially made for this purpose . . . the *cotechino* sausage, a large sausage made of lean pork, fat salt pork, white wine and spices, is often served in Italy with brown lentils or white beans, the robust, country flavour and fat juiciness of this sausage providing the perfect complement to the mealy vegetables. Try slices of *cotechino*, too, with cooked spinach, a speciality of the Cotechino restaurant in Rome. *Cotechino* and the sausage-stuffed pig's trotter from Modena called *zampone* are often used interchangeably in the famous Italian dish, *bollito misto*, mixed boiled meats. This noble dish, served at Rome's glamorous Capriccio restaurant just off the Via Veneto, combines lean beef, fat beef, veal, chicken, a calf's head and a *cotechino* sausage, simmered in salted boiling water with onions, celery, carrots and parsley. Very much like the French *pot-au-feu*, *bollito misto* is served with a *salsa verde* or a spicy tomato sauce.

Other Italian culinary sausages available in this country are the *salsicce negroni*, fat mottled sausages with a rustic flavour, and the thinner, finer *chipolate* sausages. The *negroni* are best poached in water until tender; make sure you prick several holes in each before placing in water; then dry them carefully and sauté gently in oil and butter until done. This method keeps sausages from splitting and yet assures that they are cooked through without taking on too much colour. The *chipolate* are cooked in the usual manner.

BEAN AND SAUSAGE PLATTER

8 ITALIAN SAUSAGES
2 TABLESPOONS OLIVE OIL
2 TABLESPOONS BUTTER
6–8 TABLESPOONS TOMATO PURÉE
6–8 TABLESPOONS COLD WATER
1 POUND DRY WHITE BEANS, COOKED
SALT AND FRESHLY-GROUND BLACK PEPPER

Prick holes in sausages with a fine skewer or the point of a sharp knife; place in a frying pan just large enough to hold them and cover with water. Cook over medium heat until water evaporates. Remove sausages and brown in a little oil with butter, turning them from time to time until they are cooked through and well coloured on all sides (20 to 30 minutes). In this way the sausages will be well cooked, will remain soft and keep their skins intact. Remove sausages. Then add tomato purée to fat in pan. Cook for a minute or two, stirring; then add 6 to 8 tablespoons water and simmer gently for 10 minutes.

Add cooked and drained white beans, season with salt and pepper and simmer gently for a few minutes to allow beans to absorb flavour. Return sausages to pan and heat through. Serve beans on a serving platter, topped by sausages. Serves 4.

COTECHINO WITH LENTILS

1 COTECHINO SAUSAGE
¾ POUND BROWN LENTILS
SALT
½ SPANISH ONION
2 STALKS CELERY
2 OUNCES FAT SALT PORK, DICED
1 TABLESPOON OLIVE OIL
1 TABLESPOON BUTTER
SALT AND FRESHLY-GROUND BLACK PEPPER

Prick holes in the skin of the *cotechino* with a fine skewer or the point of a sharp knife. Put *cotechino* in cold water in a pan just large enough to hold it and bring slowly to the boil. Turn down heat and let the water barely bubble for about 2 hours. While still hot, remove the skin gently and allow sausage to cool. Reserve liquid. When sausage is cool, cut it into fairly thick slices.

Wash the lentils well, picking out any impurities; cook in salted boiling water with onion and celery for about 1½ hours. When lentils are soft, drain thoroughly. Sauté diced fat salt pork in olive oil and butter until golden, in the bottom of a fire-proof casserole. Add drained lentils and moisten with a little of the liquid from the *cotechino*. Season to taste with salt and pepper; bring to the boil and then simmer gently for a few minutes until the lentils have absorbed all the liquid. Place *cotechino* slices on top; heat through and serve in the casserole. Serves 4.

SAUCISSES CHIPOLATA EN CHEMISE

2 TABLESPOONS OLIVE OIL
1 POUND CHIPOLATA SAUSAGES
½ POUND FLAKY PASTRY
TARRAGON MUSTARD
MILK
TOMATO SAUCE

Heat olive oil in a frying pan and sauté sausages in it until golden brown. Roll out flaky pastry thinly on a floured pastry board. Cut rectangles in the pastry large enough to fold over each sausage; spread rectangles with mustard, and on each place a sausage. Roll up pastry like a little package. Brush top of each with milk and bake in a fairly hot oven (400° to 425°F. Mark 5 to 6) for 15 minutes. Serve with tomato sauce and a salad. Serves 4 to 6.

SAUCISSES AU VIN ROUGE

1 OUNCE BUTTER
1 POUND TOULOUSE SAUSAGES
2 TABLESPOONS DRY BREADCRUMBS
½ PINT GOOD RED WINE
SALT AND FRESHLY-GROUND BLACK PEPPER
POWDERED THYME AND BAY LEAF

Melt butter in a frying pan and sauté sausages over a low heat until they are golden on all sides, turning them from time to time with a wooden spoon. Add breadcrumbs, turn up heat and let breadcrumbs take on colour. Add wine; bring to the boil; lower flame and simmer gently for 10 minutes. Add salt and pepper, a pinch of thyme and a bay leaf, and simmer for 5 to 10 minutes more. Serves 4 to 6.

SAUSAGE AND SAUERKRAUT CASSEROLE

4 TOULOUSE SAUSAGES
MILK
12 OUNCES COOKED SAUERKRAUT
4 MUSHROOM CAPS
1 TABLESPOON BUTTER
½ PINT RICH BROWN SAUCE

Cover sausages with hot water. Bring to the boil; remove from heat and let stand in hot water for 5 minutes. Drain and dip sausages in milk; place under grill and grill lightly until golden. Place cooked sauerkraut in baking dish; top with sausages. Chop mushrooms; sauté for 3 minutes in butter and spoon over sausages and sauerkraut. Top with brown sauce and heat under grill until bubbling. Serves 4.

SAUSAGE PATTIES

1½ POUNDS LEAN PORK
¾ POUND FAT SALT PORK
1 CLOVE GARLIC
1 LEVEL TEASPOON SALT
1 BAY LEAF, CRUSHED
ALLSPICE, GROUND
CORIANDER, GROUND
1 LEVEL TEASPOON COARSELY-GROUND BLACK PEPPER
1 EGG
1 SPANISH ONION, FINELY CHOPPED
1 TEASPOON RUBBED THYME
1 TABLESPOON FINELY-CHOPPED PARSLEY
2 TABLESPOONS BUTTER
2 TABLESPOONS OLIVE OIL

Put meat through finest blade of mincer, or have it minced by your butcher. Combine garlic, salt, crushed bay leaf, ground allspice and coriander, to taste, with coarsely-ground black pepper in mortar, and pound to a smooth paste. Add this mixture to minced meat with egg, finely-chopped onion, thyme and finely-chopped parsley. Mix thoroughly and form into patties. Sauté patties in butter and olive oil until cooked through but not dry. Serve with soft scrambled eggs. Serves 4 to 6.

GREAT DISHES OF THE WORLD

CHAPTER 11

Poultry and Game

Coq-au-Vin

I made my first contact with *coq-au-vin*, one of the undisputed glories of French cuisine, when I was eighteen. The place – a little French restaurant on New York's West Side, one of those little *bistros* run by a French family, where you could eat inexpensively yet wonderfully well.

Maman served smilingly behind the bar in the small front room with its three or four tables. Papa cooked the specialities of France in the back dining-room-cum-kitchen, separated from his clients by only a low counter, and their daughter served at table. Each night had papa's favourite speciality: Monday was a creamy *blanquette de veau*; Tuesday, a hearty sausage-and-game-filled *cassoulet*; Wednesday, a majestic *pot-au-feu*; Thursday, *navarin de mouton*, garnished with papa's own vegetables; Friday was *bouillabaisse* night. But best of all, for me at least, was Saturday, for that was the night they served *coq-au-vin*.

Papa's *coq-au-vin* was a simple affair – chicken simmered in Burgundy and chicken stock, with *lardons* of fat salt pork, tiny white onions and small new potatoes – and I returned there as often as I could after that first visit to enjoy this great country dish.

If that *coq-au-vin* was my first, it was certainly not my last, for this famous dish has travelled from its native Burgundy throughout the length and breadth of France. I do not know of a restaurant in all France that at some time does not feature a version of it. I have enjoyed chicken cooked in red wine, white wine, and even in champagne; I have had it garnished with button mushrooms, tiny white onions, *lardons* of fat salt pork or green bacon, *croûtons* of fried bread or golden pastry crescents, and even with soft-textured cockscombs as it is served today at the Restaurant La Bourgogne in Paris.

Here is my favourite recipe for this famous dish.

COQ-AU-VIN

1 3-POUND CHICKEN
3 TABLESPOONS BUTTER
2 TABLESPOONS OLIVE OIL
¼ POUND GREEN BACON (IN 1 PIECE)
12 BUTTON ONIONS
12 BUTTON MUSHROOMS
FLOUR
SALT AND FRESHLY-GROUND BLACK PEPPER
2 CLOVES GARLIC, FINELY CHOPPED
1 SPRIG THYME
2 BAY LEAVES
2 SPRIGS PARSLEY
4 TABLESPOONS COGNAC (WARMED)
½ BOTTLE GOOD RED WINE
1 LUMP SUGAR
1 TABLESPOON BUTTER
1 TABLESPOON FLOUR
2 TABLESPOONS FINELY-CHOPPED PARSLEY

Cut the chicken into serving pieces. Heat butter and olive oil together with the green bacon, cut in cubes, in a heat-proof casserole. When the bacon begins to turn golden, add the onions and cook for a minute or two, and then add the mushrooms. Sauté this mixture gently until the onions begin to turn transparent and the mushrooms to brown; remove from casserole and keep warm.

Roll chicken pieces in seasoned flour and sauté in the same fat for about 5 minutes, or until they turn golden on one side. Then, without piercing, turn chicken pieces over to brown on the other side. As each of the pieces begins to 'stiffen', remove and put in a covered dish in a warm oven. Next, return the onions, bacon, mushrooms, chicken segments and their juices to the casserole. Add salt, pepper, finely-chopped garlic, thyme, bay leaves and parsley; cover casserole and cook in a moderate oven (375°F. Mark 4) until almost tender. Remove chicken pieces, bacon and vegetables from casserole and keep warm. Skim off excess fat from the juices in casserole. Set casserole on a high flame, pour in cognac, warmed in a soup ladle, and ignite it. Allow to burn for a minute or two and then extinguish by pouring in half a bottle of good red wine. Add a lump of sugar; bring to the boil and reduce the sauce over a quick heat to half the original quantity. Thicken with a *beurre manié* made of the remaining tablespoon each of butter and flour. Strain sauce into a clean casserole; return chicken pieces, bacon and vegetables to the casserole; cover and allow to simmer in a very slow oven until ready to serve. Garnish with finely-chopped parsley. Serves 4 to 6.

QUICK CHICKEN IN WINE

1 SMALL BROILER (2–2½ POUNDS)
2 TABLESPOONS BUTTER
2 TABLESPOONS OLIVE OIL
4 SLICES BACON, DICED
4 TABLESPOONS BRANDY
¼ PINT RED WINE
1 BAY LEAF
2 CLOVES
PINCH THYME
12 SMALL WHITE ONIONS
SALT AND FRESHLY-GROUND BLACK PEPPER
12 SMALL MUSHROOMS
4 TABLESPOONS FINELY-CHOPPED PARSLEY
1 TABLESPOON FLOUR
1 TABLESPOON BUTTER

Cut chicken into 4 or 8 serving pieces and brown in frying pan with butter and olive oil. Add diced bacon and brown lightly. Heat brandy; ignite and pour over chicken. Add red wine, bay leaf, cloves, thyme, peeled onions and salt and pepper, to taste. Cover and simmer for 20 minutes. Add button mushrooms and finely-chopped parsley and cook for 5 to 10 minutes more, or until chicken is tender. Transfer chicken pieces to a hot serving dish and thicken sauce by gradually stirring in a *beurre manié* (made by kneading 1 tablespoon flour and 1 tablespoon butter to a smooth paste). Correct seasoning and pour sauce over chicken pieces. Serves 2 to 4.

CHICKEN EN COCOTTE

1 TENDER CHICKEN
SALT AND FRESHLY-GROUND BLACK PEPPER
2 TABLESPOONS BUTTER
2 TABLESPOONS OLIVE OIL
4 OUNCES FAT BACON, DICED
4 SHALLOTS, COARSELY CHOPPED
2 CARROTS, COARSELY CHOPPED
2 FLUID OUNCES COGNAC
4 TOMATOES, PEELED, SEEDED AND CHOPPED
1 BOUQUET GARNI
½ PINT RED WINE

Cut chicken into serving pieces and season to taste with salt and pepper. Heat butter and oil in an iron *cocotte* or a heavy casserole and sauté bacon pieces until golden. Remove bacon; add coarsely-chopped shallots and carrots and cook, stirring constantly, until vegetables 'soften'; then add chicken pieces and brown them on all sides. Return bacon bits to the pan; pour over cognac and flame. Then add peeled, seeded and chopped tomatoes, *bouquet garni* and red wine. Cover the casserole and let the chicken simmer over a low fire until it is very tender. Add more wine or chicken stock if the sauce reduces too quickly while cooking. Serves 4.

POULET FRANÇOIS 1er

1 3½-POUND CHICKEN
4 TABLESPOONS BUTTER
½ POUND BUTTON MUSHROOMS
½ POUND SMALL WHITE ONIONS
4 TABLESPOONS CALVADOS
¼ PINT FRESH CREAM
SALT AND FRESHLY-GROUND BLACK PEPPER
1 BOUQUET GARNI (PARSLEY THYME AND CELERY)
FRIED BREAD TRIANGLES

Cut chicken into quarters and sauté in butter until golden. Add button mushrooms, cut in quarters, and onions, and simmer gently for 5 minutes.

Pour over warmed Calvados and flame, shaking the pan until flames die out. Moisten with cream; add *bouquet garni* and salt and freshly-ground black pepper, to taste, then cover casserole and cook in a slow oven (325°F. Mark 2) for 45 minutes, or until chicken is tender.

To serve: place chicken on a heated serving dish, correct sauce for seasoning and pour over. Garnish with fried bread triangles and serve immediately. Serves 4.

MEDITERRANEAN CHICKEN

1 3½-POUND CHICKEN
½ POUND FAT GREEN BACON, DICED
2 TABLESPOONS OLIVE OIL
2 TABLESPOONS BUTTER
½ POUND GREEN OLIVES, PITTED
½ POUND BUTTON MUSHROOMS
SALT AND FRESHLY-GROUND BLACK PEPPER
6 TABLESPOONS COGNAC
1 POUND DICED SAUTÉED POTATOES
4 TOMATOES

Sauté chicken and diced green bacon in butter and olive oil in a flame-proof casserole until chicken is golden on all sides.

Add pitted green olives, which you have previously soaked in hot water for 15 minutes to remove excess salt, and button mushrooms. Season chicken to taste with a little salt and freshly-ground black pepper. Moisten with cognac. Cover casserole and cook in a slow oven (325°F. Mark 2) for 45 minutes. Add sautéed potatoes and tomatoes and simmer gently for another 15 minutes, or until chicken is tender. Serve in the casserole or on a serving dish. Serves 4.

ITALIAN CHICKEN CASSEROLE

1 3½-POUND CHICKEN
½ POUND COOKED HAM, DICED
4 TABLESPOONS FRESH BREADCRUMBS
2 CLOVES GARLIC, FINELY CHOPPED
2 TABLESPOONS FINELY-CHOPPED PARSLEY
1 BEATEN EGG
FRESHLY-GROUND BLACK PEPPER
2 TABLESPOONS BUTTER
2 TABLESPOONS OLIVE OIL
¼–½ PINT CHICKEN STOCK
2 TABLESPOONS TOMATO CONCENTRATE
FINELY-CHOPPED PARSLEY
RICE

Combine diced cooked ham, breadcrumbs, finely-chopped garlic and parsley in a bowl and mix well. Moisten with beaten egg; season to taste with freshly-ground black pepper and stuff chicken with this mixture.

Melt butter and olive oil in thick-bottomed, flame-proof casserole and sauté chicken until golden on all sides. Combine chicken stock and tomato concentrate and pour over chicken. Cover casserole and simmer gently on top of the stove or in a slow oven (325°F. Mark 2) for about 1 hour, or until chicken is tender. Correct seasoning; garnish with finely-chopped parsley and serve with rice. Serves 4.

CHICKEN À LA GRECQUE

1 3½-POUND CHICKEN
1 SPANISH ONION
2 LARGE CARROTS
2 STALKS CELERY
2 TABLESPOONS BUTTER
2 TABLESPOONS OLIVE OIL
¼–½ PINT CHICKEN STOCK
6 TABLESPOONS DRY WHITE WINE
COOKED RICE

STUFFING:
6 TABLESPOONS FINELY-CHOPPED SHALLOTS
2 TABLESPOONS BUTTER
4 OUNCES TOASTED BREADCRUMBS
2 CLOVES GARLIC
2 TABLESPOONS FINELY-CHOPPED CELERY
2 TABLESPOONS FINELY-CHOPPED PARSLEY
GRATED RIND OF ½ LEMON
SALT AND FRESHLY-GROUND BLACK PEPPER
PINCH ROSEMARY
4 TABLESPOONS COGNAC

Cut onion, carrots and celery into thin strips. Combine butter and olive oil in saucepan; add vegetables and cook, stirring continuously, until soft, about 5 minutes. Transfer to casserole. *To prepare stuffing:* Cook finely-chopped shallots in 2 tablespoons butter until transparent. Mix with remaining stuffing ingredients; fill cavity of bird and close opening with small skewers. Place bird on top of vegetables; cook in a pre-heated oven (450°F. Mark 7) for 20 minutes. Pour over chicken stock. Cover casserole; reduce heat to 325°F. (Mark 2) and cook until chicken is tender, about 30 minutes.

To serve: arrange drained vegetables and chicken on a hot serving dish. Garnish with cooked rice. Pour white wine into casserole with stock; cook rapidly for several minutes to reduce liquid slightly. Strain and serve with bird. Serves 4.

CHICKEN IN CHAMPAGNE OASIS

1 TENDER CHICKEN (ABOUT 3 POUNDS)
4–6 TABLESPOONS BUTTER
2 TABLESPOONS FINELY-CHOPPED ONION
SALT AND FRESHLY-GROUND BLACK PEPPER
1 TABLESPOON FLOUR
½ BOTTLE CHAMPAGNE
½ PINT DOUBLE CREAM
4 EGG YOLKS
2 TABLESPOONS CREAM

Cut chicken into serving pieces and simmer in butter in a fire-proof casserole with finely-chopped onion and salt and freshly-ground black pepper, to taste. Turn chicken pieces several times; cover casserole and let them steam on the lowest possible heat for 10 minutes. The chicken should not take on colour.

Sprinkle chicken pieces with flour; turn several times and then pour over champagne. Cover casserole and simmer gently for 15 minutes more, or until the chicken is tender.

Arrange chicken pieces on a warm serving dish; cover and keep warm in a low oven. Reduce pan juices in which chicken was cooked to a quarter of the original quantity over a brisk flame. Add cream and continue cooking, stirring from time to time, until sauce is reduced by half.

Whisk egg yolks and remaining cream until well blended; add a little of the hot sauce to this mixture; blend well and pour mixture into hot sauce. Simmer sauce over a very low flame, or over water, until sauce is thick and smooth. Do not allow it to boil. Correct seasoning and strain the sauce over the chicken through a fine sieve. Serve very hot. Serves 4.

SUMMER CHICKEN CASSEROLE

1 3-POUND CHICKEN
2 TABLESPOONS BUTTER
2 TABLESPOONS OLIVE OIL
12 SMALL ONIONS
1 TABLESPOON FLOUR
SALT AND FRESHLY-GROUND BLACK PEPPER
1 BOUQUET GARNI (PARSLEY, THYME, BAY LEAF)
24 BUTTON MUSHROOMS
2 TABLESPOONS BUTTER
JUICE OF 2 LEMONS
2 EGG YOLKS
½ PINT DOUBLE CREAM

Cut chicken into 8 serving pieces and then sauté in butter and oil with onions until they just begin to turn colour. Sprinkle with flour and add just enough water to cover the chicken. Season to taste with freshly-ground black pepper; add *bouquet garni*, cover casserole and cook for about 1½ hours, or until chicken is tender. Remove chicken and onions to a deep serving dish or shallow casserole. Reserve stock.

Sauté button mushrooms in butter and juice of 1 lemon until tender and add to chicken and onions. Whisk egg yolks, juice of 1 lemon and ¼ pint double cream in a bowl. Bring stock to the boil, and, whisking vigorously, add a ladle of boiling stock to the cream and egg mixture. Pour mixture into the hot stock, bring gently to the boil, whisking well until sauce is thick and creamy. Strain sauce through a fine sieve into a clean bowl and allow to cool. When it is cool, whisk remaining cream into it; correct seasoning and pour over chicken and vegetables. Toss well. Chill. Serves 4.

OLD ENGLISH CHICKEN PIE

1 TENDER CHICKEN (ABOUT 3 POUNDS)
6 TABLESPOONS FLOUR
2 TABLESPOONS BUTTER
SALT AND FRESHLY-GROUND BLACK PEPPER
SHORTCRUST PASTRY FOR 8-INCH PIE DISH
2 HARD-BOILED EGGS

WHITE FORCEMEAT:

4 OUNCES STALE BREAD
GRATED RIND OF ½ LEMON
1 TEASPOON FINELY-CHOPPED PARSLEY
¼ TEASPOON FINELY-CHOPPED THYME
PINCH GRATED NUTMEG
½ TEASPOON SALT
FRESHLY-GROUND BLACK PEPPER
2 OUNCES BUTTER
1 EGG YOLK

SAUSAGE FORCEMEAT:

LIVER AND HEART OF THE CHICKEN
4 OUNCES SAUSAGE MEAT
1 TEASPOON FINELY-CHOPPED PARSLEY
1 TEASPOON FINELY-CHOPPED CHIVES OR ONION GREENS

Bone chicken and simmer wings, neck and bones in a little seasoned water to make a light stock. Re-form the boned pieces of chicken; roll lightly in flour and sauté in 2 tablespoons butter until they are a light golden colour on all sides. Season well with salt and freshly-ground black pepper; cover pan and cook over a low flame for 20 minutes, turning occasionally.

In the meantime, prepare forcemeat balls to garnish chicken. *White forcemeat:* Grate stale bread and mix thoroughly with grated lemon rind, finely-chopped parsley and thyme, and grated nutmeg, salt and pepper, to taste. Dice butter; add to mixture together with egg yolk and work to a smooth paste with fingers.

Sausage forcemeat: Put liver and heart of chicken through mincer with sausage meat and combine this paste with finely-chopped parsley and chives or onion greens.

Form small balls the size of walnuts out of each of these two mixtures by rolling them between your hands or on a board (enough for 12 to 16 forcemeat balls). Brown them lightly in remaining butter in another pan. Line an 8-inch pie dish with shortcrust pastry and place chicken pieces in it. Garnish with forcemeat balls and quartered hard-boiled eggs.

Stir 6 tablespoons of stock into the pan in which the chicken was cooked, blending it well with the butter and remaining juices. Pour this over the contents of the pie dish and cover with top layer of pastry. Moisten the edges of pastry with water, pinch them together and cut one or two slits in the centre of crust. Bake in a moderate oven (375°F. Mark 4) for 30 minutes, or until done. Serves 4 to 6.

This pie is excellent served with a chicken *velouté* sauce.

MOROCCAN ROAST CHICKEN

1 ROASTING CHICKEN
1 TABLESPOON CHOPPED PARSLEY
1 TABLESPOON CHOPPED CHERVIL
½ SPANISH ONION, CHOPPED
4–6 TABLESPOONS BUTTER
1 LEVEL TEASPOON POWDERED CUMIN
½ LEVEL TEASPOON SALT
GENEROUS PINCH CAYENNE PEPPER

Pound chopped parsley, chervil and onion in a mortar. Add butter, cumin, salt and red pepper, and pound to a smooth paste.

Spread chicken with this mixture and roast in usual manner, basting with sauce from time to time.

MOROCCAN CHICKEN

1 CHICKEN (4–5 POUNDS)
SALT
¼ LEVEL TEASPOON PAPRIKA
¼ LEVEL TEASPOON POWDERED CUMIN
FRESHLY-GROUND BLACK PEPPER
3 OUNCES BUTTER
¾ POUND SPANISH ONIONS, SLICED
⅛–¼ LEVEL TEASPOON POWDERED SAFFRON
4 OUNCES CHICK-PEAS, SOAKED OVERNIGHT
WELL-FLAVOURED CHICKEN STOCK
4 TABLESPOONS FINELY-CHOPPED PARSLEY
1 SPRIG FRESH CORIANDER OR LEMON THYME
½ POUND RICE
2 TABLESPOONS BUTTER
LEMON JUICE

Cut chicken into serving pieces; season to taste with salt, paprika, powdered cumin and freshly-ground black pepper, and sauté chicken pieces with sliced onions in butter in a casserole until golden.

Sprinkle with powdered saffron; add chick-peas and enough well-flavoured chicken stock to cover, and simmer gently for 1 to 1½ hours, or until chicken is tender. Just before serving, add chopped parsley and coriander or lemon thyme.

To serve: spoon half of the rice (cooked in salted water with butter) into a heated serving dish; place chicken pieces on it; pour over saffron sauce; add remaining rice and sprinkle with lemon juice. Serves 6 to 8.

CHICKEN BRAISED IN WINE

1 TENDER CHICKEN (ABOUT 4 POUNDS)
2 TABLESPOONS BUTTER
2 TABLESPOONS OLIVE OIL
4 OUNCES FAT BACON, DICED
4 SHALLOTS, COARSELY CHOPPED
2 CARROTS, COARSELY CHOPPED
2 TABLESPOONS COGNAC
1 BOUQUET GARNI
SALT AND FRESHLY-GROUND BLACK PEPPER
½ PINT DRY WHITE WINE
¼ PINT CHICKEN STOCK

Heat butter and oil in an iron *cocotte* or a heavy heat-proof casserole just large enough to hold chicken. Dice bacon pieces and sauté in fat until golden. Remove bacon; add chopped shallots and carrots and cook, stirring constantly, until vegetables 'soften'; then add chicken and brown on all sides.

Return bacon bits to the pan; pour over cognac and flame. Then add *bouquet garni*, salt and freshly-ground black pepper, to taste, and dry white wine and chicken stock. Cover the bird with a piece of buttered paper cut to fit the casserole, with a small hole in the centre to allow steam to escape. Cover casserole and simmer gently over a very low heat until tender (1 to 1¼ hours). Add more wine or a little chicken stock if the sauce reduces too quickly during the cooking. Serves 4.

CHICKEN PUDDING IN BUTTER CRUST

1 POUND FLOUR
6 OUNCES BUTTER
4 EGG YOLKS, WELL BEATEN
A LITTLE WATER
1 CHICKEN, CUT INTO SERVING PIECES
½ POUND HAM IN 1 PIECE
¼ POUND BUTTON MUSHROOMS
2 TABLESPOONS FINELY-CHOPPED PARSLEY
SALT AND FRESHLY-GROUND BLACK PEPPER
½ TEASPOON EACH DRIED ROSEMARY AND TARRAGON
1 TEASPOON FRESHLY-GRATED LEMON PEEL
½ PINT WELL-FLAVOURED CHICKEN STOCK

Grease a basin; line it with a crust made of flour and butter, moistened with beaten egg yolks and, if necessary, a little water.

Cut the chicken into small serving pieces and flour them lightly. Cut the ham into strips about ½ inch thick and 2 inches long. Scatter ham, quartered mushrooms and parsley among chicken pieces. Add salt, freshly-ground black pepper, dried rosemary, tarragon and grated lemon peel.

Pour over well-flavoured chicken stock. Cover with remaining crust and pinch edges together; cover with a piece of buttered paper, then with a cloth. Tie up securely and boil for 2½ to 3 hours.

OVEN-FRIED CHICKEN

1 TENDER 2½-POUND FRYING CHICKEN
2 OUNCES FLOUR
1 TEASPOON SALT
½ LEVEL TEASPOON BLACK PEPPER, CRUSHED
1 TABLESPOON FINELY-CHOPPED PARSLEY
1 TEASPOON DRIED TARRAGON, CRUSHED
1 TEASPOON DRIED ROSEMARY, CRUSHED
GRATED RIND OF 1 LEMON
1 EGG, BEATEN
MILK
4 TABLESPOONS BUTTER
4 TABLESPOONS OLIVE OIL
THIN TRIANGLES OF BREAD, FOR FRYING

Cut chicken into serving pieces.

Combine flour, salt, pepper, finely-chopped parsley, tarragon, rosemary and grated lemon rind in a bowl. Combine beaten egg and a little milk in another bowl. Dip chicken pieces into egg mixture and then into seasoned flour. Chill.

Place butter and oil in a shallow baking dish and heat in a

moderately hot oven (400°F. Mark 5) until butter sizzles. Place chicken pieces in dish; spoon butter over them and cook for 45 to 50 minutes, or until chicken is tender and brown, turning pieces once or twice during cooking time.

Serve chicken pieces on thin slices of toast sautéed in butter until crisp. Accompany with pan juices. Serves 4.

POULET AU BLANC

1 PLUMP CHICKEN
1 PINT GOOD WHITE STOCK
12 MUSHROOM CAPS
4 TABLESPOONS BUTTER
JUICE OF 1 LEMON
2 TABLESPOONS FLOUR
2 EGG YOLKS
SALT AND FRESHLY-GROUND BLACK PEPPER

Place chicken in an earthenware casserole. Add enough stock (veal or chicken, or a combination of the two) to half-cover chicken. Cover exposed part of chicken with a piece of buttered paper; place lid on casserole and simmer in a moderate oven for about an hour, or until chicken is tender.

Simmer mushroom caps in 2 tablespoons butter and lemon juice in a small saucepan; keep warm. Remove chicken from casserole; keep warm. Make a white *roux* with remaining butter and flour. Strain pint of liquid in which chicken has been cooked into *roux* to make a *velouté* sauce. Remove sauce from heat and stir in the egg yolks. Carve chicken into serving pieces and return to clean casserole; add *velouté* sauce and mushroom caps; correct seasoning; warm through and serve in casserole. Serves 4.

POULE-AU-POT HENRI IV

Good King Henry's chicken in the pot

1 FINE FAT CHICKEN (3½–4½ POUNDS)

COURT-BOUILLON:
1 VEAL KNUCKLE
1 TEASPOON SALT
FRESHLY-GROUND BLACK PEPPER
2 CARROTS
2 LEEKS
2 TURNIPS
2 POTATOES
FEW CABBAGE LEAVES, IF AVAILABLE
1 SPANISH ONION, STUCK WITH 2 CLOVES
1 BOUQUET GARNI (CELERY, PARSLEY, BAY LEAF)

STUFFING:
¼ POUND GREEN BACON
¼ POUND FRESH PORK
2–3 CLOVES GARLIC
¼ POUND DRY BREADCRUMBS
MILK, TO MOISTEN
2–3 TABLESPOONS FINELY CHOPPED PARSLEY
½ LEVEL TEASPOON DRIED TARRAGON OR CHERVIL
GENEROUS PINCH MIXED SPICE
2 EGGS
SALT AND FRESHLY-GROUND BLACK PEPPER

To make court-bouillon: Combine gizzard, heart, wing-tips, neck and feet of the chicken with veal knuckle, salt, pepper, vegetables and *bouquet garni* in a large saucepan. Add 3 quarts of water and bring to the boil. Skim, lower heat and simmer, covered, for 1 hour.

To make stuffing: Put chicken liver, green bacon, fresh pork and garlic through the finest blade of the mincer. Moisten breadcrumbs with milk; combine with minced meats and add finely-chopped parsley, dried herbs, mixed spice, eggs and salt and pepper, to taste. Mix well, adding more milk if necessary to make fairly loose mixture.

Stuff chicken; sew up openings and truss bird. Poach, covered, in *court-bouillon* for approximately 1 hour, or until tender. If there is any stuffing left over, tie it in cabbage leaves and poach with chicken for last 20 minutes of cooking time.

To serve: For a family luncheon: the hot broth is served first, followed by the chicken surrounded by freshly-poached vegetables . . . choose among carrots, turnips, onions, green beans and potatoes.

For a company dinner: place chicken on a heated serving dish and surround with individual pastry shells filled with glazed carrots, onions or French-style peas. Just before serving, spoon a little chicken *velouté* sauce over chicken and serve remaining sauce separately. Serves 4 to 6.

POULET À LA CRÈME – I

1 3½-POUND CHICKEN
¼ POUND BUTTER
1 MEDIUM ONION, FINELY CHOPPED
SALT AND FRESHLY-GROUND BLACK PEPPER
HOT WATER, TO COVER
½ PINT CREAM
4 EGG YOLKS

Cut chicken into 8 serving pieces. Melt butter in a large, heavy-bottomed frying pan or flame-proof casserole and sauté chicken pieces gently without letting them colour.

Add finely-chopped onion, salt and freshly-ground black pepper, to taste; cover with hot water and simmer gently until tender.

Just before serving, combine cream and egg yolks and pour over chicken. Heat through for 5 minutes, stirring continuously, taking care that sauce never comes to the boil. Correct seasoning and serve immediately. Serves 4.

POULET À LA CRÈME – II

1 3½-POUND CHICKEN
BOILING WATER AND WINE, TO COVER
1 ONION, STUCK WITH A CLOVE
2 CARROTS
2 LEEKS
1 STALK CELERY
1 BAY LEAF
PEPPERCORNS
1 BOUQUET GARNI
SALT
2 TABLESPOONS BUTTER
2 TABLESPOONS FLOUR
1 TABLESPOON CURRY POWDER
3 EGG YOLKS
6 TABLESPOONS CREAM

Place the chicken in a deep saucepan and cover with boiling water and dry white wine in equal quantities. Add the onion stuck with a clove, carrots, leeks, celery, bay leaf, a few peppercorns and a *bouquet garni*. Cover tightly and simmer gently – do not boil – for 1 hour. Add salt to taste and continue simmering until the chicken is tender.

Cut the chicken into serving pieces and serve accompanied by the following sauce: make a *roux* by melting 2 tablespoons butter with 2 tablespoons flour and 1 tablespoon curry powder. Before this mixture changes colour, moisten with chicken stock (about ¾ pint). Thicken the sauce by stirring in 3 egg yolks mixed with 6 tablespoons cream. Cook for several minutes without allowing it to boil, and pour over the chicken pieces. Serves 4.

The broth in which the chicken has been cooked will make an excellent *consommé*.

POULE AU RIZ AU SAFRAN

1 FAT CHICKEN
1 SPANISH ONION, STUCK WITH 2 CLOVES
2 LARGE CARROTS
1 BOUQUET GARNI
1 STALK CELERY
2 CLOVES GARLIC
1 GLASS DRY WHITE WINE
1 QUART WHITE STOCK (CHICKEN OR VEAL, OR BOTH)
SALT AND PEPPERCORNS

SAFFRON RICE:
1 TABLESPOON BUTTER
1 SPANISH ONION
½ POUND RICE
HALF OF THE CHICKEN STOCK, STRAINEDSALT AND FRESHLY-GROUND BLACK PEPPER
FRESHLY-GRATED NUTMEG
1 GENEROUS PINCH SAFFRON

CHICKEN VELOUTÉ SAUCE:
2 TABLESPOONS FLOUR
2 TABLESPOONS BUTTER
REMAINDER OF CHICKEN STOCK
2 EGG YOLKS
JUICE OF 1 LEMON

Clean, singe and truss chicken; place in a casserole with an onion stuck with cloves; add carrots, a *bouquet garni*, celery and garlic, and moisten with dry white wine and a good white stock. Season to taste with salt and a few peppercorns, and simmer gently for about 1½ hours, or until chicken is tender.

Remove chicken and keep warm. Strain chicken stock and use for saffron rice and for chicken *velouté* sauce.
To make saffron rice: Melt butter in a saucepan; add finely-chopped onion and stir for a minute over the heat until transparent. Stir in rice; add half of the strained chicken stock and salt, pepper, a little freshly-grated nutmeg and saffron, to taste, and simmer very gently, covered, for about 25 minutes, or until rice is tender but not mushy.
To make chicken velouté: Make a white *roux* with flour and butter; add remaining chicken stock and bring slowly to the boil, stirring constantly. Simmer, stirring from time to time, until sauce is thick and smooth. Correct seasoning and just before serving add egg yolks and lemon juice.

The Festive Duck

The duck is a festive bird. It is ideal for a special occasion. I am always disappointed when I hear cooks in this country recommending that it should be served 'plain roast with green peas and sauce'. I far prefer the Continental methods – French, Italian and Greek – of dealing with this delicious bird, half-way in flavour between poultry and game. It is rich, meltingly tender when young, and fairly cries out to be simmered with wine, herbs and brandy in the Provençal manner. It can be filleted raw, marinated in Madeira and herbs, and encased with the remainder of the meat, pounded and mixed with truffles and fat salt pork, in a terrine or *pâté en croute*, or stuffed with rice or wheat and pine nuts and herbs *à la grecque*, before being roasted in the oven.

I remember delicious country meals in France at which duck was the star performer: duck *en gelée*, the duck simmered in a rich stock with carrots, onions and celery, cooled in its own liquids and then served whole in its own jelly, surrounded by young vegetables; duck *en casserole*, the duck cut into serving pieces and marinated overnight in wine and brandy, flavoured with garlic, herbs, onions and carrots, and then simmered in the marinade juices until tender. I also remember duck stuffed with diced green bacon, sauerkraut and diced green apples and roasted in the oven, bathed in dry white wine and its own juices.

But perhaps best of all, I like to roast my ducks to the half-way mark and then finish them with a variety of sweet and savoury ingredients. Duck goes wonderfully with oranges, olives, apples, cherries, herbs and spices, sauerkraut, wild rice, wines, cognac and gin.

Be imaginative with duck at your next dinner party. One

5- or 6-pound duck, or two smaller ones, will serve 4 to 8 people easily.

DUCK NOTES

Ducks mature rapidly and reach their prime about 9 to 12 weeks after they hatch, when they weigh about 5 to 7 pounds.

You can judge the age of a duck by pressing its beak with your finger. A young duck's beak should be soft and flexible, while an older bird's beak will be hard and firm. A duck is a very fat bird so you will not need to add additional fat when roasting. I usually cut all visible fat from openings before cooking and pour off excess fat occasionally as it accumulates in the pan.

ROAST DUCKLING

Preparation: Trim wing-tips and cut off the neck of a 5- or 6-pound duckling. Wipe the bird with a damp clean cloth inside and out, and sprinkle the cavity with salt and freshly-ground black pepper. Rub the cavity with lemon juice or brandy and fill it with ½ sliced onion, ½ peeled and sliced apple and a few celery leaves.

Preliminary roasting: Prick the skin of the bird with a fork; rub with a cut clove of garlic and sprinkle with salt and pepper. Place duckling, breast side up, on a rack in a roasting pan and cook in a moderate oven (375°F. Mark 4) for ½ hour. Remove duck and keep warm.

To finish bird: Skim excess fat from the pan, add ½ pint dry white wine and continue to roast the bird until tender, basting frequently and allowing about 20 minutes cooking time to the pound.

DUCKLING WITH OLIVES

Preparation: As above.
Preliminary roasting: As above.
To finish bird: Pour off all but 2 tablespoons of fat from the pan. Stir in 1 tablespoon flour and cook, stirring continuously, until flour is golden. Add ¼ pint chicken stock and ¼ pint dry white wine and cook, stirring, until the sauce is smooth and slightly thickened. Transfer sauce to an oven-proof casserole large enough to hold duck; season sauce to taste with salt and pepper, and add a *bouquet garni* (3 sprigs parsley, 1 bay leaf, 1 stalk celery, 1 sprig thyme).

Place duck in the casserole and cook, covered, for about 1 hour, or until duck is tender. Pit 24 green olives and poach them in water for 5 minutes to remove excess salt. Place duck on a heated serving platter; add the drained olives to the sauce and pour it over the bird. Serve immediately.

DUCKLING WITH ORANGES

Preparation: As above.

Preliminary roasting: As above, but continue roasting, basting from time to time, until duck is tender, allowing about 20 minutes cooking time to the pound. Remove duck from the pan and keep warm.

To finish bird: Skim fat from pan juices and add ¼ pint chicken stock to the pan, scraping in all the crusty bits from bottom and sides of pan. Stir in the juice of 2 oranges and 1 lemon, and 2 tablespoons cognac. Blend 2 tablespoons each of sugar and water in another pan and cook until sugar turns to caramel. Add this to the sauce and simmer gently until it is reduced by half.

To serve: Carve the duckling; place on a heated serving platter; pour sauce over it and sprinkle with the rinds of 2 Seville oranges cut into thin strips and blanched in boiling water. Garnish with fresh orange segments and watercress.

DUCK EN DAUBE

1 TENDER DUCK
SALT AND FRESHLY-GROUND BLACK PEPPER
1 STALK CELERY, CHOPPED
2 CARROTS, SLICED
2 LARGE ONIONS, SLICED
4 FLUID OUNCES COGNAC
¾ PINT DRY RED WINE
4 OUNCES FAT BACON, DICED
1 TABLESPOON OLIVE OIL
1 BOUQUET GARNI
1 CLOVE GARLIC
½ POUND MUSHROOMS, SLICED

Cut duck into serving pieces and place in a porcelain or earthenware bowl. Add salt and freshly-ground black pepper, celery, carrots, sliced onions, cognac and red wine, and marinate the duck in this mixture for at least 2 hours.

Remove duck from the marinade; drain and dry with a clean cloth. Sauté diced bacon in olive oil until golden. Remove bacon bits and brown duck pieces in the resulting fat. Place bacon bits and duck pieces with pan juices in a large oven-proof casserole and cook, covered, for 20 minutes.

Add the marinade, *bouquet garni*, garlic and mushrooms. Cook over a low flame for 1½ hours, or until duck is tender. Remove *bouquet garni*; skim fat; correct seasoning and serve in casserole. Serves 4.

PINEAPPLE DUCK

1 DUCK, CUT INTO SERVING PIECES
OLIVE OIL
1 TIN PINEAPPLE SLICES
1 GLASS RED WINE
1 CLOVE GARLIC, FINELY CHOPPED
SALT AND FRESHLY-GROUND BLACK PEPPER

PINEAPPLE AND ORANGE SAUCE:
½ OUNCE CORNFLOUR
JUICE AND RIND OF 1 ORANGE
JUICES FROM THE DUCK, MADE UP TO ½ PINT WITH WATER
2 OUNCES SEEDLESS RAISINS

Place the duck, cut into serving pieces, in a roasting pan, and brush well with olive oil. Pour the juice from the tin of pineapple into the pan with the red wine, finely-chopped garlic, and salt and black pepper, to taste. Cook in a moderate oven (375°F. Mark 4) for 40 minutes or until well cooked. Baste frequently with the juices. Serve with pineapple and orange sauce. Serves 4.

To make sauce: Mix cornflour to a smooth paste with orange juice. Heat pan juices, skimmed of fat and made up to ½ pint with water, and pour over the cornflour mixture. Return to the pan and cook until thick. Add chopped pineapple slices, raisins and grated rind of orange, and heat through.

DUCK WITH SAUERKRAUT AND APPLE STUFFING

1 DUCK (4–5 POUNDS)
6 OUNCES FAT SALT PORK
1 LARGE ONION, COARSELY CHOPPED
2 COOKING APPLES
2 TABLESPOONS BROWN SUGAR
SALT AND FRESHLY-GROUND BLACK PEPPER
THYME
1 TEASPOON CARAWAY SEED
1½ POUNDS SAUERKRAUT

Dice salt pork and heat in frying pan until transparent. Add coarsely-chopped onion and fry until transparent. Add apples which have been peeled, cored and diced, and toss with onion and salt pork. When apples and onion are golden, add brown sugar, salt, pepper, thyme and caraway seed. Remove from the heat. Drain sauerkraut and toss with apple and onion mixture.

Wash duck inside and out. Rub cavity with a little salt and pepper. Stuff with apple-sauerkraut and truss. Prick well with a fork and place duck on rack over a roasting pan. Roast in a slow oven (350°F. Mark 3) for about 2½ hours, pricking duck from time to time to allow fat to escape. When the leg joint moves freely, the bird is done. Serves 4.

ROAST GOOSE

1 GOOSE (8–10 POUNDS)
FLOUR
SALT AND FRESHLY-GROUND BLACK PEPPER
DRY BREADCRUMBS

Stuff and tie goose and sprinkle lightly with flour. Roast in a fairly hot oven (425°F. Mark 6) for 15 minutes; reduce heat to 350°F. (Mark 3) and continue roasting until goose is tender (about 25 minutes per pound if stuffed).

Do not baste goose during cooking time as it is already fat enough. Remove fat several times during cooking. It will keep indefinitely in a cool place.

If you cover goose with aluminium foil, remove foil at least ¾ hour before end of cooking time; 15 minutes before end of cooking time, sprinkle lightly with dry breadcrumbs; raise oven heat to 425°F. (Mark 6) and cook for final 15 minutes.

STUFFED GOOSE NECK

1 GOOSE NECK (SKIN ONLY)
4–6 TABLESPOONS BRANDY
2 CLOVES GARLIC, FINELY CHOPPED
2 TABLESPOONS FINELY-CHOPPED PARSLEY
FRESHLY-GROUND BLACK PEPPER
1 GOOD PINCH POWDERED CINNAMON
1 GOOD PINCH POWDERED CLOVES
1 POUND SAUSAGE MEAT
1 SMALL DUCK'S LIVER, CHOPPED
2 TRUFFLES, COARSELY CHOPPED
½ LEVEL TEASPOON POWDERED MACE
SALT
½ GLASS DRY WHITE WINE
FAT, FOR FRYING

Remove skin from fat goose neck by separating skin from neck at one end with a sharp knife. Peel back the skin and pull it off, inside out, as you would a glove.

Marinate skin overnight in brandy seasoned with finely-chopped garlic, parsley and freshly-ground black pepper, to taste, and a good pinch each of cinnamon and powdered cloves.

Make a stuffing of sausage meat, chopped duck's liver and truffles, and season to taste with powdered mace, salt and pepper. Moisten with dry white wine and the marinade juices and mix well. Turn skin right side out and stuff with mixture; then tie or sew it firmly at both ends so that stuffing cannot fall out during cooking.

Sauté the stuffed neck in goose fat or lard over low heat until the dressing is cooked through and the neck is brown. Serve the stuffed goose neck sliced, hot or cold.

AUSTRIAN STUFFING FOR GOOSE OR TURKEY

1 SPANISH ONION, FINELY CHOPPED
LARD
½ POUND SAUSAGE MEAT
2 TABLESPOONS FINELY-CHOPPED PARSLEY
4 ANCHOVY FILLETS, FINELY CHOPPED
2 EGGS
JUICE OF ½ LEMON
THYME AND MARJORAM
SALT AND FRESHLY-GROUND BLACK PEPPER
½ POUND POULTRY LIVERS, CHOPPED
2–3 OUNCES DRY BREADCRUMBS

Sauté finely-chopped onion in lard until transparent. Add sausage meat and sauté with onion until golden. Combine onion and sausage mixture in a bowl with finely-chopped parsley and anchovy fillets, eggs, lemon juice, thyme, marjoram, and salt and freshly-ground black pepper, to taste. Sauté chopped poultry livers in remaining fat; add breadcrumbs and toss until golden. Combine with other ingredients and stuff bird.

CONFIT D'OIE (PRESERVED GOOSE)

1 FAT GOOSE
1 LEVEL TEASPOON SALT
1 LEVEL TEASPOON POWDERED MIXED SPICES
¼ LEVEL TEASPOON CRUSHED THYME
SALT
GOOSE FAT
2 GLASSES WATER
MELTED LARD, TO COVER (IF NECESSARY)

Cut goose into 8 or 10 pieces, reserving all goose fat. Pound salt, spices and thyme in a mortar; mix well and rub goose pieces with this mixture. Place pieces in a large casserole and add ¾ ounce salt per pound of goose. Mix well and leave in a cool place for 24 to 36 hours.

continued on page 265

Illustration on facing page

Osso Buco

– veal marrow bones simmered in a rich tomato sauce and served with saffron rice – is one of the great dishes served at London's Tiberio Restaurant. Our photograph shows this dish against the red glass wall that separates Tiberio's elegant dining-room from the beautifully designed kitchen. (Recipe on page 212.)

Illustration on following page

Pork and Lobster Balls, Sweet and Sour

– is an exotic Chinese delicacy, easily translatable to Western kitchens. The traditional Sweet and Sour sauce so beloved by Chinese cooks adds authentic excitement to this Chinese dish as served at The China Garden Restaurant, London. (Recipe on page 240.)

Dice goose fat; combine with water in a large saucepan and melt fat gently over a low heat. When fat is melted, add goose pieces from which you have brushed salt and simmer gently for 2½ hours, or until goose is tender.

Wash deep earthenware or pyrex containers with boiling water; dry well and arrange pieces of preserved goose in them. Continue to cook the fat until froth forms on the surface; skim thoroughly; remove from heat and cool for 10 minutes.

Pour fat through a fine sieve to cover goose pieces. If there is not enough fat to cover all pieces, melt enough fresh lard to cover them completely. Allow to cool; seal container with greaseproof paper and tie securely. A well-prepared *confit* will keep in a cool place for several months, to be used little by little, either by itself (served hot with puréed potatoes), or as one of the star ingredients in a *cassoulet*.

ROAST TURKEY

1 MEDIUM TURKEY (10–12 POUNDS)
STRIPS OF PORK FAT OR GREEN BACON
SALT AND FRESHLY-GROUND BLACK PEPPER
½ POUND BUTTER, MELTED
JUICE OF 1 LEMON

Place turkey, breast side up, in a roasting pan and cover breast with thin strips of pork fat or green bacon. Season to taste with salt and freshly-ground black pepper and roast in a fairly hot oven (425°F. Mark 6) for 15 minutes; then reduce temperature to 350°F. (Mark 3) and cook until juices run clear when turkey is stuck with a skewer at the leg joint (10 to 15 minutes per pound or 20 minutes per pound if stuffed), basting frequently with melted butter and lemon juice.

If turkey has not become golden towards the end of cooking time, bring heat up to 425°F. (Mark 6) again and roast for 10 or 15 minutes more.

Illustration on previous page

Coq-au-Vin

These are the raw ingredients for one of France's most famous dishes. There are as many recipes for coq-au-vin as there are cooks in France. (Recipe on page 248.)

Illustration on facing page

Caneton de Colette

Restaurant Lapérouse, Paris

Pressed duck – with a sauce made rich with mashed duck livers, cognac, port, butter and allspice – is one of the most famous dishes served at Lapérouse.

PINTADEAU RÔTI ET FLAMBÉ À LA RICHE

2 GUINEA FOWL
½ PINT BURGUNDY
GRATED RIND OF 1 LEMON
4–6 TABLESPOONS COGNAC
DIJON MUSTARD
4 OUNCES BUTTER
4 OUNCES FOIE GRAS
1–2 TABLESPOONS LEMON JUICE
SALT AND FRESHLY-GROUND BLACK PEPPER

Roast guinea fowl in a moderately hot oven (400°F. Mark 5) for 25 to 30 minutes, or until almost cooked. Cut birds into serving pieces.

Reduce wine with grated lemon rind to a third of its original quantity. Add birds to pan and heat through. Flame with warmed cognac. Stir in mustard, to taste, and continue to simmer for a few minutes, turning birds from time to time.

Mix butter and *foie gras* to a smooth paste and add to pan, stirring in all the juices. Add lemon juice. Stir pieces of guinea fowl into sauce, making sure they are well covered. Season to taste with salt and freshly-ground black pepper and serve immediately. Serves 4 to 6.

Magdalen Venison

Most of us imagine that a medieval banquet would have consisted of a series of great set pieces like Sir Osbert Sitwell's recipe: 'You first captured a swan – having previously been granted, of course, the necessary royal permission – and then stuffed it with a peacock, inside which you had placed a pheasant, which contained a partridge, and so *ad infinitum*.' But the first written recipes in English, produced by Richard II's cooks in 1391, have an amazingly modern ring about them. I was surprised by the variety of fruits and vegetables available; the numbers of ways of preparing fish, both salt and 'green'; the different recipes for meat and game; the imaginative use of seasonings, wines and herbs; and the great variety of the recipes themselves. One, for example, advocates the use of grapes to stuff a chicken, together with garlic, parsley and sage.

But the modern ring of these ancient dishes is not so surprising. The High Tables of the Plantagenet kings and of the great houses of the Tudor nobility have their direct descendants today in the High Tables at Oxford and Cambridge, where the rulers of the college still dine on a raised dais, separated from the commoners below them.

Famous feasts linger long in the memory of a place like Oxford. Gaudies and Bump Suppers, banquets to royalty and to visiting statesmen, even ordinary fish and flesh days, all have given rise to recipes that are handed down throughout the years from chef to chef in the college kitchens . . . the

Christmas Boar's Head at Queen's, the legendary Cherry Pie at All Souls, the superb Meringues of Christ Church, and at Magdalen, the seventeen-day ritual of Magdalen Venison.

One of Oxford's greatest dishes, Magdalen Venison, which has been served for two and a half centuries at the yearly Restoration Dinner, is a saddle of venison from the College's own herd, marinated for days, braised in Château wine, garnished with glazed chestnuts, glazed onions and sautéed mushrooms, and served with a heady port wine sauce.

Tradition has it that there should be only as many deer in the park as there are Fellows in College . . . and so every year at the Restoration Dinner venison is served.

According to a centuries-old recipe, 'second year' beasts are selected from the herd, killed, blooded and stripped, dusted with rock salt and powdered ginger, and allowed to hang for at least ten days. Then the choicest bits – the saddle, leg or haunch – are cut for High Table and marinated for three days to one week to improve the flavour and tenderise the meat.

MAGDALEN VENISON

6- OR 7-POUND SADDLE OF VENISON
4 TABLESPOONS BUTTER
4 TABLESPOONS OLIVE OIL
½ POUND DICED SALT PORK

MARINADE:
1 SPANISH ONION
2 CARROTS
2 TABLESPOONS BUTTER OR OLIVE OIL
1 BOTTLE CHÂTEAU WINE, EITHER BURGUNDY OR CLARET
3 SPRIGS PARSLEY
1 SPRIG THYME
1 BAY LEAF
2 CLOVES GARLIC
4–5 BLACK PEPPERCORNS
1–2 CRUSHED JUNIPER BERRIES

SAUCE:
MARINADE JUICES, REDUCED
BEURRE MANIÉ (1 TABLESPOON EACH BUTTER AND FLOUR)
1 WINEGLASS OF PORT
2 TABLESPOONS REDCURRANT JELLY

GARNISH:
GLAZED CHESTNUTS
GLAZED BUTTON ONIONS
SAUTÉED BUTTON MUSHROOMS

To make marinade: Slice onion and carrots and 'sweat' them gently in a little butter or olive oil. Place vegetables in a china or earthenware casserole, not metal, and add wine, parsley, thyme, bay leaf, garlic, pepper and juniper berries. Soak venison in this mixture for 3 days to a week in a cool place, turning 3 or 4 times a day so that all surfaces of the meat are evenly exposed to the marinade and keep well moistened. The longer the meat is marinated, the gamier the flavour.

To cook the meat: Combine butter and olive oil in a heavy-bottomed metal pan or iron casserole with a tight cover. Add diced salt pork and sauté until pork cubes are crisp and golden. Then drain venison from the marinade, wipe it dry with a damp cloth, and brown it lightly in the fats.

Boil down the juices of the marinade to half the original quantity, and strain sauce over the venison. Cover and cook in a moderately slow oven (325°F. Mark 2) until meat is tender.

When meat is tender, remove it from the casserole to a warm serving platter and keep it in a warm place.

To make the sauce: Reduce sauce to half the original quantity by cooking over a high flame. Thicken, if necessary, with a *beurre manié* made by combining 1 tablespoon flour with the same amount of butter. Add 1 wineglass of port and 2 tablespoons of redcurrant jelly and blend all together, taking care to dislodge all the crusty bits at the sides of the pan.

Strain the sauce, which should be dark and rich, over the venison and serve garnished with alternate clusters of glazed chestnuts, glazed button onions and sautéed button mushrooms. Serves 8 to 10.

VENISON IN PORT

¼ PINT OLIVE OIL
¼ POUND BUTTER
2 CARROTS, SLICED
1 SPANISH ONION, SLICED
2 CLOVES GARLIC
1 SPRIG THYME
1 BAY LEAF
6- OR 7-POUND SADDLE OF VENISON
SALT AND FRESHLY-GROUND BLACK PEPPER
⅓ BOTTLE PORT
1 TABLESPOON BUTTER
1 TABLESPOON FLOUR
1 TABLESPOON REDCURRANT JELLY

GARNISH:
GLAZED CHESTNUTS
GLAZED BUTTON ONIONS
MUSHROOM CAPS SAUTÉED IN BUTTER
FRIED CROÛTONS

Combine olive oil and butter in a braising pan. Add sliced carrots, onion, garlic, thyme and bay leaf. Place saddle of venison, seasoned with salt and freshly-ground black pepper, on this bed of aromatics. Cover the pan and cook in a moderate oven (375°F. Mark 4) until the saddle begins to brown. Pour ⅓ bottle of good port over the roast and cook, basting continually with meat and wine juices, until tender.

Remove saddle to a serving platter and keep in a warm place. Skim away fat from the pan and strain the sauce into a small saucepan. Reduce the sauce by boiling down to half the original quantity; thicken it with a *beurre manié* (made by kneading butter and flour to a smooth paste), and add 1 tablespoon of redcurrant jelly. Correct seasoning.

Carve the saddle and serve on the bone, surrounded with glazed chestnuts, glazed button onions and mushroom caps sautéed in butter. Just before serving, strain the sauce over the venison and surround with fried *croûtons.*

VENISON STEAKS

3 POUNDS VENISON STEAK
FAT SALT PORK, FOR LARDING
¼ POUND BUTTER
SALT AND FRESHLY-GROUND BLACK PEPPER
CRUSHED JUNIPER BERRIES
DRIED ROSEMARY
1 SPANISH ONION, GRATED
¼ PINT RICH BEEF STOCK
¼ PINT RED BURGUNDY
¼ PINT THICK SOUR CREAM
¼ POUND MUSHROOMS, SLICED
REDCURRANT JELLY

Have leg or loin of venison cut into 4 thick steaks. Lard with thin strips of fat salt pork; trim off larding ends into a thick-bottomed frying pan and add butter (reserving 1 tablespoon for later use), salt, freshly-ground black pepper, crushed juniper berries and dried rosemary (a good pinch per steak). Heat; add steaks and brown until done on both sides, about 5 minutes per side, or until tender. Remove steaks and keep warm. Cut heat down to a simmer; add grated onion, beef stock and red wine to the pan. Mix well, scraping in all crusty bits from sides of pan. Reduce gently until sauce is rich and thick; add sour cream; simmer and strain. Clean pan and sauté sliced mushrooms in remaining butter until tender; add steaks to pan and pour sauce over them. Heat through and serve with redcurrant jelly. Serves 4.

PIGEONS CONFITS AUX RAISINS

4 PIGEONS
SALT AND FRESHLY-GROUND BLACK PEPPER
4–6 TABLESPOONS COGNAC
6 FLUID OUNCES MELTED CHICKEN FAT OR LARD
FEW DROPS WATER
4 OVAL PASTRY CASES OR RECTANGULAR CANAPÉS (EACH LARGE ENOUGH TO HOLD A PIGEON)
1 SMALL TIN MOUSSE DE FOIE GRAS
BLACK TRUFFLES
PEELED AND SEEDED WHITE GRAPES
ASPIC JELLY

Season pigeons with salt and freshly-ground black pepper and flame with cognac.

Melt chicken fat with a few drops of water over a low heat. As soon as the fat is nearly melted, add pigeons; bring fat to a moderate boil and simmer for 45 minutes to 1 hour.

Remove pigeons from fat; place them in a stone or earthenware crock, cover with strained fat and cool.

Prepare 4 oval-shaped pastry cases and bake in the usual manner, or use 4 rectangular *canapés*. Spread with *mousse de foie gras* and place 1 pigeon (from which you have removed the fat) in the centre of each. Decorate pigeons with small pieces of black truffle, surround each bird with 6 large peeled and seeded white grapes and glaze with aspic jelly.

RABBIT IN CREAM

1 RABBIT (OR HARE)
¼ POUND LEAN BACON, THINLY SLICED
¼ POUND FAT SALT PORK, THINLY SLICED
FRESH HERBS
2 TABLESPOONS BUTTER
6 TABLESPOONS FINE CHAMPAGNE
SALT AND FRESHLY-GROUND BLACK PEPPER
¾ PINT FRESH CREAM
STOCK OR DRY WHITE WINE

Cut rabbit (or hare) into serving pieces. Line an earthenware casserole just large enough to hold rabbit, with alternating thin strips of lean bacon and fat salt pork. Cover this bed with aromatic herbs (tarragon, thyme, rosemary); sauté rabbit pieces in butter until golden; place them on bed of herbs and pour over *fine champagne* or other quality brandy. Season to taste with salt and pepper.

Place casserole on an asbestos mat and start cooking at a low heat. After 30 minutes cover rabbit pieces with fresh cream and a little stock or dry white wine. Cover casserole and simmer for about 3 hours. Serve from casserole. Serves 4.

VINTNER'S STEW OF RABBIT OR HARE

1 RABBIT OR HARE

MARINADE MIXTURE:
1 SPANISH ONION, SLICED
2 CARROTS, SLICED
2 CLOVES GARLIC
½ PINT RED BURGUNDY
4 SPRIGS PARSLEY
1 SPRIG THYME
SALT AND FRESHLY-GROUND BLACK PEPPER
4 TABLESPOONS OLIVE OIL

FOR COOKING:
4 TABLESPOONS OLIVE OIL
2 TABLESPOONS FLOUR
SALT AND FRESHLY-GROUND BLACK PEPPER
½ PINT BEEF STOCK
1 PINT RED BURGUNDY

GARNISH:
12 BUTTON MUSHROOMS
12 GLAZED ONIONS
¼ POUND FAT SALT PORK, DICED
CROÛTONS
2 TABLESPOONS CHOPPED PARSLEY

Skin and clean rabbit or hare; cut into serving pieces and marinate in the marinade mixture for 2 days, turning pieces several times each day so that they will be well marinated.

Dry rabbit pieces with a damp cloth; season well with salt and pepper and sprinkle liberally with flour. Sauté pieces in hot olive oil until golden; skim fat and add marinade mixture, beef stock and enough red wine, as necessary, to cover the meat. Bring to the boil, skim and allow to simmer slowly for about 1½ hours, by which time the meat should be almost done. Remove meat to a serving platter and keep warm. Strain sauce into a clean casserole; skim fat and correct seasoning.

Add rabbit pieces, button mushrooms, glazed onions and sautéed, diced, fat salt pork to the sauce and cook for ½ hour more, or until rabbit pieces are tender. Serve with *croûtons* and finely-chopped parsley. Serves 4 to 6.

RABBIT AUX DEUX MOUTARDES

1 FAT TENDER RABBIT
2 TABLESPOONS FLOUR
SALT AND FRESHLY-GROUND BLACK PEPPER
2 TABLESPOONS OLIVE OIL
2 TABLESPOONS BUTTER
4 OUNCES FAT BACON, DICED AND BLANCHED
4 SHALLOTS, CHOPPED
1 BOUQUET GARNI
¼ PINT DRY WHITE WINE
¼ PINT CHICKEN STOCK
1 TEASPOON DIJON MUSTARD
1 TEASPOON ENGLISH MUSTARD
½ PINT DOUBLE CREAM

Cut rabbit into serving pieces; roll pieces in flour, add salt and pepper and sauté until golden in olive oil and butter with diced, blanched bacon. Add chopped shallots and a *bouquet garni*; moisten with white wine and stock, and cook gently, covered, until rabbit is tender.

Drain rabbit pieces; place them on a heated serving platter and keep warm. Skim fat from the sauce; whisk Dijon mustard and English mustard thoroughly with fresh cream and add to the sauce in the pan. Correct seasoning, adding a little more mustard, salt and pepper, if desired. Add rabbit pieces; heat through and serve in the casserole. Serves 4.

CASSEROLED PHEASANT

2 YOUNG PHEASANTS
6 OUNCES COOKED HAM, FINELY CHOPPED
6 TABLESPOONS COOKED RICE
6 TABLESPOONS COGNAC
1 EGG
SALT AND FRESHLY-GROUND BLACK PEPPER
POWDERED THYME AND MARJORAM
FAT SALT PORK
4 TABLESPOONS BUTTER
4 TABLESPOONS OLIVE OIL
2–4 SHALLOTS, FINELY CHOPPED
2 TABLESPOONS COGNAC, WARMED
1 POUND BUTTON MUSHROOMS
2 CLOVES GARLIC
JUICE OF ½ LEMON

Clean birds and stuff with the following mixture: finely-chopped pheasant livers combined with finely-chopped ham and cooked rice, moistened with cognac and egg and flavoured to taste with salt, freshly-ground black pepper, powdered thyme and marjoram.

Truss birds firmly; wrap each in fat salt pork and brown birds on all sides in a fire-proof casserole with 2 tablespoons each of butter and olive oil and the finely-chopped shallots.

Pour over 2 tablespoons warmed cognac and ignite. When flames die down, cover casserole and simmer pheasants on a low flame or in a slow oven until almost done, adding a little more liquid if necessary.

Sauté mushrooms and garlic in the remaining butter and oil. Season well and pour over birds. Finish cooking on an asbestos mat or in a low oven and just before serving, sprinkle with lemon juice. Serves 6 to 8.

NORMANDY PHEASANT

2 PLUMP PHEASANTS
4 TABLESPOONS BUTTER
2 LARGE TART APPLES
1 WINEGLASS CALVADOS
½ PINT FRESH CREAM
JUICE OF ½ LEMON
SALT AND FRESHLY-GROUND BLACK PEPPER

Clean and truss 2 plump pheasants and sauté in half the butter in a heavy-bottomed frying pan until they are nicely browned on all sides. Remove and keep warm.

Peel, core and slice apples and sauté them in remaining butter until golden. Place apples in the bottom of an earthenware casserole: arrange pheasants on top; baste with the pan juices thinned down with Calvados and cook the birds in a moderate oven (375°F. Mark 4) for about 30 minutes.

Add cream and the juice of ½ lemon, and season to taste with salt and freshly-ground black pepper. Return the casserole, covered, to the oven and cook until the birds are tender and the sauce is thick and creamy. Serves 6 to 8.

PHEASANT À LA CRÈME

1 TENDER PHEASANT
4 TABLESPOONS BUTTER
2 TABLESPOONS OLIVE OIL
2 TABLESPOONS FINELY-CHOPPED CARROT
2 TABLESPOONS FINELY-CHOPPED ONION
1 GOOD PINCH THYME
1 BAY LEAF, CRUMBLED
2–4 TABLESPOONS COGNAC, HEATED
½ PINT DOUBLE CREAM
PHEASANT LIVER
BUTTER
COGNAC
BREAD
SALT AND FRESHLY-GROUND BLACK PEPPER

Clean and truss pheasant and brown on all sides in butter and olive oil in a flame-proof casserole. Add finely-chopped carrot and onion, thyme and bay leaf. Cover casserole and simmer for 20 minutes. Pour off excess fat and flame with heated cognac. Moisten with cream; cover casserole and simmer until pheasant is tender and sauce has reduced a little.

Mash the pheasant liver with a little butter and cognac and spread a *canapé* of white bread with this mixture. Remove bird; pass the sauce through a fine sieve and correct seasoning.

Place pheasant on the *canapé* and cover with sauce, which should be quite thick. Serves 4.

PHEASANT WITH GREEN APPLES

1 PHEASANT
¼ POUND GREEN BACON, DICED
½ SPANISH ONION, FINELY CHOPPED
1 CLOVE GARLIC, FINELY CHOPPED
2 TABLESPOONS BUTTER
2 TABLESPOONS OLIVE OIL
4 SMALL COOKING APPLES
4 TABLESPOONS COINTREAU
½ PINT CREAM
SALT AND FRESHLY-GROUND BLACK PEPPER

Sauté diced green bacon and finely-chopped onion and garlic in butter and oil in a fire-proof casserole until golden. Remove bacon and vegetables; reserve. Then brown pheasant on all sides in resulting mixture of fats. Remove pheasant and keep warm.

Peel, core and slice apples thickly and sauté in remaining fat until they start to turn golden. Pour over Cointreau. Remove apples from casserole. Skim fat from pan juices. Return pheasant to casserole; surround with apple slices, bacon bits, onion and garlic, and allow to simmer, covered, for 10 minutes. Stir in the cream, add salt and freshly-ground black pepper, to taste; cover the casserole and cook in a slow oven (275°F. Mark ½) until the pheasant is tender.

When ready to serve, remove the pheasant and bacon bits to a clean casserole and keep warm; purée sauce and apples. Correct seasoning; re-heat the sauce; pour over pheasant and serve immediately.

PHEASANT À LA SOUVAROFF

2 YOUNG PHEASANTS
4 OUNCES PÂTÉ DE FOIE GRAS, DICED
1 TRUFFLE, THINLY SLICED
1 TABLESPOON COGNAC
SALT AND FRESHLY-GROUND BLACK PEPPER
BUTTER
DRY WHITE WINE
2–3 SLICES FAT SALT PORK OR GREEN BACON
DICED TRUFFLES
4 TABLESPOONS MADEIRA
2 TABLESPOONS COGNAC
3 TABLESPOONS TRUFFLE JUICE
3 TABLESPOONS DEMI-GLACE (IF AVAILABLE)
FLOUR AND WATER PASTE

Clean your pheasants (partridge and quail are also excellent cooked in this way, and I have often made a delicious casserole with a fine fat capon) and stuff with the following mixture: diced *pâté de foie gras*, thinly-sliced truffle, cognac, and salt and freshly-ground black pepper, to taste.

Truss wings and legs of birds; sew up openings and place in a buttered roasting pan with a little butter and some dry white wine. To prevent birds from drying out in cooking, cover breasts with several slices of fresh fat pork or green bacon and cook for about 40 minutes in a hot oven (400°F. Mark 5). Remove pork strips from breasts, cut strings and place birds in an oval casserole just large enough to hold them comfortably. Cover casserole. Set pan juices aside to cool; you will use them later. All the above can be done before your guests arrive.

About 25 minutes before you wish to serve the birds, dice 3 or 4 small truffles and toss them in a little hot butter to bring out their flavour. Then skim solidified fat from roasting pan and add 4 tablespoons Madeira, 2 tablespoons cognac, 3 tablespoons truffle juice, and, if available, the same of *demi-glace* sauce, to the pan juices. Stir this mixture over a low heat until it nearly reaches boiling point and strain sauce over the pheasants in the casserole.

Cover casserole and seal the edges with a band of stiff dough made of flour and water. Bake in moderate oven (375°F. Mark 4) for 20 minutes. Bring the sealed casserole to the table and break seal just before serving. Serves 4 to 6.

PHEASANT IN RED WINE

2 YOUNG PHEASANTS
4 SHALLOTS, FINELY CHOPPED
2 TABLESPOONS OLIVE OIL
3 TABLESPOONS BUTTER
1 PINT RED BURGUNDY
MUSHROOM STALKS
SALT AND FRESHLY-GROUND BLACK PEPPER
1 TABLESPOON FLOUR

GLAZED ONIONS:
12 SMALL ONIONS
1 TABLESPOON BUTTER
1 TABLESPOON GRANULATED SUGAR

SAUTÉED MUSHROOM CAPS:
12 BUTTON MUSHROOMS
1 TABLESPOON BUTTER
SALT AND FRESHLY-GROUND BLACK PEPPER

Clean birds. Put 2 finely-chopped shallots and the pheasant liver into the cavity of each bird. Heat olive oil and 2 tablespoons butter in a large thick pan and sauté pheasants gently until they are golden on all sides and almost tender.

Transfer pheasants to a large oven-proof casserole and keep warm. Pour red wine into the pan in which you have cooked birds and cook over a high flame, combining wine with the pan juices. Add mushroom stalks and continue to cook until the liquid is reduced by half. Thicken the sauce with the remaining butter and flour. Simmer for a few minutes; strain through a fine sieve into a bowl and allow to cool slightly so that the grease can be skimmed off the surface.

Pour wine sauce over the pheasants, correct seasoning and add glazed onions and sautéed mushroom caps. Cover casserole and cook in a moderate oven until pheasants are tender.

To make glazed onions: Cook small white onions in boiling salted water until they are tender; drain well. Melt butter in a saucepan; add sugar and stir until well blended. Add onions and cook slowly until they are glazed. Keep warm.

QUAIL WITH WHITE GRAPES

4 QUAIL
SALT AND WHITE PEPPER
2 TABLESPOONS FLOUR
4 TABLESPOONS BUTTER
¼ PINT DRY WHITE WINE
2 TABLESPOONS LEMON JUICE
3 OUNCES SEEDLESS GRAPES
2 TABLESPOONS BLANCHED ALMONDS, SLICED

Clean quail; rub with a mixture of salt, pepper and flour. Melt the butter in a thick-bottomed casserole and sauté the birds in it until they are golden on all sides. Add wine and lemon juice; cover and cook over low heat for 15 to 20 minutes. Add seedless grapes and sliced blanched almonds and cook for 5 to 10 minutes more, or until the birds are tender. Serves 4.

PARTRIDGE WITH JUNIPER BERRIES

2 PARTRIDGES
4 TABLESPOONS MELTED BUTTER
SALT AND FRESHLY-GROUND BLACK PEPPER
4 TABLESPOONS SHREDDED BREAD
2 TABLESPOONS FINELY-CHOPPED HAM
4–6 JUNIPER BERRIES, CRUSHED
GRATED RIND OF ½ LEMON
SALT, FRESHLY-GROUND BLACK PEPPER AND MARJORAM
1 BEATEN EGG
FAT SALT PORK
6 TABLESPOONS DRY WHITE WINE
¼ PINT RICH CHICKEN STOCK
1 CARROT, FINELY CHOPPED
1 SMALL ONION, FINELY CHOPPED

Clean partridges inside and out. Brush cavities with melted butter and season liberally with salt and pepper. Combine remaining melted butter, shredded bread, chopped ham, crushed juniper berries and grated lemon rind; season to taste with salt, pepper and marjoram; mix in beaten egg and stuff birds with this mixture.

Truss birds; wrap a thin piece of fat salt pork around each and roast in a moderate oven (375°F. Mark 4) for about 1 hour, or until tender, basting from time to time with dry white wine, chicken stock and finely-chopped carrot and onion. Serves 4.

VEAL AND PARTRIDGE PIE

½ POUND LEAN VEAL
½ POUND LEAN PORK
¼ POUND FAT SALT PORK
SALT AND FRESHLY-GROUND BLACK PEPPER
PARSLEY, MARJORAM AND THYME
1 PLUMP PARTRIDGE
¼ POUND BACON, DICED
¼ PINT BEEF STOCK
SHORTCRUST PASTRY, TO COVER
1 EGG YOLK

Pass veal, lean pork and fat salt pork twice through the finest blade of your mincer; season generously with salt, freshly-ground pepper and finely-chopped parsley, marjoram and thyme. Cut partridge into serving pieces. Line a deep pie dish with minced meat mixture, on this place a layer of pieces of bird, then a few cubes of bacon and more minced meats. Continue to add layers of these until the dish is well filled. Moisten with beef stock; cover with a shortcrust pastry; decorate and brush with yolk of egg. Bake in a moderate oven (375°F. Mark 4) for 1 to 1½ hours. Serve hot or cold.

PARTRIDGE WITH LENTILS

2 PARTRIDGES
SALT AND FRESHLY-GROUND BLACK PEPPER
2 TABLESPOONS BUTTER
2 TABLESPOONS OLIVE OIL
¼ POUND FAT SALT PORK, DICED
1 SPANISH ONION, SLICED
2 CARROTS, SLICED
¼ PINT WHITE WINE
¼ PINT CHICKEN STOCK

LENTILS:
12 OUNCES LENTILS
1 ONION, STUCK WITH 2 CLOVES
2 CLOVES GARLIC
1 SPRIG FRESH THYME
2 SPRIGS FRESH PARSLEY
SALT AND FRESHLY-GROUND BLACK PEPPER

Clean and prepare partridges in the usual way; then sprinkle cavities with a little salt and freshly-ground pepper and sauté the birds in a fire-proof casserole in butter and oil with diced fat salt pork, sliced onion and carrots. When birds are golden on all sides, add dry white wine and cook until wine is reduced by half. Add chicken stock and season to taste with salt and freshly-ground black pepper; cover casserole and cook over a low flame until partridges are tender, about 45 minutes.

To prepare lentils: Soak the lentils overnight. Drain and cover with water, adding onion, garlic, thyme, parsley, and salt and pepper, to taste. Bring to the boil, reduce heat and allow to simmer until tender but not too soft. Each lentil should be separate, not mushy. When cooked, drain lentils and remove onion, garlic and herbs.

To serve: Place partridges on hot serving dish and surround with cooked lentils. Skim fat from pan juices; strain and pour over birds. Serves 4.

SALMIS OF WOODCOCK

4 WOODCOCK
4 TABLESPOONS DRY WHITE WINE
4 TABLESPOONS RICH BEEF STOCK
2 LEMONS
SALT, FRESHLY-GROUND BLACK PEPPER AND NUTMEG
1–2 TABLESPOONS DRY MUSTARD
2–3 OUNCES MUSHROOMS, SLICED
1 TABLESPOON BUTTER
1 TABLESPOON FLOUR
2 TABLESPOONS FINELY-CHOPPED PARSLEY

Roast woodcock slightly (until about half cooked) and cut them into serving pieces. Be sure to cut woodcock on a serving dish to catch blood and juices. Arrange pieces in the blazer pan of a chafing dish.

Crush livers and giblets into serving dish containing juices; add dry white wine, beef stock and juice of 2 lemons; stir in the finely-grated peel of 1 lemon, and season to taste with salt, freshly-ground black pepper, nutmeg and mustard.

Add sliced mushrooms and pour this mixture over woodcock; place over heater and cook, stirring to moisten each piece of meat thoroughly and to prevent it from sticking to the dish.

Do not let the *salmis* come to the boil. Just before serving, stir in a *beurre manié* made of butter and flour. Sprinkle with finely-chopped parsley. Serves 4.

SALMIS OF GROUSE

3 YOUNG GROUSE
$\frac{1}{4}$ POUND BUTTER
1 SPANISH ONION, FINELY CHOPPED
2 SMALL CARROTS, FINELY CHOPPED
2 CLOVES GARLIC, FINELY CHOPPED
6 FLUID OUNCES GOOD RED WINE
1 ROUNDED TABLESPOON FLOUR
$\frac{3}{4}$ PINT WELL-FLAVOURED STOCK
2 SPRIGS THYME
1 BAY LEAF
SALT AND FRESHLY-GROUND BLACK PEPPER
$\frac{1}{2}$ POUND BUTTON MUSHROOMS
JUICE OF $\frac{1}{2}$ LEMON
12 SMALL BREAD TRIANGLES
FINELY-CHOPPED PARSLEY

Clean and truss birds; spread with a little softened butter and roast in the oven until partially cooked. Cut into serving pieces and reserve.

Sauté finely-chopped onion, carrots and garlic in 4 tablespoons butter until golden. Pour in wine and simmer, stirring continuously, until wine reduces a little. Add flour and stir vigorously until sauce thickens; then add stock, trimmings and juices from birds, thyme, bay leaf, and salt and freshly-ground black pepper, to taste. Cover the pan and simmer gently for 1 hour.

Sauté sliced mushrooms in 2 tablespoons butter and lemon juice until tender. Strain sauce; add drained mushrooms and grouse to the sauce and simmer for 5 minutes, or until they are heated through and the flavour of the sauce has permeated the birds.

Fry bread triangles in remaining butter and place 6 on a heated serving dish; cover with *salmis*; sprinkle with finely-chopped parsley; garnish with remaining *croûtons*. Serves 6.

GREAT DISHES OF THE WORLD

CHAPTER 12

Vegetables

Red Cabbage Normandy

Many men are known to be ardent, if furtive, members of the anti-vegetable school. And who can blame us if we are apt to recoil surreptitiously from the tasteless, soggy blobs of greenery that all too often masquerade on dinner plates throughout the country under the misleading names of 'peas', 'string beans', 'cauliflower' and 'cabbage'? Why, when the waiter offers us that old standby, 'a cut off the joint with two veg', do we instinctively know that the 'two veg' will almost certainly consist of boiled cabbage and potatoes, perhaps ennobled by the terminology 'boiled greens' or, more euphemistically, 'spring greens'?

I for one would like to start a counter-revolution against the habit of serving vegetables in their own water. Let us take courage in both hands and borrow from the cuisines of other lands to give vegetables a fighting chance on our dinner tables. Let us cook them – as do the Chinese – until they are just tender, not waterlogged and mushy. Let us serve them – like the French – as a fresh-tasting first course, or as a separate vegetable course to be served *after* the meat, so much easier on the cook and so much more inviting for the diner.

Of all vegetables, cabbage particularly seems to suffer from this lack of imagination. Yet the culinary potential of this year-round vegetable is as rich as its history. The ancient Greeks served cabbage with savoury stuffings of meat and rice, flavoured with pine nuts, currants, grated lemon peel and herbs. It was known and used in China as far back as the first century. Indeed, sour cabbage, known throughout the world today as sauerkraut, was, in fact, an early Chinese invention.

The Mediterraneans have used cabbage as the main ingredients for stews and soups for centuries; the Poles call it 'little pigeons' – braised cabbage leaves deliciously stuffed with finely-chopped meat, onion, tomatoes and herbs. The Russians immortalise it in a superb peasant soup called *stchi*, made of cabbage, onions, tomatoes and beets simmered in stock; the Germans poach it until tender and stuff it with buttered noodles flavoured with caraway seed; and the Austrians even use this versatile vegetable in a sweet cabbage *strudel.*

There are three main varieties of cabbage. The common or green cabbage, sold everywhere, is bright green in the summer months, whiter, firmer and larger in the winter. The Savoy cabbage – a bright, deep green in colour with a curly leaf – is much more delicate in flavour. I like to use its tender leaves for stuffed cabbage recipes.

White cabbage is used commercially for the preparation of sauerkraut and is also used extensively for salads and cole slaw.

Red cabbage is delicious either raw or cooked. Always add lemon juice or vinegar to water when cooking this attractive vegetable or it will turn purple in cooking. Red cabbage must be firm and the outer leaves must be bright in colour. Cut the head in quarters and remove the heavy veins, then shred the rest of the leaves on a coarse shredder. Often served as an *hors-d'œuvre* salad in France, red cabbage is delicious when shredded in this way, drained to the last drop of the water in which it was cooked, and then simmered gently in butter or lard with diced apples and spices, a wonderful accompaniment to all pork dishes, goose and many forms of veal and hare.

Perhaps the most noble version of this dish is red cabbage cooked in the fashion of the Norman French.

RED CABBAGE WITH APPLES

1 RED CABBAGE (ABOUT 2 POUNDS)
4 TABLESPOONS BUTTER
1 POUND COOKING APPLES
½ POUND ONIONS
2 CLOVES GARLIC, FINELY CHOPPED
¼ TEASPOON EACH OF POWDERED NUTMEG, ALLSPICE, CINNAMON, THYME AND CARAWAY SEED
SALT AND FRESHLY-GROUND BLACK PEPPER
1 TEASPOON GRATED ORANGE RIND
2 TABLESPOONS BROWN SUGAR
½ PINT RED WINE
2 TABLESPOONS WINE VINEGAR

Wash and shred cabbage, removing central core, ribs and outer leaves. Cook in butter, in a covered saucepan, for 5 minutes. Peel and core apples and cut into quarters; slice onions. Place these ingredients in a deep oven-proof casserole in layers, beginning with a layer of cabbage, then onions, then apples, and continue until casserole is full. Season each layer with finely-chopped garlic, spices and salt and pepper, to taste, and grated orange rind. Sprinkle brown sugar over the top and add wine, wine vinegar and a little hot water.

Cover and simmer very slowly in a moderate oven (375°F. Mark 4) until tender, adding a little more wine if necessary. Serves 4 to 6.

BUTTERED CABBAGE – I

Remove and discard discoloured outer leaves from 1 head of green cabbage. Wash, core and cut into shreds or wedges. Soak cabbage in cold salted water for ½ hour. Drain and cook, covered, in a small amount of boiling salted water or well-flavoured stock, until just tender. Drain well. Season with salt and freshly-ground black pepper, and serve with finely-chopped parsley and melted butter. Serves 4 to 6.

BUTTERED CABBAGE – II

Prepare cabbage as above; soak in cold salted water for ½ hour; drain. Melt 4 tablespoons butter in a large saucepan; add cabbage; season to taste with salt, freshly-ground black pepper and the juice of ½ lemon and simmer, covered, until cabbage is just tender, but not browned. Stir in a little finely-chopped parsley and serve. Serves 4 to 6.

SCALLOPED CABBAGE

- 1 HEAD CABBAGE
- 4 TABLESPOONS BUTTER
- ½ PINT RICH CREAM SAUCE
- SALT AND FRESHLY-GROUND BLACK PEPPER
- 4 TABLESPOONS FRESHLY-GRATED PARMESAN

Shred cabbage and soak in salted cold water for ½ hour. Drain well. Melt butter; add shredded cabbage and simmer, covered, until cabbage is just tender, but not browned.

Line a large casserole with half the simmered cabbage. Add half of the cream sauce; sprinkle with freshly-ground black pepper and half the grated Parmesan. Add remaining cabbage; pour remaining sauce over the top and add more pepper and remainder of Parmesan. Place in a slow oven (350°F. Mark 3) and cook until the casserole bubbles and the top is golden brown – about ½ hour. Serves 4 to 6.

SAFFRON CABBAGE

- 1 SMALL HEAD CABBAGE
- 1 PINT RICH BROWN STOCK
- 1 GENEROUS PINCH POWDERED SAFFRON
- 4–6 TABLESPOONS FINELY-CHOPPED HAM
- ½ SPANISH ONION, THINLY SLICED
- SALT AND FRESHLY-GROUND BLACK PEPPER
- 1 GENEROUS PINCH CAYENNE

Shred cabbage and soak in salted cold water for ½ hour. Drain well. Combine in saucepan with beef stock and simmer for 15 minutes, or until half cooked.

Mix saffron with a little water and add to cabbage together with finely-chopped ham, finely-sliced onion, salt, pepper and cayenne.

Stir well and simmer until cabbage is tender, adding a little more stock or water if necessary. Serves 4.

MY COLCANNON

1 CABBAGE
4–6 POTATOES
4–6 YOUNG CARROTS
4–6 YOUNG TURNIPS
4 TABLESPOONS BUTTER
SALT AND FRESHLY-GROUND BLACK PEPPER
¼ PINT DOUBLE CREAM
2 EGG YOLKS
FRESHLY-GRATED BREADCRUMBS
FRESHLY-GRATED CHEESE
BUTTER

Cook cabbage and potatoes in water until tender.

Peel and slice carrots and turnips in thin strips and blanch in sufficient water to cover. Pour off water; add butter and 4 tablespoons water to pan; cover and simmer until vegetables are tender. Season to taste with salt and pepper.

Chop cabbage finely and mash with potatoes until smooth. Combine with cream, egg yolks, additional butter and freshly-ground black pepper and salt, to taste.

Spread half of the cabbage-potato mixture in the bottom of a well-buttered oven-proof gratin dish. Arrange a layer of alternating strips of carrots and turnip down the centre and cover with remaining cabbage-potato mixture. Sprinkle with freshly-grated breadcrumbs; top with a little freshly-grated cheese (optional) and dot with butter. Cook in a moderate oven (375°F. Mark 4) for 30 minutes, or until golden.

Cauliflower à la Polonaise

The cabbage family is a large and powerful clan which ranges from the earthy tones of cabbage and sprouts to the more sophisticated flavour of cauliflower, the undoubted aristocrat of the family. I like cauliflower steamed or simmered in salted water with a little lemon juice until it is just tender, not mushy, and then served with melted butter or a delicious sauce.

When buying cauliflower, choose heads that are very white and very firm, with small compact flowers squeezed tightly together. A yellow cauliflower has a very strong flavour and if the flowers are loosely separated from each other, this is usually a sign of excess maturity.

HOW TO COOK CAULIFLOWER

WHOLE: Cut off stem and remove green leaves from a medium-sized cauliflower. Soak the head for ½ hour in cold water to which you have added ½ teaspoon salt and the juice of ½ lemon to free it from insects. Fill a deep saucepan with enough water to cover cauliflower; add ½ teaspoon salt and bring to the boil. Put cauliflower into the boiling water; cover saucepan and simmer gently, about 20 minutes, or until the cauliflower is just tender when pierced at the stem end with a fork. Do not overcook.

Drain well; arrange on a heated serving dish or bowl and top with butter. Season to taste with salt and freshly-ground black pepper.

FLOWERETS: If you do not intend to cook the head whole, break or cut cauliflower into flowerets. Prepare as above, but cook for 10 to 15 minutes only, so that flowerets are tender but not mushy. Drain and serve as above, or with any of the sauces below.

CAULIFLOWER VARIATIONS

Prepare cauliflower as above, either whole or cut into flowerets.

CAULIFLOWER HOLLANDAISE: Serve hot cauliflower with a *sauce hollandaise*.

CAULIFLOWER AMANDINE: Sauté 4 tablespoons blanched slivered almonds in butter; pour sauce over hot cauliflower and season to taste with salt and freshly-ground black pepper.

CHEESED CAULIFLOWER: Melt 4 tablespoons butter; add 4 tablespoons toasted breadcrumbs, ½ teaspoon grated onion, 4 tablespoons finely-grated Gruyère, and salt and freshly-ground pepper, to taste. Cook over low heat, stirring continuously, until cheese is melted, and pour over cooked hot cauliflower.

CAULIFLOWER À LA POLONAISE

1 HEAD CAULIFLOWER
SALT
4 TABLESPOONS BUTTER
4 TABLESPOONS FRESH BREADCRUMBS
JUICE OF ½ LEMON
2 TABLESPOONS FINELY-CHOPPED HAM
2 TABLESPOONS FINELY-CHOPPED HARD-BOILED EGG
2 TABLESPOONS FINELY-CHOPPED PARSLEY
SALT AND FRESHLY-GROUND BLACK PEPPER

Remove outer green leaves from cauliflower; wash and leave in cold salted water for ½ hour. Measure enough water to cover cauliflower into a deep saucepan; add salt to taste, and bring to the boil. Put cauliflower into the boiling water; cover saucepan and simmer gently for about 20 minutes, or until the cauliflower is just tender when pierced at the stem end with a fork. Do not overcook.

Drain well, arrange on a heated serving dish and top with Polonaise sauce. Serves 4.

To make Polonaise sauce: Melt butter in a frying pan. Add fresh breadcrumbs and cook until crumbs are a light brown. Stir in the juice of ½ lemon and 2 tablespoons each of finely-chopped ham, hard-boiled egg and parsley. Season to taste.

CAULIFLOWER AU GRATIN

1 HEAD CAULIFLOWER
SALT
4 TABLESPOONS BUTTER
4 TABLESPOONS FLOUR
1 PINT HOT MILK
4 OUNCES FRESHLY-GRATED GRUYÈRE
1 LEVEL TEASPOON MUSTARD
JUICE OF ½ LEMON
SALT AND FRESHLY-GROUND BLACK PEPPER
2 TABLESPOONS WHIPPED CREAM
2 TABLESPOONS FRESH BREADCRUMBS
BUTTER

Remove outer green leaves from cauliflower; wash and leave in cold salted water for ½ hour. Cut cauliflower into flowerets and poach in salted water for 20 minutes, or until tender. Drain.

To make sauce: melt butter in top of double saucepan; blend in flour and cook over water, stirring constantly, until smooth. Add hot milk gradually and cook, stirring constantly, until sauce comes to the boil. Add cheese and cook, stirring, until cheese melts. Season to taste with mustard, lemon juice, salt and freshly-ground black pepper.

Place cooked cauliflower in a buttered baking dish; pour sauce over; spread with whipped cream; sprinkle with fresh breadcrumbs and dot with butter. Bake in a moderate oven (375°F. Mark 4) for about 20 minutes, or until top is golden. Serves 4.

FRENCH FRIED CAULIFLOWER

1 CAULIFLOWER
OIL FOR DEEP-FRYING
1 EGG
¼ PINT MILK
¼ POUND FLOUR
1 TEASPOON SALT
TOMATO SAUCE

Heat oil to 375°F. To make batter: beat egg in a bowl; add milk and beat. Add flour and salt and beat until smooth.

Clean and prepare cauliflower as above. Separate into small flowerets and poach in boiling water for 5 minutes. Dip flowerets into batter. Deep-fry until golden. Drain and serve immediately with tomato sauce. Serves 4.

CAULIFLOWER À LA NIÇOISE

1 CAULIFLOWER
1 SPANISH ONION, FINELY CHOPPED
2 CLOVES GARLIC, FINELY CHOPPED
3 TABLESPOONS OLIVE OIL
2 TABLESPOONS BUTTER
6 TOMATOES, PEELED AND DICED, OR 1 TIN ITALIAN PEELED TOMATOES
2 TABLESPOONS FINELY-CHOPPED PARSLEY
SALT AND FRESHLY-GROUND BLACK PEPPER
1 TABLESPOON BREADCRUMBS

Prepare and cook cauliflower as in poached cauliflowerets recipe, for about 5 minutes. Sauté onion and garlic until transparent in olive oil and butter. Add diced peeled tomatoes or tinned tomatoes, and 2 tablespoons finely-chopped parsley. Season with salt and freshly-ground pepper. Add cooked cauliflowerets and breadcrumbs and simmer for a further 10 minutes, or until tender. Serves 4.

Gratin Dauphinois

'Let the sky rain potatoes,' cried Sir John Falstaff deliriously as Mistress Ford appeared in the last scene of *The Merry Wives of Windsor*. For the sudden arrival of the potato from America had caused uproar throughout Europe. Denounced as an aphrodisiac from the pulpits of England, prohibited by the Parliament of Besançon as a cause of leprosy, the potato was stolidly ignored by the poor to whom it would have been so useful. But the rich seized on it as a new fad. Elizabeth Tudor feasted on potatoes from Raleigh's Irish estate. Louis XVI brought their flower into high fashion by accepting a bouquet of them from Parmentier – collectors know how widespread was the use of the potato flower as a decorative design for plates. Francis Bacon lauded them with stately phrases in his *History of Life and Death*.

This first excitement soon waned and as they became more common, potatoes slowly sank to the bottom of the menu, following all other vegetables. The problem? We eat them too much; they have become a necessity, not a pleasure. In this country we tend to look at them without imagination, without desire. But give a French chef a potato and he will create a hundred succulent dishes. So do not take the potato for granted. Give it a little credit. Treat it – as the French do – with *panache*!

Select potatoes best suited to your purpose:

BAKING POTATOES are large with a fine, mealy texture when cooked. Use floury potatoes for baking and for soups and purées.

NEW POTATOES range in size from tiny ones no bigger than a walnut to those of the size of a regular potato. The smallest are delicious cooked whole with their skins left on and served with butter or butter and lemon juice. When SALAD POTATOES are hard to come by, larger new potatoes are good for potato salads and cooked dishes such as *gratin dauphinois* for which you want potato slices to keep their shape. Never bake new potatoes.

Whenever possible, cook potatoes with their skins on. Most of the food value of a potato lies just under the skin and is lost if peeled away. After cooking, the skins will slip off easily enough if you prefer serving them without their jackets.

If you peel potatoes when raw, put them immediately into a bowl of cold water to keep them from changing colour.

The major mistake in potato cookery – as with most vegetables – is overcooking. When you boil potatoes, test them with a fork. They are done when you can pierce them easily. Do not allow them to become watery and mushy.

On special occasions that call for a little more than the usual baked, sautéed or puréed potato, apply the Gallic touch and dress your potatoes for company. Cut them in slices or cubes; shape them with a knife to resemble olives. Parboil them for 5 minutes in salted water; drain, then sauté in clarified butter until they are soft and golden. Serve with finely-chopped sautéed onions and parsley, crumbled cooked bacon, or a combination of finely-chopped parsley, chervil and chives. To clarify butter: place as much butter as desired in a container over hot water until butter has melted. Pour off butter carefully and discard remaining sediment.

Follow on in the French tradition by serving thinly-sliced potatoes paired off with the flavours of butter, cream, freshly-grated Gruyère or Parmesan and finely-chopped onions. *Gratin dauphinois* (recipe below) combines layers of thinly-sliced potatoes with cream and freshly-grated cheese, dots the whole with knobs of butter and bakes it in a gratin dish in the oven until bubbling and golden-crusted. Serve this delicious dish as a hot first course (as the Italians do *gnocchi* or *pasta*) or with a roast. Potatoes Lyonnaise sautées thin slices of boiled new potatoes in butter and serves them with gently-fried chopped onions. *Pommes de terre Anna* sets overlapping layers of sliced raw potatoes in a small buttered baking dish or round mould, each layer dotted with butter, and the whole then baked in a hot oven until cooked through. The potatoes are turned out of the mould like a crisp, golden cake just before serving.

GRATIN DAUPHINOIS

1 POUND NEW POTATOES
¼ PINT DOUBLE CREAM
8 TABLESPOONS FRESHLY-GRATED GRUYÈRE
4 TABLESPOONS FRESHLY-GRATED PARMESAN
BUTTER
SALT AND FRESHLY-GROUND BLACK PEPPER

Butter a shallow fire-proof casserole or deep gratin dish. Peel and slice potatoes thinly and soak in cold water for a few minutes. Drain and dry thoroughly with a clean tea towel.

Place layer of sliced potatoes on bottom of dish in overlapping rows; pour over a quarter of the cream, sprinkle with 2 tablespoons grated cheese (mixed Gruyère and Parmesan), dot with butter and season to taste with salt and freshly-ground black pepper. Continue this process until dish is full, finishing with layer of grated cheese. Dot with butter and cook in a slow oven (350°F. Mark 3) for about 1 hour, or until potatoes are cooked through. If top becomes too brown, cover with aluminium foil. Serve very hot. Serves 4.

GRATIN SAVOYARD

1 POUND NEW POTATOES
¼ PINT WELL-FLAVOURED BEEF STOCK
6 TABLESPOONS FRESHLY-GRATED GRUYÈRE
2 TABLESPOONS FRESHLY-GRATED PARMESAN
SALT AND FRESHLY-GROUND BLACK PEPPER
BUTTER

Butter a heat-proof shallow casserole or gratin dish. Peel and slice potatoes thinly and soak in cold water for a few minutes. Drain and dry thoroughly with a clean tea towel.

Place layer of sliced potatoes on bottom of dish in overlapping rows; pour over a quarter of the stock; sprinkle with 2 tablespoons grated cheese (mixed Gruyère and Parmesan); dot with butter and season to taste with salt and freshly-ground black pepper (not too much salt). Continue this process until dish is full, finishing with a layer of grated cheese. Dot with butter and cook in a slow oven (350°F. Mark 3) for about 1 hour, or until potatoes are cooked through. If top becomes too brown, cover with aluminium foil. Serve very hot. Serves 4.

POTATOES LYONNAISE

1 POUND BOILED NEW POTATOES, SLICED
4 TABLESPOONS BUTTER
1 SMALL ONION, THINLY SLICED
SALT AND FRESHLY-GROUND BLACK PEPPER
2 TABLESPOONS FINELY-CHOPPED PARSLEY

Sauté sliced potatoes in butter over a medium heat until golden on both sides. Remove potatoes and sauté sliced onion in remaining fat until golden. Return potatoes to the pan; season to taste with salt and freshly-ground black pepper and continue cooking until potatoes are heated through. Sprinkle with finely-chopped parsley. Serves 4.

POMMES DE TERRE ANNA

1 POUND NEW POTATOES
2–3 OUNCES SOFTENED BUTTER
SALT AND FRESHLY-GROUND BLACK PEPPER

Peel and slice potatoes thinly and soak in cold water for a few minutes. Drain and dry thoroughly with a clean tea towel.

Butter a shallow fire-proof casserole or gratin dish and place in it a layer of sliced potatoes overlapping around sides of dish. Place a layer of sliced potatoes on bottom of dish in overlapping rows; spread potatoes with 1 tablespoon softened butter and season to taste with salt and freshly-ground black pepper. Repeat layers as above with a final spreading of butter on top. Bake in a 425°F. oven (Mark 6) for 45 minutes to 1 hour, or until the potatoes are cooked through. To serve, invert golden-brown potato 'cake' on to a heated serving dish and serve immediately. Serves 4.

LATKES (JEWISH POTATO PANCAKES)

4 LARGE RAW POTATOES, PEELED AND GRATED
1 SPANISH ONION, PEELED AND GRATED
2 EGGS, BEATEN
2 TABLESPOONS FLOUR
½ LEVEL TEASPOON BAKING POWDER
SALT AND FRESHLY-GROUND BLACK PEPPER
BUTTER AND OLIVE OIL, FOR FRYING

Combine grated potatoes and onion in a mixing bowl; stir in beaten eggs, flour and baking powder and add salt and freshly-ground black pepper, to taste.

Heat a little butter and olive oil in frying pan. Drop potato mixture in spoonfuls and fry *latkes* until browned on both sides. Drain well.

HASH-BROWNED POTATOES

6 LARGE POTATOES, BAKED IN JACKETS
1 SPANISH ONION, COARSELY GRATED
SALT AND FRESHLY-GROUND BLACK PEPPER
3 TABLESPOONS BUTTER
3 TABLESPOONS LARD

Chill potatoes; peel and shred coarsely. Add grated onion and salt and pepper, to taste. Melt butter and lard in frying pan.

Put potatoes into pan, leaving ½-inch space around edge. Brown 10 to 12 minutes. When crusty and hot, hold serving dish over pan and invert.

Serve hash-browned potatoes with minute steaks or chops; garnish with glazed onion rings.

ITALIAN POTATO BALLS

1½ POUNDS POTATOES
2 EGG YOLKS
4 TABLESPOONS FRESHLY-GRATED PARMESAN
1 TABLESPOON FINELY-CHOPPED ONION
1 TABLESPOON BUTTER
2 TABLESPOONS FINELY-CHOPPED PARSLEY
SALT AND FRESHLY-GROUND BLACK PEPPER
2 EGGS
FLOUR
BREADCRUMBS
FAT, FOR FRYING

Peel potatoes and boil in salted water until cooked. Mash and combine with egg yolks and cheese in a large mixing bowl.

Sauté finely-chopped onion in butter until golden, but not brown. Add to potato mixture with parsley and generous amounts of salt and pepper. Mix to a smooth paste and form into small balls the size of a large walnut. Makes about 24 balls.

Beat eggs with a fork until well blended. Roll potato balls in flour and then in beaten egg. Coat with breadcrumbs and chill until ready to use.

Heat fat (I prefer a mixture of olive oil and lard) to frying temperature. Fry a few potato balls at a time until they are golden in colour and heated through. Serves 6.

LEMON DILL POTATOES

1½ POUNDS NEW POTATOES
SALT
1 TABLESPOON OLIVE OIL
1 TABLESPOON BUTTER
1½ TABLESPOONS FLOUR
½ PINT MILK
1 LEVEL TEASPOON DILL SEED
2 TABLESPOONS LEMON JUICE
1 TABLESPOON FINELY-CHOPPED PARSLEY
SALT AND FRESHLY-GROUND BLACK PEPPER

Peel or scrape new potatoes. Cook until just tender in boiling water to which you have added salt and olive oil. Drain and keep warm.

Melt butter in a saucepan; blend in flour and gradually stir in milk. Add dill seed and cook, stirring constantly, until sauce is smooth and thick. Add lemon juice, finely-chopped parsley and salt and freshly-ground black pepper, to taste, and pour over hot potatoes. Serves 4.

Artichokes

The French believe that if you eat old vegetables you yourself become old. Not for them the jumbo carrots or the giant cabbages so beloved by English housewives. It is the infant vegetables they use. In Italy, too, where the artichoke is very popular, tiny raw artichokes no bigger than a baby's fist are eaten raw as an appetiser, preserved in olive oil as an integral part of an Italian *antipasto* platter, or dipped in batter and fried, either alone, or with tiny octopus and prawns in an Italian mixed fry called *fritto misto del mare*.

In Rome, tender young artichokes are often cooked in olive oil, lemon and herbs, *alla romana*, and served as a marvellously flavoured hot or cold *hors-d'œuvre*. I like artichoke hearts done in this manner, too, flavoured with a little finely-chopped garlic and *oregano*. In France, artichokes *au vin blanc* top the bill, the artichokes simmered in dry white wine with a little olive oil and seasonings. Artichokes *à la provençale*, *à la barigoule*, *à la grecque*, are all exalted variations on this basic theme.

There are so many ways to serve this delicate, nutty-flavoured vegetable – rich in iron, mineral salts and iodine – that I cannot understand why so many people consider it an acquired taste. I like them baked, fried, stuffed, puréed with rich cream as an accompanying vegetable, and even in a soup. But my favourite way of dealing with this sophisticated vegetable is to cook it in boiling water with a little salt, olive oil and lemon juice, and serve it cold with a *vinaigrette* sauce as a first course, or hot as a separate vegetable course. Whole, halved or quartered, a hot artichoke served with a *sauce hollandaise* or melted butter and lemon makes an unbeatable dish; each leaf should be pulled off separately, the large succulent end dipped in the sauce and the soft fleshy bits prised gently off with the teeth.

Atichoke hearts, found at the base of each vegetable, make one of the best garnishes for cold dishes imaginable if cooked and then chilled. They can be served as a vegetable, stuffed with various ingredients or used as the decorative base for a host of salads and *hors-d'œuvre* dishes.

ITALIAN ARTICHOKES WITH MUSHROOM SAUCE

4 SMALL ARTICHOKES
SALT
JUICE OF ½ LEMON
BUTTER

MUSHROOM SAUCE:
4 TABLESPOONS FINELY-CHOPPED MUSHROOMS
2 TABLESPOONS BUTTER
2 TABLESPOONS FINELY-CHOPPED SHALLOTS
4–6 TABLESPOONS DRY WHITE WINE
2 TABLESPOONS TOMATO CONCENTRATE
1 TABLESPOON FINELY-CHOPPED PARSLEY

Cut small artichokes into quarters; trim tough outer leaves and tips of tender leaves and remove chokes. Poach artichokes for 5 minutes in boiling water to which you have added a little salt and lemon juice. Drain and arrange in a buttered shallow casserole. Cook for 2 minutes on a high flame; spoon over mushroom sauce, cover casserole and simmer until tender. Serves 4.

To make sauce: Melt butter in a frying pan and sauté finely-chopped mushrooms and shallots until almost golden; moisten with white wine and simmer for 3 minutes. Add tomato concentrate and finely-chopped parsley.

ARTICHOKE HEARTS WITH FOIE GRAS

4 ARTICHOKES
1 LEMON
2 TABLESPOONS OLIVE OIL
SALT AND FRESHLY-GROUND BLACK PEPPER
4 TABLESPOONS BUTTER
4 SLICES TINNED PÂTÉ DE FOIE GRAS
4 TABLESPOONS SAUCE BÉARNAISE

Choose tender artichokes. Cut the hearts out carefully. Rub each heart with ½ lemon and place immediately in a bowl of cold water to keep colour fresh.

Bring water to the boil with olive oil and juice of ½ lemon. Add salt and pepper to taste and poach artichoke hearts in this liquid until they are tender, about 15 to 20 minutes, according to their size. Drain.

Melt butter in a flame-proof gratin dish or shallow casserole; place artichoke hearts in this upside-down and let them simmer in the butter for a few minutes; turn them delicately and when done place a round of *pâté de foie gras* in each heart; cover each with a spoonful of *sauce béarnaise* and place the dish under the grill for a few seconds to brown the sauce. Serve immediately. Serves 4.

ARTICHOKES AU VIN BLANC

4 MEDIUM ARTICHOKES
2 TABLESPOONS OLIVE OIL
¼ PINT DRY WHITE WINE
2 CLOVES GARLIC, FINELY CHOPPED
1 SMALL ONION, FINELY CHOPPED
1 TABLESPOON FINELY-CHOPPED PARSLEY
PINCH SAVORY
SALT AND FRESHLY-GROUND BLACK PEPPER

Cut off tops of artichokes and remove chokes.

Combine olive oil, dry white wine, finely-chopped garlic and onion, parsley, savory, salt and freshly-ground black pepper, to taste. Place trimmed artichokes in a saucepan just large enough to hold them and pour mixture over them.

Cover tightly and simmer slowly for 45 minutes, adding a little more wine and olive oil if necessary. When tender, remove and serve with sauce poured over them. Serves 4.

ARTICHOKES VINAIGRETTE

4 ARTICHOKES
SALT
JUICE OF ½ LEMON
VINAIGRETTE DRESSING

Remove the tough outer leaves of artichokes and trim tops of inner leaves. Trim the base and stem of each artichoke with a sharp knife. Cook until tender (30 to 40 minutes) in a large quantity of salted boiling water to which you have added the juice of ½ lemon. Artichokes are cooked when a leaf pulls out easily.

Turn artichokes upside-down to drain. Serve artichokes cold with a well-flavoured *vinaigrette* dressing. Pull off a leaf at a time; eat tender base of each leaf. Remove choke and eat artichoke heart.

Artichokes are delicious served as a hot *hors-d'œuvre* or separate vegetable course with seasoned melted butter, or for more special occasions, a *sauce hollandaise*. Serves 4.

STUFFED PEPPERS

4 GREEN PEPPERS
1 TABLESPOON OLIVE OIL
2 OUNCES BUTTER
SALT AND FRESHLY-GROUND BLACK PEPPER
4 OUNCES RAW RICE
HOT CHICKEN STOCK
½ SPANISH ONION, FINELY CHOPPED
2 OUNCES CHOPPED MUSHROOMS
2 TABLESPOONS OLIVE OIL
4 OUNCES FINELY-CHOPPED HAM
2 TABLESPOONS TOMATO PURÉE
½ PINT HOT BEEF STOCK
2 TABLESPOONS CHOPPED PARSLEY

Remove the tops of the peppers and reserve. Remove pith and seeds. Place peppers in boiling water and olive oil and leave for 5 minutes; drain well and dry. Place a small piece of butter in bottom of each pepper (using half the butter), and season well.

Melt remaining butter in a frying pan. Add the rice and sauté until golden. Cover with hot chicken stock and cook, stirring constantly, until the mixture comes to the boil; reduce the heat, cover the pan and cook slowly for about 30 minutes, adding a little more chicken stock if necessary. Sauté the chopped onion and mushrooms in oil and add to rice mixture. Mix in the finely-chopped ham, season well and fill the peppers. Replace pepper caps and arrange in a flat, oven-proof dish. Blend tomato purée with hot beef stock; pour over the stuffed peppers and bake in a moderate oven for 30 to 40 minutes, or until done, basting frequently. Sprinkle with chopped parsley. Serves 4.

CHILES RELLENOS (CHEESE-STUFFED GREEN PEPPERS)

4 LARGE GREEN PEPPERS
½ POUND MOZZARELLA, FINELY CHOPPED
SALT AND FRESHLY-GROUND BLACK PEPPER
4 EGGS, SEPARATED

½ POUND MILD CHEDDAR, FINELY CHOPPED
TABASCO OR CHILI SAUCE
2 LEVEL TABLESPOONS FLOUR
FAT FOR DEEP-FRYING

Roast green peppers under the grill, turning them from time to time until skins are charred. Remove charred skins under cold water; dry peppers and make a small cut down the side without opening the pepper full length. With a spoon, scrape out the seeds and all the pith.

Mix finely-chopped cheeses together and season to taste with salt and pepper and a little Tabasco or chili sauce; fill peppers with the cheese mixture. Re-shape the peppers and roll them lightly in flour. Beat egg whites until they are stiff and fold in lightly-beaten egg yolk with 2 level tablespoons flour.

Dip stuffed peppers in batter and fry them in deep hot fat until they are golden brown. Serve immediately. Serves 4.

PEPPERS ALLA ROMANA

6 LARGE PEPPERS
½ SPANISH ONION, FINELY CHOPPED
1 CLOVE GARLIC, FINELY CHOPPED
2 TABLESPOONS OLIVE OIL
2 TABLESPOONS LARD
4 TOMATOES, PEELED AND CHOPPED
2 TABLESPOONS TOMATO PURÉE
¼ PINT DRY WHITE WINE
SALT AND FRESHLY-GROUND BLACK PEPPER

Wash peppers; remove stalks and seeds and slice thinly. Sauté finely-chopped onion and garlic in olive oil and lard until golden. Add peeled and chopped tomatoes, tomato purée and dry white wine and simmer for 5 minutes.

Add sliced peppers and salt and pepper, to taste; cover pan and simmer gently for 30 minutes, or until peppers are tender, adding more liquid if necessary. Serves 6.

RATATOUILLE

8 TABLESPOONS OLIVE OIL
2 SPANISH ONIONS, SLICED
2 GREEN PEPPERS, DICED
2 AUBERGINES, DICED
2 BABY MARROWS, CUT IN ½-INCH SLICES
4–6 RIPE TOMATOES, PEELED, SEEDED AND CHOPPED
SALT AND FRESHLY-GROUND BLACK PEPPER
1 TABLESPOON CHOPPED PARSLEY
1 PINCH MARJORAM OR OREGANO
1 PINCH BASIL
1 LARGE CLOVE GARLIC

Heat the olive oil in a large frying pan, add onion slices and sauté until they are transparent. Add the diced green pepper and aubergines and, 5 minutes later, the baby marrows and tomatoes. The vegetables should not be fried but stewed in the oil, so simmer gently in a covered pan for 30 minutes. Add salt and pepper to taste, chopped parsley, marjoram, basil and crushed garlic; then cook, uncovered, for about 10 to 15 minutes, or until *ratatouille* is well mixed and has the appearance of a *ragoût* of vegetables—which it is. Serve hot from the casserole, or cold as a delicious beginning to a summer meal. Serves 4.

PROVENÇAL STUFFED VEGETABLES

VEGETABLE CASES:
4 SMALL AUBERGINES
4 BABY MARROWS
4 MEDIUM ONIONS
4 SMALL TOMATOES

PROVENÇAL STUFFING:
6 OUNCES GROUND VEAL
1 OUNCE DICED FAT SALT PORK
1 ONION, FINELY CHOPPED
OLIVE OIL
1 CLOVE GARLIC, CRUSHED
FINELY-CHOPPED FRESH TARRAGON
FINELY-CHOPPED FRESH PARSLEY
1 EGG, BEATEN
1 TABLESPOON GRATED PARMESAN
4 TABLESPOONS BOILED RICE
MARROW AND AUBERGINE PULP
SALT AND FRESHLY-GROUND BLACK PEPPER
BUTTER

Poach baby marrows, aubergines and onions whole for 1 minute in boiling salted water. Cut tops off tomatoes, aubergines, marrows and onions. Scoop out interiors of vegetables and keep pulp of aubergines and marrows for stuffing.

To make stuffing: Sauté meats and onion in olive oil. Mix other ingredients in a bowl and then add them to the meat and onion mixture. Add pepper and salt, to taste. Sauté for a few minutes, stirring continuously, and then stuff scooped-out vegetables with the mixture.

Place stuffed vegetables in an oven-proof baking dish to which you have added a little olive oil; place a knob of butter on each vegetable and bake in a moderate oven (375°F. Mark 4) for ½ hour. Serve one of each vegetable as a main course. Serves 4.

STUFFED TOMATOES PROVENÇAL

12 LARGE RIPE TOMATOES FOR CASES
OLIVE OIL AND BUTTER

PROVENÇAL STUFFING:
6 OUNCES GROUND VEAL
1 OUNCE FAT SALT PORK, DICED
1 ONION, FINELY CHOPPED
1 CLOVE GARLIC, CRUSHED
FINELY-CHOPPED FRESH TARRAGON
FINELY-CHOPPED FRESH PARSLEY
1 EGG, BEATEN
1 TABLESPOON GRATED PARMESAN
4 TABLESPOONS BOILED RICE
TOMATO PULP
SALT AND FRESHLY-GROUND BLACK PEPPER

Cut tops off tomatoes, scoop out interiors and keep pulp for stuffing.

To make stuffing: Sauté meat and onion in olive oil. Mix remaining ingredients in a bowl and then add them to the meat and onion mixture. Add pepper and salt to taste. Sauté for a few minutes, stirring continuously, and then stuff scooped-out tomatoes with the mixture.

Place stuffed tomatoes in an oven-proof baking dish to which you have added a little olive oil; place a knob of butter on each tomato and bake in a moderate oven (375°F. Mark 4) for 30 minutes. Serve as a main course. Serves 4 to 6.

AUBERGINE CASSEROLE

4–6 AUBERGINES
SALT
2 TABLESPOONS OLIVE OIL
FRESHLY-GROUND BLACK PEPPER
8 TABLESPOONS GRATED PARMESAN
¼ PINT FRESH CREAM
4–6 TOMATOES, PEELED AND SLICED
4 TABLESPOONS BREADCRUMBS
1 TABLESPOON BUTTER

Peel the aubergines; cut in thin slices; sprinkle with salt and let them 'sweat' in a dish for 2 hours. Drain the aubergine slices; wipe them and fry lightly in olive oil until they are soft and golden. Drain.

Butter a deep oven-proof casserole; place a layer of aubergine slices in the bottom; season with freshly-ground black pepper and sprinkle generously with grated Parmesan and fresh cream.

Add a layer of sliced raw tomatoes, then add pepper and a little more cream and cheese, followed by another layer of aubergine slices and so on, until the dish is full.

Finish with cream on the top; cover with breadcrumbs and grated Parmesan; dot with butter and cook in a moderate oven (375° F. Mark 4) for approximately 45 minutes. Serves 4.

STUFFED AUBERGINES

4 MEDIUM-SIZED AUBERGINES
SALT
OLIVE OIL
2 SPANISH ONIONS, SLICED
2 CLOVES GARLIC, FINELY CHOPPED
2 TABLESPOONS FINELY-CHOPPED PARSLEY
6 RIPE TOMATOES, SEEDED AND CHOPPED
4 WHOLE TOMATOES
SUGAR
SALT AND FRESHLY-GROUND BLACK PEPPER

Trim aubergines; cut in half lengthwise and scoop out some of the aubergine flesh, leaving shell about ¼ inch thick. Make 4 incisions lengthwise in each half, being careful not to cut through the skin. Salt aubergine halves, making sure salt goes into incisions, and leave for 20 minutes. Wash aubergines, squeeze dry and sauté in olive oil until soft and pliable. Reserve oil.

Sauté sliced onions in fresh olive oil in another frying pan until transparent. Add finely-chopped garlic, parsley and seeded, chopped tomatoes, and sauté for a few minutes more, stirring from time to time. Allow to cool.

Place sautéed aubergines, cut side up, in a fairly deep baking dish or shallow casserole. Stuff with onion and tomato mixture, spooning any left over around aubergines.

Slice 4 whole tomatoes and place 3 slices on top of each stuffed aubergine; sprinkle with a little sugar, salt and pepper, to taste.

Pour over the reserved oil; add a little water and cook in a slow oven (325°F. Mark 2) for 1 hour, or until tender. Serve cold as appetiser. Serves 4 to 6.

BOUILLABAISSE D'ÉPINARDS

1½ POUNDS COOKED SPINACH
6 TABLESPOONS OLIVE OIL
1 SPANISH ONION, FINELY CHOPPED
2 CLOVES GARLIC, FINELY CHOPPED
¾ POUND POTATOES, THINLY SLICED
SALT AND FRESHLY-GROUND BLACK PEPPER
¼ TEASPOON POWDERED SAFFRON
1 BOUQUET GARNI (PARSLEY, THYME, FENNEL AND BAY LEAF)
1 PIECE LEMON PEEL
1 EGG PER PERSON
1 FRIED TOAST TRIANGLE PER PERSON

Heat olive oil in frying pan and sauté finely-chopped onion and garlic in it until they are transparent but not golden. Add thinly-sliced potatoes and let them sauté a minute on both sides without taking colour. Transfer to an earthenware casserole; add salt and freshly-ground black pepper and pour over ¾ pint boiling water in which you have dissolved ¼ teaspoon powdered saffron. Drain cooked spinach, press it between your hands to get rid of all the moisture, chop finely and stir into the casserole, being careful not to break potato slices. Add *bouquet garni* and lemon peel; cover and allow to simmer in a slow oven (350°F. Mark 3) for at least 1 hour, or until the potatoes are cooked. When ready to serve, break into the pan 1 egg for each person and cook gently until egg whites set. One toast triangle fried in butter for each guest accompanies this country dish which is so popular in Provence.

SPINACH AU GRATIN

2 POUNDS SPINACH
SALT

GRATIN INGREDIENTS:
2 TABLESPOONS WHIPPED CREAM
1–2 TABLESPOONS FRESH BREADCRUMBS
BUTTER

SAUCE INGREDIENTS:
4 TABLESPOONS BUTTER
4 TABLESPOONS FLOUR
1 PINT HOT MILK
4 OUNCES FRESHLY-GRATED GRUYÈRE
1 LEVEL TEASPOON MUSTARD
JUICE OF ½ LEMON
SALT AND FRESHLY-GROUND BLACK PEPPER

Wash spinach several times in cold water. Poach in a little salted water for 15 to 20 minutes, or until tender. Drain; squeeze dry and chop finely.

To make sauce: Melt butter in top of double saucepan; blend in flour and cook over water, stirring constantly, until smooth. Gradually add hot milk and cook, stirring constantly, until sauce comes to the boil. Add cheese and cook, stirring, until cheese melts. Flavour to taste with mustard, lemon juice, salt and freshly-ground black pepper.

To finish 'gratin': Place chopped, cooked spinach in a buttered baking dish; pour sauce over; spread with whipped cream; sprinkle with fresh breadcrumbs and dot with butter.

Bake in a moderate oven (375°F. Mark 4) for about 20 minutes or until top is golden. Serves 4.

SPINACI CON SALSICCIA

2 POUNDS SPINACH
4 TABLESPOONS OLIVE OIL
2 TABLESPOONS BUTTER
1 SMALL CLOVE GARLIC
½ POUND DRY ITALIAN SAUSAGE, DICED
SALT AND FRESHLY-GROUND BLACK PEPPER
LEMON WEDGES

Bring about ¼ pint of water to a vigorous boil in the bottom of a large saucepan; add carefully-washed spinach leaves; cover and boil rapidly for about 3 minutes, adding a little more water if necessary. When spinach is tender, but not too soft, drain thoroughly.

Heat olive oil and butter in a large frying pan and sauté garlic in this mixture until golden. Remove garlic; add diced sausage and sauté until thoroughly cooked. Stir in the cooked spinach and heat through. Add salt and pepper to taste. Serve with lemon wedges. Serves 4.

SAUTÉED SPINACH

1 SPANISH ONION, FINELY CHOPPED
1 CLOVE GARLIC, FINELY CHOPPED
6 TABLESPOONS BUTTER
2 TABLESPOONS OLIVE OIL
3 POUNDS SPINACH, COOKED AND DRAINED
6 TABLESPOONS DOUBLE CREAM
4 TABLESPOONS DRY BREADCRUMBS
4 TABLESPOONS FRESHLY-GRATED PARMESAN
SALT AND FRESHLY-GROUND BLACK PEPPER
GRATED NUTMEG
2 SLICES WHITE BREAD

Sauté finely-chopped onions and garlic until transparent in 2 tablespoons each of butter and oil. Drain cooked spinach; chop finely and add to vegetable mixture. Cook over low heat, stirring constantly, until fats are absorbed.

Stir in cream, breadcrumbs and cheese; season to taste with salt, freshly-ground black pepper and grated nutmeg. Heat thoroughly, but do not allow to boil.

Trim crusts from bread; cut into cubes and sauté in remaining butter until golden. Just before serving, stir into spinach. Serves 6.

BAKED SPINACH MORNAY

2 SMALL PACKETS FROZEN SPINACH (ABOUT 11 OUNCES)
6 TABLESPOONS BUTTER
SALT AND FRESHLY-GROUND BLACK PEPPER
4 TABLESPOONS DOUBLE CREAM
3 SLICES BREAD

MORNAY SAUCE:
2 TABLESPOONS BUTTER
2 TABLESPOONS FLOUR
½ PINT MILK
½ TEASPOON DRY MUSTARD
6 TABLESPOONS FRESHLY-GRATED PARMESAN
PINCH CAYENNE PEPPER

Place thawed spinach in saucepan with 4 tablespoons butter, salt and pepper, to taste. Cook slowly for 3 to 6 minutes, stirring from time to time. Stir in cream. Trim crusts from bread; dice and fry in 2 tablespoons butter until golden. Fold *croûtons* into spinach and spoon mixture into a buttered, shallow, oven-proof dish.

To make sauce: Melt 2 tablespoons butter in the top of a double saucepan; add flour and cook, stirring continuously, until the mixture is smooth. Pour in milk and stir over hot water until the mixture begins to thicken. Add mustard, 5 tablespoons grated cheese and a little cayenne pepper, and simmer slowly for 5 minutes.

Pour over spinach and sprinkle top with remaining cheese. Dot with butter and brown quickly under the grill. Serves 4.

MUSHROOMS À LA GRECQUE

2 CARROTS, COARSELY CHOPPED
1 SPANISH ONION, COARSELY CHOPPED
2 TABLESPOONS OLIVE OIL
2 TABLESPOONS CORN OIL
¼ PINT DRY WHITE WINE
SALT AND FRESHLY-GROUND BLACK PEPPER
1 BOUQUET GARNI
1 FAT CLOVE GARLIC
1 POUND BUTTON MUSHROOMS
½ POUND TOMATOES, PEELED AND SEEDED
2 TABLESPOONS OLIVE OIL
2 TABLESPOONS CHOPPED PARSLEY

Coarsely chop carrots and onion and sauté in oil (half olive and half corn) until they are soft and golden. Moisten with white wine; add salt and freshly-ground black pepper to taste, a generous *bouquet garni* (2 sprigs parsley, 2 sprigs thyme, 2 bay leaves, 1 branch celery) and a clove of garlic.

Wash mushrooms well; trim stems and add to vegetables with peeled and seeded tomatoes and a little more wine if necessary. There should not be too much liquid at this stage as the mushrooms will add liquid in cooking.

Cook, uncovered, for about 15 to 20 minutes. Remove from heat; allow to cool; remove herbs and add raw olive oil. Sprinkle with freshly-chopped parsley and serve cold as *hors-d'œuvre*. Serves 4 to 6.

BAKED STUFFED MUSHROOMS

12 LARGE MUSHROOMS
4 TABLESPOONS OLIVE OIL
2 OUNCES BACON, FINELY CHOPPED
2 SHALLOTS, FINELY CHOPPED
SALT AND FRESHLY-GROUND BLACK PEPPER
1 EGG
2 TABLESPOONS DOUBLE CREAM
1 TABLESPOON COGNAC
2 TABLESPOONS BREADCRUMBS
2 TABLESPOONS BUTTER

Stem and wash 12 large mushrooms. Dry caps; brush them with olive oil and bake in a hot oven for 5 minutes, or until they are half cooked. Heat remaining olive oil in a frying pan and gently sauté finely-chopped bacon, mushroom stems and shallots for 10 minutes. Add salt and freshly-ground black pepper, to taste. Stir in egg, beaten with double cream and cognac, and cool.

Place mushroom caps on a buttered baking sheet and fill them with the stuffing, piling it up in the centre. Sprinkle with breadcrumbs, place a dab of butter on each mound and brown under the grill. Serves 4.

CRAB-STUFFED MUSHROOMS

16 LARGE MUSHROOM CAPS
¼ POUND CRABMEAT
4 TABLESPOONS DRIED BREADCRUMBS
2 EGGS, BEATEN
2 TABLESPOONS CREAM
2 TABLESPOONS FINELY-CHOPPED PARSLEY
1 TABLESPOON FINELY-CHOPPED ONION
BUTTER
SALT AND FRESHLY-GROUND BLACK PEPPER
LEMON JUICE

Wash mushroom caps and cut off stalks.

Combine crabmeat, breadcrumbs, eggs, cream and parsley in a mixing bowl. Sauté finely-chopped onion in 1 tablespoon butter until soft. Stir into crab mixture and season to taste with salt, pepper and lemon juice. Fill mushroom caps with this mixture. Dot with butter; arrange mushroom caps in a lightly-buttered baking dish and place in a moderate oven (375°F. Mark 4) for 15 to 20 minutes, or until mushrooms are tender. Serve with Mornay sauce. Serves 4.

LEEKS AU GRATIN

12 LEEKS
4 TABLESPOONS BUTTER
4 TABLESPOONS FLOUR
¾ PINT HOT MILK
4 OUNCES FRESHLY-GRATED GRUYÈRE
1 LEVEL TEASPOON MUSTARD
JUICE OF ½ LEMON
SALT AND FRESHLY-GROUND BLACK PEPPER
2 TABLESPOONS FRESH BREADCRUMBS
BUTTER

Wash leeks; cut off roots and green tops to within an inch of white. Split leeks from top almost to root end and wash thoroughly under running water. Simmer in boiling salted water for 20 minutes, or until tender. Drain thoroughly.

Melt butter in top of double saucepan; blend in flour and cook over water, stirring constantly, until smooth. Add hot milk gradually and cook, stirring constantly, until sauce comes to the boil. Add cheese and cook, stirring, until cheese melts. Flavour to taste with mustard, lemon juice, salt and freshly-ground black pepper.

Place leeks in buttered baking dish; pour sauce over them. Sprinkle with fresh breadcrumbs and dot with butter; bake in moderate oven (375°F. Mark 4) for about 20 minutes, or until top is golden. Serves 4 to 6.

GARLIC-STUFFED ONIONS

6 SPANISH ONIONS
12 FAT CLOVES GARLIC
OLIVE OIL
SALT AND FRESHLY-GROUND BLACK PEPPER
6 TABLESPOONS FINELY-CHOPPED PARSLEY
FRESH BREADCRUMBS
BUTTER

Simmer onions and garlic in boiling salted water until tender. Scoop out centres of onions. Combine scooped-out flesh of onions with cooked garlic, chop very finely and then pound together until smooth with olive oil, salt, freshly-ground black pepper, finely-chopped parsley and 6 tablespoons fresh breadcrumbs. Stuff onions with this mixture; place on a greased baking dish and sprinkle with breadcrumbs; dot with butter and cook in the oven until cooked through. Serves 6.

GLAZED WHITE ONIONS

1 POUND SMALL WHITE ONIONS
4 LEVEL TEASPOONS BUTTER
4 TABLESPOONS CHICKEN STOCK
1 TABLESPOON SUGAR
SALT

Peel onions and place in a small saucepan; cover with cold water and cook over a high flame until the water boils. Remove from the heat and drain.

Replace blanched onions in the saucepan; add butter and chicken stock; season with sugar and salt, to taste, and simmer over a low flame until onions have absorbed the liquid without burning and have taken on a little colour. Serves 4.

BRAISED CELERY

2 HEADS CELERY
¼ SPANISH ONION, THINLY SLICED
2 SMALL CARROTS, THINLY SLICED
¼ PINT CHICKEN STOCK
SALT AND FRESHLY-GROUND BLACK PEPPER
2 TEASPOONS BUTTER
2 LEVEL TEASPOONS FLOUR
FINELY-CHOPPED PARSLEY

Clean celery; cut each in half lengthwise and trim off tops. Blanch in boiling water for 10 minutes. Drain carefully and put in a heat-proof dish with thinly-sliced onion, carrots and chicken stock.

Season to taste with salt and freshly-ground black pepper, then cover pan and cook slowly until tender (30 to 40 minutes). About 5 minutes before you remove vegetables from heat, stir in butter and flour which you have mixed to a smooth paste. Just before serving, sprinkle with finely-chopped parsley. Serves 4.

GLAZED CARROTS

1 POUND SMALL CARROTS
4 LEVEL TABLESPOONS BUTTER
4 TABLESPOONS CHICKEN STOCK
1 TABLESPOON SUGAR
SALT

Scrape carrots; slice thickly and place in a small saucepan; cover with cold water and blanch. Drain.

Simmer blanched carrots with butter, chicken stock, sugar and salt, to taste, until carrots have absorbed the liquid without burning and have taken on a little colour. Serves 4.

FRENCH-STYLE PEAS

1 POUND FROZEN PEAS
4 LEVEL TEASPOONS BUTTER
4 TABLESPOONS CHICKEN STOCK
1 TABLESPOON SUGAR
SALT

Place peas in a small saucepan; cover with cold water and blanch. Drain.

Simmer blanched peas with butter, chicken stock, sugar and salt, to taste, until peas have absorbed the liquid and are tender. Serves 4.

SLICED CARROTS AND MUSHROOMS

1 BUNCH YOUNG CARROTS
2 TABLESPOONS BUTTER
1 TABLESPOON OLIVE OIL
1 SMALL ONION, FINELY CHOPPED
½ CLOVE GARLIC, FINELY CHOPPED
6 FRESH MUSHROOMS, SLICED
SALT AND FRESHLY-GROUND BLACK PEPPER
PINCH CRUSHED ROSEMARY
PINCH CRUSHED CARDAMOM (OPTIONAL)
2–4 TABLESPOONS CREAM

Scrape carrots and slice diagonally. Combine butter, olive oil, finely-chopped onion and garlic in a saucepan and sauté for 1 minute. Add sliced carrots, mushrooms and seasonings; cover saucepan and cook over a low heat for 10 to 15 minutes, or until vegetables are just tender. Stir in cream and season to taste. Serves 4 to 6.

PETITS POIS AU LARD

2 POUNDS FRESHLY-SHELLED PEAS
¼ POUND DICED SALT PORK OR BACON
4 TABLESPOONS BUTTER
12 TINY WHITE ONIONS
2 LETTUCE LEAVES, SHREDDED
4 TABLESPOONS WATER
SALT AND FRESHLY-GROUND BLACK PEPPER
1 TABLESPOON SUGAR

Parboil diced salt pork for 5 minutes in water to cover. Drain. Melt the butter gently in a saucepan; sauté the diced bacon until golden. Add peas, peeled onions, shredded lettuce, water, and salt and pepper, to taste. Cover saucepan and simmer gently for about 30 minutes. Add sugar after peas have cooked for 20 minutes. Serve hot. Serves 4 to 6.

GREAT DISHES OF THE WORLD
CHAPTER 13

Pasta and Rice

Pasta

Inexpensive, easy to prepare, wonderfully filling and practically imperishable in storage, *pasta* – as typically Italian as Grand Opera and Chianti – has much to recommend it as one of the great dishes of the world.

Though all *pasta* is made of the same basic wheat flour dough, the different shapes and sizes it comes in are as varied as the different towns and regions of Italy. Some varieties – *pasta asciutta* – are eaten with sauce and freshly-grated Parmesan; others are stuffed with finely-chopped meats, spinach, *ricotta* cheese and other ingredients. Still others – *pasta in brodo* – are meant to be served in soups.

Most of us are familiar with several varieties of *pasta.* Italians have more than a hundred different shapes and sizes to choose from – ranging from tiny golden specks called *pastina*, used mainly in light soups and invalid broths, to huge ribbed *rigatoni*, so large and hearty that they are individually stuffed with meat, cheese and tomatoes.

The delightful names the Italians give to these shapes are proof of their great affection for *pasta*. *Spaghetti* (which means little strings) and *macaroni* are, of course, best known to us, but they are just two of the immense *pasta* family: *amorini*, little cupids; *farfalletti*, little bows or butterflies; *conchiglie*, little shells; *cappelletti*, little hats; *tirabaci*, kiss-bringers . . . are a few of the other delicious forms that *pasta* takes. And strange as it seems, the cut and shape of *pasta*, in one or another of these many forms, alters the taste of the finished dish, for it affects the cooking and the amount of sauce included with each mouthful.

Even more important than the size and shape of the *pasta* is the kind of sauce that accompanies it. Not all Italian *pasta* sauces are tomato-based. One of my favourite recipes serves well-drained *spaghetti* with only butter and freshly-grated Parmesan cheese; another adds one or two raw egg yolks and a little cream to this basic recipe for a really superb sauce. An 'emergency shelf' sauce that I find useful for *pasta* features finely-chopped onions sautéed in butter and olive oil, and moistened with thinned clam broth; the whole is simmered for ten minutes and coarsely-chopped tinned clams and fresh cream are added just before serving. I like, too, a sauce made of pounded anchovies and finely-chopped onion and garlic; or, when fresh basil is available, the famous *pesto* or 'green sauce' of Genoa, made by pounding fresh basil with garlic and olive oil. But best of all, perhaps, and certainly the most famous, is *spaghetti alla bolognese*, *spaghetti* served with a rich meat and tomato sauce.

One pint of sauce is enough for a pound of *pasta*, as there should be just enough to flavour, moisten and coat each strand or piece of *pasta*, but not enough to leave a pool of sauce in the bottom of the serving dish.

HOW TO COOK PASTA PERFECTLY

One pound of *pasta* serves 4 people for a main course, 6 people for a first course. Cook *pasta* in boiling, well-salted water (3 to 4 quarts of water per pound of *pasta*).

Let water boil briskly for a minute before adding *pasta*. Instead of breaking long *spaghetti* or *macaroni*, hold a handful at one end and dip the other into the boiling water. As the *pasta* softens, curl it round in the pan until the whole length goes in. Do not cover; use a kitchen fork or a long wooden spoon to stir at the start of the cooking to prevent *spaghetti* from sticking to the pan. Stir frequently during cooking.

Cook *pasta* until tender, but still firm – '*al dente*', as the Italians say, which means just firm enough to bite comfortably but not so soft that it is mushy. And remember, cooking time varies with the shape, thickness and freshness of *pasta*. Dried *pasta* – the commercial variety available in this country – should be cooked for 12 to 15 minutes. *Pasta fatta in casa* – the home-made kind – takes only about 5 minutes to cook. Lift out one strand with a fork and bite it to test whether it is ready.

Be careful not to overcook *pasta*. When done, drain at once in a big colander, shaking it to remove as much water as possible. For best results, serve *pasta* immediately.

TO KEEP PASTA HOT

If it is impractical to serve *pasta* as soon as it is cooked, set the colander of drained *pasta* over a saucepan containing a small amount of boiling water. Cover with a damp towel until ready to serve.

BASIC RECIPE FOR HOME-MADE EGG PASTA

1 POUND SIFTED FLOUR
1 LEVEL TEASPOON SALT
3 WELL-BEATEN EGGS
4–5 TABLESPOONS WATER

Mix flour, salt and eggs and a little water with a fork until *pasta* dough is just soft enough to form into a ball, adding a little more water if mixture seems too dry.

Sprinkle a large pastry board with flour and knead the dough until smooth and elastic (about 15 minutes) on this board with the flat of your hand, sifting a little flour on hands and board from time to time.

Divide dough into 6 equal parts and, using a rolling pin, roll out a piece at a time into paper-thin sheets. To do this, roll out in one direction, stretching the *pasta* dough as you go, and then roll out in the opposite direction. Sprinkle with flour, fold over and repeat. The dough should be just dry enough not to stick to the rolling pin. Repeat this process of rolling, stretching and folding the dough another 2 or 3 times. Repeat with other pieces of *pasta* dough.

To make Tagliatelle: Prepare egg *pasta* as above. Dust liberally with flour. Fold loosely and cut into ¼-inch strips. Spread on a clean cloth to dry for at least 1 hour before cooking in the usual way.

To make Lasagne: Prepare egg *pasta* as above. Dust with flour. Fold loosely and cut into 2-inch strips. Spread on a clean cloth to dry for at least 1 hour before cooking in the usual way.

To make Cannelloni: Prepare egg *pasta* as above. Cut into 3-inch by 4-inch rectangles. Dry for 1 hour. Drop into boiling salted water, 6 to 8 at a time, and boil for 5 minutes. Remove and drop immediately into cold water. Drain and spread on a clean cloth to dry. Fill as desired and bake until stuffing is cooked through. Serve with tomato sauce and freshly-grated Parmesan.

SPAGHETTI ALLA BOLOGNESE

1 POUND SPAGHETTI
2 TABLESPOONS BUTTER
4 TABLESPOONS OLIVE OIL
¼ POUND FAT SALT PORK OR GREEN BACON, FINELY CHOPPED
1 ONION, FINELY CHOPPED
2 CARROTS, FINELY CHOPPED
1 STALK CELERY, FINELY CHOPPED
½ POUND SIRLOIN OF BEEF, MINCED
1 STRIP OF LEMON PEEL
1 BAY LEAF
4 TABLESPOONS TOMATO PURÉE
½ PINT RICH BEEF STOCK
¼ PINT DRY WHITE WINE
SALT, FRESHLY-GROUND BLACK PEPPER AND GRATED NUTMEG
4 TABLESPOONS DOUBLE CREAM
FRESHLY-GRATED PARMESAN
BUTTER

Heat butter and olive oil in a large thick-bottomed frying pan; add finely-chopped fat salt pork (or green bacon), onion, carrots and celery, and sauté over a medium heat, stirring occasionally, until meat browns. Stir in raw minced beef and brown evenly, stirring continuously. Add lemon peel, bay leaf, tomato purée, beef stock and dry white wine, and season to taste with salt, freshly-ground black pepper and nutmeg. Cover pan and simmer the sauce very gently for ½ hour, stirring occasionally. Remove lemon peel and bay leaf and simmer, uncovered, for ½ hour, or until sauce has thickened slightly. Add cream and simmer for 2 to 3 minutes more.

Cook *spaghetti* in boiling salted water until *al dente*. Drain. Serve with Bolognese sauce and freshly-grated Parmesan. Dot with butter. Serves 4.

SPAGHETTI SOUFFLÉ

2 TABLESPOONS BUTTER
2 TABLESPOONS FLOUR
½ PINT MILK
4 OUNCES GRATED PARMESAN
1 TEASPOON MUSTARD
CAYENNE PEPPER AND SALT
¼ POUND SPAGHETTI
5 EGGS
TOMATO SAUCE

Melt butter in the top of a double saucepan. Add flour and blend well. Add milk and stir until sauce begins to thicken; then add grated Parmesan and stir until sauce is smooth and thick. Season to taste with mustard, cayenne pepper and salt.

Cook *spaghetti* in boiling salted water until tender. Drain well. Separate eggs and stir yolks, one by one, into slightly-cooled cheese mixture. Stir *spaghetti* into cheese mixture. Beat egg whites until they are stiff, but not dry. Fold gently into *spaghetti* and cheese mixture and pour into a well-buttered soufflé dish. Cook in a pre-heated oven (350°F. Mark 3) for about 25 minutes, or until done. Serve immediately with well-flavoured tomato sauce. Serves 4.

SPAGHETTI ALLA MATRICIANA

1 POUND SPAGHETTI
¼ POUND FAT SALT PORK, DICED
1 SPANISH ONION, FINELY CHOPPED
2 CLOVES GARLIC, FINELY CHOPPED
2 TABLESPOONS OLIVE OIL
1 LARGE TIN ITALIAN PEELED TOMATOES
2 TABLESPOONS TOMATO CONCENTRATE
½ LARGE RED PEPPER, DICED
SALT AND FRESHLY-GROUND BLACK PEPPER
FRESHLY-GRATED PARMESAN
BUTTER

Sauté diced fat salt pork, finely-chopped onion and garlic in olive oil until golden. Add Italian peeled tomatoes, tomato concentrate, diced red pepper; season to taste with salt and freshly-ground black pepper and simmer for 1 hour.

Cook *spaghetti* in boiling salted water until *al dente*. Drain. Serve with sauce and freshly-grated Parmesan. Dot with butter. Serves 4.

SPAGHETTI ALLA BERSAGLIERA

1 POUND SPAGHETTI
1 ONION, FINELY CHOPPED
4 TABLESPOONS OLIVE OIL
¼ POUND SALAME, CUT IN STRIPS
4 TABLESPOONS DRY WHITE WINE
2 POUNDS TOMATOES, PEELED AND SEEDED
SALT AND FRESHLY-GROUND BLACK PEPPER
¼ POUND PROVOLONE CHEESE, CUT IN STRIPS
FRESHLY-GRATED PARMESAN
BUTTER

Sauté finely-chopped onion in olive oil until golden. Cut *salame* in thin strips and add to onion mixture. Allow *salame* to take on colour; moisten with dry white wine and cook, stirring, until wine evaporates. Stir in tomatoes, which you have peeled and seeded. Season to taste with salt and pepper and simmer gently for at least 45 minutes. Keep warm.

Cook *spaghetti* in salted water until *al dente*. Cut *provolone* cheese into thin strips and when *pasta* is almost cooked, add it to the tomato and *salame* sauce and mix well. Drain; cover with sauce and sprinkle with grated Parmesan. Serve with butter and additional Parmesan. Serves 4.

TAGLIATELLE VERDE

1 POUND GREEN NOODLES
6 TABLESPOONS BUTTER
1 TIN ITALIAN WHITE TRUFFLES
4 EGG YOLKS
¼ PINT CREAM
1 PINCH NUTMEG
FRESHLY-GRATED PARMESAN
BUTTER

Boil green noodles in salted water until they are cooked to *al dente* tenderness. Drain. Melt half the butter in a large saucepan. Slice truffles thinly and sauté for a minute in butter. Add the noodles and pour over the egg yolks beaten with cream and a grating of nutmeg. Stir for a minute; remove from heat and add remaining butter.

The sauce should be creamy and the eggs should not begin to solidify. Serve with additional quantities of butter and freshly-grated Parmesan.

SPAGHETTI WITH MUSHROOM SAUCE

1 POUND SPAGHETTI
4 TABLESPOONS OLIVE OIL
4 TABLESPOONS BUTTER
2 ONIONS, COARSELY CHOPPED
1 POUND MUSHROOMS, SLICED THINLY
2 CLOVES GARLIC, CRUSHED
1 TEASPOON SALT
FRESHLY-GROUND BLACK PEPPER
1¼ POUNDS PEELED TOMATOES
½ TEASPOON OREGANO, BASIL OR MARJORAM
FRESHLY-GRATED PARMESAN
BUTTER

Combine olive oil and butter in a heavy-bottomed iron *cocotte* or casserole and sauté chopped onions until they are golden but not brown. Add sliced mushrooms, crushed garlic, salt and pepper to taste, and simmer with onions, stirring frequently, for 10 minutes. Add tomatoes and herbs and simmer for 30 minutes.

While sauce is simmering, cook *spaghetti* in rapidly boiling salted water until just tender. Drain and place on a hot serving dish. Pour over sauce and serve with a generous knob of butter and grated Parmesan. Serves 4.

SPAGHETTI ALLA MARINARA

1 POUND SPAGHETTI
1 SPANISH ONION, FINELY CHOPPED
2 CLOVES GARLIC, FINELY CHOPPED
4 TABLESPOONS OLIVE OIL
1 POUND RIPE TOMATOES
SALT AND FRESHLY-GROUND BLACK PEPPER
1–2 TEASPOONS BROWN SUGAR
½ TEASPOON OREGANO, BASIL OR MARJORAM
1 POUND PRAWNS, CHOPPED IF LARGE
¼ PINT DRY WHITE WINE
4 TABLESPOONS FINELY-CHOPPED PARSLEY
BUTTER

Sauté finely-chopped onion and garlic in olive oil until transparent. Skin, seed and coarsely chop tomatoes. Add chopped tomatoes, salt, pepper, brown sugar, and *oregano*, basil or marjoram to onion mixture, and simmer gently for 15 to 20 minutes.

Combine prawns and dry white wine in another saucepan and simmer gently for 5 minutes. Add prawns to tomato sauce with finely-chopped parsley and simmer for 10 minutes longer. Correct seasoning.

While sauce is simmering, cook *spaghetti* in rapidly boiling salted water until just tender. Drain and place on a hot serving dish. Pour over sauce and serve with a generous knob of butter. Serves 4.

SPAGHETTI AL TONNO

1 POUND SPAGHETTI
1 CLOVE GARLIC
4 TABLESPOONS OLIVE OIL
6–8 TABLESPOONS TOMATO CONCENTRATE
½ PINT WATER
¼ POUND TUNA FISH
4 ANCHOVY FILLETS
SALT AND FRESHLY-GROUND BLACK PEPPER
FINELY-CHOPPED PARSLEY
BUTTER

Sauté garlic in olive oil until golden. Discard garlic. Mix tomato concentrate with water and add to the oil. Simmer for 30 minutes.

Chop tuna fish coarsely; chop anchovies finely; add to tomato mixture. Season to taste with salt and pepper and simmer for 15 minutes, stirring occasionally.

Cook *spaghetti* in boiling salted water until *al dente*. Drain and mix with sauce; sprinkle with finely-chopped parsley; dot with butter and serve. Serves 4.

FETTUCINE WITH PESTO SAUCE

1 POUND FETTUCINE
2–3 CLOVES GARLIC, FINELY CHOPPED
4–6 TABLESPOONS FINELY-CHOPPED FRESH BASIL
4–6 TABLESPOONS FINELY-CHOPPED PARSLEY
1 TABLESPOON PINE NUTS
6–8 TABLESPOONS GRATED CHEESE (ROMANO, PECORINO OR PARMESAN)
OLIVE OIL
FRESHLY-GROUND BLACK PEPPER
BUTTER

Pound finely-chopped garlic, basil, parsley, pine nuts and grated cheese in a mortar until smooth. Gradually add olive oil and whisk until sauce is thick and smooth. Season to taste with freshly-ground black pepper.

Cook *fettucine* in rapidly boiling salted water until just tender. Drain and place on a hot serving dish. Spoon *pesto* sauce over and serve with a generous knob of butter and grated cheese. Serves 4.

ITALIAN SPAGHETTI

1 POUND SPAGHETTI
1 SPANISH ONION, FINELY CHOPPED
1 CLOVE GARLIC, FINELY CHOPPED
2–4 TABLESPOONS OLIVE OIL
1 SMALL TIN MUSHROOMS, SLICED
1 LARGE TIN ITALIAN PEELED TOMATOES
6 TABLESPOONS ITALIAN TOMATO CONCENTRATE
1 BAY LEAF
1 SMALL STRIP LEMON PEEL
1 BEEF STOCK CUBE
SALT AND FRESHLY-GROUND BLACK PEPPER
1 TABLESPOON WORCESTERSHIRE SAUCE
FRESHLY-GRATED PARMESAN
BUTTER

Sauté finely-chopped onion and garlic in olive oil in a large, thick-bottomed frying pan until transparent. Add sliced tinned mushrooms and sauté for a minute or two more. Then add peeled tomatoes, tomato concentrate, bay leaf, lemon peel, beef stock cube, and salt and pepper, to taste. Simmer gently, covered, stirring from time to time, for 1 hour. Just before serving, stir in Worcestershire sauce.

Cook *spaghetti* in boiling salted water until just tender. Drain. Serve with sauce and freshly-grated Parmesan and butter. Serves 4.

SPAGHETTI WITH OIL AND GARLIC SAUCE

- 1 POUND SPAGHETTI
- 4 CLOVES GARLIC, FINELY CHOPPED
- 4 TABLESPOONS PARSLEY, FINELY CHOPPED
- 4 TABLESPOONS BUTTER
- 4 TABLESPOONS OLIVE OIL
- SALT AND FRESHLY-GROUND BLACK PEPPER
- FRESHLY-GRATED PARMESAN
- BUTTER

Cook *spaghetti* in boiling salted water until tender, but not mushy. Drain and keep warm.

Simmer finely-chopped garlic and parsley in butter and olive oil until sauce is hot, but do not allow garlic to take on colour.

Add drained *spaghetti* to oil and garlic mixture and stir until thoroughly moistened, adding a little more warm oil if necessary. Season to taste with salt and freshly-ground black pepper.

Turn *spaghetti* into a heated serving dish, sprinkle with freshly-grated Parmesan, dot with butter and serve immediately. Serves 4.

TAGLIATELLE CON TARTUFI

- 1 POUND EGG NOODLES
- 4 TABLESPOONS BUTTER
- 2 RAW EGG YOLKS
- 6 TABLESPOONS FRESHLY-GRATED PARMESAN
- 6 TABLESPOONS DOUBLE CREAM
- SALT AND FRESHLY-GROUND BLACK PEPPER
- TINNED WHITE TRUFFLES
- FRESHLY-GRATED PARMESAN
- BUTTER

Boil a pound of *tagliatelle*, or egg noodles, in salted water until they are cooked to *al dente* tenderness. Drain and place them in a hot serving bowl or chafing dish, with butter, egg yolks, grated cheese and cream. Toss noodles in this mixture until the heat of the noodles 'cooks' the egg and cream sauce. Season to taste with salt and freshly-ground pepper; sprinkle with finely-sliced white truffles and serve immediately with additional quantities of butter and freshly-grated Parmesan. Serves 4.

LASAGNE AL FORNO

1 POUND LASAGNE NOODLES
½ POUND MOZZARELLA CHEESE
¼ POUND COOKED ITALIAN SAUSAGE
2 HARD-BOILED EGGS
2 OUNCES FRESHLY-GRATED PARMESAN
½ POUND RICOTTA CHEESE
TOMATO SAUCE
BUTTER

TOMATO SAUCE:
3 POUNDS TOMATOES
3 TABLESPOONS TOMATO PURÉE
3 LARGE CARROTS, CHOPPED
1 SPANISH ONION, CHOPPED
3 STALKS CELERY, CHOPPED
2 CLOVES GARLIC, CHOPPED
FINELY-CHOPPED PARSLEY
GRATED RIND OF ½ LEMON
SALT AND FRESHLY-GROUND BLACK PEPPER
2 TABLESPOONS OLIVE OIL
2 TABLESPOONS BUTTER

Cook the *lasagne*, 6 or 8 at a time, in boiling salted water until they are half done; drain carefully. Line a well-buttered baking dish with a layer of *lasagne*; add a layer of diced *mozzarella* cheese, a layer of coarsely-chopped Italian sausage, a layer of sliced hard-boiled eggs; sprinkle generously with grated Parmesan and crumbled *ricotta* cheese and moisten with well-seasoned tomato sauce. Repeat, using the same quantities, finishing with tomato sauce as before. Dot with butter and bake in a moderate oven (375°F. Mark 4) for about 30 minutes. Serves 4.

To make sauce: Combine the coarsely-chopped tomatoes with 3 tablespoons tomato purée and the carrots, Spanish onion and celery, all coarsely chopped. Stir in chopped garlic, finely-chopped parsley and the grated rind of ½ lemon.

Simmer this mixture for 1½ hours and press it through a sieve; add salt and pepper and simmer until thick. Just before using, stir in 2 tablespoons each olive oil and butter.

CANNELLONI RIPIENI

1 POUND CANNELLONI
1 POUND BUTTON MUSHROOMS, CHOPPED
½ POUND COOKED HAM OR VEAL, DICED
½ SPANISH ONION, CHOPPED
2 TABLESPOONS OLIVE OIL
2 TABLESPOONS BUTTER
2 TABLESPOONS GRATED PARMESAN
SALT AND FRESHLY-GROUND BLACK PEPPER
FRESHLY-GRATED PARMESAN

CHEESE SAUCE:
2 TABLESPOONS BUTTER
2 TABLESPOONS FLOUR
1 PINT HOT MILK
4 TABLESPOONS GRATED PARMESAN
SALT AND FRESHLY-GROUND BLACK PEPPER

To make pastry: Follow recipe on page 305, or buy *cannelloni* ready-made, and prepare as below.

To make filling: Sauté the chopped mushrooms, diced ham or veal and onion in butter and olive oil until vegetables are cooked. Cool. Add cheese, and salt and pepper, to taste. Place 2 tablespoons mushroom filling on each square and roll it carefully around filling. Arrange filled *cannelloni* in a buttered shallow baking dish; cover with sauce; sprinkle generously with grated cheese and bake in a slow oven (350°F. Mark 3) for about 30 minutes, or until golden brown.
To make sauce: Melt butter in the top of a double saucepan; stir in flour to make a smooth *roux*. Add hot milk gradually, stirring continuously; season to taste with grated cheese, salt and freshly-ground black pepper and cook, stirring from time to time, until sauce is smooth and thick.

Illustration on facing page

The Cauliflower

This is the undoubted aristocrat of the cabbage family, a large and powerful clan which includes green, white, red and Savoy cabbage as well as Brussels sprouts, broccoli and cauliflower.

Illustration on following page

The Artichoke

There are many ways to serve this delicate and attractive vegetable, rich in iron, mineral salts and iodine. I like it best poached in water with a little salt, lemon juice and olive oil, and served hot with clarified butter or a *sauce hollandaise* or cold with a well-seasoned *vinaigrette* dressing.

CHINESE SHO M'AI

1 POUND FLOUR
½ PINT WATER
½ POUND MINCED RAW PORK
4 TABLESPOONS FINELY-CHOPPED WATER CHESTNUTS
4–6 CHINESE MUSHROOMS, SOAKED AND FINELY CHOPPED
1 SLICE FRESH GINGER ROOT, FINELY CHOPPED
2 SPRING ONIONS, FINELY CHOPPED
1–2 TABLESPOONS SAKE OR DRY SHERRY
1–2 TABLESPOONS SOY SAUCE
1 TABLESPOON CORN OR OLIVE OIL
FRESHLY-GROUND BLACK PEPPER
SOY SAUCE, SAKE (OR DRY SHERRY) AND STOCK

To make thin pastry dough: mix flour and water in a large bowl. When well mixed, knead dough for 15 minutes. Cover with a damp cloth and leave for 30 minutes.

Combine minced pork with finely-chopped water chestnuts, Chinese mushrooms, ginger root, spring onions and *sake* (or dry sherry), soy sauce, oil and freshly-ground black pepper to taste.

When ready to serve: roll dough into a long roll (1 inch in diameter). Slice roll thinly; flatten each piece with the palm of your hand and roll out on a floured board to a circle (3 to 4 inches in diameter).

Place a tablespoon of filling in the middle of each circle and bring edges up over filling, pinching top together to contain filling.

Place *sho m'ai* in a wet towel and steam them in a steamer for 15 minutes. Serve with a sauce made of soy sauce, *sake* (or sherry) and stock. Makes about 3 dozen.

Illustration on previous page

Pasta

Inexpensive, easy to prepare, wonderfully filling and practically imperishable in storage, *pasta* – as typically Italian as Grand Opera or Chianti – has much to recommend it as one of the great dishes of the world.

Illustration on facing page

Creole Jambalaya

– a popular Creole dish from Louisiana – is a hearty concoction of ham, prawns and rice, enriched with wine, tomatoes and herbs. (Recipe on page 315.)

Creole Jambalaya

For me, one of the most romantic places in the United States, and perhaps the world, is the shadowy, unreal swampland of Louisiana, where the grey streamers of Spanish moss trail heavily from the branches of oak trees, removing all sense of depth and turning the *bayoux* into a series of dreamy backdrops for some gigantic ballet.

The trees, growing straight out of the water, seem to float in space, balanced precariously over their own writhing reflections. Strange creatures of these wastes – alligators, raccoons and swimming snakes – contest possession of the dark waterways with men in canoes, Cajun Indians, who have lived in this area for centuries and yet (almost the strangest fact of all about this lost land) speak among themselves perfect seventeenth-century French.

It was from this magic country and its capital, New Orleans, where Indian, Spanish, Negro and French cultures have combined to produce the Creole, that I first discovered how foreign and exotic American regional food could be. It was here that I first tasted baked *pompano* with spicy Creole sauce, red snapper *court-bouillon*, fluffy oyster cutlets, feathery-light beaten biscuits, and the heady delights of Creole *gumbos* (high-flavoured soups of chicken, oysters, shrimps and crabs, seasoned with okra and powdered sassafras) and Creole *jambalaya*, my favourite of them all.

This great Creole speciality seems to sum up the troubled history of Louisiana, combining the subtlety of the French, the exoticism of the *Conquistadores* and the earthy magic of the Negro plantation cooks. Ham and shrimps or prawns are a necessity for this dish; hot Spanish sausage (*chorizo*) and cubed poached chicken are often added for festive occasions; and even chick-peas can go into the pot with the spices, herbs, rice and tomatoes that give such character and flavour to this great dish.

Creole *jambalaya* takes time to prepare and more time to cook but the results make the operation more than worth the extra effort involved. I particularly like this dish for its easy stretchability. The recipe below feeds six lavishly, will stretch comfortably to eight, and can be doubled for twelve. Easily manageable with a fork, it is an admirable standby for buffet party suppers.

CREOLE JAMBALAYA

¾ POUND COOKED HAM
¾ POUND JUMBO PRAWNS, SHELLED
½ POUND CHORIZO SAUSAGE
4 TABLESPOONS OLIVE OIL
2 TABLESPOONS BUTTER
2 TABLESPOONS LARD

VEGETABLES:
1 SPANISH ONION, FINELY CHOPPED
¾ POUND RISOTTO RICE
1 STALK CELERY, CHOPPED
1 GREEN PEPPER, FINELY CHOPPED
6 TOMATOES, PEELED, SEEDED AND CHOPPED
1 SMALL TIN TOMATO CONCENTRATE

SEASONINGS:
1 BAY LEAF, CRUMBLED
½ TEASPOON OREGANO
⅛ TEASPOON THYME
⅛ TEASPOON GROUND CLOVES
2 CLOVES GARLIC
SALT, PEPPER AND CAYENNE

2 PINTS WELL-FLAVOURED CHICKEN STOCK
1 SMALL GLASS DRY WHITE WINE
4 TABLESPOONS FINELY-CHOPPED PARSLEY
PITTED BLACK OLIVES

Cut ham into 1-inch squares; shell and clean prawns and cut into smaller pieces if they seem a little large; slice *chorizo* sausage (if not available, substitute pork or garlic sausage).

Heat olive oil in a thick-bottomed frying pan and sauté ham chunks, prawns and sausage until they are golden brown. Reserve.

Melt butter and lard in the bottom of a large flame-proof casserole and sauté finely-chopped Spanish onion until transparent. Stir in Italian rice (the kind you use to make a risotto) and cook over a low heat, stirring gently until the rice is golden. Add ham, prawn and sausage mixture to rice; and stir in chopped celery, pepper, tomatoes and tomato concentrate, and seasonings.

Bring chicken stock to the boil and pour over *jambalaya* mixture. Cover casserole and simmer over a low flame for 25 to 30 minutes – or until the rice is tender, but still separate – adding a little more liquid from time to time if necessary. Just before serving, stir in dry white wine, correct seasoning and keep warm in the lowest of ovens – or on a candle warmer – until ready to serve. A little finely-chopped parsley or a handful of pitted black olives may be added if desired. Serves 6

QUICK JAMBALAYA

2 TABLESPOONS BUTTER
2 TABLESPOONS OLIVE OIL
1 SPANISH ONION, FINELY CHOPPED
1 GREEN PEPPER, FINELY CHOPPED
1 CLOVE GARLIC, FINELY CHOPPED
½ POUND COOKED HAM, DICED
½ POUND JUMBO PRAWNS, SHELLED
¼ PINT DRY WHITE WINE
1 LARGE TIN ITALIAN PEELED TOMATOES
½ LEVEL TEASPOON THYME
¼ LEVEL TEASPOON BASIL OR OREGANO
¼ TEASPOON TABASCO SAUCE
½ POUND RICE

Heat butter and olive oil in a thick-bottomed, flame-proof casserole and sauté onion, pepper and garlic until onion is transparent. Stir in ham and prawns and sauté for a few minutes longer. Add wine, tomatoes and seasonings and bring slowly to the boil. Stir in rice gradually; reduce heat, cover casserole and simmer gently, adding more liquid if necessary, for about ½ hour or until rice is tender. Serves 4.

Spanish Paella

One of the prime pleasures of travelling is the chance we have to sample foods that differ from our own. Spain is famous for its *empanados*, deep-fried 'little pies' of finely-chopped seafood or meat, served in tiny pastry cases for *hors-d'œuvre*, slightly larger for luncheon or supper; its savoury *tortillas*, thick flat omelettes rich with vegetables and meats; and *gazpacho*, a cold tomato and garlic-based soup with finely-chopped trimmings – spring onions, radishes, pimento, cucumber, green pepper, hard-boiled egg and ripe olives – served in individual bowls on the side so that *aficionados* may flavour it as they see fit.

Hearty soups – *cocida*, a knife-and-fork soup that blends the flavours of chicken, beef, smoked ham, chick-peas and other vegetables – and fragrant combinations of beans, beans and pork, chicken and rice, or lobster and rice, are intrinsic parts of this exotic fare, as rich in tradition as the country itself. But perhaps the most famous and most exciting of all is the famous *päella valenciana* – one of the great dishes of the world – which combines many of these ingredients in one delicious dish.

Paella gets its name from the flat, round frying pan with two handles in which this dish is traditionally cooked and served. In Spain these pans range from six inches in diameter for one portion to about two feet for parties.

I always think of *paella* as the perfect party dish – glamorous and attractive and as easy to make as it is easy to serve. It combines its four essential ingredients – saffron, pimentos, Spanish onion and rice – with a selection of the following: fried chicken, diced bacon, ham, veal or pork, *chorizo* sausage, mussels or cockles, prawns or shrimps, and (for gala occasions) a lobster.

SPANISH PAELLA

12 MUSSELS, WITH SHELLS
6 TABLESPOONS DRY WHITE WINE
2 TABLESPOONS FINELY-CHOPPED ONION
4 TABLESPOONS FINELY-CHOPPED PARSLEY
1 FRYING CHICKEN, CUT IN PIECES
½ POUND LEAN PORK, DICED
¼ POUND CHORIZO OR PORK SAUSAGE, SLICED
¼ PINT OLIVE OIL
1 SMALL LOBSTER, CUT IN PIECES
8 LARGE WHOLE PRAWNS
1 SPANISH ONION, FINELY CHOPPED
4 SMALL CLOVES GARLIC, FINELY CHOPPED
4 LARGE TOMATOES, PEELED AND CHOPPED
2 TINNED PIMENTOS, CUT IN STRIPS
SALT AND FRESHLY-GROUND BLACK PEPPER
¼ TEASPOON CAYENNE PEPPER
½ TEASPOON POWDERED SAFFRON
¾ PINT CHICKEN STOCK OR WATER, BOILING
1 POUND UNCOOKED RICE FOR RISOTTO

Steam mussels in dry white wine with 2 tablespoons each finely-chopped onion and parsley until shells open. Reserve mussels. Strain liquor and reserve.

Sauté chicken, pork and sausage in olive oil in a *paella* or large frying pan until golden on all sides. Remove meats and reserve. Sauté lobster and prawns in same pan. Remove and reserve. Add finely-chopped Spanish onion and 2 cloves finely-chopped garlic to pan and sauté until transparent. Then add peeled and chopped tomatoes and sliced tinned pimentos and simmer mixture for about 5 minutes, stirring constantly.

Return sautéed chicken, pork, sausage and half the lobster, prawns and mussels to pan; add mussel liquor; season to taste with salt, pepper and cayenne pepper, and heat through.

Mix remaining garlic, parsley and powdered saffron in 1 cup boiling stock or water; add to remaining stock or water and pour over meat and seafood mixture; stir well and slowly bring to the boil again. Add rice and cook, uncovered, for 15 minutes without stirring. Stir well with a wooden spoon; garnish with remaining lobster, prawns and mussels, and cook for 10 to 15 minutes more, or until rice is tender. Serves 4 to 6.

QUICK PAELLA

1 SPANISH ONION, FINELY CHOPPED
2 TABLESPOONS BUTTER
2 TABLESPOONS OLIVE OIL
¾ POUND RISOTTO RICE
1½ PINTS HOT CHICKEN STOCK (MADE WITH 2 CHICKEN STOCK CUBES)
½ TEASPOON POWDERED SAFFRON
1 SMALL TIN PRAWNS
1 TIN MINCED CLAMS, WITH LIQUID
1 SMALL TIN MUSHROOMS, QUARTERED
1 SMALL TIN PEAS
1 SMALL TIN PIMENTOS, DICED
SALT AND FRESHLY-GROUND BLACK PEPPER

Place chopped onion in a deep saucepan with butter and olive oil. Cook slowly, stirring constantly, until onion is transparent. Add rice and cook over medium heat, stirring constantly with a wooden spoon. After a minute or two, stir in a cup of hot chicken stock in which you have dissolved the powdered saffron. Stir in prawns, minced clams with liquid and quartered mushrooms, and continue cooking, adding chicken stock as needed and stirring gently from time to time, until rice is cooked (15 to 18 minutes). Add drained peas and diced pimentos, correct seasoning and cook for a few minutes more until all the stock in the pan is absorbed by the rice and the rice is tender but still moist. Serves 4 to 6.

Italian Rice

Italians love rice and are wonderfully creative in their methods of cooking it. Not for them the pallid plain-boiled variety so often served here as a sop for undistinguished gravies of curry and casserole. Instead they combine rice with butter, finely-chopped onion and rich chicken stock, and simmer it gently until it is magically tender – neither mushy soft nor unpleasantly hard – but *al dente* just like their *spaghetti*. And then they flavour it with saffron, wild mushrooms or, for more special occasions, chicken, shrimps, prawns or thinly-sliced white truffles.

Italian cooks respect rice: rarely do they wash it under the tap. Instead they clean it by placing it in cold water for a few minutes, carefully picking out the bits of grit, and then they rub it dry, after draining it, between the folds of a clean tea towel.

For the best results rice should be cooked in only as much liquid as it can absorb, and special care is required in handling it once it is cooked. The grains mash very easily and so, once cooked, they should never be stirred with a spoon, but tossed lightly with a fork. Serve your rice as soon as possible after cooking.

THE RISOTTO

One of the easiest and most delicious methods of cooking rice I know is the *risotto*. Wash *risotto* or Italian rice in cold water. Drain and dry thoroughly. Add 3 to 4 tablespoons butter; season to taste with salt and pepper and then add enough chicken stock and dry white wine, beef stock, or a combination of the three, to cover the rice. Bring to the boil, stirring; reduce flame, cover tightly and simmer gently for 15 to 18 minutes, adding a little more liquid if necessary. Uncover, toss lightly with a fork, add a little extra butter and some grated Parmesan cheese and serve. The rice should have absorbed all the liquid and all the grains will be separate and moist.

If a rich chicken stock is used in cooking the rice, and you have sautéed the rice with a little finely-chopped onion before adding the liquid, it will take on extra strength and flavour. Try adding to it ½ pound diced cooked chicken or lamb that has been heated in a little stock with ½ Spanish onion, finely-chopped and cooked until golden in 2 tablespoons butter. Substitute cooked prawns, shrimps, lobster or diced white fish. Then add to any of these a teaspoon or two of curry powder, or ¼ teaspoon of powdered saffron. Chopped nuts, diced raw apples or raisins will also do much to change the taste and quality of your *risotto*. This with a salad, followed by a sweet or cheese and fruit, will make a delicious and satisfying meal.

RISOTTO ALLA MILANESE

½ SPANISH ONION, FINELY CHOPPED
4 TABLESPOONS BUTTER
4 TABLESPOONS DICED RAW BEEF MARROW
¾ POUND RICE
1½–2 PINTS HOT BEEF STOCK
¼ TEASPOON POWDERED SAFFRON
SALT AND FRESHLY-GROUND BLACK PEPPER
FRESHLY-GRATED PARMESAN
BUTTER

Place chopped onion in a deep saucepan with butter and diced beef marrow. Cook slowly for 2 to 4 minutes, taking care that the onion does not become brown. Add the rice and cook over medium heat, stirring constantly with a wooden spoon. After a minute or so stir in a cup of hot beef stock in which you have dissolved the powdered saffron.

Continue cooking, adding stock as needed and stirring from time to time, until rice is cooked (15 to 18 minutes). Correct seasoning. By this time all the stock in the pan should have been absorbed by the rice, leaving rice tender but still moist. Serve rice immediately with extra butter and freshly-grated Parmesan. Serves 4 to 6.

EASY SAFFRON RICE

½ TEASPOON POWDERED SAFFRON
6 TABLESPOONS DRY WHITE WINE
1½ PINTS HOT CHICKEN STOCK
¾ POUND RICE
SALT AND FRESHLY-GROUND BLACK PEPPER

Dissolve saffron in white wine; add it to hot chicken stock and combine in a large saucepan with rice and salt and pepper, to taste. Cover pan and simmer until all the liquid is absorbed and the rice is tender (about 30 minutes). Serves 4.

SAFFRON RICE SALAD

¾ POUND RICE, COOKED AS ABOVE
6–8 TABLESPOONS OLIVE OIL
2 TABLESPOONS WINE VINEGAR
4 TABLESPOONS FINELY-CHOPPED PARSLEY
1–2 CLOVES GARLIC, FINELY CHOPPED
DRY MUSTARD
¾ POUND FLAKED COOKED HADDOCK
SALT AND FRESHLY-GROUND BLACK PEPPER
4 TOMATOES, SLICED
RIPE OLIVES

Make a highly-flavoured dressing with olive oil, wine vinegar, parsley, garlic and dry mustard, to taste. Toss cooked saffron rice and flaked cooked fish in a bowl with dressing and season generously with salt and pepper, adding more oil and vinegar if necessary. Garnish salad with sliced tomatoes and ripe olives. Serves 4.

RISI E BISI

1 SPANISH ONION, CHOPPED
2 SLICES BACON, CHOPPED
4 TABLESPOONS BUTTER
½ POUND SHELLED FRESH PEAS
2 TABLESPOONS CHOPPED PARSLEY
1½–2 PINTS BEEF OR CHICKEN STOCK
¾ POUND RICE
SALT AND FRESHLY-GROUND BLACK PEPPER
FRESHLY-GRATED PARMESAN
BUTTER

Sauté chopped onion and bacon in butter until onion is soft and lightly golden. Stir in peas and parsley; pour over half the stock; cover and simmer for 15 to 20 minutes (5 minutes only if frozen peas are used). Add rice; cover and cook for 15 to 18 minutes, stirring occasionally. Add stock from time to time when needed. Season to taste with salt and pepper. When rice is done, all the stock in the pan should have been absorbed by the rice, which should be quite moist. Serve sprinkled with cheese and dotted with butter. Serves 4.

ITALIAN GREEN RICE

¾ POUND RICE
1 CLOVE GARLIC
½ TEASPOON SAGE
¼ POUND BUTTER
2 TABLESPOONS COOKED STRAINED SPINACH OR WATERCRESS
2 OUNCES GRATED PARMESAN

Cook rice in boiling salted water for 15 to 18 minutes. A few minutes before rice is done, gently sauté garlic and sage in butter, being careful not to let butter become brown. Discard garlic as soon as it becomes lightly golden. Drain rice and place in serving dish. Stir in cooked strained spinach or watercress, and pour hot butter over it. Mix well. Sprinkle with cheese and serve. Serves 4.

RISOTTO PROVENÇAL

4 TABLESPOONS OLIVE OIL
1 SPANISH ONION, FINELY CHOPPED
½ POUND RICE
HOT WATER
SALT AND FRESHLY-GROUND BLACK PEPPER

RISOTTO SAUCE:
2 TABLESPOONS ONION, FINELY CHOPPED
4 TABLESPOONS OLIVE OIL
¼ PINT DRY WHITE WINE
4–6 TOMATOES
SALT AND FRESHLY-GROUND BLACK PEPPER
2 CLOVES GARLIC
4 TABLESPOONS FINELY-CHOPPED PARSLEY
¼ TEASPOON POWDERED SAFFRON
½ GREEN PEPPER, FINELY CHOPPED

Heat oil in a thick-bottomed saucepan and sauté onion until golden. Stir in rice and cook, stirring continuously, until rice is golden. Moisten with ½ pint hot water and simmer gently, stirring from time to time and adding more hot water as liquid is absorbed by the rice. Continue cooking in this way until rice is cooked through, but not mushy. Correct seasoning. Serve with risotto sauce.

To make sauce: Sauté the finely-chopped onion in olive oil until transparent. Stir in dry white wine and tomatoes which you have peeled, seeded and chopped coarsely. Season to taste with salt and freshly-ground black pepper; add 2 whole cloves garlic, finely-chopped parsley and the saffron. Simmer gently for 20 minutes. Add chopped green pepper and simmer for a further 10 minutes. Serves 4.

CHINESE FRIED RICE

2 EGGS
1 TABLESPOON BUTTER
4 TABLESPOONS CORN OIL
½ SPANISH ONION, FINELY CHOPPED
4 CUPS COLD COOKED RICE
4 TABLESPOONS DICED COOKED PORK
4 TABLESPOONS DICED COOKED CHICKEN
4 TABLESPOONS DICED ITALIAN SAUSAGE
4 MUSHROOMS, DICED
2 TEASPOONS SOY SAUCE
SALT AND FRESHLY-GROUND BLACK PEPPER

Make a thin omelette with eggs and butter; cut in strips and set aside. Heat corn oil in a large frying pan, and when it is very hot add chopped onion and sauté until golden. Add next five ingredients and sauté gently for 3 to 5 minutes. Just before serving, add egg strips, soy sauce and salt and pepper, to taste. Serve immediately. Serves 4.

ORANGE RICE WITH BANANAS

2 STALKS CELERY
1 ONION
2 CLOVES GARLIC
6 TABLESPOONS BUTTER
¾ POUND RISOTTO RICE
2 TABLESPOONS FINELY-CHOPPED PARSLEY
SALT AND FRESHLY-GROUND BLACK PEPPER
JUICE OF 1 ORANGE
½ PINT CHICKEN STOCK
2 BANANAS, SLICED
2 TEASPOONS GRATED ORANGE RIND

Chop finely celery, onion and garlic; melt 4 tablespoons butter and sauté vegetables until soft but not brown. Stir in rice and fry, stirring continuously, until golden. Add parsley, season to taste with salt and black pepper and add the orange juice and chicken stock. Cover and simmer for 12 to 15 minutes, or until rice is cooked but not mushy. Sauté sliced bananas in 2 tablespoons butter until golden. Sprinkle with grated orange rind and stir gently into rice mixture. Serves 4.

RISOTTO AL TONNO

4 TABLESPOONS OLIVE OIL
2 TABLESPOONS BUTTER
½ SPANISH ONION, FINELY CHOPPED
2 TABLESPOONS TOMATO PASTE
6 TABLESPOONS DRY WHITE WINE
6 OUNCES TUNA FISH, POUNDED
½ SPANISH ONION, FINELY CHOPPED
4 TABLESPOONS BUTTER
¾ POUND RICE
6 TABLESPOONS DRY WHITE WINE
1½–2 PINTS HOT CHICKEN STOCK
SALT AND FRESHLY-GROUND BLACK PEPPER
FRESHLY-GRATED PARMESAN
BUTTER

For the sauce: combine olive oil and butter in a deep saucepan and sauté the finely-chopped onion until golden. Combine tomato paste and dry white wine and stir into onion mixture with pounded tuna fish. Heat through, stirring constantly, and keep warm.

For the risotto: sauté ½ finely-chopped Spanish onion in 4 tablespoons butter until transparent. Add rice and cook, stirring continuously, until rice is golden. Add dry white wine and hot chicken stock and simmer, covered, until rice is tender.

Five minutes before serving, stir in tuna sauce. Correct seasoning and serve with additional butter and grated Parmesan. Serves 4.

RICE PILAFF

4 TABLESPOONS BUTTER
½ SPANISH ONION, FINELY CHOPPED
¾ POUND UNCOOKED RICE
1–1½ PINTS BOILING CHICKEN STOCK
SALT AND FRESHLY-GROUND BLACK PEPPER
2 TABLESPOONS BUTTER
¼ POUND SLICED MUSHROOMS

Melt butter in a casserole and brown finely-chopped Spanish onion in it. Add uncooked rice and stir for a minute or two, until the grains of rice are coated with butter. Add 1 pint of boiling chicken stock and salt and pepper, to taste, and cover the casserole tightly. Bake the rice in a moderate oven (375°F. Mark 4) for about 30 minutes, or until the grains are tender, stirring occasionally and adding a little more chicken stock if necessary. Or cook the rice in a tightly-covered pan over direct heat for about 25 minutes. Remove the rice to a serving dish, add 2 tablespoons butter and sliced mushrooms sautéed in butter and toss with a fork. Serves 4.

RISOTTO ALLA PAESANO

4 OUNCES RED KIDNEY BEANS, SOAKED OVERNIGHT
4 TABLESPOONS BUTTER
2 TABLESPOONS OLIVE OIL
3 SLICES BACON, DICED
1 SMALL ONION, FINELY CHOPPED
2 OUNCES CARROTS, DICED
2 BABY MARROWS, DICED
2 OUNCES CELERY, DICED
½ PINT HOT BEEF STOCK
¾ POUND RICE
FRESHLY-GRATED PARMESAN
SALT AND FRESHLY-GROUND BLACK PEPPER

Place beans in saucepan with lightly salted water. Bring to the boil; cover and cook for 1 hour, or until tender. Reserve.

Combine butter and oil in a large frying pan and sauté diced bacon and onion until onion is transparent. Add prepared carrots, baby marrows and celery and continue to cook, uncovered, for 3 or 4 minutes, stirring occasionally.

Pour over hot beef stock and simmer uncovered until almost all the liquid has evaporated. Add rice to this mixture and cook for 2 minutes, stirring occasionally, over low flame.

Drain beans, reserving stock. Add beans to rice, together with 3 cups of bean stock; cook over medium flame for 15 to 18 minutes, stirring occasionally, and continue adding bean stock as needed until rice is done. When rice is tender, season to taste with salt and pepper. Add cheese and serve. Serves 6.

GREAT DISHES OF THE WORLD

CHAPTER 14

Salads

Tossed Green Salad

What is simpler or more summery than a fresh green salad? The very sound of the word evokes visions of crisp green lettuce leaves, carefully washed and dried leaf by leaf, liberally bathed with fruity olive oil and flavoured with a touch of wine vinegar, a hint of garlic and a dusting of salt and freshly-ground black pepper.

There are two secrets to perfect salad-making: the preparation of the salad itself and the preparation of the dressing. Salad greens must be thoroughly washed and dried and preferably chilled before being mixed with the dressing. No water should be allowed to drip from the greens into the dressing. If you do not own a salad basket, an easy way to dry well-washed salad greens is to pile them loosely in the centre of a clean tea towel and pat the leaves dry. Then gather up the edges and corners of the towel; shake out any remaining moisture over the sink and chill in the refrigerator until crisp.

There seems to be a mystery about a simple so-called French dressing; so many people put sugar, water, paprika or mustard into it; some use Worcestershire sauce or Tabasco. Others depend on bottled preparations rather than use their own initiative and skill to achieve what should be one of the most individual dishes of the meal.

I usually prefer to mix my salad dressing directly in the salad bowl – a wooden one, of course, and washed as seldom as possible – blending the olive oil and vinegar with pepper, salt, garlic and herbs, before I add the lettuce and salad greens. Then all one has to do at table is to give a final toss to the ingredients to ensure that every leaf is glistening with the dressing. A final check for flavour, and the salad is ready to serve.

SALAD DRESSINGS

Here is my recipe for salad dressing to make a tossed salad for 4.

French dressing: To 2 tablespoons of wine vinegar add coarse salt and freshly-ground black pepper to taste; stir the mixture well; add 6 to 8 tablespoons olive oil and beat with a fork until the mixture thickens. For a creamier dressing, put an ice cube in the mixing bowl and stir the dressing for a minute or two longer. Remove the cube and serve.

Tarragon dressing: Add 1 teaspoon chopped fresh tarragon leaves to French dressing.

Curry dressing: Add ½ teaspoon curry powder and 1 teaspoon finely-chopped shallots to French dressing.

Caper dressing: Add 1 teaspoon chopped capers, ½ clove garlic, crushed, and anchovy paste to taste.

Roquefort dressing: Add 2 to 4 tablespoons crumbled Roquefort cheese to French dressing and blend well. Chill thoroughly before using.

TO MAKE SALAD

Break into the bowl some tender lettuce leaves, well washed and dried. Leaves should be left whole, or torn, never cut. Wash them well in a large quantity of water. Drain well and dry thoroughly in a cloth or a salad basket so that there is no water on them to dilute the dressing.

For variety's sake, the lettuce can be augmented with other salad greens in season – Cos lettuce, endive, chicory, spinach leaves if they are very young and tender, watercress and French *mâche*. Fresh green herbs – chervil, basil and tarragon – are often used to add flavour and freshness to green salads. I also like eau-de-Cologne mint, which lends a certain purple spiciness to a summer salad, or even a chopped nasturtium leaf or two from the garden.

Shallots, so finely chopped they are almost minced, are excellent in a tossed green salad, as are chives, especially when combined with diced or finely-sliced avocado pear as a garnish.

Sometimes a little 'crunch appeal' seems warranted in a summer salad; in these cases I use a little chopped celery, green pepper, or *finocchi*, the green-white root of fennel, with its delicate aniseed flavour.

SALADE NIÇOISE

4 TOMATOES, SEEDED AND QUARTERED
½ SPANISH ONION, SLICED
1 SWEET GREEN PEPPER, SLICED
8 RADISHES
2 LETTUCE HEARTS
4 STALKS CELERY, SLICED
1 TIN TUNA FISH
8 ANCHOVY FILLETS
2 HARD-BOILED EGGS, QUARTERED
8 RIPE OLIVES

SALAD DRESSING:
2 TABLESPOONS WINE VINEGAR OR LEMON JUICE
6 TABLESPOONS PURE OLIVE OIL
SALT AND FRESHLY-GROUND BLACK PEPPER
12 LEAVES OF FRESH BASIL, COARSELY CHOPPED

Combine prepared vegetables in a salad bowl, placing neatly on top the tuna fish, anchovies and quartered eggs. Dot with ripe olives. Mix salad dressing of wine vinegar, olive oil, seasoning and herbs, and sprinkle over the salad.

CHILLED WATERCRESS SALAD

4 BUNCHES WATERCRESS
2 ORANGES
6–8 TABLESPOONS OLIVE OIL
2 TABLESPOONS WINE VINEGAR
1 TABLESPOON LEMON JUICE
1 LEVEL TABLESPOON CURRY POWDER
SALT AND FRESHLY-GROUND BLACK PEPPER
1 TEASPOON FINELY-CHOPPED SHALLOTS

Prepare watercress and chill in a damp towel.

Peel oranges, cut into thin slices and chill.

Prepare curry dressing: combine olive oil, wine vinegar, lemon juice and curry powder. Season to taste with salt and pepper and chill. Just before serving, place watercress in a salad bowl; arrange orange slices on top; add finely-chopped shallots to curry dressing and pour over salad.

Toss at table so that each leaf is glistening. Serves 4 to 6.

TOSSED GREEN SALAD WITH HERBS

2 HEADS LETTUCE
CHOICE OF SALAD GREENS: ENDIVE, YOUNG SPINACH, WATERCRESS, CHICORY, DANDELION, MÂCHE, ETC.
1 CLOVE GARLIC, FINELY CHOPPED
1 TEASPOON EACH FINELY-CHOPPED FRESH BASIL, MARJORAM, CHERVIL AND CHIVES
OLIVE OIL
WINE VINEGAR
SALT AND FRESHLY-GROUND BLACK PEPPER

Wash and prepare lettuce and salad greens of your choice. Shake dry in a salad basket, or dry each leaf carefully in a clean tea towel. Wrap in tea towel and allow to crisp in refrigerator until ready to use.

Make salad as above, adding finely-chopped garlic and fresh herbs to dressing. Serves 4 to 6.

TOSSED GREEN SALAD WITH AVOCADO

2 HEADS LETTUCE
1 BUNCH WATERCRESS
1 CLOVE GARLIC
2 TEASPOONS FINELY-CHOPPED CHIVES
OLIVE OIL
WINE VINEGAR
SALT AND FRESHLY-GROUND BLACK PEPPER
1 AVOCADO PEAR, PEELED AND SLICED
LEMON JUICE

Wash and prepare lettuce and watercress. Shake dry in a salad basket, or dry each leaf carefully in a clean tea towel. Wrap in tea towel and allow to crisp in refrigerator until ready to use.

Rub wooden salad bowl with cut clove of garlic. Arrange lettuce and watercress in bowl. Chop garlic and chives finely; sprinkle over the salad and dress with an olive oil and wine vinegar dressing (3 to 4 parts oil to 1 part vinegar), and season to taste with coarse salt and freshly-ground black pepper.

Garnish with wedges of avocado which you have marinated in lemon juice to prevent it from going brown. Just before serving, toss salad until each leaf is glistening. Serves 4 to 6.

DELMONICO SALAD

2 HEADS LETTUCE
6–8 TABLESPOONS OLIVE OIL
2 TABLESPOONS WINE VINEGAR
2 TABLESPOONS CREAM
2 TABLESPOONS ROQUEFORT CHEESE
FRESHLY-GROUND BLACK PEPPER
DASH OF TABASCO
1 HARD-BOILED EGG, FINELY CHOPPED
1 RASHER COOKED BACON, FINELY CHOPPED

Wash and prepare lettuce. Shake dry in a salad basket, or dry each leaf carefully in a clean tea towel. Wrap in tea towel and allow to crisp in refrigerator until ready to use.

To make dressing: combine olive oil, wine vinegar, cream and crumbled Roquefort in a small bowl and whisk until smooth. Add freshly-ground black pepper and Tabasco, to taste, and stir in finely-chopped egg and crumbled bacon.

Arrange lettuce in a salad bowl. Pour over dressing; toss and serve. Serves 4 to 6.

CHASEN'S CAESAR SALAD

2 HEADS COS LETTUCE
JUICE OF 1½ LEMONS
2 TABLESPOONS GARLIC OIL (CUT 1 CLOVE GARLIC INTO A LITTLE OLIVE OIL. LEAVE FOR 2 HOURS. REMOVE GARLIC)
1½ TEASPOONS WORCESTERSHIRE SAUCE
6 TABLESPOONS FRENCH DRESSING
1 ONE-MINUTE CODDLED EGG
4 SLICES TOAST, CUT INTO ½-INCH SQUARES
FRESHLY-GROUND BLACK PEPPER
4 TABLESPOONS GRATED PARMESAN CHEESE

Wash, dry and break Cos lettuce into fairly big pieces.

Combine lemon juice, garlic oil, Worcestershire sauce, French dressing and coddled egg in a small bowl and whisk lightly until well blended.

Just before serving, place salad greens in a large salad bowl; add toast *croûtons*, freshly-ground black pepper and freshly-grated Parmesan cheese. Pour over salad dressing and toss until each leaf is coated and there is no excess dressing left in the bottom of the bowl. Serve immediately. Serves 4 to 6.

CAESAR SALAD WITH HAM

1 HEAD COS LETTUCE
6–8 TABLESPOONS OLIVE OIL
2 TABLESPOONS WINE VINEGAR
6 TABLESPOONS FINELY-GRATED PARMESAN
1–2 FAT CLOVES GARLIC, MASHED
SALT AND FRESHLY-GROUND BLACK PEPPER
LEMON JUICE
2 SLICES BREAD, DICED
2 TABLESPOONS BUTTER
½ POUND DICED COOKED HAM
2 RAW EGG YOLKS
6 ANCHOVY FILLETS

Prepare Cos lettuce; wash and drain. Combine olive oil, wine vinegar, grated cheese and garlic in a large salad bowl and season to taste with salt, freshly-ground black pepper and lemon juice. Sauté diced bread in butter with a little garlic. Add diced ham and torn lettuce, and toss lightly. Then add egg yolks and toss salad until every leaf glistens. Top off with garlic *croûtons* and anchovy fillets. Serves 4 to 6.

SALADE PAYSANNE

2 HEADS LETTUCE, WASHED AND CHILLED
¼ POUND FAT SALT PORK, DICED
2 TABLESPOONS OLIVE OIL
2 HARD-BOILED EGGS, CHOPPED
SALT AND FRESHLY-GROUND BLACK PEPPER
1 TABLESPOON FINELY-CHOPPED CHERVIL, TARRAGON OR BASIL
WINE VINEGAR

Wash and dry lettuce leaves thoroughly and chill. Sauté finely-diced fat salt pork in olive oil until it is golden brown.

Place lettuce in salad bowl; sprinkle with diced pork and hot fat. Add chopped eggs, salt, freshly-ground black pepper, herbs and vinegar, to taste. Mix well and serve immediately. Serves 4 to 6.

RUSSIAN SALAD

1 POUND COOKED NEW POTATOES, DICED
½ POUND COOKED STRING BEANS, SLICED
4–6 COOKED CARROTS, SLICED
¼ POUND DRIED BEANS, BOILED
1 CUP COOKED PEAS
2 TABLESPOONS WINE VINEGAR
2 TABLESPOONS OLIVE OIL
SALT AND FRESHLY-GROUND BLACK PEPPER
1 TABLESPOON CAPERS
1 TABLESPOON CHOPPED PICKLES
2 TABLESPOONS FINELY-CHOPPED PARSLEY
2–3 HARD-BOILED EGGS
½–¾ PINT WELL-FLAVOURED MAYONNAISE

Combine diced cooked potatoes with sliced cooked string beans and carrots and cooked dried beans and peas, reserving a few of each vegetable for garnish. Moisten with wine vinegar and olive oil and season to taste with salt and freshly-ground black pepper. Toss and chill.

Add capers, chopped pickles and parsley, chopped egg whites and enough mayonnaise to bind mixture loosely. Toss ingredients and mound in salad bowl. Decorate top and sides with remaining mayonnaise and assorted vegetables. Sprinkle sieved egg yolks over top.

CHEF'S SALAD

1 HEAD LETTUCE
¼ POUND COOKED CHICKEN
¼ POUND SMOKED OX TONGUE
¼ POUND COOKED HAM
¼ POUND SWISS CHEESE
2 HARD-BOILED EGGS
4 TOMATOES, CUT IN WEDGES
1 BUNCH WATERCRESS
¼ PINT FRENCH DRESSING

Wash and dry lettuce carefully, leaf by leaf; chop coarsely and arrange in the bottom of a large salad bowl. Cut chicken, tongue, ham and cheese into thin strips and arrange according to colour on bed of lettuce with hard-boiled eggs, cut in quarters, and raw tomatoes, cut in wedges. Place a cluster of prepared watercress in centre and serve with well-flavoured French dressing. Serves 4 to 6.

SALADE CAROLINE COCHONNE

¾ POUND GRUYÈRE CHEESE, DICED
¾ POUND HAM, DICED
6–8 TABLESPOONS OLIVE OIL
2–3 TABLESPOONS WINE VINEGAR
SALT AND FRESHLY-GROUND BLACK PEPPER
1 HEAD LETTUCE
FINELY-CHOPPED PARSLEY

Combine diced Gruyère cheese and ham in large bowl. Prepare salad dressing; pour over cheese and ham; toss well. Allow to marinate in refrigerator for 1 hour.

Just before serving, place washed and dried lettuce leaves in the bottom of salad bowl. Pile diced cheese and ham in the centre. Sprinkle with finely-chopped parsley or fresh herbs. Serve with additional salad dressing. Serves 4 to 6.

ITALIAN VEGETABLE SALAD

4 TOMATOES
OLIVE OIL
WINE VINEGAR
SALT AND FRESHLY-GROUND BLACK PEPPER
1 SMALL CUCUMBER
2 SMALL GREEN PEPPERS
¼ POUND BUTTON MUSHROOMS
1 TABLESPOON FINELY-CHOPPED PARSLEY
2 HARD-BOILED EGGS
LETTUCE

ITALIAN DRESSING:
¼ PINT OLIVE OIL
4 ANCHOVY FILLETS, FINELY CHOPPED
JUICE OF 1 LARGE LEMON
SALT AND FRESHLY-GROUND BLACK PEPPER
1 TEASPOON CAPERS

Quarter tomatoes and toss lightly in a small bowl with a little wine vinegar, olive oil, salt and pepper. Peel cucumber and slice thinly; place in a small bowl with a little wine vinegar, olive oil, salt and pepper. Remove the seeds and pith from green peppers; slice in thin strips and place in a small bowl with the same dressing as above. Wash and slice raw mushrooms into thin slices. Dress with a little wine vinegar and olive oil and add 1 tablespoon finely-chopped parsley.

Just before serving, assemble salads on a bed of lettuce in a large wooden bowl. Garnish with quartered hard-boiled eggs and sprinkle liberally with Italian dressing.

Italian dressing: Warm slightly ¼ pint olive oil and add finely-chopped anchovy fillets, mashing them with a fork until they are well blended with the oil. Add lemon juice and salt, pepper and capers, to taste. Serves 4 to 6.

BEAN AND RAW SPINACH SALAD

¾ POUND KIDNEY OR BROAD BEANS
6–8 TABLESPOONS OLIVE OIL
3 TABLESPOONS WINE VINEGAR
1 TEASPOON CHOPPED FRESH MARJORAM
1 TEASPOON CHOPPED FRESH BASIL
2 TEASPOONS CHOPPED FRESH PARSLEY
1 CLOVE GARLIC, FINELY CHOPPED
SALT AND FRESHLY-GROUND BLACK PEPPER
1 POUND RAW SPINACH LEAVES
1 SMALL ONION, THINLY SLICED

Cook kidney or broad beans until tender; cool and drain. Mix with a dressing made of olive oil, wine vinegar or lemon juice, finely-chopped herbs and garlic, and season to taste with salt and freshly-ground black pepper. Serve on tender young spinach leaves and garnish with onion rings. Serves 4 to 6.

ROASTED OR GRILLED PEPPERS FOR SALADS

Perfectionists prefer to peel the sweet pepper. The easiest way I know of preparing peppers for use in appetiser salads and other dishes, is to grill or roast the peppers as close to the heat as possible, turning them until the skin is charred on all sides. The skins can then be easily rubbed off under running cold water. The peppers are then cored, seeded, sliced into thick strips and marinated in a well-flavoured French dressing. Peppers prepared in this way will keep a long time under refrigeration if packed in oil in tight sterilised jars. Serve as a salad on a bed of lettuce with a lattice of anchovy fillets for garnish.

PROVENÇAL PEPPER SALAD

2 LARGE GREEN PEPPERS
2 LARGE SWEET RED PEPPERS
6 FIRM RIPE TOMATOES
6 HARD-BOILED EGGS
24 ANCHOVY FILLETS
24 RIPE OLIVES

HERB DRESSING:
2 CLOVES GARLIC, FINELY CHOPPED
1 TABLESPOON EACH FINELY-CHOPPED PARSLEY, TARRAGON, CHERVIL AND CHIVES
6–8 TABLESPOONS OLIVE OIL
3 TABLESPOONS WINE VINEGAR
SALT AND FRESHLY-GROUND BLACK PEPPER

Prepare herb dressing by combining finely-chopped garlic and fresh herbs with oil, vinegar, salt and freshly-ground black pepper, to taste.

Prepare peppers as follows: wash and dry whole; place under grill, as close to flames as possible. Cook, turning peppers continually, until skin on all sides has charred. Remove charred skin under cold water. Cut peppers in lengths – 4 or 6 to each pepper – and wash off seeds and excess fibre; drain on absorbent paper. Slice raw tomatoes thickly and cover bottom of a large flat serving dish with slices. Sprinkle with a quarter of the salad dressing; add a layer of prepared green pepper slices; sprinkle with salad dressing; add a layer of red pepper slices and sprinkle with dressing. Shell eggs and slice into rings; cover red pepper with a layer of sliced eggs and pour over the rest of the dressing. Arrange anchovy fillets in a lattice on top and place a ripe olive in the centre of each lattice square. Chill in refrigerator for at least 30 minutes before serving. Serves 6.

WALDORF SALAD

6 RED-SKINNED EATING APPLES
JUICE OF 2 LEMONS
6 STALKS CELERY
2 OUNCES HALVED WALNUTS
1 HEAD LETTUCE
MAYONNAISE OR FRENCH DRESSING

Core and dice apples and sprinkle with lemon juice. Add sliced celery and walnut halves. Toss together in mayonnaise or French dressing according to taste, and pile into salad bowl lined with lettuce leaves. Serves 4 to 6.

CHICKEN WALDORF

Make salad as above; but add ¾ pound diced cooked chicken.

GERMAN POTATO SALAD

2 POUNDS NEW POTATOES
1 TABLESPOON SUGAR
2 TABLESPOONS WINE VINEGAR
¼ PINT SOUR CREAM
1 TEASPOON MUSTARD
½ SPANISH ONION, FINELY CHOPPED
1 TEASPOON CELERY SEED
LEMON JUICE
SALT AND FRESHLY-GROUND BLACK PEPPER
LETTUCE
2 TABLESPOONS FINELY-CHOPPED PARSLEY
TOMATO WEDGES
2 HARD-BOILED EGGS, SLICED

Scrub new potatoes; cook in boiling salted water until just tender, 15 to 20 minutes; drain, peel and slice. Place potatoes in a bowl and sprinkle with sugar and wine vinegar. Add sour cream blended with mustard, finely-chopped onion, celery seed, and lemon juice, salt and freshly-ground black pepper, to taste. Toss well and serve in lettuce-lined bowl. Garnish with finely-chopped parsley, tomato wedges and sliced hard-boiled eggs. Serves 4 to 6.

WATERCRESS AND RADISH SALAD

1 HEAD LETTUCE
1 BUNCH WATERCRESS
1 BUNCH RADISHES

FRENCH DRESSING:
2 TABLESPOONS WINE VINEGAR
6–8 TABLESPOONS OLIVE OIL
DRY MUSTARD
SALT AND FRESHLY-GROUND BLACK PEPPER
1 CLOVE GARLIC, FINELY CHOPPED (OPTIONAL)

Wash and trim lettuce and watercress. Dry thoroughly. Trim radishes and slice paper-thin. Chill.

To assemble salad: arrange lettuce leaves in a salad bowl and spread watercress on top. Scatter thinly-sliced radishes over this. Make French dressing and just before serving add dressing and toss until every ingredient glistens. Serves 4 to 6.

ITALIAN TUNA SALAD

1 HEAD LETTUCE
4 BOILED NEW POTATOES, SLICED
4 RIPE TOMATOES, SLICED
4 BLACK AND 4 GREEN OLIVES, QUARTERED
2 STALKS CELERY, SLICED
1 TIN TUNA FISH, FLAKED
SALT AND FRESHLY-GROUND BLACK PEPPER
2 TABLESPOONS LEMON JUICE
4–6 TABLESPOONS OLIVE OIL
1 TABLESPOONS CHOPPED ANCHOVY FILLETS
2 TABLESPOONS FINELY-CHOPPED PARSLEY

Line a salad bowl with leaves of lettuce. Place a layer of sliced potatoes on this; top with a layer of sliced tomatoes; sprinkle with quartered olives, sliced celery and flaked tuna fish.

Make a dressing by combining lemon juice, olive oil, chopped anchovy fillets and parsley. Season to taste with salt and freshly-ground black pepper and pour over salad. Just before serving, toss. Serves 4 to 6.

LEEK AND TOMATO SALAD

4 RIPE TOMATOES
1 HEAD COS LETTUCE
2 RAW LEEKS
1 TEASPOON EACH FINELY-CHOPPED PARSLEY AND BASIL

FRENCH DRESSING:
2 TABLESPOONS WINE VINEGAR
6–8 TABLESPOONS OLIVE OIL
DRY MUSTARD
SALT AND FRESHLY-GROUND BLACK PEPPER
1 CLOVE GARLIC, FINELY CHOPPED (OPTIONAL)

Cut tomatoes in wedges. Wash and drain lettuce and arrange in salad bowl. Wash leeks carefully; cut white parts coarsely and add to salad with tomato wedges. Sprinkle with finely-chopped parsley and basil; pour over French dressing and toss. Serves 4 to 6.

APPLE HERRING SALAD

2 FILLETED SALT HERRINGS
OLIVE OIL
VINEGAR
4 BOILED POTATOES, SLICED
4 TART APPLES, DICED
2 HARD-BOILED EGGS, CHOPPED
1 DILL PICKLE, CHOPPED
4 TABLESPOONS SLICED STUFFED OLIVES
1 SMALL ONION, FINELY CHOPPED
SALT AND FRESHLY-GROUND BLACK PEPPER

Cut filleted herrings in small pieces and marinate in olive oil and vinegar. Combine potatoes, apples, eggs, pickle, olives and onion in a bowl. Add herrings. Make a dressing of 3 parts olive oil to 1 part vinegar; add salt and freshly-ground black pepper and toss salad just before serving. Serves 4 to 6.

SPANISH SEAFOOD SALAD

½ POUND COOKED PRAWNS
½ POUND COOKED LOBSTER MEAT
½ POUND COOKED WHITE FISH
½ POUND COOKED CRABMEAT
1 HEAD LETTUCE, WASHED AND CHILLED
1 HEAD COS LETTUCE, WASHED AND CHILLED
4 RIPE TOMATOES
8 LARGE RIPE OLIVES

SAFFRON DRESSING:
¼ PINT MAYONNAISE
4 TABLESPOONS LEMON JUICE
2 TABLESPOONS GRATED ONION
1 TEASPOON PREPARED MUSTARD
SALT AND WHITE PEPPER
1 GENEROUS PINCH SAFFRON

Line salad bowl with lettuce and Cos leaves. Arrange prawns, lobster, white fish and crabmeat, cut in cubes, on bed of salad

greens. Garnish with wedges of ripe tomato, and ripe olives. Serve with a well-flavoured French or saffron dressing.
To make dressing: Combine mayonnaise with lemon juice, grated onion and prepared mustard, and season to taste with salt and white pepper. Dissolve saffron in a little hot water and stir into dressing. Chill.

TRUFFLED CHICKEN SALAD

4 TABLESPOONS STIFF MAYONNAISE
TRUFFLE JUICE
SALT, CELERY SALT AND FRESHLY-GROUND BLACK PEPPER
2 TABLESPOONS FINELY-SLICED BLACK TRUFFLES
1 HEAD LETTUCE, FINELY SHREDDED
3 HARD-BOILED EGGS, FINELY CHOPPED
¾ POUND CHICKEN, DICED
4 STALKS CELERY, DICED
¼ POUND TUNA FISH, DICED

Thin mayonnaise with juice from a small tin of black truffles and season to taste with salt, celery salt and freshly-ground black pepper. Add finely-sliced black truffles to sauce and combine with shredded lettuce, finely-chopped eggs, diced chicken, celery and tuna fish. Mix well. Add more mayonnaise and seasoning if desired. Serves 4.

CAULIFLOWER SALAD

1 CAULIFLOWER
6 ANCHOVY FILLETS, FINELY CHOPPED
12 BLACK OLIVES, PITTED AND CHOPPED
3 TABLESPOONS FINELY-CHOPPED PARSLEY
1 CLOVE GARLIC, FINELY CHOPPED
1 TABLESPOON FINELY-CHOPPED CAPERS
6 TABLESPOONS OLIVE OIL
2 TABLESPOONS WINE VINEGAR
SALT AND FRESHLY-GROUND BLACK PEPPER

Remove green leaves from cauliflower, trim stem and cut off any bruised spots. Break or cut into flowerets and poach in lightly-salted water for about 5 minutes. Drain and place in a bowl of cold salted water until ready to use. Drain well. Mix finely-chopped anchovies, olives, parsley, garlic and capers with oil and vinegar; add cauliflower and season to taste. Serves 4 to 6.

RAW MUSHROOM SALAD

1 POUND BUTTON MUSHROOMS
JUICE OF 1 LEMON
8 TABLESPOONS OLIVE OIL
SALT AND FRESHLY-GROUND BLACK PEPPER
1 TEASPOON FINELY-CHOPPED CHIVES
1 TEASPOON FINELY-CHOPPED PARSLEY

Remove stems from mushrooms; wash and dry caps but do not peel. Slice caps thinly, arrange them in a salad bowl and pour well-flavoured lemon and olive oil dressing over them. Toss carefully and chill in refrigerator for 2 hours before serving. Sprinkle with chopped chives and parsley. Serves 6.

SARDINE SALAD

2 TINS SARDINES
1 SMALL ONION
4 HARD-BOILED EGGS
1 SMALL COOKED BEETROOT
LETTUCE
6 TABLESPOONS OLIVE OIL
2 TABLESPOONS LEMON JUICE
SALT AND FRESHLY-GROUND BLACK PEPPER
2 TABLESPOONS FINELY-CHOPPED PARSLEY

Drain sardines. Cut onion into rings. Slice hard-boiled eggs into quarters. Dice beetroot. Prepare lettuce and arrange in a salad bowl. Combine olive oil and lemon juice and season to taste with salt and freshly-ground black pepper. Toss onion rings, eggs and beetroot in this dressing, and pile on bed of salad greens. Arrange sardines in the centre. Sprinkle with finely-chopped parsley. Serves 4.

COURGETTES EN SALADE

8 COURGETTES (4 INCHES LONG)
½ SPANISH ONION, FINELY CHOPPED
1 CLOVE GARLIC, FINELY CHOPPED
WELL-FLAVOURED FRENCH DRESSING
LETTUCE
4 TOMATOES, PEELED AND FINELY CHOPPED
½ SMALL GREEN PEPPER, FINELY CHOPPED
¼ SPANISH ONION, FINELY CHOPPED
1 TABLESPOON CAPERS, FINELY CHOPPED
1 TEASPOON EACH FINELY-CHOPPED PARSLEY AND BASIL
SALT AND FRESHLY-GROUND BLACK PEPPER

Simmer *courgettes*, unpeeled, in salted water for about 8 minutes. Cut them in half lengthwise, and carefully scoop out seeds. Lay *courgettes*, cut sides up, in a flat dish. Combine finely-chopped onion and garlic and cover *courgettes* with this mixture. Sprinkle half the French dressing over them; cover with aluminium foil and allow to marinate in this mixture in the refrigerator for at least 4 hours.

When ready to serve, remove onion and garlic mixture and drain off the marinade. Arrange *courgette* halves on crisp lettuce leaves and fill the hollows with remaining French dressing to which you have added finely-chopped tomatoes, pepper, onion, capers, parsley and basil, and salt and pepper, to taste.

COLE SLAW

1 HEAD CABBAGE (ABOUT 2 POUNDS)
4 TABLESPOONS TARRAGON VINEGAR
2 TABLESPOONS SUGAR
SALT AND FRESHLY-GROUND BLACK PEPPER
PAPRIKA
1 SMALL GREEN PEPPER, CHOPPED
1 TABLESPOON FINELY-CHOPPED SPRING ONIONS
¼ TEASPOON CELERY SEED
¼ TEASPOON CARAWAY SEED
6 TABLESPOONS MAYONNAISE
¼ PINT SOUR CREAM

Shred the cabbage and then crisp in cold water for ½ hour. Drain and dry thoroughly.

Combine vinegar, sugar, salt, pepper and a sprinkling of paprika in a salad bowl. Add shredded cabbage, toss well and marinate for 1 hour. Add green pepper, spring onions, celery seed and caraway seed and toss lightly.

Combine mayonnaise and sour cream and pour over the cabbage mixture. Toss lightly, correct seasoning and serve. Serves 4 to 6.

RED CABBAGE SALAD

1 RED CABBAGE (ABOUT 2 POUNDS)
TARRAGON VINEGAR
SALT AND FRESHLY-GROUND BLACK PEPPER
4 HARD-BOILED EGG YOLKS
½ PINT CREAM
JUICE OF 1 LARGE LEMON
1 TABLESPOON EACH FINELY-CHOPPED CHERVIL, CHIVES AND FENNEL
½ CUCUMBER, THINLY SLICED
RADISHES, THINLY SLICED

Wash cabbage leaves and shred them. Blanch strips in boiling salted water. Drain; place in cold water; then drain again. Allow to marinate for at least 1 hour in tarragon vinegar with salt and pepper, turning from time to time. Remove and drain.

Pass the hard-boiled egg yolks through a fine sieve; combine with cream and lemon juice and add salt and pepper to taste. Add herbs to this dressing and mix well with red cabbage. Serve decorated with thin rounds of cucumber and radish.

RED BEAN SALAD

- $\frac{3}{4}$ POUND KIDNEY BEANS
- SALTED WATER
- 1 SPANISH ONION, FINELY CHOPPED
- FINELY-CHOPPED PARSLEY
- 6 TABLESPOONS OLIVE OIL
- 4 TABLESPOONS WINE VINEGAR
- SALT AND FRESHLY-GROUND BLACK PEPPER
- GENEROUS PINCH DRY MUSTARD
- LETTUCE

Soak kidney beans overnight in salted water. Bring the beans to the boil in their liquid and simmer for about 2 hours or until tender.

Drain the beans. Add finely-chopped onion and parsley; moisten with olive oil and wine vinegar and season to taste with salt, freshly-ground pepper and a pinch of dry mustard. Mix the salad lightly and chill it. Serve bean salad on lettuce leaves and sprinkle generously with finely-chopped parsley.

MOROCCAN ORANGE SALAD

- 6 RIPE ORANGES
- 6–8 DATES, CHOPPED
- 6–8 BLANCHED ALMONDS, SLIVERED
- ORANGE FLOWER WATER (OR LEMON JUICE AND POWDERED SUGAR)
- POWERED CINNAMON

Peel oranges, removing all pith, and slice crosswise. Place in a salad bowl with chopped dates and slivered almonds and flavour to taste with orange flower water or lemon juice and sugar.

Chill. Just before serving, sprinkle lightly with powdered cinnamon. Serves 6 to 8.

SUMMER FRUIT SALAD

1 RIPE CANTALOUPE MELON
JUICE OF 2 LEMONS
RIPE CHERRIES, PITTED
STRAWBERRIES, HULLED
2 PEACHES, PEELED AND SLICED
2 ORANGES, PEELED AND SLICED
2 PEARS, UNPEELED, DICED
2 RED APPLES, UNPEELED, DICED
SPRIGS OF MINT, TO GARNISH

PAPRIKA DRESSING:
6 TABLESPOONS PINEAPPLE JUICE
6 TABLESPOONS LEMON JUICE
3 EGGS, BEATEN UNTIL LIGHT
3 OUNCES SUGAR
PINCH SALT
1 LEVEL TEASPOON PAPRIKA

Cut a ripe cantaloupe melon partway down in 6 or 8 sections so that it opens out slightly. Remove the seeds carefully; brush segments with lemon juice; cover with aluminium foil and chill in refrigerator until ready to use. Reserve lemon juice for diced apples and pears.

Just before serving, place cut melon on a large serving platter. Pile assorted fruits – pitted cherries, hulled strawberries, sliced peaches and oranges, and unpeeled apples and pears, diced, and brushed with lemon juice to prevent discolouration. Serve with paprika dressing.

Paprika dressing: Combine all ingredients in the top of a double saucepan and cook over boiling water until thick, stirring constantly. Chill.

PEARS VINAIGRETTE

4 RIPE DESSERT PEARS

MINT VINAIGRETTE SAUCE:
6 TABLESPOONS OLIVE OIL
3 TABLESPOONS WINE VINEGAR
2 TABLESPOONS CHOPPED FRESH MINT
2 TABLESPOONS CHOPPED FRESH PARSLEY
SALT, FRESHLY-GROUND BLACK PEPPER AND MUSTARD
LETTUCE, TO GARNISH

Peel, core and slice pears.

To make sauce: Combine olive oil, vinegar, finely-chopped mint and parsley in a mixing bowl. Season to taste with salt, freshly-ground black pepper and a little dry mustard. Mix well.

Toss pears in *vinaigrette* sauce and serve on lettuce leaves.

ORANGE VINAIGRETTE

6 RIPE ORANGES

OLIVE AND HERB VINAIGRETTE SAUCE:
6 TABLESPOONS OLIVE OIL
2 TABLESPOONS WINE VINEGAR
12–18 BLACK OLIVES, PITTED AND FINELY CHOPPED
½ SPANISH ONION, FINELY CHOPPED
1 TABLESPOON CHOPPED FRESH MINT
1 TABLESPOON CHOPPED FRESH PARSLEY
1 TABLESPOON CHOPPED FRESH BASIL
SALT, FRESHLY-GROUND BLACK PEPPER AND CAYENNE

Peel oranges, removing all pith, and slice crosswise.
To make sauce: Combine olive oil, vinegar, finely-chopped olives, onion and herbs in a mixing bowl. Season to taste with salt, pepper and cayenne. Mix well.

Toss orange slices in *vinaigrette* sauce. Serves 6 to 8.

APPLE AVOCADO SALAD

4 EATING APPLES
1 AVOCADO PEAR
JUICE OF 2 LEMONS
1–2 OUNCES SALTED MIXED NUTS
CRISP WATERCRESS
FRENCH DRESSING

Core apples but do not pare. Slice into wedges ⅛ inch thick. Slice avocado in half, remove stone, pare and slice ⅛ inch thick. Cover apple and avocado slices with lemon juice to prevent discolouration. Just before serving, drain; add salted nuts and watercress and toss with a good French dressing (made with olive oil, some of the drained lemon juice, pepper, salt and a little sugar). Serves 6 to 8.

GREAT DISHES OF THE WORLD

CHAPTER 15

Desserts

Rum Baba

King Stanislas of Poland, father-in-law of Louis XV of France, Duke of Lorraine and Bar, was an ardent cook. Among the many creations credited to this noble *cuisinier* is the *baba-au-rhum*, one of the world's most delicious sweets. History tells us that Stanislas dunked his favourite *kugelhupf* in a rum-flavoured syrup and declared the result a triumph! Later generations of cooks added a scattering of raisins to the dough, and the baba as we know it was born. Based on a *savarin* recipe (see below), the rum baba is a featherlight concoction of flour, sugar and eggs, made airy with powdered or granulated yeast and moistened with syrup and rum. At London's famous Caprice restaurant, this sweet is baked in a ring mould and filled with a *macédoine* of fresh fruits.

The *savarin* cake mixture, which is the basis of rum baba as well as many other famous sweets, is quite easy to make if you follow these rules:

Dissolve yeast in liquid (water, milk, or a mixture of the two) just a little warmer than body temperature. The liquid should feel warm, not hot.

Warm a mixing bowl with boiling water. Dry it thoroughly. Sift flour, sugar and salt into warm bowl; gradually add yeast mixture and beaten eggs and blend batter ingredients by hand. (The warmth of your hand is important to the handling of the yeast.)

Beat by hand until batter is smooth and well blended, cover it with a towel and leave to rise in a warm place protected from draughts.

Do not allow batter to stand too long, at most 45 minutes to an hour, or until it doubles in bulk.

Punch the batter down and beat it again, using the bread hook of your electric mixer, if you have one, to facilitate this task, until the dough leaves the sides of bowl (about 5 minutes with mixer).

Butter moulds; fill one-third to one-half full with yeast batter; cover with a towel and leave for final rising (about 45 minutes). When batter rises to top of the mould, the cakes are ready for baking and should be put into the oven immediately.

Bake small shapes in a moderately hot oven (400°F. Mark 5). Larger shapes are baked in a very hot oven (450°F. Mark 7) for 10 minutes, then the temperature is reduced to moderate (375°F. Mark 4) and the cake is baked for 30 to 40 minutes longer until it acquires a rich brown colour.

To turn out: invert mould on a wire cake rack for 5 to 10 minutes; then loosen with a knife and turn out of mould. Saturate with hot syrup while the cake is still warm, spooning the syrup over the cake until most of it is absorbed.

BASIC SAVARIN RECIPE

¼ OUNCE POWDERED OR GRANULATED YEAST
4 TABLESPOONS WARM WATER
4 TABLESPOONS WARM MILK
8 OUNCES FLOUR
2 OUNCES SUGAR
1 PINCH SALT
2 EGGS, BEATEN
½ TEASPOON VANILLA ESSENCE
2 OUNCES SOFTENED BUTTER

Step 1. Mix yeast with warm water and milk and leave for 5 minutes. Sift flour, sugar and salt into a warm mixing bowl. Beat eggs with vanilla essence. Make a well in the centre, add yeast mixture, then the beaten eggs, little by little, mixing the soft, sticky dough very lightly with your hand.

Step 2. When dough is well blended, distribute softened butter in small quantities over it; cover lightly with a towel and leave for 1 hour, or until it has doubled in bulk. Punch the batter down and beat it again, using bread hook of your electric mixer, until dough leaves sides of bowl, about 5 minutes.

Step 3. Butter a deep cake tin or *savarin* mould and half-fill it with dough; put in a warm place until dough rises to top of tin (about 45 minutes). Tie a band of buttered paper around top (and 2 inches above) and bake in a moderately hot oven (400°F. Mark 5) for 10 minutes, then lower heat to 350°F. (Mark 3) for 25 to 30 minutes, or until the cake is a rich brown. Leave to cool and then turn out.

BABA-AU-RHUM

1 BASIC SAVARIN RECIPE
2 TABLESPOONS CURRANTS
1 TABLESPOON SULTANAS

SYRUP FOR BABA:
6 TABLESPOONS RUM
SYRUP (½ POUND SUGAR AND ½ PINT WATER)

Step 1. Follow basic recipe.
Step 2. Follow basic recipe.
Step 3. Add currants and sultanas and mix well. Then put dough into a large, well-buttered ring mould, or into small individual moulds, filling moulds only up to one-third of their height. Put mould in a warm place, covered with a towel, until dough rises to top of tin. Bake large mould in a hot oven (450°F. Mark 7) for 10 minutes, then reduce temperature to 375°F. (Mark 4); small moulds are baked at 400°F. (Mark 5) until the cakes are golden. Leave to cool and then turn out. Pour syrup over the cake and sprinkle with more rum just before serving.
To make syrup: Combine sugar and water in a saucepan. Simmer gently until it thickens. Stir in rum. Prick cake all over with a fork and spoon syrup over it. If desired, pour a little more rum over baba just before serving.

GÂTEAU À L'ANANAS

1 BASIC SAVARIN RECIPE

GARNISH:
1 LARGE TIN PINEAPPLE SLICES
3 TABLESPOONS SUGAR
6 TABLESPOONS KIRSCH
GLACÉ CHERRIES (OPTIONAL)

To make savarin: Follow basic *savarin* recipe, baking mixture in a buttered cake tin.
To make syrup for garnish: Pour pineapple juice into a saucepan. Add sugar and simmer gently until it thickens. Stir in Kirsch. Prick cake all over with a fork and spoon half of the syrup over it. Cook remainder until it is reduced by half. Cut pineapple slices into segments; arrange in concentric rings on cake; garnish with glacé cherries and, just before serving, cover with thickened caramel sauce.

SAVARIN AUX POMMES

1 BASIC SAVARIN RECIPE

CRÈME PÂTISSIÈRE:
4 EGG YOLKS
2 OUNCES SUGAR
2 TEASPOONS FLOUR
½ PINT WARM MILK
¼ TEASPOON VANILLA ESSENCE

POACHED APPLE HALVES:
3–4 RIPE EATING APPLES
WATER
4 TABLESPOONS SUGAR
JUICE OF 1 LEMON
VANILLA ESSENCE

RUM-FLAVOURED APPLE SAUCE:
½ PINT APPLE SAUCE
2–4 TABLESPOONS JAMAICA RUM

4–6 TABLESPOONS APRICOT JAM, WARMED
½ PINT DOUBLE CREAM, WHIPPED

To make savarin ring: Follow basic *savarin* recipe, making mixture in a buttered ring mould.
To make crème pâtissière: Beat yolks and sugar together until mixture is lemon-coloured. Mix in flour, then add milk and vanilla and mix thoroughly. Place mixture in saucepan over low flame and cook, stirring constantly, until it reaches boiling point. Cook until thick; remove from heat; put through sieve and allow to cool.
To poach apples: Peel and core eating apples; slice in half and poach gently in water with lemon juice, sugar and vanilla essence, until they have softened slightly. Drain.
To assemble cake: Fill centre of *savarin* ring with equal quantities of *crème pâtissière* and rum-flavoured apple sauce (add 4 to 6 tablespoons rum to ½ pint apple sauce). Place a ring of well-drained, poached apple halves on *savarin* ring. Brush apples with warmed apricot jam and serve with whipped cream.

KUGELHUPF

1 LEVEL DESSERTSPOON POWDERED OR GRANULATED YEAST
4 TABLESPOONS WARM WATER
2 TABLESPOONS SUGAR
1 POUND SIFTED FLOUR
6 TABLESPOONS ICING SUGAR
½ LEVEL TEASPOON SALT
½ TEASPOON VANILLA ESSENCE
GRATED RIND OF 1 LEMON
2 EGGS
2 OUNCES BUTTER, MELTED
½ PINT WARM MILK
2 OUNCES RAISINS

Dissolve granulated yeast thoroughly in warm water in a bowl and add sugar. Cover the mixture with a warm towel and put in a warm place for ½ hour.

Sift flour, icing sugar and salt into a warm mixing bowl. Add vanilla essence and grated lemon rind and mix well. Make a well in the centre of the flour and pour in the yeast mixture. Stir well, incorporating as much flour into the mixture as possible. Stir in beaten eggs and melted butter gradually, and continue to mix flour in with hands. Work in enough warm milk (about ½ pint) to form a smooth dough. Dust with flour, cover with a warm towel and let it rise in a warm place for 2 hours, or until it doubles in bulk.

Add raisins and beat until they are well distributed. Half-fill a well-buttered *kugelhupf* mould or a tube pan with the mixture. Cover with a towel and allow to rise in a warm place until it is double in bulk and the pan is almost full. Cover with a piece of aluminium foil and bake in a moderate oven (375°F. Mark 4) for about 1 hour.

Unmould on a cake rack; cool and dust with icing sugar. Leave cake to stand overnight before slicing.

GENOESE SPONGE

4 EGGS
4 OUNCES CASTOR SUGAR
½ TEASPOON VANILLA ESSENCE OR GRATED RIND OF ½ LEMON
3 OUNCES FLOUR
1 OUNCE CORNFLOUR
8 TABLESPOONS MELTED UNSALTED BUTTER

Combine eggs, sugar and vanilla or grated lemon rind, and whisk mixture in the top of a double boiler until it is very light and thick and lukewarm. Transfer mixture to electric mixer and beat at high speed for 3 to 5 minutes, or until mixture holds shape.

Sift flour and cornflour and fold carefully into the mixture a little at a time until thoroughly blended. Melt butter in the top of double boiler, taking care that it does not bubble or separate; add it immediately to batter and pour batter into a buttered and floured sandwich tin. Bake in a slow oven (350°F. Mark 3) for 45 minutes, or until golden brown. If desired, the mixture may be put in two shallow tins and baked for 15 minutes. Invert cake on a wire rack to cool. Slice into two layers; sandwich and ice to choice. Excellent for all layer cakes, iced cakes and *petits fours*.

SPONGE CAKE

6 EGG YOLKS
8 OUNCES SUGAR
2 TABLESPOONS LEMON JUICE OR WATER
GRATED RIND OF ½ LEMON
1 GENEROUS PINCH SALT
3 OUNCES FLOUR (SIFTED 4 TIMES)
1 OUNCE CORNFLOUR
6 EGG WHITES

Beat yolks, sugar, lemon juice or water, lemon rind and salt until light and fluffy (5 minutes at high mixer-speed). Sift flour and cornflour and mix into egg yolk mixture a little at a time. Whisk egg whites until soft peaks form and fold gently into yolk mixture.

Pour into unbuttered cake tins. Cut through mixture gently several times to break up any large air bubbles. Bake for 25 to 30 minutes in a slow oven (350°F. Mark 3). Test by denting lightly with finger; if the cake is done, the dent will spring back.

Invert layers on wire racks. When cool, loosen edges and remove from tins.

SUMMER LEMON CAKE

CAKE MIXTURE:
6 EGGS, SEPARATED
6 OUNCES SUGAR
2 TABLESPOONS WATER
GRATED RIND OF 1 LEMON
1 GENEROUS PINCH SALT
3 OUNCES FLOUR
1 OUNCE CORNFLOUR

LEMON TOPPING:
1 EGG
5 OUNCES SUGAR
GRATED RIND AND JUICE OF 1 LEMON MADE UP TO ¼ PINT WITH WATER
1 OUNCE FLOUR
½ PINT DOUBLE CREAM, WHIPPED
4 OUNCES CHOPPED TOASTED ALMONDS

The cake: Beat yolks, sugar, water, lemon rind and salt until light and fluffy (5 minutes in mixer at high speed). Sift flour and cornflour and gradually blend into egg yolk mixture. Whisk egg whites until stiff but not dry and fold gently into yolk mixture. Place equal quantities of batter into three round 8-inch cake tins which have been buttered and lightly dusted with flour. Bake in a moderately slow oven (350°F. Mark 3) for 45 minutes, or until golden brown. Invert layers on wire racks. When cool, loosen edges and remove from pans.

The topping: Beat egg, sugar and lemon rind together until foamy; add sifted flour and lemon juice and cook in the top of a double boiler, stirring all the time, until smooth and thick. Cool. Fold in whipped cream. Spread 2 cake layers with lemon topping and put together. Cover top and sides of cake with topping and pat chopped almonds firmly around sides. Makes 8 to 12 portions.

LEMON DEVIL'S FOOD

3 TABLESPOONS COCOA
3 LEVEL TABLESPOONS SUGAR
3 TABLESPOONS WATER
¼ PINT MILK
1 TEASPOON VANILLA ESSENCE
¼ POUND BUTTER
½ POUND BROWN SUGAR
3 EGG YOLKS
3 OUNCES PLAIN FLOUR
1 OUNCE CORNFLOUR
1 LEVEL TEASPOON BAKING SODA
PINCH SALT
3 EGG WHITES, BEATEN UNTIL STIFF

LEMON ICING:
10 OUNCES ICING SUGAR
½ POUND SOFTENED BUTTER
GRATED RIND AND JUICE OF 2 LEMONS
2 TABLESPOONS GRAND MARNIER (OPTIONAL)

The cake: Combine cocoa, sugar and water in top of double saucepan and cook over water, stirring, until smooth and thick. Stir in milk and vanilla essence; blend well and set aside to cool.

Cream butter and sugar. Beat in egg yolks one at a time; then beat in chocolate mixture. Sift flour and cornflour 3 times with baking soda and salt and beat into cake mixture.

Fold in egg whites. Pour into cake tins and bake for 30 to 35 minutes in a slow oven (350°F. Mark 3).

To make icing: Cream sugar and softened butter. Add grated lemon rind and juice, and Grand Marnier, to taste. Beat until smooth and creamy. Spread between layers and top cake.

CHOCOLATE DATE NUT TORTE

6 OUNCES SUGAR
2 TABLESPOONS FLOUR
1 LEVEL TEASPOON BAKING POWDER
2 EGGS
4 OUNCES COARSELY-CHOPPED WALNUTS
8 OUNCES COARSELY-CHOPPED DATES
2 OUNCES FINELY-GRATED BITTER CHOCOLATE
¼ TEASPOON CINNAMON
WHIPPED CREAM

Sift 5 ounces sugar together with the flour and baking powder. Beat the eggs until light and fluffy. Add dry ingredients and mix well. Fold the coarsely-chopped nuts, dates and finely-grated chocolate into the mixture. Pour into a well-greased and floured 9-inch cake tin. Sprinkle with a mixture of remaining sugar and the cinnamon. Bake in a very slow oven (300°F. Mark 1) for 30 to 40 minutes, until golden brown. Serve warm with whipped cream. Makes 6 to 8 portions.

TROPICAL BANANA CAKE

2 RIPE BANANAS
¼ POUND BUTTER
1 TEASPOON GRATED LEMON RIND
½ POUND CASTOR SUGAR
½ TEASPOON VANILLA ESSENCE
2 EGGS
½ POUND SIFTED PLAIN FLOUR
1 LEVEL DESSERTSPOON BAKING POWDER
¾ TEASPOON SALT
4 TABLESPOONS MILK

BANANA ICING:
1 POUND ICING SUGAR
½ TEASPOON SALT
¼ POUND BUTTER
1 RIPE BANANA, MASHED
1–2 TEASPOONS RUM

Combine butter, lemon rind, sugar and vanilla in a mixing bowl and beat until light and fluffy. Scrape sides with a rubber scraper and beat in eggs, one at a time, until thoroughly mixed.

Sift flour, baking powder and salt into a bowl. Peel bananas and mash to a pulp.

Add dry ingredients to egg mixture in 3 portions, alternately with banana pulp and milk. Beat after each addition until smooth. Pour into two 9-inch pans. Bake in a pre-heated oven (375°F. Mark 4) for 25 minutes. Cool and frost with icing.

To make icing: Beat the sugar, salt and butter until mixture is glossy and smooth. Add remaining ingredients and beat until well mixed. Use to frost cake layers.

CAPRICE SAINT SYLVESTRE

CAKE MIXTURE:
- 4 EGGS
- 4 OUNCES CASTOR SUGAR
- 4 OUNCES FLOUR
- 1 OUNCE POWDERED UNSWEETENED COCOA
- 4 OUNCES MELTED BUTTER
- FINELY-CHOPPED ALMONDS

GARNISH:
- 2–4 TABLESPOONS JAMAICAN RUM
- 2–4 TABLESPOONS VANILLA SYRUP
- ½ PINT CRÈME CHANTILLY
- 8 MARRONS GLACÉS
- ¼ POUND MELTED CHOCOLATE

Place sugar and eggs in a large mixing bowl. Whisk for 5 minutes. Sift the flour and cocoa together; fold into the egg mixture, followed by cooled, melted butter.

Pour the mixture into a well-buttered, round cake tin or ring mould which you have sprinkled with finely-chopped almonds. Bake in a moderately hot oven (400°F. Mark 5) for 25 to 30 minutes.

When the cake detaches itself slightly from the sides of the mould, it is cooked. Remove from oven and allow to cool.

Split cake in two, moisten the cut sides with equal quantities of rum and vanilla syrup, and spread with *crème chantilly* to which you have added 4 coarsely-chopped *marrons glacés.*

Ice cake with slightly sweetened, melted chocolate and decorate with remaining *marrons glacés.* Serve with remaining *chantilly.* Makes 6 to 8 portions.

GÂTEAU BASQUE

CRÈME PÂTISSIÈRE:
- 4 EGG YOLKS
- 2 OUNCES SUGAR
- 2 TEASPOONS FLOUR
- ½ PINT WARM MILK
- ¼ TEASPOON VANILLA ESSENCE

CAKE MIXTURE:
- 8 OUNCES FLOUR
- 4 OUNCES BUTTER
- 2 EGGS
- 5 OUNCES SUGAR
- CRÈME PÂTISSIÈRE
- EGG OR MILK, TO GLAZE

Crème pâtissière: Beat yolks and sugar together until mixture is lemon-coloured. Mix in flour, then add milk and vanilla essence and mix thoroughly. Place mixture in top of a double saucepan and cook over water, stirring constantly, until smooth and thick; remove from heat, put through sieve and allow to cool.

The cake: Mix flour, butter, eggs and sugar. Knead lightly to a smooth dough. Form into two equal-sized, round layers. Cover first layer with *crème pâtissière.* Top with second layer of dough. Brush with egg or milk and bake in a moderate oven (375°F. Mark 4) for about 40 minutes or until golden brown. Serve cold.

AMERICAN STRAWBERRY SHORTCAKE

SHORTCAKE MIXTURE:

½ POUND FLOUR
3 LEVEL TEASPOONS BAKING POWDER
½ TEASPOON SALT
2 TABLESPOONS SUGAR
4–6 TABLESPOONS BUTTER
2 EGG YOLKS, LIGHTLY BEATEN
¼ PINT MILK

BERRY MIXTURE:

FRESH STRAWBERRIES
SUGAR
JUICE OF ½ LEMON

SOFTENED BUTTER
½ PINT CREAM

Sift flour with baking powder, salt and sugar. Work in softened butter with a fork. Add milk and eggs little by little, stirring continuously, until mixture holds together but is still soft.

Turn out on to a floured board. Roll out or pat into 4 rounds; place on a greased baking sheet and bake for 10 to 15 minutes in a fairly hot oven (425°F. Mark 6).

To serve: split carefully with fork; spread with softened butter and spoon halved strawberries (to which you have added sugar and lemon juice) between layers and on top. Serve warm with cream.

AMERICAN BAKING POWDER BISCUITS

½ POUND PLAIN FLOUR
3 LEVEL TEASPOONS BAKING POWDER
½ LEVEL TEASPOON SALT
4–6 TABLESPOONS BUTTER
¼ PINT MILK

Sift flour, baking powder and salt into a mixing bowl. Rub softened butter into mixture with pastry blender or your fingers; then add milk, stirring mixture quickly, until you have a soft but not sticky dough.

Knead dough with floured fingertips on a lightly-floured board just enough to shape it into a smooth ball; roll or pat out lightly to ½-inch thickness and cut in rounds with a floured glass or biscuit cutter. Bake on a greased baking sheet in a hot oven (450°F. Mark 7) for about 15 minutes, or until biscuits are golden brown. Makes 12.

The Bombe

Ice cream first reached these shores eight centuries ago in the form of a recipe for orange ice, brought back from the Crusades by Richard Cœur de Lion. It was given to him by Saladin, the great warrior Sultan of Egypt and Syria. Ever since, ices have been firm favourites of the English; the ice-houses buried in hillsides on great estates all over the country bear solid witness to that. Unprotected by our blanket of smog, winters were colder in the past, summers hotter, and only by burying the thick blocks of ice sawn from rivers and ponds after Christmas could they be preserved throughout the summer to provide the delights of iced sweets.

'Take two Pewter Basons, one larger than the other,' wrote Mrs. Glasse in 1747. 'The inward one must have a close Cover, into which you are to put your Cream, and mix it with Raspberries or whatever you like best, to give it a Flavour and a Colour. Sweeten it to your Palate; then cover it close, and set it into the larger Bason. Fill it with Ice, and a Handful of Salt; then let it stand in this Ice three Quarters of an Hour, then uncover it, and stir the Cream well together; cover it close again, and let it stand Half an Hour longer, after that turn it into your Plate.'

The method was cumbersome but the principle was sound. Fresh fruit and fresh cream are the only possible foundation for ice cream, even if you do only have to pop it into the refrigerator to freeze. The juice of peaches, of white grapes, of plums and strawberries and currants, of apples and pears even, will provide the climax to any summer meal.

But to get this perfection, you will have to make the ice cream yourself. Gunter's used to make fresh fruit ice cream in London before the war; many shops in Paris still do. But it is in the tiny village of St. Tropez that the best ices in the world exist. In a side turning at the end of the port, Mme. Lamponi makes ice cream of such perfection that her customers have been down on bended knees, begging her to open in Paris. They have promised her backing, they have found her a shop, they have guaranteed her a clientele, but nothing will budge her. As the last yacht leaves the harbour in the autumn, she puts up her shutters and firmly remains closed until spring brings the first boats nosing once more into the little port. Then she opens again and all summer long a procession of people can be seen leaving her shop, bearing the round cylinders in which the best ice cream in the world is packed. Mme. Lamponi is wise. By opening during the summer months only, she need use nothing but fresh fruit purées in her confections . . . and fresh is the operative word, for no finer tastes have been devised than the blends of fresh fruits, butterscotch and praline that she makes in her little shop.

Experiment yourself with different flavours. Quince and tangerine, fresh lime or banana will amaze you with their flavour in this new setting. Almost anything will work, as I found myself from Mme. Lamponi. I had heard of a legendary ice served by Gunter's at garden parties before the war – a grape ice cream. When I asked Mme. Lamponi to make some for me, she told me indignantly that it could not be done – the flavour was too subtle to be captured. Disappointed, I gave up; but she did not. Behind her closed shutters she worked away all winter, experimenting, until she had perfected the new flavour. And when I visited St. Tropez the next year, Grape Ice Cream was her top seller!

Home-made fresh fruit ices, iced soufflés and glamorous iced *bombes* can add enormously to the excitements of summer entertaining. A *bombe*, so named because it is usually made in a round or conical-shaped mould, is always a combination of two or more creams or ices frozen together. In most cases an ice or ice cream is used to line the mould and a creamy *bombe* mousse is used to fill the centre.

Bombes make a wonderfully elegant ending to a meal. And as they can be prepared the day, or even days, before the event, they provide a perfect iced pudding for a small dinner party. Well-flavoured fruit ices or ice creams can be bought in most areas for the outside casing and all that is required is a home-made centre to give a personal touch to your *bombe* recipe.

A delicious basic *bombe* mixture for the filling can be made of egg yolks, sugar and water. It will keep in a well-sealed jar in the refrigerator for a week and is added to whipped cream with the desired flavourings and garnishes when ready to use. Fruits, nuts, crushed macaroons, cake crumbs, raisins or coarsely-grated chocolate are wonderful additions to *bombe* mixtures.

BASIC BOMBE MIXTURE

Bring 5 ounces granulated sugar and ¼ pint water to the boil, stirring continuously, and cook over medium heat until thermometer reads 217°F. Set aside to cool.

Beat 5 egg yolks until light and creamy. Place beaten yolks over boiling water in the top of a double saucepan and add cooled sugar syrup gradually, beating constantly, until well mixed. Cook the mixture, still beating, until it is thick and doubled in volume, about 15 minutes.

Remove from heat; set in a pan of iced water and whisk again until mixture is smooth and cold. Use immediately or store in a sealed container in the refrigerator for up to 7 days.

Add ½ pint whipped cream flavoured with vanilla essence, rum, cognac or the liqueur of your choice. Stir in any one of the following garnishes and pour into the centre of a well-chilled mould lined with ice or ice cream of a contrasting colour. Chill until ready to serve (2 to 4 hours).

BOMBE GARNISHES

Coarsely-grated chocolate, crumbled macaroons, finely-chopped glacé cherries, chopped toasted almonds, halved strawberries, crushed raspberries, chopped peaches, bananas or pears and chopped nuts.

RASPBERRY BOMBE

½ RECIPE BASIC BOMBE MIXTURE
2 PINTS RASPBERRY ICE
½ PINT CREAM, WHIPPED UNTIL STIFF
1 TABLESPOON GRATED ORANGE RIND
1–2 TABLESPOONS GRAND MARNIER
1–2 TABLESPOONS COARSELY-CHOPPED NUTS
1 EGG WHITE, BEATEN STIFF

Line a chilled mould with raspberry ice and smooth into a coating about ¾ inch thick. Chill lined mould.

In the meantime, whip cream and flavour to taste with grated orange rind and Grand Marnier. Whisk into basic *bombe* mixture. Fold in stiffly-beaten egg white and chopped nuts and pour into lined mould. Freeze until ready to serve. Serves 4 to 6.

BOMBE AU CHOCOLAT

½ RECIPE BASIC BOMBE MIXTURE
2 PINTS CHOCOLATE ICE CREAM
1–1½ TEASPOONS INSTANT COFFEE
2 TABLESPOONS KIRSCH
½ PINT CREAM, WHIPPED STIFF
1 EGG WHITE, BEATEN STIFF

Line a chilled mould with chocolate ice cream and smooth into a coating about ¾ inch thick. Chill lined mould.

In the meantime, dissolve instant coffee in Kirsch and whisk into basic *bombe* mixture. Fold mixture gently into whipped cream. Fold in stiffly-beaten egg white and pour into lined mould. Freeze until ready to serve. Serves 4 to 6.

ICED SOUFFLÉS

4 TABLESPOONS DICED SPONGE CAKE
4 TABLESPOONS GRAND MARNIER
4 EGGS
4 OUNCES SUGAR
GRATED RIND OF 1 ORANGE
2 TABLESPOONS ORANGE JUICE
½ PINT CREAM
POWDERED CHOCOLATE

Soak diced sponge cake in 2 tablespoons Grand Marnier. Separate eggs and beat yolks with sugar until the mixture is lemon-coloured and thick. Stir in remaining Grand Marnier, orange juice and grated orange rind.

Whisk cream and egg whites separately and fold into mixture. Half-fill individual soufflé dishes or custard cups; divide diced sponge cake among the cups; add the remaining soufflé mixture and freeze soufflés for 4 hours. Dust with powdered chocolate or cocoa. Serves 8.

CHOCOLATE ICE CREAM

4 EGG YOLKS
¼ POUND SUGAR
1 PINCH SALT
¾ PINT SINGLE CREAM
2 OUNCES MELTED CHOCOLATE
1 TEASPOON VANILLA
½ PINT DOUBLE CREAM, WHIPPED

Beat egg yolks, sugar and salt until light and lemon-coloured. Scald single cream and add to egg and sugar mixture, whisking until mixture is well blended.

Pour mixture into top of a double saucepan and cook over water, stirring continuously, until custard coats spoon.

Strain through a fine sieve; stir in melted chocolate and vanilla and set aside to chill.

Mix whipped cream with chocolate custard mixture and freeze for at least 3 hours.

ORANGE ICE

¾ POUND SUGAR
1½ PINTS WATER
¾ PINT ORANGE JUICE
¼ PINT LEMON JUICE
FINELY-GRATED RIND OF 1 ORANGE AND 1 LEMON

Bring sugar and water to the boil; boil for 5 minutes. Cool slightly and add orange juice, lemon juice and grated orange and lemon rind. Cool; strain through a fine sieve and freeze.

ICED COFFEE SOUFFLÉS

4 EGGS
4 OUNCES SUGAR
2 TABLESPOONS POWDERED COFFEE
2 OUNCES CHOCOLATE
2 TABLESPOONS WATER
2 TABLESPOONS RUM
½ PINT DOUBLE CREAM
GRATED CHOCOLATE (FOR DECORATION)

Separate eggs and beat yolks with sugar and powdered coffee until mixture is thick and creamy. Melt chocolate and water in a small saucepan; add rum and stir into egg and coffee mixture.

Whip cream and fold into soufflé mixture. Whisk egg whites and fold into mixture. Pour into individual soufflé dishes or custard cups and freeze for 4 hours. Decorate with grated chocolate.

FROZEN BANANA CREAM

3–4 BANANAS, MASHED
2 OUNCES SUGAR
PINCH SALT
6–8 TABLESPOONS PINEAPPLE JUICE
2 TABLESPOONS LEMON JUICE
2 TABLESPOONS RUM
½ PINT DOUBLE CREAM, WHIPPED
2 TABLESPOONS CHOPPED TOASTED ALMONDS

Combine mashed bananas, sugar, salt, pineapple and lemon juices and rum. Fold in the cream. Turn into a freezing tray. Freeze in the freezer compartment of the refrigerator until firm. Turn into a bowl and whisk until frothy. Fold in chopped toasted almonds; return to tray and freeze until set. Serves 6 to 8.

COUPE CRÉOLE

¼ PINT MILK
½ PINT DOUBLE CREAM
4 EGG YOLKS
4 OUNCES CASTOR SUGAR
½ TEASPOON VANILLA ESSENCE
4 TABLESPOONS CRÈME DE MARRONS
½ PINT CREAM, WHIPPED
HOT MELTED CHOCOLATE
4 MARRONS GLACÉS
TOASTED SLIVERED ALMONDS

To make vanilla ice cream: combine milk and cream in a saucepan and bring to the boil. Place the egg yolks in a bowl and whisk, adding sugar slowly, until mixture is light-coloured and creamy. Pour hot cream mixture over egg and sugar mixture, stirring well. Cook over very low heat until thickened sufficiently to coat back of wooden spoon. Do not let it come to the boil or it will curdle.

Strain through a fine sieve into freezer tray and allow to cool. Stir in vanilla essence and freeze, stirring from time to time.

Just before serving, place a tablespoon of *crème de marrons* at the bottom of individual *coupes* or champagne glasses, together with a little whipped cream. Place a large ball of ice cream on top and cover with hot melted chocolate. Top with a *marron glacé* and garnish with whipped cream and toasted slivered almonds. Serves 4.

TULIPE GLACÉE

5 OUNCES FLOUR
5 OUNCES ICING SUGAR
2 EGG YOLKS
3 EGG WHITES
1 FRESH PINEAPPLE, PEELED, CORED AND DICED
KIRSCH
VANILLA ICE CREAM
DOUBLE CREAM, WHIPPED
1 LARGE ORANGE, GREASED, TO FORM PASTRY SHAPES

Sift flour and icing sugar into a mixing bowl; add egg yolks and whites and mix well.

Grease a cold baking sheet and mark 4 circles on it with a saucer. Spread 1 dessertspoon of mixture over each circle, using back of teaspoon. Bake in a slow oven (350°F. Mark 3) for 5 to 6 minutes, or until just turning brown at edges.

Remove each round from baking sheet; turn over and, working quickly, place each circle over top of a greased orange. Place tea towel over pastry to prevent burning hands and mould pastry to fit orange. Remove and continue as above, baking 2 to 4 circles each time and shaping them over oranges as you go. Cases will keep for days in a biscuit tin. This recipe makes 12 to 16 *tulipes*.

To serve: fill 8 cases with diced fresh pineapple which you have marinated in Kirsch; add a scoop of vanilla ice cream and decorate with whipped cream. Serves 8.

ANANAS GLACÉ 'LAURENT'

4 SLICES FRESH PINEAPPLE
ORANGE QUARTERS, PEELED
4 SCOOPS VANILLA ICE CREAM
¼ PINT DOUBLE CREAM, WHIPPED
CHOCOLATE VERMICELLI
TOASTED SLIVERED ALMONDS

Remove hard central core from a slice of pineapple. Arrange on a plate; add orange quarters in a flower shape; keep cool. Just before serving, place a scoop of vanilla ice cream in the hollow of the pineapple; top with whipped cream and sprinkle with chocolate vermicelli and toasted slivered almonds. Serves 4.

ORANGE APRICOT CHANTILLY

1 POUND DRIED APRICOTS
1 ORANGE (RIND AND PULP), FINELY SHREDDED
4 OUNCES GRANULATED SUGAR
2–4 TABLESPOONS COINTREAU
¼ PINT CREAM, WHIPPED
2 TABLESPOONS BLANCHED SLIVERED ALMONDS

Rinse apricots well and put them in a saucepan with shredded orange pulp, rind and just enough water to cover. Simmer gently, uncovered, for 15 minutes. Stir in sugar and continue to cook over a very low heat until most of the liquid is absorbed and the apricots are cooked through, adding more water if necessary.

Allow apricot mixture to cool and purée it in an electric blender or rub through a fine sieve. Add Cointreau to taste, stir in whipped cream and blanched slivered almonds, and chill in individual soufflé dishes or *pots de crème*. Serves 6.

BAKED APPLE COMPOTE

2 POUNDS COOKING APPLES
RIND AND JUICE OF 1 LEMON
6 OUNCES BROWN SUGAR
2 OUNCES BUTTER
DOUBLE CREAM

Slice peeled and cored cooking apples into a buttered baking dish. Sprinkle the slices with lemon juice, grated lemon rind and brown sugar and dot with butter. Bake, uncovered, in a moderate oven (375°F. Mark 4) for 30 minutes, or until tender. Serve with double cream. Serves 4.

POIRES À LA BOURGUIGNONNE

2 POUNDS SMALL PEARS
8 OUNCES SUGAR
¼ PINT WATER
CINNAMON
¼ PINT RED BURGUNDY

Peel pears but do not core them. Put them in a saucepan with the sugar, water and cinnamon. Simmer, covered, for about 15 minutes. Add Burgundy and continue to cook over a low heat, uncovered, for 15 minutes.

Put pears in a deep serving dish. Reduce liquid to the consistency of a light syrup. Pour syrup over the pears and chill. Serve very cold with whipped cream.

POIRES BELLE DIJONNAISE

4 RIPE PEARS
VANILLA SYRUP
VANILLA ICE CREAM
BLACKCURRANT JELLY
1–2 TABLESPOONS KIRSCH
CRYSTALLISED VIOLETS

Peel, core and halve pears. Poach lightly in vanilla syrup. Cool in syrup and then put in refrigerator until ready to use.

Just before serving, spoon slightly softened vanilla ice cream into a chilled serving bowl; arrange halved poached pears on this bed and cover pears with blackcurrant jelly thinned with Kirsch. Decorate with crystallised violets. Serves 4.

MARQUISE À L'ANANAS

2 SMALL FRESH PINEAPPLES
SUGAR
½ PINT PINEAPPLE JUICE
¼ PINT WATER
8 OUNCES SUGAR
RIND AND JUICE OF 1 LEMON
½ PINT CREAM, WHIPPED
3 TABLESPOONS KIRSCH

Cut pineapples in half lengthwise, leaving on the green tops. With a fork, scrape the flesh and juice into a bowl, discarding the hard core and being careful not to break through the shell. Sprinkle the insides of the shells with a little sugar and chill in the refrigerator until ready to use.

Mash flesh of the two pineapples with a fork. Add pineapple juice, water, sugar and the grated lemon rind. Bring to the boil and boil for 5 minutes. Strain; add lemon juice and freeze in the usual way.

Whisk with a fork, fold in whipped cream and Kirsch and return to freezer. Just before serving, spoon mixture into chilled pineapple shells and serve immediately. Serves 4.

FRESH FRUIT COMPOTE

1 MEDIUM-SIZED PINEAPPLE
4 PEARS
4 COX'S ORANGE PIPPINS
4 PLUMS
1 BUNCH GRAPES
ICING SUGAR
2 TABLESPOONS BRANDY
2 TABLESPOONS LEMON JUICE
¼ BOTTLE CHAMPAGNE

Peel, core and slice pineapple into rings. Reserve top. Slice each ring in half and combine in a mixing bowl with peeled, cored and sliced pears and apples, sliced plums and halved, seeded grapes. Dust with icing sugar to taste; moisten with brandy and lemon juice; toss well and chill.

Just before serving, transfer to serving bowl; pour over champagne and decorate with pineapple top.

BAKED PEARS IN WHITE WINE

6 PEARS
WHITE WINE, TO COVER
SUGAR
WHIPPED CREAM

Peel pears and place in an oven-proof baking dish with dry white wine and sugar, to taste. Cover and bake in a moderate oven (375°F. Mark 4) for about 45 minutes. Serve cool or chilled with whipped cream.

FIGS IN WINE AND HONEY

1 POUND FRESH FIGS
WHITE WINE, TO COVER
4 FLUID OUNCES HONEY
FRESH CREAM

Place figs in a saucepan with enough white wine to cover. Bring to the boil; add honey and simmer until figs are tender. Chill. Serve with fresh cream. Serves 4.

RUM CHARLOTTE

¼ PINT WATER
¼ POUND CASTOR SUGAR
6 TABLESPOONS RUM
4 OUNCES UNSWEETENED CHOCOLATE
¼ PINT COFFEE
2 TABLESPOONS BROWN SUGAR
2 OUNCES BUTTER
4 EGGS
SPONGE FINGERS
UNSWEETENED WHIPPED CREAM

Make a rum syrup by boiling water, sugar and rum together for 3 to 5 minutes. Make a chocolate sauce by melting chocolate in a small saucepan. Add coffee and cook for 5 minutes. Remove saucepan from the heat; add brown sugar, butter and egg yolks, and mix well. Fold in stiffly-beaten egg whites. Line small moulds with sponge fingers which have been sprinkled with some of the rum syrup and pour in the chocolate mixture.

Arrange more sponge fingers over the top of the moulds to cover filling completely. Chill for 12 hours. Unmould, sprinkle with remaining syrup and serve with whipped cream. Serves 4 to 6.

ELIZABETH MOXON'S LEMON POSSET

1 PINT DOUBLE CREAM
GRATED RIND AND JUICE OF 2 LEMONS
¼ PINT DRY WHITE WINE
SUGAR
WHITES OF 3 EGGS

Add the grated lemon rind to 1 pint of double cream and whisk until stiff. Stir in lemon juice and dry white wine. Add sugar to taste. Whisk egg whites until they form peaks and fold into whipped cream mixture. Serve in a glass serving dish or in individual glasses. Serves 4 to 6.

ENGLISH TRIFLE

- 1 TIN WHOLE PEELED APRICOTS
- 1 SPONGE CAKE
- ¼ PINT SWEET MARSALA
- 2 TABLESPOONS CORNFLOUR
- 2 TABLESPOONS SUGAR
- ½ PINT HOT MILK
- 3 EGGS
- 1 CUP CRUMBLED MACAROONS
- 1 PINT DOUBLE CREAM
- ½ TEASPOON VANILLA ESSENCE
- SUGAR
- FRESH OR CRYSTALLISED FRUITS

Drain syrup from a can of whole peeled apricots. Remove pits and purée apricots in an electric blender. Cut sponge cake into 2 layers and spread half the apricot purée between layers. Assemble cake again and cut into pieces 2 inches by 1 inch.

Arrange cake strips in the bottom of a large glass serving bowl. Pour Marsala over cake and spread remaining apricot purée on top.

Prepare custard: mix cornflour and sugar to a smooth paste with a little milk; combine with remaining hot milk in the top of a double saucepan and bring to the boil. Cook over water, stirring continuously, until the mixture thickens. Remove from heat and beat in eggs, one by one. When well blended, simmer gently over water, stirring continuously, for 10 minutes. Stir in crumbled macaroons and leave to soak until soft. Beat well to dissolve macaroons. Cool custard and pour over apricot purée. Chill for 2 hours.

Just before serving, whisk double cream with vanilla essence and sugar until thick. Cover custard with whipped cream and decorate with fresh or crystallised fruits. Serves 8 to 10.

FRENCH RICE PUDDING

- 2–3 OUNCES RICE
- 1 PINT MILK
- WATER
- ¼ POUND SUGAR
- ¼ TEASPOON SALT
- 2 EGG YOLKS
- 2 EGG WHITES, STIFFLY BEATEN
- ½ TEASPOON VANILLA ESSENCE

Cook rice in milk and a little water with sugar and salt until tender but not mushy. Beat egg yolks and add hot rice mixture slowly. Cook in the top of a double saucepan until thick. Cool slightly and fold in beaten egg whites. Flavour with vanilla essence and, if necessary, more sugar.

Bake pudding in a fairly hot oven (425°F. Mark 6) for 5 to 10 minutes or until golden brown. Serves 4 to 6.

ZABAGLIONE PUDDING

6 EGG YOLKS
2 OUNCES GRANULATED SUGAR
6–8 TABLESPOONS MARSALA OR SHERRY
¼ OUNCE GELATINE
2 TABLESPOONS COLD WATER
3 TABLESPOONS BRANDY
⅜ PINT DOUBLE CREAM

ZABAGLIONE SAUCE:
3 EGG YOLKS
1 OUNCE GRANULATED SUGAR
3–4 TABLESPOONS MARSALA OR SHERRY
1½ TABLESPOONS BRANDY

To make pudding: In the top of a double boiler, combine the egg yolks with sugar and Marsala or sherry, and whip the mixture over hot, but not boiling, water until it thickens. Stir in gelatine, softened in cold water and dissolved over hot water. Put the pan in a bowl of ice and stir the *zabaglione* well until it is thick and free of bubbles. When it is almost cold, fold in brandy and whipped cream and pour into individual moulds. Chill the *zabaglione*, unmould it, and serve with *zabaglione* sauce. Serves 4.

To make the sauce: Combine egg yolks and sugar in the top of a double saucepan. Whisk mixture over hot, but not boiling, water until sauce coats the back of a spoon. Stir in Marsala (or sherry) and brandy, and serve immediately. For cakes, puddings, sweet soufflés and ice cream.

CRÈME RENVERSÉE AU GRAND MARNIER

¾ PINT SINGLE CREAM
3 TABLESPOONS GRAND MARNIER OR OTHER LIQUEUR
4 WHOLE EGGS
4 EGG YOLKS
¼ POUND SUGAR

Scald cream with Grand Marnier and let it cool slightly. Beat whole eggs and egg yolks with sugar until light and lemon-coloured. Add cream, stirring constantly until the mixture is well blended together. Strain through a fine sieve into a buttered baking dish. Set the dish in a pan of hot water; cover and bake in the oven (350°F. Mark 3) for 35 to 45 minutes, or until the custard is set and a knife inserted near the centre comes out clean.

To serve: cool custard, loosen it from the sides of the dish with a knife and invert the mould on to a serving platter. Serves 4 to 6.

BREAD AND BUTTER PUDDING

1 OUNCE CURRANTS
4 SLICES BREAD
BUTTER
4 EGG YOLKS
3 EGG WHITES
4 OUNCES SUGAR
NUTMEG
1 PINT WARM MILK
¼–½ TEASPOON VANILLA ESSENCE

Wash and pick 1 ounce of currants and scatter a few in the bottom of a well-buttered quart baking dish. Trim crusts from 4 slices of bread; cut each slice in half; butter each piece generously and place in layers in baking dish, scattering currants between each layer.

Twenty minutes before you are ready to bake the pudding: beat egg yolks and egg whites together with sugar and a little nutmeg. Stir in warm milk and vanilla essence and pour over sliced bread and currants. Bake in a moderate oven (375°F. Mark 4) for about ¾ hour, or until pudding is set and lightly browned.

Illustration on facing page

Salade Niçoise

I like basking by the lazy blue of the Mediterranean, with a glass of chilled *vin rose* in my hand, or better yet, an iced glass of smoke-filled Pernod. Who could ask for anything more? Lunch in the sun, perhaps, under the striped awning of a *quai*-side restaurant, on a hillside terrace, or in the cool depths of a summer garden.

Lunch would be a refreshing Provençal salad – a combination of both cooked and raw vegetables, with hard-boiled eggs, tuna fish and anchovies in the Mediterranean manner. I like *Salade Nicoise*, quartered tomatoes and eggs, sliced sweet onions, celery and green peppers, black olives, tuna fish and anchovies, bathed in a rich dressing of Provençal olive oil and wine vinegar made from the robust red wines of the Var.

4 TOMATOES, SEEDED AND QUARTERED
½ SPANISH ONION, SLICED
1 SWEET GREEN PEPPER, SLICED
8 RADISHES
2 HEARTS OF LETTUCE
4 STALKS CELERY, SLICED
1 TIN TUNA FISH
8 FILLETS OF ANCHOVY
2 HARD-BOILED EGGS, QUARTERED
8 RIPE OLIVES
Salad Dressing:
2 TABLESPOONS WINE VINEGAR OR LEMON JUICE
6 TABLESPOONS PURE OLIVE OIL
SALT AND FRESHLY-GROUND BLACK PEPPER
12 LEAVES OF FRESH BASIL, COARSELY CHOPPED

Combine prepared vegetables in a salad bowl, placing neatly on top the tuna fish, anchovies and quartered eggs. Dot with ripe olives. Mix salad dressing of wine vinegar, olive oil, seasoning and herbs, and sprinkle over the salad.

OLIVE
MARTIN

Crêpes Suzette

Pancakes, in one form or another, have been a universal delight since man first discovered that if he mixed crushed grain with water and baked it, he would have a new kind of food.

Under more elaborate conditions – and a host of different names and fillings – they have been enjoyed around the world for centuries. In Mexico, it is the peasant *tortilla*; in China, the crisp egg roll; while America prefers hers for breakfast, swimming in melted butter and maple syrup; and the Russians like theirs as *blini*, a delicious appetiser topped with caviare and sour cream.

But of all the pancake recipes in the world, the greatest – *Crêpes Suzette* – originated in France. The legends of the origin of this famous dish are as varied as the recipes for making it. The one I like best is the version recounted by Morrison Wood in his excellent cookery book, *With a Jug of Wine*. According to Mr. Wood, a well-known French chef, Henri Carpentier, was preparing *crêpes* in liqueur for Edward VII when the dish accidentally burst into flames. Chef Henri, not at all abashed at this misadventure, carried the flaming pan in which the *crêpes* were immersed to the table, and when the fire had died out, he served the little pancakes to the king and his party.

Edward pronounced them delicious and asked what they were called. 'They have just been invented, sir,' Henri replied, 'and they shall be called *Crêpes Princesse*.' The king smiled, but shook his head. 'Where is your gallantry, Henri?' he asked. Then, indicating the young daughter of his host, he announced: 'They shall be called *Crêpes Suzette*, in Mademoiselle's honour.' Whatever you call them, these paper-thin pancakes are wonderfully easy to make. They can be prepared hours or even the day before you plan to serve them, as their flaming sauce calls more for showmanship than for skill.

You will need a good *crêpes* pan made of cast iron or lined copper, for the delicate pancakes may scorch in lighter materials. It should be the size of the ultimate pancake (about 5 inches across), for the batter should be so creamy and thin that it will run ragged over a larger pan. And your pan should have rounded or sloping sides so that you will be

continued on page 362

Illustration on facing page

Baba-au-Rhum

Caprice Restaurant, London
The *baba* – first cousin of the *savarin* – a deliciously light addition to the sweet trolley, is served by Mario Gallati at the Caprice with a moist filling of fresh fruits. (Recipe on page 342–3.)

able to turn the pancakes over with your spatula without tearing them.

Season your *crêpes* pan before using: fill it with vegetable oil; bring the oil slowly to a simmer; remove from heat and let the oil-filled pan stand until oil is cold. Then pour out the oil and wipe the pan clean with cloth or kitchen paper. To keep your pan in prime condition: wipe it out with oil, never with water, after every use, and your *crêpes* will never stick.

BASIC CRÊPES MIXTURE

8 OUNCES FLOUR
1 LEVEL TABLESPOON SUGAR
SALT
3 EGGS
¾ PINT MILK
2 TABLESPOONS MELTED BUTTER OR OIL
2 TABLESPOONS COGNAC OR RUM

Sift together flour, sugar and salt. Beat eggs and add them to the dry ingredients. Mix in the milk, melted butter and cognac gradually to avoid lumps. Strain through a fine sieve and leave batter to stand for at least 2 hours before cooking the *crêpes*. Batter should be as thin as cream. (Add a little water if too thick.) For each *crêpe*, spoon about 2 tablespoons batter into heated pan, swirling pan to allow batter to cover entire surface thinly; brush a piece of butter around edge of hot pan with the point of a knife and cook over a medium heat until just golden, but not brown (about 1 minute each side). Repeat until all *crêpes* are cooked, stacking them on a plate as they are ready. If *crêpes* are to be filled, cover with waxed paper or aluminium foil to prevent drying. Makes 20 to 24 golden *crêpes*.

LEMON CRÊPES MIXTURE

4 OUNCES FLOUR
1 TABLESPOON SUGAR
1 PINCH SALT
2 EGGS
2 EGG YOLKS
¾ PINT MILK
2 TABLESPOONS MELTED BUTTER
1 TEASPOON GRATED LEMON RIND
2 TABLESPOONS LEMON JUICE

Sift together flour, sugar and salt. Beat together whole eggs and egg yolks and add them to the dry ingredients. Mix in the milk, melted butter, grated lemon rind and lemon juice smoothly. Strain through a fine sieve and let batter stand for at least 2 hours before cooking the *crêpes*. Batter should be as thin as cream.

For each *crêpe*, melt 1 teaspoon butter in a small thick-bottomed frying pan (6 to 8 inches in diameter); add about 2 tablespoons batter, swirling pan to allow batter to cover entire bottom of pan thinly; brush a piece of butter around edge of hot pan with the point of a knife and cook over a medium heat until just golden (about 1 minute each side). Makes 20 to 24 thin lemon pancakes.

VARIATIONS ON THE BASIC CRÊPES THEME

1. APPLE CRÊPES

Simmer 3 to 4 apples, peeled and sliced, with ½ teaspoon cinnamon, 4 tablespoons brown sugar and 4 tablespoons butter for 15 minutes, or until apples are soft. Cook *crêpes* as above; place 1 or 2 tablespoons of apple filling on each; roll up and brown in butter. Sprinkle with cinnamon and sugar before serving.

2. FRESH BERRY CRÊPES

Cook *crêpes* as above and fill with crushed raspberries or strawberries mixed with whipped cream. Garnish with whole berries.

3. APRICOT CRÊPES

Cook *crêpes* as above and fill with a combination of chopped pineapple and apricot jam flavoured with Kirsch.

4. MARRON CRÊPES

Cook *crêpes* as above. Keep warm. When ready to serve, butter them generously with *crème de marrons* (tinned puréed chestnuts); roll them up and cover with a sauce made of heated apricot jam. Top with toasted slivered almonds.

CRÊPES SUZETTE

½ BASIC CRÊPES MIXTURE
¼ POUND BUTTER
2 OUNCES ICING SUGAR
1 TABLESPOON GRATED LEMON RIND
GRATED RIND AND JUICE OF 1 ORANGE
6 TABLESPOONS COINTREAU
4 TABLESPOONS COGNAC

Cream butter and icing sugar together; add grated lemon and orange rind, orange juice and 4 tablespoons Cointreau. (You can substitute either curaçao or Grand Marnier for the Cointreau.)

Make *crêpes* as in basic recipe.

When ready to serve: heat orange-flavoured butter in a hot chafing dish (or electric frying pan) for about 5 minutes or until it bubbles and reduces a little. Dip each cooked *crêpe* into this hot mixture; then fold in quarters, using a fork and spoon, and push to one side of the pan. When all *crêpes* are used, sprinkle with a little sugar and add remaining Cointreau to the pan with cognac. Stand well away from the pan and light the liquid with a match. Spoon the flaming liquid over the *crêpes* and serve with the sauce as soon as the flames die down. Serves 4.

PALATSCHINKEN

½ BASIC CRÊPES MIXTURE
APRICOT JAM
2 TABLESPOONS COGNAC
CHOPPED ALMONDS
ICING SUGAR

Make about 12 *crêpes*, transferring them to a warm plate as you cook them. Combine apricot jam, cognac and 1 ounce finely-chopped almonds; spread *crêpes* with apricot-nut mixture; roll them up neatly, place on an oven-proof serving dish and keep hot in a very slow oven (250°F. Mark ½) until ready to serve. Just before serving, dust *palatschinken* with icing sugar.

CRÊPES AU MOCHA

4 OUNCES FLOUR
1 TABLESPOON SUGAR
PINCH SALT
1 TABLESPOON POWDERED CHOCOLATE
1 TABLESPOON POWDERED COFFEE
2 EGGS
2 EGG YOLKS
¾ PINT MILK
2 TABLESPOONS MELTED BUTTER
½ PINT CREAM, WHIPPED
1 TABLESPOON RUM
SUGAR

Sift together flour, sugar, salt and powdered chocolate and coffee. Beat together whole eggs and egg yolks and add them to the dry ingredients. Mix in the milk and melted butter smoothly. Strain through a fine sieve and let batter stand for at least 2 hours before cooking the *crêpes*. Batter should be as thin as cream.

Melt a bit of butter for each *crêpe* in a small thick-bottomed frying pan (6 or 8 inches in diameter); add about 2 tablespoons batter, swirling pan to allow batter to cover entire bottom of pan thinly; brush a piece of butter around edge of hot pan with the point of a knife and cook over a medium heat until crisp (about 1 minute each side). Makes 20 to 24 thin *crêpes*.

Fill *crêpes au mocha* with whipped cream flavoured to taste with rum and sugar.

DESSERT CRÊPES

½ LEMON CRÊPES RECIPE
8 OUNCES STRAWBERRY JAM
12 OUNCES PINEAPPLE CHUNKS
4 TABLESPOONS KIRSCH
1 TABLESPOON CURAÇAO
SLIVERED ALMONDS
ZABAGLIONE SAUCE (PAGE 105)

Make 12 lemon *crêpes*. Mix strawberry jam and pineapple chunks. Flavour with Kirsch and a little curaçao. Add slivered almonds. Fill *crêpes*, roll them and dress them on a platter. Garnish with *zabaglione* sauce.

STRAWBERRY DESSERT PANCAKES

½ LEMON CRÊPES RECIPE
1 PUNNET STRAWBERRIES
SUGAR
KIRSCH OR GRAND MARNIER
BLANCHED, SHREDDED AND LIGHTLY-TOASTED ALMONDS
WHIPPED CREAM, FLAVOURED WITH KIRSCH OR GRAND MARNIER

Make about 12 *crêpes*, using either an electric griddle or a thick-bottomed frying pan. Slice strawberries; add sugar and a little Kirsch or Grand Marnier to taste and spoon 2 tablespoons sliced and sugared strawberries on to each pancake.

Roll the *crêpes* to enclose the filling and arrange the rolls side by side in a shallow buttered baking dish. Sprinkle *crêpes* with blanched, shredded and lightly-toasted almonds and put the dish under the grill for a few minutes. Serve hot with whipped cream, sweetened and flavoured with a little Kirsch or Grand Marnier.

English Apple Pie

It is quite amazing the subtleties of flavour that our ancestors managed to create when you realise how few ingredients they had to play with.

Sated as we are with the riches of the world (asparagus from Kenya, strawberries from California and *courgettes* from Morocco as early as January), we can hardly imagine that the cabbage and the carrot were once exotic imported vegetables, that Henry VIII himself brought back from the Field of the Cloth of Gold the first cherries ever to be seen here, and that the pineapple was considered so extraordinary when it first arrived on these shores that the reigning monarch, Charles II, was painted receiving the first specimen as if it was a rare treasure.

But for nearly two thousand years, ever since the Romans first planted apple trees in Somerset and found that the flavour of the fruit surpassed that of any in all their Empire, the apple has been our dominant fruit, and by far and away our favourite.

Along with roast beef, game and salmon, the apple pie is one of the great dishes of this island, and one that has spread right round the world, recognisably British still, perfected over the centuries, impossible to improve.

I find a special satisfaction, in these days of quick and easy cooking, in making this traditional dish just for the sheer pleasure of it. The warm and spicy smell of apple pie baking in the oven – its filling rich with cinnamon and nutmeg and the tart rind of lemon, its crust part butter, part flour and part poetry – is one of the most tantalising and appetising aromas I know. For British cooks have been making superb apple pies ever since 1296 when the first British cooking apple of real importance, the Costard, came on the scene.

Costards are no longer to be had today, for time has marched over them. But from those far-off origins stem their descendants, the Lord Derby, the Grenadier, the Newtown Wonder, and my own personal favourite, Bramley's Seedling.

The Bramley keeps firm and well, and cooks to perfection. Tart, but not too tart; juicy, but not too juicy; its highly-flavoured flesh breaks down when cooked to a fluffy mass that is as delicious hot as it is cold. It is the perfect apple for making apple sauce and baked apples and, of course, apple pie.

ENGLISH APPLE PIE

1½ POUNDS COOKING APPLES
JUICE OF ½ LEMON
PASTRY FOR SHELL AND TOP
4 OUNCES GRANULATED SUGAR
2 OUNCES DARK BROWN SUGAR
1 TABLESPOON FLOUR
⅛ LEVEL TEASPOON GRATED NUTMEG
¼ LEVEL TEASPOON POWDERED CINNAMON
GRATED PEEL OF ½ ORANGE
GRATED PEEL OF ½ LEMON
2 OUNCES CHOPPED RAISINS AND SULTANAS
1–2 TABLESPOONS ORANGE JUICE
1–2 TABLESPOONS BUTTER

Pare and core apples and slice thickly. Soak them in water to which you have added lemon juice to keep their colour. Line a deep 9-inch pie dish with pastry, using your own favourite recipe or one of the new mixes.

Combine granulated sugar, brown sugar, flour, nutmeg and cinnamon and rub a little of this mixture into pastry lining. Add grated peels to remaining sugar mixture. Cover bottom of pastry shell with sliced apples and sprinkle with a few chopped raisins and sultanas and some of the sugar mixture, to taste. Repeat layers until pie shell is richly filled.

Sprinkle with orange juice; dot with butter and fit top crust over apples, pressing the edges together or fluting them. Decorate pastry; cut slits in top crust to release steam and bake in a moderately hot oven (400°F. Mark 5) for 35 to 40 minutes, or until tender. Serve warm, with cream or Cheddar cheese

FRENCH APPLE FLAN

1 BAKED PASTRY SHELL

FRENCH PASTRY CREAM:
¼ POUND SUGAR
3 TABLESPOONS CORNFLOUR
¾ PINT MILK
5 EGG YOLKS
½–1 TEASPOON VANILLA ESSENCE
2 TEASPOONS KIRSCH

1½ POUNDS COOKING APPLES
2 TABLESPOONS BUTTER

APRICOT GLAZE:
6 TABLESPOONS APRICOT JAM
3 TABLESPOONS WATER
1 TABLESPOON RUM, BRANDY OR KIRSCH

To make French pastry cream: Combine sugar and cornflour in the top of a double saucepan. Stir in milk and cook over direct heat, stirring all the time, until mixture comes to the boil. Boil for 1 minute. Beat yolks slightly, add a little hot milk mixture and pour into milk and sugar mixture, stirring. Cook, stirring, over hot but not boiling water for 5 to 10 minutes. Strain and cool. Add vanilla essence and Kirsch; cover with waxed paper and chill well. Half-fill baked pastry shell with this mixture.

To prepare apples: Peel, core and slice apples as thinly as possible. Arrange in overlapping concentric circles on top of French pastry cream. Dot with knobs of butter and bake under pre-heated grill for 3 to 5 minutes, or until apple slices are nicely browned. Coat with apricot glaze.

To prepare glaze: Heat apricot jam and water in small saucepan, stirring constantly, until mixture melts. Strain and if desired stir in rum, brandy or Kirsch. Keep warm until ready to use.

CREAMY APPLE PIE

1 PASTRY SHELL
2 POUNDS COOKING APPLES
6 OUNCES SUGAR
1 OUNCE FLOUR
¼ TEASPOON SALT
¼ TEASPOON CINNAMON
½ PINT DOUBLE CREAM

Prepare a 9-inch unbaked pastry shell. Bake 'blind'. Peel, core and slice apples thickly to fill. Combine sugar, flour, salt and cinnamon and add to apples. Toss lightly and turn into a pastry shell. Pour double cream over top and bake in a hot oven (400°F. Mark 5) for 35 to 40 minutes, or until firm. Serve warm. Serves 4 to 6.

LEMON MERINGUE PIE

4 TABLESPOONS CORNFLOUR
½ LEVEL TEASPOON SALT
10 OUNCES SUGAR
¾ PINT BOILING WATER
1 TABLESPOON BUTTER
6 TABLESPOONS LEMON JUICE
GRATED RIND OF ½ LEMON
4 EGG YOLKS, SLIGHTLY BEATEN
1 BAKED PASTRY SHELL
4 EGG WHITES
SALT AND SUGAR

Combine first four ingredients in the top of a double saucepan and cook, stirring continuously, until mixture comes to the boil. Turn down heat and simmer gently for 15 minutes, stirring from time to time.

Beat in butter and lemon juice and rind. Stir in egg yolks and cook over water until thick. Cool. Fill baked pastry shell.

Make a meringue with egg whites, beaten until stiff with a pinch of salt and sugar. Spoon meringue on to pie and bake until golden brown in a fairly hot oven (425°F. Mark 6).

FRENCH LEMON TARTS

PASTRY:
4 OUNCES BUTTER
2 OUNCES ICING SUGAR
JUICE OF 1 LEMON
6 OUNCES FLOUR
½ LEVEL TEASPOON SALT

FILLING:
1 EGG
5 OUNCES SUGAR
1 LEMON
2 OUNCES SOFTENED BUTTER

Pastry: Cream butter and sugar; add lemon juice and flour sifted with salt. Mix quickly to a firm paste, using a little water if necessary. Chill for 15 minutes. Roll out and fit into tart cases. Prick bases lightly and bake 'blind' at 450°F. (Mark 7) for 10 minutes.

Filling: Beat egg with sugar until light and creamy; add juice and grated rind of lemon and softened butter, and continue beating until it is a smooth paste. Fill tart shells with this mixture and bake in a slow oven (325° to 350°F. Mark 2 to 3) for 10 to 15 minutes, or until filling is firm. Cool before serving. Makes 16 to 20 tarts.

STRAWBERRY FLAN CHANTILLY

1 POUND STRAWBERRIES
6 TABLESPOONS GRAND MARNIER
SUGAR
1 EGG WHITE
½ PINT CREAM, WHIPPED
1 BAKED FLAN CASE

Wash, hull and slice strawberries into a bowl. Pour Grand Marnier over them; add sugar to taste; stir and let them marinate in the refrigerator for at least 30 minutes. Beat egg white stiff and fold into whipped cream.

Just before serving, fold sliced strawberries and liquid into *chantilly* mixture; correct flavouring and pile into baked flan case. Serve immediately.

ENGLISH TREACLE TART

SHORTCRUST PASTRY
1 COOKING APPLE
1 CUP FRESHLY-GRATED BREADCRUMBS
JUICE AND GRATED RIND OF 1 LEMON
1 SALTSPOON SALT
1 SALTSPOON GROUND GINGER
1 TABLESPOON SUGAR
2 TABLESPOONS MILK
2 TABLESPOONS WARMED GOLDEN SYRUP
MILK
CASTOR SUGAR

Butter pie tin and line with shortcrust pastry. Grate peeled and cored apple and mix with breadcrumbs, juice and grated rind of lemon, salt, ginger, sugar, milk and golden syrup. Blend well and spread evenly over pastry.

Make thin strips of pastry out of remaining dough; lay in lattice fashion over treacle filling; brush lightly with a little milk and sprinkle with castor sugar. Bake in a moderate oven (375°F. Mark 4) for 40 minutes.

BRIOCHES AUX PÊCHES

6 SMALL PEACHES
8 OUNCES SUGAR
¼ PINT WATER
CINNAMON
¼ PINT RED BURGUNDY
6 BRIOCHES
4 OUNCES BUTTER

Pour boiling water over peaches in a bowl and peel. Slice in half and remove stones. Poach peaches, uncovered, in syrup made of sugar and water with cinnamon to taste, for about 15 minutes. Add Burgundy and continue to cook, uncovered, over a low heat until fruit is tender (about 15 minutes).

Put peaches in a deep bowl. Reduce liquid to the consistency of a light syrup. Pour syrup over the peaches and chill in the refrigerator.

Slice off tops of *brioches* and remove the interiors, leaving a thin shell. Coat insides of *brioches* with soft butter and bake in the oven until crisp and golden. Set re-formed peach inside each case and glaze with reduced syrup. Serves 6.

Index

APPETISERS

SOUPS

SAUCES

EGGS

FISH

SHELLFISH

BEEF

LAMB

VEAL

PORK

POULTRY AND GAME

VEGETABLES

PASTA AND RICE

SALADS

DESSERTS

GROWING, FREEZING & COOKING

Keith Mossman and Mary Norwak

Growing, Freezing & Cooking provides a complete reference book for all who want the best results from their garden produce. It provides information on basic methods of gardening and freezing, and an alphabetical guide to many vegetables, herbs and fruits; under each heading will be found advice on cultivation and choice of varieties, followed by freezing recommendations, and recipes for each product.

For all those households where gardening and cooking are regular activities, and for the ever-burgeoning ranks of freezer-owners, this book by two experts will prove invaluable.

60p

CALENDAR OF HOME FREEZING

Mary Norwak

In this month-by-month guide to successful home freezing Mary Norwak helps you to use your freezer to the best advantage, and to make the most of seasonal produce. The leading expert on home freezing, she provides invaluable advice on bulk buying for home freezing, seasonal buying and preservation, prepare-ahead meals and menus and recipes for home freezing.

Calendar of Home Freezing is an excellent handbook for use the whole year through – no freezer-owning household should be without it!

60p

Illustration on facing page

The Dessert Trolley

at the Four Seasons Restaurant, New York, is photographed in front of the showpiece of the restaurant, a twenty-foot-square pool of white marble, whose softly-lit waters are set off by exotic shrubbery tended by a full-time landscape gardener. The confection at the top is the 'Four Seasons Fancy Cake', a great 'cabbage' of thinnest chocolate containing a rum-filled Bavarian cream.

Illustration on following page

English Apple Pie

A decorated pastry case (heresy to the hide-bound) with a filling of sliced cooking apples enriched with the juices and grated rinds of orange and lemon, makes one of the most exciting apple pies imaginable. Shown here in its pristine purity just before it goes into the oven. (Recipe on page 366.)